T3-BOJ-684

UNIVERSITY OF DAYTON ROESCH LIBRARY

OUR LADY IN CATHOLIC LIFE

By Lawrence G. Lovasik, s.v.d.

STEPPING STONES TO SANCTITY
Practical Hints for Religious and Lay People

PRAYING THE GOSPELS
*Meditations in Prayer on the Life of Christ
According to the Four Evangelists*

OUR LADY IN CATHOLIC LIFE

OUR LADY
in Catholic Life

By

The Reverend Lawrence G. Lovasik, s.v.d.
DIVINE WORD MISSIONARY

232.931
L896o

New York, 1957

THE MACMILLAN COMPANY

DAYTON and MONTGOMERY COUNTY
PUBLIC LIBRARY
UNIVERSITY OF DAYTON ROESCH LIBRARY

IMPRIMI POTEST
Raymond J. Weisenberger, s.v.d.
Provincial, Girard, Pa.

NIHIL OBSTAT
A. H. Wiersbinski, LL.D.
Censor

IMPRIMATUR
✠ John M. Gannon, D.D., D.C.L., LL.D.
Archbishop, Bishop of Erie

© *Lawrence G. Lovasik 1957*

Published simultaneously in Canada

All rights reserved—no part of this book may be re-
produced in any form without permission in writing
from the publisher, except by a reviewer who wishes
to quote brief passages in connection with a review
written for inclusion in magazine or newspaper.

First Printing

Printed in the United States of America

Library of Congress catalog card number: 57-7500

DAYTON and MONTGOMERY COUNTY
PUBLIC LIBRARY

DISCARDED
FROM
UNIVERSITY OF DAYTON
ROESCH LIBRARY

Dedication

TO MARY IMMACULATE,
THE MOTHER OF GOD AND OUR MOTHER,

*through whose intercession I have been privileged to become
a missionary priest (August 14, 1938)
and to found the Congregation of the Sisters of the Divine Spirit
(August 22, 1955),
in memory of the hundredth anniversary of her apparitions at
Lourdes (1858–1958), when she declared, "I am the Immaculate
Conception,"
as a tribute of sincerest gratitude and love,
I dedicate this work.*

FATHER LAWRENCE G. LOVASIK, S.V.D.

† † †

"Surely, she who bears toward us the affection of a Mother, and who
through her interest in the affairs of all mankind is solicitous for our
salvation, and who has been appointed by the Lord as Queen of heaven
and earth, and has been exalted above all the choirs of the angels and
the ranks of the saints, surely, she, standing at the right hand of her
only-begotten Son, Our Lord Jesus Christ, and with a mother's prayer,
is most influential in her intercession, and obtains what she asks and
cannot be denied."

—POPE PIUS IX, in his definition of the dogma of
the Immaculate Conception, December 8, 1854

57–56774
Main

Before Meditation

COME, HOLY SPIRIT, fill the hearts of Your faithful and enkindle in them the fire of Your love.

V. Send forth Your Spirit and they shall be created.

R. And You shall renew the face of the earth.

Let us pray.

O God, who instructed the hearts of the faithful by the light of the Holy Spirit, grant us in the same Spirit to be truly wise, and ever to rejoice in His consolation. Through Christ Our Lord. Amen.

Indulgence of 5 years (287)

† † †

DIVINE SPIRIT, Spirit of Truth, impart to my soul a tender love, unbounded veneration, and a childlike devotion to my beloved Mother, Mary Immaculate. She is Your Immaculate Bride. She was given to me as Mother by Jesus, my Savior.

Make me believe of Mary what the Church believes of her, and love her as the Church loves her, more and more as Jesus loves her, and as You love her. Give me, by the Gift of Piety, a singular devotion to her, so characteristic of all the saints. Through her kind prayers, and Your divine grace, may I become more like Jesus. Amen.

Foreword

The purpose of this book is to help you to know and love Mary, the Mother of God and Our Mother. It is made up of two major parts: an explanation and a meditation for each of the feasts of Our Lady and each of her titles as they are expressed in the Litany of Loreto.

Our Lady's Feasts are the Church's own tribute of honor and affection for the Blessed Virgin Mary. Apart from public devotion of the faithful, we have in the sacred liturgy itself—the official prayer of the Church composed by the special help of the Holy Spirit for the Mystical Bride of Christ—most convincing evidence of the place accorded by her to Mary, as standing ever between the Fount of all grace and mercy and the prayers of our afflicted race. The yearly calendar shows that some major and minor feasts occur each month, the Mass and Office on such occasions being specially adapted to bring out and to emphasize the wonderful prerogatives of Mary and the confidence of her children in her all-powerful intercession. The actual liturgical prayers, along with other devotions for the Feasts of Our Lady, are contained in my prayerbook *Mary My Hope* (Marian Action Publications, Tarentum, Pa.). In the following pages, however, I wish to offer a more detailed explanation of each feast and material for meditation which will enable you to prepare for and celebrate each feast day more fruitfully.

Our Lady's Titles touch on all those dominant qualities that make her so pleasing to God and lovable to her children. Just as a jewel will be more delightful to look at and more appreciated if viewed from different angles, so, too, Mary—the Masterpiece of the Divine Spirit—will appear in greater splendor if you *prayerfully* examine the many titles with which her devoted children have addressed her down through the ages. These titles are found in the Litany of Loreto. It is especially at prayer that you will receive choice graces from God to understand and to appreciate the virtues

vii

and privileges of Mary and the wonders with which the Holy Spirit has blessed His Immaculate Bride.

By making a Novena for each major feast and a Triduum for each minor feast, and by meditating on one of the titles of Our Lady on each Saturday, *you will be spending the year in close union with Mary.* This is surely a very practical and fruitful way of living a holy life and preparing your soul for eternity, because Mary will lead you to Jesus, Who is "the Way and the Truth and the Life."

FATHER LAWRENCE G. LOVASIK, S.V.D.

Feast of the Apparition of Mary Immaculate, February 11, 1957
Divine Word Seminary
Girard, Pennsylvania

† † †

O MARY, conceived without sin,
pray for us who have recourse to thee!

Contents

Part I OUR LADY'S FEASTS

December

January

February

March

ix

Part II OUR LADY'S TITLES

January

February

March

April

May

June

July

August

September

October

Part I

OUR LADY'S FEASTS

*Meditations on the Church's major
and minor feast days in honor of the
Blessed Virgin Mary*

The angels and saints have been favored by God and are distinguished above other creatures by a special supernatural excellence, and therefore are deserving of special honor. By this subordinate cult of saints (*dulia*) the Church indirectly glorifies God, Who shows His perfections in the graces He has bestowed upon His chosen creatures. The Liturgy of the Church singles out the Blessed Virgin Mary, the Mother of Christ, and honors her by a special cult (*hyperdulia*). In this respect the Liturgy is but imitating the example of the angel Gabriel who greeted Mary as "full of grace" and "blessed among women."

The Church has established feast days in honor of God's Mother. There are in all some 25,000 feasts in the Church in honor of Mary, although only about sixteen are included in the universal Church Calendar. But whatever their number, we know that many are purely local in some dioceses or religious houses, and many others of her titles or pilgrimages have no special fixed feast. Part I of this book is concerned with the major as well as the most popular minor feasts of Our Lady. Mary's glories are a constantly recurring theme of the Church's Liturgy, in order that the faithful may realize in their lives the value of Mary's position in the economy of salvation. Her Liturgy is a medium to teach the truth about the Mother of God and our Mother and to extol her dignity.

Mother! whose virgin bosom was uncrost
With the least shade of thought to sin allied;
Woman! above all women glorified,
Our tainted nature's solitary boast;
Purer than foam on central ocean tost;
Brighter than eastern skies at daybreak strewn
With fancied roses, than the unblemished moon
Before her wane begins on heaven's blue coast;
Thy Image falls to earth. Yet some, I ween,
Nor unforgiven the suppliant knee might bend,
As to a visible Power, in which did blend
All that was mixed and reconciled in Thee
Of mother's love with maiden purity,
Of high with low, celestial with terrene.

—WORDSWORTH

The Immaculate Conception

Background:

The Immaculate Conception of the Blessed Virgin Mary consists essentially in her exemption from original sin. From the first moment of her existence her soul was adorned with sanctifying grace which made her a beloved child of God. She was never in that state of separation from God in which all men find themselves before baptism. Mary was preserved from sin in view of the merits of her Son. The grace of the Redeemer prevented her from being tainted by original sin; whereas, we have been rescued from this sin through baptism.

The main reason which demanded the Immaculate Conception for Mary was her divine maternity. It was fitting that the Mother of God be always without sin, even original sin. The *Son of God* could create for Himself a mother most pure; and He certainly has done so. His filial love is infinitely greater than ours. If Mary had been conceived in sin, she would have been in a state of enmity toward her Son before He had chosen her as His Mother. Since He had come as Savior to redeem mankind, it was fitting that He redeem His Mother in a more excellent way than the rest of mankind, that is, by preserving her from sin instead of only delivering her from it. Mary is the privileged daughter of the *Heavenly Father.* He had to make her at least equal to Eve, His first daughter, whom He created immaculate. The *Holy Spirit* made Mary His bride. It was only just that this Spirit of love sanctify her soul in a more sublime manner than all other souls by preventing sin from entering, instead of merely driving it out.

The Immaculate Conception entails a great number of *heavenly favors.* With her original grace she received the principal gifts which God gave Adam for the perfection of his nature—gifts which are not restored to us with the grace of baptism. In Mary there were no unruly desires of the flesh, no moral or religious ignorance that would have caused disorder, no weakness in the will, no bodily infirmities. Her sufferings were sufferings of love—love for her Son and for us. Like Him, she was also to die, but her death was an ecstasy of love.

The Fathers, the early writers of the Church, believed that Mary was free from sin in her conception. Later there were some writers who doubted the Immaculate Conception because they thought that it implied that Mary had not been redeemed by Christ and had no need of such redemption. This doubt can be explained in the light of the following facts: first, the doctrine of the Immaculate Conception was not yet defined, nor thoroughly understood or discussed; second, the gift of infallibility belongs to the Roman Pontiff alone, and not to individual writers. The doubters would accept the doctrine as defined by the Roman Pontiff were they now living. Moreover, a few dissenting voices cannot avail against the moral agreement of ecclesiastical writers taken as a whole.

In 1453 the Immaculate Conception was defined as a pious belief, in harmony with the devotion of the Church, reason, and Holy Scripture. In the sixteenth century, at the time of the Council of Trent, Pope Leo X considered defining the dogma. But not until the nineteenth century were positive steps to define the dogma taken. Pope Pius IX named a commission to examine the question, and Rome asked the opinion of the bishops of the whole world. Of 626 answers, only four were negative, and these were later reduced to one.

On December 8, 1854, Pope Pius IX, in the presence of 53 cardinals and 143 bishops from all parts of the world, solemnly promulgated the beloved dogma in these words: *We pronounce and define that the doctrine which states that the Most Blessed Virgin Mary was, in the first instant of her conception, by the singular grace and privilege of God, in view of the merits of Jesus Christ, the Savior of the human race, preserved immune from all stain of original sin, has been revealed by God and is therefore to be firmly and unswervingly believed by all the faithful.*

Inspired by the fiftieth anniversary of the definition of the dogma of the Immaculate Conception, *St. Pius X* gave the world the encyclical *Ad diem illum,* about Our Lady's part in the restoration of all things to Christ which this great Pope made the rule of his pontificate. According to St. Pius X, these were the *lessons of the Immaculate Conception definition:*

"Let the nations believe and profess that the Virgin Mary, in the first moment of her conception was free from all stain, and they must admit original sin, the redemption of mankind by Christ, the Gospel, the Church and even the law of suffering. This plague [the rejection of all authority], which is equally destructive of civil and Christian society, is destroyed by the dogma of the Immaculate Conception of the Mother of God. For by it we are all constrained to recognize in the Church a power to which one must submit not only the will but also the intellect, since it is through this subjection of the reason that the Christian people sing to the Mother

of God: 'Thou art all fair, O Mary, and there is no original stain in thee.'
So again we conclude that the Church rightly attributes to the august Virgin this: that she by herself destroyed all the heresies in the whole world."

Devotion to Mary Immaculate will lead you to imitate the sinlessness of Our Lady and her perfect love for Jesus. Take the Immaculate Virgin as the special protectress of the purity of your body and soul. Say three "Hail Marys" each morning and evening in honor of her Immaculate Conception, particularly for the grace of holy purity.

The United States was dedicated to the Immaculate Conception by the Third Plenary Council of Baltimore in 1846. Pray to Mary Immaculate for our country, that she may bless and protect it.

Prayer

(1) MARY, MOTHER OF GOD, *I believe what Holy Mother Church teaches about your Immaculate Conception:* that from the first moment of your conception you possessed justice and holiness—that is, sanctifying grace, even the fullness of grace, with the infused virtues and gifts of the Holy Spirit, and with integrity of nature; yet you remained subject to death and other pains and miseries of life that your Son Himself willed to undergo.

For the first time after four thousand years God, in His wisdom and power and love, created again a human being in that state in which He had created our first parents. Immaculate Virgin, you are that human being. Because of sanctifying grace infused into your soul, you were from the first moment of your existence most intimately united with God and endowed with the most precious gifts of heaven. You possessed a perfect faith, a firm hope, a burning charity, a deep humility, a purity greater than that of the angels. Your soul is the creation and the masterpiece of almighty workmanship. The Archangel Gabriel expressed this very clearly: "Hail, full of grace"—there was no room left for sin; "the Lord is with thee"—where God dwells, Satan can have no rights; "blessed art thou among women"—you were elevated above all other women in the world.

MARY, MY MOTHER, you were never without grace. From the first moment of your existence the Holy Spirit made you His temple and blessed you with the fullness of His grace. Your Immaculate Conception, purchased by the Precious Blood of the Son of God Himself and freely bestowed upon you as the highest gift of God, is the most wonderful work of sanctification that the world has ever seen.

(2) MARY, MOTHER OF GOD, no stain of original sin ever defiled your pure soul. *This privilege separated you from all the rest of the children of Adam.* As the Mother of the Incarnate Son you were so preserved from inheriting original sin that never for a moment was so much as a shadow cast by sin upon your spotless soul. You were the only one who was exempt from the universal curse that had fallen on the whole human race. You were never under the power of the serpent, whose head you crushed in giving a Redeemer to the world. Your Immaculate Conception is a triumph over Satan, the author of evil, who, under your heel, suffered his first complete defeat. It is but a symbol of the endless victories which you are to win over him to the last day. Hence the Church sings of you, "You are all fair, O Mary, and the original stain is not in you."

But you needed the redeeming Savior to obtain this exemption, deliverance from the universal debt of being subject to original sin. Being the new Eve who was to be the Mother of the new Adam, you were, by the eternal decree of God and by the merits of Christ, withdrawn from the general law of original sin. Your redemption was the very masterpiece of Christ's redeeming wisdom. He paid the debt that original sin might not be incurred.

MARY, MY MOTHER, what joy for you never to have been, even for a single instant, in the state of enmity toward God! You know that you are the well beloved Daughter of the Father; you embrace the Son; you are united to the Holy Spirit with a simplicity, a confidence, and a delicacy of love which belong to you alone, for in you alone there cannot be the remembrance of a moment in which you were opposed to God. I share in this joy. I am happy at the thought that you, a human creature, have escaped completely from the clutches of Satan; that, born of a race universally tainted, you are more pure and more brilliant than the most sublime of the angels; and that you are my Mother.

(3) MARY, MOTHER OF GOD, *your greatness began at the first instant of your existence with the privilege of your Immaculate Conception.* After Almighty God and the Sacred Humanity of Jesus, there is no being so great as you. It is true, you are a creature, and, therefore, far beneath the Supreme Being. But you are a creature so holy and so perfect that you are superior to all other creatures. You are above not only patriarchs, prophets, apostles, martyrs, and all the saints

but even all angels. You stand alone on a throne of greatness and perfection far above the rest of creatures.

It was fitting that you, a Virgin Mother, should conceive the Man Who was also the Son of God. It was fitting that you should be adorned with the greatest purity ever possible to a creature. You are the Virgin to whom God the Father decreed to give His only Son— the Divine Word, equal with Himself in all things—that entering the natural order He might become your Son as well as His. You are the immaculate Virgin whom the Son Himself chose to make His Mother. You are the immaculate Virgin whom the Holy Spirit willed to make His bride and in whom He would work the tremendous miracle of the Incarnation. The privilege of the Immaculate Conception was suitable to your dignity. It was possible for God to confer it, and He did confer it!

MARY, MY MOTHER, help me to imitate your sinlessness by keeping my soul free from every willful sin by the faithful observance of God's commandments. Help me to imitate your fullness of grace by receiving Holy Communion frequently, where I shall obtain the sanctifying grace that will make my soul holy and pleasing to God, more like your own, and where I shall obtain the actual graces I need to practice virtue and to walk in your footsteps. Through prayer may grace fill my soul with the life of God and transform me into a living image of Jesus, just as you were.

Thou art all fair, O Mary,
There is no spot in thee.
Thou art the Mother of Wisdom,
The spouse of Infinity.
O morning star of Jacob,
O boast of Israel's pride,
Through thee came the gift from Heaven
For which the hills long sighed.

Thou art all bright, O Mary,
The moon serene and sweet
That mirrors the Face of Justice
To the world beneath thy feet.
O Woman clothed with sunlight,
O Virgin crowned with stars,
Through thee God opened Heaven,
Released earth's sin-chained bars.

Thou art all pure, O Mary,
White wings thy thoughts enfold;
Thy breast is an ivory altar,
Thy heart a house of gold.
No thing defiled can enter
Thy sanctuary wall,
For thou dost shrine in thy sweet flesh
Our God, our life, our all.

† † †

O God, Who by the Immaculate Conception of the Virgin Mary have prepared a worthy dwelling place for Your Son, we humbly beg of You, that as through the Death of Your Son, which You foreknew, You have kept her free from all sin, so by her intercession enable us also to come to You with pure hearts. Through the same Christ Our Lord. Amen.

PRAYER FOR THE MARIAN YEAR
1954
By the Sovereign Pontiff Pius XII

Enraptured by the splendor of your heavenly beauty, and impelled by the anxieties of the world, we cast ourselves into your arms, O Immaculate Mother of Jesus and our Mother, Mary, confident of finding in your most loving heart appeasement of our ardent desires, and a safe harbor from the tempests which beset us on every side.

Though degraded by our faults and overwhelmed by infinite misery, we admire and praise the peerless richness of sublime gifts with which God has filled you, above every other mere creature, from the first moment of your Conception until the day on which, after your Assumption into Heaven, He crowned you Queen of the Universe.

O crystal Fountain of faith, bathe our minds with the eternal truths! O fragrant Lily of all holiness, captivate our hearts with your heavenly perfume! O Conqueress of evil and death, inspire in us a deep horror of sin, which makes the soul detestable to God and a slave of hell!

O well-beloved of God, hear the ardent cry which rises up from every heart in this year dedicated to you. Bend tenderly over our aching wounds. Convert the wicked, dry the tears of the afflicted and oppressed, comfort the poor and humble, quench hatred, sweeten harshness, safeguard the flower of purity in youth, protect the holy Church, make all men feel the attraction of Christian goodness. In your name, resounding harmoniously in heaven, may they recognize that they are brothers, and that the nations are members of one family, upon which may there shine forth the sun of a universal and sincere peace.

Receive, O Most Sweet Mother, our humble supplications, and above all obtain for us that, one day, happy with you, we may repeat before your throne that hymn which today is sung on earth around your altars: You are all-beautiful, O Mary! You are the glory, you are the joy, you are the honor of our people! Amen.

Transferring of the Holy House of the Blessed Virgin Mary

FEAST, December 10 (TRIDUUM, December 7–9)

Background:

Eighteen miles south of Ancona, and about three miles from the Adriatic coast of Italy, stands the city of Loreto on the summit of a hill. A vast basilica with a great dome forms the most treasured of all the Pope's "extra-territorial" Vatican State properties, enshrining as it does perhaps the most sacred and important of all Our Lady's Shrines—the Home of the Holy Family, *the Holy House of Loreto.*

Written at the door of the basilica are these words: "The whole world has no place more sacred. . . . For here was the Word made Flesh, and here was born the Virgin Mother. . . ." On entering the basilica, one finds beneath the central dome, and just behind the high altar, a rectangular edifice of white marble, richly adorned with statues. The white marble, however, forms only a protective crust. The contrast between the exterior richness and the poverty of the interior is startling. Inside, are the plain, rough walls of a cottage of great antiquity, 30 feet long by 15 feet wide and about 15 feet high.

The tradition is that toward the end of the thirteenth century, *the Holy House was borne by the hands of angels,* first from Galilee to Dalmatia, and thence to Loreto, where it has remained ever since.

The House of Our Lady stood undestroyed in Nazareth for more than twelve hundred years. It was set apart from secular uses by the Apostles. Then when the Empress, St. Helen, visited the Holy Places, she went to Nazareth and found there the House, where she built a beautiful church to the Mother of God. It was a common practice to enshrine entire houses associated with saints beneath churches. St. Louis, King of France, heard Mass in Nazareth in 1253 "in the exact chamber where the Virgin Mary was declared the Mother of God," and then heard another Mass at the High Altar above.

In 1291 some Dalmatian shepherds found a strange building in their field. Since the materials in the structure were not obtainable in Dalmatia, the

Governor of Dalmatia sent envoys to Nazareth. The Holy House could no longer be found there, but the length and breadth of the walls of the cottage agreed exactly with those of the foundations beneath the Basilica of the Annunciation.

Three and a half years later, on December 10, 1294, the same Holy House was removed from Dalmatia and set down at Loreto. It was visited there by innumerable persons. Pope Boniface VIII deputed a commission to inquire into and report fully on the matter, both at Dalmatia and Nazareth, as well as at Loreto. From 1294 onward, pilgrims began to throng the roads to Loreto. Some forty-seven Popes have knelt there. Pope after Pope has added to the testimony in favor of belief. The Sacred Congregation of Rites has paid tribute by appointing December 10th as the Feast "of the Translation of the Holy House" with special Mass and Office.

By order of Benedict XIV, a number of experts dug around the base of the little sanctuary and proved beyond a doubt that the building rested on no foundations at all, but stood directly on the surface of an ancient road. Recently experts have examined the materials, stones and mortar of the walls and compared them with stones in the remains of the foundations at Nazareth. They were judged to be identical.

At Loreto is the actual house in which Our Lady dwelt and where Our Lord spent the years of His childhood. Loreto is the foremost shrine in Christendom in honor of Our Lady. From it, the Litany of Loreto takes its name. This shrine still remains to bring us in truth and spirit the message of the Archangel Gabriel, "Hail, full of grace, the Lord is with thee!"

Prayer

(1) MARY, MOTHER OF GOD, *in your humble home of Nazareth the great mystery of the Incarnation was accomplished.* In your person God awaited the response of the humanity to which He wished to unite Himself. You gave your reply, "Behold the handmaid of the Lord, be it done to me according to thy word." At that moment the Divine Word, the Second Person of the Holy Trinity, took flesh of you and became man. This was the greatest event in the history of the world, for the salvation of man depended upon it.

I venerate you as the Mother of God. Through the power of the Holy Spirit you conceived Jesus and yet remained a Virgin. You were chosen from all eternity for this exalted honor. You alone, among all the children of men, were conceived immaculate, born full of grace, and blessed among women. Your immaculate Heart was unstained by any evil. All the virtues that could ripen in a human soul through divine grace were found in you. All this holiness made you worthy of being the Mother of God. I thank God for the great things He has done for you in your little home of Nazareth.

MARY, MY MOTHER, your most glorious title is that of Mother of God. It makes you all-powerful with Jesus, your Son. Pray to Jesus for me that I may show my gratitude to Him for becoming man to save my soul. My best gratitude consists in becoming more like Jesus through love. As it was your joy to form Jesus in your own body, may your joy now be to form Jesus in my soul. The Holy Spirit worked in you the great miracle of the Incarnation of Jesus. Through the Holy Spirit Jesus takes up His abode in me in Holy Communion. He continues to dwell in me by letting me share in His own divine life by grace. Make my heart glow with the same love that filled your Heart when you adored the living presence of Jesus within you. Help me to imitate your humility, sinlessness and love, for which God chose you to be His Mother.

(2) MARY, MOTHER OF GOD, *your Divine Motherhood was the source and cause of all your glory.* You became the Mother of a Son Who is almighty, eternal, and infinite in all perfection. You became the Mother of God without ceasing to be a virgin, and your happy fruitfulness only consecrated and increased your purity. By it you saw yourself raised above all the saints and angels.

I believe that to be the Mother of God is the greatest grace which can be conferred on a creature. God could make a greater world, a greater Heaven, but He cannot exalt a creature more than by making her His Mother—and this He has done for you. You received a kind of infinite dignity by becoming the Mother of God, a God clothed in human flesh. By your humility you became the Mother of your Creator. The Creator in His goodness became your Son—the Son of His own creature.

MARY, MY MOTHER, you prepared yourself for that dignity by the constant practice of the highest virtue. But you merited this dignity only in the sense that it was eminently proper that God should give to His Son the purest of virgins for His Mother, and that a Virgin as rich as you in privileges and in merits should have no other son than a God made Man. You first had to conceive the Son of God in your heart before conceiving Him in your flesh. By the extraordinary purity of your heart, the beauty and splendor of your virtues, the treasure of your merits, you deserved that the Son of God should choose you for His Mother. When you had freely done your part to prepare for Him a worthy dwelling within you, the Son of God, attracted by your charms, gladly made choice of you, in order that He might take from you our human nature, and as a Son of man might make due atonement for our sins. I praise and thank God for this wonderful dignity of Divine Motherhood which was bestowed upon you in your humble home of Nazareth. I beg you, for the love of God Who was so generous to you, help us in our needs of soul and body by your prayers in the presence of God.

(3) MARY, MOTHER OF GOD, *by your wonderful maternity you became a co-operator in the Redemption of the human race.* You nourished and prepared the holy Victim, Who was offered to the Eternal Father in expiation of our sins. From you were derived the Precious Blood which was shed upon the cross for our salvation, and the adorable Body which, after having been made the price of our Redemption, has become the nourishment of our souls in the Holy Eucharist.

MARY, MY MOTHER, thank you for the supreme generosity which urged you to go so far to prove your love for God and your fellow men as to want to give us a Savior. We are indebted to you for our Redeemer, and in our Redeemer, for the life of grace, and all the blessings that have come to us through Him. Thank you for all you have given us in Jesus—our salvation, our spiritual life of grace. I need your help if I am to progress in my spiritual life. As a child needs its mother, so I need your unfailing love and fostering care as my spiritual Mother. Teach me how to imitate your virtues, especially your humility, your purity, your love of God, so that I may merit to be sheltered under the protecting folds of your maternal mantle. With your aid I shall be ever on my guard against the enemies of my soul and shall fight them courageously. I shall be devoted to the service of God. Help me and forsake me not, till my enemies are conquered and heaven is won.

> Rejoice, O Mary, by whose mighty hand
> The Church has victory o'er Her foes achieved,
> Since thou to Gabriel's word of quickening power
> In lowliness hast listened, and believed—
> Thou, still a Virgin, in thy blessed womb
> Hast God Incarnate of thy flesh conceived,

And still of Heaven, of that virginity
Remainest after childbirth unbereaved.
                    —Matins, Feast of the Annunciation

† † †

O God, Who mercifully sanctified the house of the Blessed Mary ever Virgin through the mystery of the Incarnation and placed it in the bosom of Your Church in a wonderful manner, grant that we may avoid the dwellings of sinners and someday live in Your holy home. Through Christ our Lord. Amen.

Our Lady of Guadalupe

Background:

Guadalupe, in the Aztec Indian tongue, means "She shall crush thy head," but has been extended to the church containing the picture and to the town that grew up around it. Guadalupe is three miles northeast of Mexico City, Mexico. Pilgrimages have been made to this shrine almost uninterruptedly since 1531.

The picture which has aroused all this devotion is a representation of the Immaculate Conception, with the sun, moon, and stars, accompaniments of the text in the Apocalypse. Mary, clothed in a blue robe dotted with stars, stands on the crescent moon. Underneath the crescent is a supporting angel. The rays of the sun shoot out on all sides from behind the central figure.

According to tradition the Blessed Virgin appeared to a fifty-five-year-old neophyte named Juan Diego, who was hurrying to hear Mass in Mexico City, on Saturday, December 9, 1531. She sent him to Bishop Zumarraga to ask that a temple be built on the spot where she stood. She was at the same place that evening and Sunday evening to get the bishop's answer. After cross-questioning Juan, the bishop ordered him to ask for a sign from the lady who had said she was the Mother of God. Juan was occupied all Monday with Bernardino, an uncle, who seemed dying of fever. On Tuesday, December 12th, the grieved nephew had to run for a priest and, to avoid the apparition, slipped around where the well chapel now stands. But the Blessed Virgin crossed down to meet him and said, "What road is this thou takest, son?" A tender dialogue ensued. Reassuring Juan about his uncle— whom at that instant she cured and in an apparition to him also called herself Holy Mary of Guadalupe—she bade him go again to the bishop. Without hesitating he joyously asked for a sign. She told him to go up to the rocks and gather roses. He knew it was neither the time nor the place for roses, but he obeyed. Gathering the roses into the long cloak worn by Mexican Indians, he returned to the Blessed Mother, who rearranged them and warned him to keep them untouched and unseen till he reached the bishop. When he arrived at the bishop's home, Juan unfolded his cloak and

17

the roses fell out. Startled to see the bishop and his attendants kneeling before him, he looked at the cloak and saw glowing there the life-sized figure of the Virgin Mother, just as he had described her. The picture was venerated in the bishop's chapel and soon after carried in procession to the first shrine.

The coarsely woven material which bears the picture is as thin and open as poor sacking. It is made of vegetable fiber and consists of two strips, about seventy inches long by eighteen wide, held together by weak stitching. The chief colors imprinted on this material are deep gold in the rays and stars, blue-green in the mantle, and rose in the flowered tunic.

In 1709 a rich *shrine* was erected; in 1904 it was made a basilica. Nineteen Popes favored the shrine and its tradition. Pope Pius X decreed that Our Lady of Guadalupe should be the national patron, and made December 12th a holy day of obligation and ordered a special Mass and Office.

When Our Lady imprinted her image on the cloak of Juan Diego, there was no United States. From the Gulf to the St. Lawrence was one continent, and that continent had been dedicated to Our Lady by the Spaniards. The United States was dedicated to the Immaculate Conception by the Third Plenary Council of Baltimore in 1846. *The Image of Our Lady of Guadalupe is the image of the Immaculate Conception. She is* THE WOMAN of the Apocalypse, clothed with the Sun, standing on the Moon, and, though without the crown of stars, wears them on her mantle. Significantly, the Child Jesus does not appear. The apparition of Our Lady of Guadalupe is Mary's only recorded appearance in North America. Pope Pius XII said, "We are certain that so long as you [Our Lady of Guadalupe] are recognized as Queen and Mother, America and Mexico are saved."

By reason of the fact that we live and work for God in one section of the earth, joined together by common interests and common needs, the people of the Americas are bound to love one another with a special charity. The force of charity by which the peoples of the Western Hemisphere must be bound together is one of those graces which the Mother of God can and will procure for her children in Christ. As the patroness of Pan-American unity, Our Lady of Guadalupe influences her children to turn toward one another in common affection for her and for Our Lord.

Prayer

(1) MARY, MOTHER OF GOD, *in honoring you as Our Lady of Guadalupe, we honor you as the Immaculate Conception.* The picture you imprinted on the cloak of the Indian at Guadalupe was the image of the Immaculate Conception. You appeared as the Woman of the Apocalypse, clothed with the sun, standing on the moon.

I believe the doctrine of the Church concerning your Immaculate Conception, which teaches that at the first moment of your conception you were, by the singular grace and privilege of the omnipotent God, in virtue of the merits of Jesus Christ, Savior of the human race, preserved from all stains of original sin. The foundation of this doctrine is to be found in Sacred Scripture where we are taught that God, the Creator of all things, after the sad fall of Adam, addressed the serpent in words which the Church applies to you: "I will put enmities between thee and the woman, and thy seed and her seed; she shall crush thy head" (Gen. 3:15). If at any time you had been without Divine grace, even for the shortest moment, there would not have come between you and the serpent that everlasting enmity spoken of by God.

Since the angel saluted you "full of grace" and "blessed . . . among women" (Luke 1:28), you were the abode of all divine graces, adorned with the Gifts of the Holy Spirit, so that you were never subjected to the evil spirit.

This doctrine was received in the early Church and handed down by the Fathers who praised you with extraordinary titles and most important writings.

MARY, MY MOTHER, may the example of your sinlessness urge us to that innocence and purity of life which flees from and abhors even the slightest stain of sin. Forming with your Divine Son one spiritual body, we experience the rage of Satan until the end of time. But we, too, by our union with Jesus, and by the power of His grace, will also be united with Him in His victory over the devil. As the seed of the serpent includes all those descendants of the first man and woman who by their sinful lives bear within them the traits of the devil, so, too, the seed of the Woman includes all who in the course of ages will take their stand with your Son, Jesus Christ, in His ceaseless conflict with the enemy of God.

(2) MARY, MOTHER OF GOD, *your apparition at Guadalupe teaches me that devotion to you is a source of great graces.* The Church has always taught that God has entrusted to your hands all heavenly treasures, and many of the saints assure me that you give to your clients as much of these treasures as you wish and when you wish to do so.

How consoling it is to know that you have these heavenly blessings at your disposal! I have but to ask for them for the salvation of my

soul. There is nothing you want more than to give them to me, because you are even more anxious to save my soul than I am, for you
know better than anyone else the price your Son has paid for it
and the precious worth of each grace He so graciously offers to me
through you.

*Devotion to you brings with it sweetness and consolation for the
soul.* As a child runs to its mother in every need, and finds comfort
in her glance and kind word, I can turn to you for help when I need
it, for you are truly my Mother, whose heart is overflowing with
kindness and mercy.

MARY, MY MOTHER, the Church puts these words of the Canticle
on your lips: "I love those who love me." I want to love you with
all my heart that I may in some way merit that you love me in
return. I already know of your great love for me for the sake of
your Son Who entrusted the care of my soul to you. But I want to be
loved by you even more; hence, give me an ever growing love for you.
This love for you was the source of great joy in the hearts of the
saints. May I have more of their love for you so that I may experience more of their joy in being devoted to you. Take my cold heart;
put it into your own and inflame it with a fire of love like your own.

(3) MARY, MOTHER OF GOD, because the United States was dedicated to your Immaculate Conception, be pleased to *take our country
under your special protection* and grant that, guided by justice and
nurtured by charity, it may serve God faithfully and be blessed with
peace and prosperity. Continue to work wonders on our shores for
our spiritual and material prosperity and keep us in peace and charity. Intercede for us that we may win the victory over evil and that
we may live and reign with Jesus, your Son. Our Lady of Guadalupe,
whom we acclaim our Queen and Mother, lead our country to God.

MARY, MY MOTHER, *your apparition at Guadalupe as the Immaculate Conception is your only recorded appearance in North
America.* Bless the people of the Americas, to which uncounted
thousands have come to seek refuge and livelihood. Preserve their
faith, assailed at every hour by the forces opposed to Christ. Petition
God that their hope may never fail amid the troubles and the cares
of this life. We beg you for a burning charity for God to imitate the
works of Christ. We ask you to procure for us, by your prayers, the
great grace of final perseverance so that those who are joined to

honor you in the kingdom of your Son on earth may be together always in heaven.

Indulgenced Prayer

Our Lady of Guadalupe, mystical rose, make intercession for holy Church, protect the Sovereign Pontiff, help all those who invoke you in their necessities, and since you are the ever Virgin Mary and Mother of the true God, obtain for us from your most holy Son the grace of keeping our faith, sweet hope in the midst of the bitterness of life, burning charity and the precious gift of final perseverance. Amen.   (500 days)

Note: This prayer was approved and enriched with an indulgence of five hundred days by Pope Pius X at an audience held on August 18, 1908, and was included in the official edition of approved indulgenced prayers (1950).

Sign of Salvation with Jesus the Light,
Clothed with the Sun thou art radiant bright!
Promised of old as the serpent's defeat,
Queenly adorned with the moon 'neath thy feet!

Garden of Eden, where sin has no part,
Life-giving Tree, bearing Christ in our heart.
Ark, where the Manna was hidden away,
Holy of Holies, Immaculate Way!

City of God, with the Lamb as thy Light,
Dawn of Eternal Day knowing no night!
Bride of the Spirit and Form of our God,
Heavenly Path which the Blessed have trod!

† † †

O God, Who bestowed upon us unceasing favors by having placed us under the special protection of the Most Blessed Virgin Mary, grant us, Your humble servants, who rejoice in honoring her today upon earth, the happiness of seeing her face to face in heaven. Through Christ our Lord. Amen.

The Expectation of the Blessed
Virgin Mary

FEAST, December 18
(TRIDUUM, December 15–17 or daily until Christmas)

Background:

The Liturgical Year opens with *the season of Advent*. This period of preparation for the great solemnity celebrating the coming of the Son of God among men represents the long period of waiting which preceded the appearing of the Redeemer. It is a time of hope, full of the longings and aspirations not only of the Prophets who announced the promised Savior, but especially of the Blessed Virgin Mary who awaits the fulfillment of the message brought by the Angel.

At the tenth Council of Toledo, in the year 656, the bishops of Spain decreed that *a solemn feast* with an Octave should be celebrated in that country on December 18th, in honor of the Annunciation. By choosing this date the Spanish Church could celebrate a joyous festival which falls in the Lenten season. For a long period this day in Advent, a week before the feast of the Nativity, was observed throughout Spain in commemoration of the angel's message and the mystery of the Incarnation. However, eventually the Spanish hierarchy conformed to the general custom of the Western Church. But since December 18th had become very dear to the people as one of Our Lady's feasts and was considered a day of special graces for expectant mothers, it continued to be observed, but under a new title—the feast of the Expectation of the Blessed Virgin Mary. In 1725 Pope Benedict XIII introduced this feast into the Roman States, and gradually it spread to other lands. It never became a feast of the universal Church.

The spirit from which this feast had its origin should pervade the devotional life of Catholics, the spirit which animated the Blessed Virgin when the time of her Son's birth was drawing near. It is impossible to form any adequate idea of the thoughts that flooded the mind and heart of Mary. Her heart burned with a fervor of divine love such as never before or since

22

has enkindled a human heart, save the Heart of the God-Man, hidden for nine months in her chaste womb.

Holy Mother Church wishes you to be filled with the interior dispositions in which Our Lady expected the coming of the Savior, and thus you will prepare for His last advent on Judgment Day. In union with Mary your heart should yield itself up to an absolute confidence in Him Who is to come so that the graces of His Nativity may be brought to you in abundance, and Jesus may be born anew within your heart.

Prayer

(1) MARY, MOTHER OF GOD, *how sacred was the life of Jesus in your womb while you awaited His coming!* It was a life of concealment, and yet Jesus is infinite, the light of the angels and of the whole world. It was a life of silence, and yet He is the Word of the Father, the expression of His glory, the teacher of the prophets. It was life of the utmost weakness and helplessness, and yet His is the strength of God Himself.

During this long period of concealment in your womb, you perfected His bodily faculties for our benefit. You formed His Body in order that it might be given us in death and in the Blessed Sacrament. You formed His eyes, to look upon us with mild and pitying glance and to weep over us. You formed His lips, to teach us. You formed His feet, to search after and seek us as a Good Shepherd; His hands, to heal us and to be pierced for us; and His shoulders to carry the cross. You formed His Heart, to love us; and His Precious Blood, to shed for us and to be given to us for our drink. You formed His whole Self, to die for us as a sacrificial Lamb.

Yet Jesus was active in your womb adoring and praising God. He found joy in God, His Heavenly Father, and in the Holy Spirit, joy in all the wonderful perfections of God. He also found joy in His Divine Sonship and glorious human nature; joy in His intellect, with its immeasurable knowledge and the contemplation of God; joy in His will, with its freedom, sinlessness, holiness and unbounded power; joy in His destiny as our Redeemer; joy in the future kingdom of His Church, which was to arise from His life and death. But with these joys were also mingled bitter sorrows. He saw sin and its terrible effects in God's kingdom and in souls; He saw the sufferings of His Church and His own and your sufferings.

MARY, MY MOTHER, in your womb, the sanctuary of the living God,

Jesus was occupied with the sanctification and government of the world. From Him there flowed heavenward an unceasing stream of glory; the waves of His grace ever poured over the earth. He already occupied Himself with the salvation of all souls, and as the hidden Ruler of the world He judged all who departed this life.

But Jesus was constantly sanctifying you, His loving Mother, transforming you ever more and more into Himself by wondrous graces of knowledge of the mystery of the Incarnation, and by graces of love which united you to Him. You became more and more filled with His spirit; you grew into Him, as it were, and became in your soul ever more the Mother of God and Mother of Jesus. It was indeed a divine life that Jesus led in Your womb, a life most active, and yet one of unbroken calm.

(2) MARY, MOTHER OF GOD, *how wonderful was your own interior life as you carried the Son of God in your womb and awaited His coming!* It was a life of closest union with Jesus—a union of body as well as of soul. There is no more intimate bodily union than that of mother and child, for they are one life, one heartbeat sustaining the life of both. The Supreme God rested and worked in you.

Your life with Jesus was one of deepest recollection, which gathered all the powers of your soul around the God-Man. The divine light, received from Him, led you deeper into the mystery of the Redemption and its effects in the past and in the future.

Your life with Jesus was one of the purest, most fervent, most perfect emotions of love to God, Whom you sheltered within yourself. How can I ever imagine the emotions of longing and most eager expectation of the Birth of the Divine Child! How great must have been that longing! You were longing to see the Face of God and to be happy in the vision. You were soon really to see the Face of God, the created image of divine perfection, the sight of which rejoices heaven and earth, from which all beings derive life and joy; the Face Whose features enraptured God from all eternity; the Face for which all ages had expectantly yearned. You were to see this Face unveiled, in all the beauty and grace of childhood as the face of your own Child.

Indeed, all were awaiting your Son: the world, to gain rest and peace; the angels, to see God's plans fulfilled; the Heavenly Father Himself, to behold His created Image; and all this longing was united in your heart. While you bore the Author of all things in your womb, and your heart was beating quickly with love, adoration, and longing, still your face told nothing of this, and no one knew that such marvelous things were taking place in you.

MARY, MY MOTHER, I rejoice with you in the joyful expectation of your little Son. Though it is impossible for me to form any idea of the thoughts that flooded your mind and heart, I beg you to give me at least a spark of that fervor of divine love that burned in your soul. Let me feel some of the sentiments of loving expectation that you felt while waiting for the birth of your Child, so that I may prepare myself for His coming and the graces of the mystery of His Nativity may bear fruit in my soul. To you I entrust the preparation of my soul for the coming of my Savior on Christmas Day.

(3) MARY, MOTHER OF GOD, *make my interior life of union with Jesus more like your own.* After Holy Communion Jesus is with me as God and Man, with His Body and Blood, Soul and Divinity. Jesus is in me, too, through sanctifying grace; I bear within me the supernatural image of the Divine Sonship. He works in my soul by His grace. He forms Himself in me by supernatural principles, which He implants in my mind; by supernatural intentions and meritorious actions. He follows up in my heart also the aim that brought Him into your womb—He wishes to be born in me, to grow, rule, and reveal Himself. Thus my soul in sanctifying grace is always, in a spiritual manner, like your womb—a sanctuary of the living God!

As you led an interior life and centered all your thoughts and life upon the Word Incarnate in your womb, so help me to lead an interior, supernatural life, always guided and directed by supernatural principles, having always supernatural intentions and performing supernatural actions.

MARY, MY MOTHER, I beg you to aid me in being watchful over myself, guarding my exterior and interior senses, avoiding all outward haste and inward passion, trying to make a virtuous action of everything I do, and by talking to God frequently in prayer. May my life thus become a copy of your own life, especially during this time of your expectation!

I earnestly want to be filled with the dispositions in which you expected the coming of the Savior and thus prepare myself for His coming into my soul by faith and divine charity, as well as for His coming at the hour of my death and judgment. In union with you may my heart yield itself up to childlike confidence in Jesus so that

the graces of His Nativity may be brought to my soul in abundance,
and He may be born anew within my heart.

> A world in sin and sadness had turned in hope to thee
> To speak the word of gladness and set the sinner free;
> The ends of God's creation were filled with expectation;
> God sought to be thy Son! "Thy holy will be done!" Maria!
>
> An angel bore the message with joy so undefiled;
> Yet what the years would presage for thy beloved Child!
> The prophet's clear prediction foretold His dire affliction!
> And He thy loving Son? "Thy holy will be done!" Maria!
>
> In trial's grim oppression along life's weary way
> Thy childlike love's profession shall prompt my heart to say,
> Though sin its war is waging, though Satan's might is raging,
> And clouds obscure the sun: "Thy holy will be done!" Maria!

Grant, we beg of You, Almighty God, that we who are weighed down by
the old yoke of sin, may be freed by the new birth of Your only-begotten
Son for which we long, Who lives and reigns forever. Amen.

Christmas

Background:

After her visit of three months to Elizabeth, Mary returned to Nazareth. Joseph had not as yet been informed of the angel's visit to Mary. Seeing that she was to become a mother, and not wishing to accuse her, for "he was a just man" and could not question her virtue, he decided to send her away secretly. An angel appeared to him in a dream and said, "Joseph, son of David, fear not to take unto thee Mary, thy spouse, for that which has been formed in her is the work of the Holy Spirit." Joseph did as the Lord had commanded: he took his spouse to his home.

Emperor Augustus ordered that a census be taken. Since all had to enroll in their home town, Joseph went up from Nazareth in Galilee to the city of David in Judea, called Bethlehem, because he was of the house and family of David; he went up with Mary, his espoused wife, who was with child. The trip took about four days. Because of the many travelers, there was no room for them in the inn. They found shelter in a stable, where *Mary brought into the world her firstborn Son,* wrapped Him in swaddling clothes, and laid Him in a manger. She adored her little Son Who was also her God. An angel informed the shepherds of the birth of a Savior, and they hastened to adore Him also. Mary kept these things, pondering over them in her heart. It is to her that we owe the details concerning the birth and childhood of Jesus.

The first Lateran Council, held in 649 under Pope St. Martin I, gave the dogmatic definition of *the perpetual virginity of Mary.* The occasion was the condemnation of Monothelism, which held there was only one will in Christ; namely, the divine will: "If anyone does not in accord with the Holy Fathers acknowledge the holy and ever virgin and immaculate Mary as really and truly the Mother of God, inasmuch as she, in the fullness of time, and without seed, conceived by the Holy Spirit, God the Word Himself, Who before all time was born of God the Father, and without loss of integrity brought Him forth, and after His birth preserved her virginity inviolate, let him be condemned."

27

Especially in the Incarnation and Redemption God's infinite goodness and mercy shine forth. His eternal plan of sending His own Son into the world to redeem the human race, broken and bruised by sin, and of restoring to it the children's inheritance and heavenly beatitude, is the masterpiece of His wisdom and love. The Blessed Virgin Mary had a very important part in this eternal plan as the Mother of the Redeemer.

Christmas recalls the wonderful mystery of the Incarnation which renders God visible in order that we may listen to Him, imitate Him and unite ourselves to Him. It renders God able to suffer, for He finds in His humanity the means wherewith to suffer, to expiate, to merit, to enrich us with graces. The Word of God assumed our human nature to redeem us and to make us holy by giving us a share in His Divinity. It was through the Virgin Mary that Jesus received His humanity; hence the feast of Christmas belongs both to Christ and to His Blessed Mother. The gift of Christ was perfectly accomplished at the moment of His birth. Today there is grave danger that, in celebrating a Christmas without the Mother, we may soon reach a point where we shall celebrate Christmas without the Infant. Just as there can never be a Christmas without a Christ, so there can never be a Christ without a Mary.

Holy Church wills that the celebration of the mystery of Our Lord's Incarnation should bring us the grace that we may live a new life, more free from sin and attachment to ourselves and creatures. *She would have us understand above all that Christ, in exchange for the humanity which He takes from us, wishes to make us partakers of His Divinity by sanctifying grace, that He may possess us more completely.* The grace of His new Divine birth in us is the true meaning and spirit of Christmas. Just as Our Blessed Mother had an intimate share in giving Jesus to us, she also has an intimate share in obtaining the graces of Christmas for us.

Prayer

(1) MARY, MOTHER OF GOD, *how wondrous was the birth of your Divine Son!* To fulfill the prophecy that the Messias would be born in Bethlehem, the city of David, God made use of the edict of a pagan emperor. With Joseph you went up from Galilee into Judea, to Bethlehem, the city of David, because you were of the house and family of David, to be enrolled. In your delicate condition, in winter, and without even the necessities of life for yourself or your Child, you obediently traveled to a distant and strange land. You did not question the plans of God but hastened to fulfill them, for your confidence in God matched your love of Him.

You conceived Him by the Holy Spirit with all purity, and with all purity you brought Him forth, not in the pangs of childbirth but in the happiness of yearning love. In a poor cave of Bethlehem the Son of God was born miraculously. His human soul and body were substantially and inseparably united to His Divine nature in one Divine Person, being the soul and body of God Incarnate. Through this birth, the Divine Majesty lost nothing of Its splendor, and you became the Mother of God and yet remained a virgin. This mystery and your dignity amaze heaven and earth. Never had God submitted to man, and He submitted to you. Never had God consulted man, and He consulted you. Never had God made His actions depend on man, and He made the most wonderful of His actions depend on you! From the moment you pronounced the words, "Be it done to me according to thy word," God dwelt bodily within you. The angels adored this mystery of the abasement of the Son of God, as well as His compassion and love for men, and rejoiced in your dignity, greatness, and power, for you are truly His Mother.

MARY, MY MOTHER, I can picture you lovingly embracing your little Son and adoring Him as your God; wrapping Him in swaddling clothes and gently laying Him on the straw in the manger. There were only two spectators to witness the birth of God's own Son. Only your deep faith could fully appreciate this extreme poverty. The God of infinite power was now a helpless Infant, subject to the suffering of frail mortals. Externally, He was like every other child. He knew all things, since He was God; but He could not even speak. His cries proved His helplessness. You adored the God Whom the heaven of heavens could not contain, cribbed and confined in the narrow manger.

(2) MARY, MOTHER OF GOD, I cannot even imagine *the joy that filled your heart as you gazed at your Child* with wondering awe, lifted Him from the manger, cradled Him in your arms and pressed Him to your heart. The love that welled up in His little Heart was Divine Love, and you must have received it with the utmost humility, never for a moment deeming yourself worthy of it, but returning the favor with all the love of your own immaculate heart. Such love set your heart on fire with love of your Infant Son; not merely as your Son, but as your God and Savior, since you have already shared in the merits of His Passion and death. You loved Him according to the measure of the grace with which you were full. I

have but a very faint notion of the delight that overflowed your soul as a result of such love.

MARY, MY MOTHER, the love of your Divine Child, which was the reason for your great joy, was also the cause of your bitter *sorrow*. You knew that this little Son of yours was God's Son and that God had not given Him to you for yourself alone, but for the whole world. That little shivering Infant in the manger was your own flesh and blood. Your advent work was done—you had formed Christ of your own life, in yourself; and now that you had brought Him forth, you lived in Him. Your life was in Christ. But someday you would give that life of Jesus as a sacrifice for the salvation of the world. Calvary and the cross loomed up before you, and you seemed to feel some of the pain already. Your suffering equaled your love. But the peace of your soul was undisturbed. You received both joy and sorrow with perfect resignation to the Divine Will.

(3) MARY, MOTHER OF GOD, *how great was your love for Jesus!* When the little Jesus was not yet born, from the depths of your humble soul you sent your prayers to Him. When men's heartlessness thrust Jesus and you from Bethlehem to the cold stable, your caresses warmed the shivering Savior. When Herod's cruelty drove you into the Egyptian desert, your virginal breast was the only safe resting place for your little Son. When Jesus began to develop, your pure eyes guarded Him day and night. And when He struggled with death on Calvary, then again it was you, His Mother, who stood faithfully at the foot of the cross with the sword of pain piercing your heart.

MARY, MY MOTHER, *like you, help me to strive with every power within me to love Jesus for His own sake.* May that love impress itself on all my thoughts, words, and actions. Like you, let me not long for divine comfort, but willingly accept and bear the cross in the spirit of a true follower of my crucified Master.

Your soul was stirred with sentiments of admiration for the wondrous providence of God when you saw the first adorers of your Divine Child who had been led to the crib by the message of an angel. Never had you realized God's love of poverty, humility, and simplicity until you saw He wanted to be adored by poor, simple shepherds. You fully appreciated the meaning of your own poverty and kept all these things, pondering them in your heart. Help me to learn the lesson of humility, poverty, and self-denial which Jesus preached from His first pulpit, the little crib.

O Mother of Fair Love, it was not alone
Christ whom you mothered on the first Christmas night,
not alone the Orient, the Splendor that outshone
daylight and suns and all created light.
It was not only this new dearness, kissed and held
in love and lullabies among the straw,
warmed by the breath of oxen that still smelled
of clover and sweet fields. But in deep awe
there crept in with the shepherd and his sheep
and bowed down with the Oriental king
your other children who will always keep
the joy of your mysterious mothering,
Cause of our Joy, Heaven's Gate, at once our Mother,
on that first Christmas night, through Christ, our Brother.
　　　　　　　　　　—SISTER MARIS STELLA

† † †

O God, Who has made this most holy night to shine forth with the brightness of the true Light, grant, we beg of You, that we who have known the mystery of His light on earth, may also experience His joys in heaven, Who with You lives and reigns forever. Amen.

Feast of the Holy Family

FEAST, Sunday within the Octave of Epiphany

Background:

All that the Gospels tell us of *Christ's hidden life* at Nazareth with Mary and Joseph is that "He was subject to them" and that He advanced in wisdom and age and grace before God and men. "Having gone so far as to take a nature like ours, sin excepted, He wished also to be "obedient unto death." Jesus could say of His Mother and foster father what He said of His Heavenly Father, "I do always the things that please them." Out of a life of thirty-three years, Jesus, who is Eternal Wisdom, chose to pass thirty years in silence and obscurity, obedience and labor. Truly, He is a hidden God! It was in this hidden life at Nazareth that Mary had the rare privilege of observing the example of her Divine Son and of becoming more like Him in grace and virtue.

The Holy Family is a model for all Christian families. In the family life of Jesus, Mary, and Joseph are exemplified the proper relations that should exist between husband and wife, parents and children. There was filial devotion to God in that family circle of the three holiest persons who ever lived. While Joseph supported the Holy Family by handwork, Mary managed the household, and Jesus assisted both of them. They were united in their daily tasks which they made holy by prayer and meditation. By practicing the domestic virtues of charity, obedience and mutual help, they sanctified family life. We should often pray to them to sanctify our families by their example and intercession.

Prayer

(1) MARY, MOTHER OF GOD, *how wonderful and yet at times how painful were the experiences of your hidden life with Jesus!* After the Annunciation, the most joyful experience of your life was the birth of Jesus at Bethlehem. With all purity you had conceived Him, with all purity you had brought Him forth, not in the pains of childbirth, but in the bliss of love. You adored and loved Him

in the company of St. Joseph. Later, encouraged by your smile, poor shepherds drew near to the crib to pay homage to your newly born Son. And when they told you about the message of the angel, you kept these things, pondering over them in your heart.

On the eighth day you were present at *the circumcision* of your Child when He was given the name Jesus. This name, meaning Savior, must have recalled for you the mission for which Jesus had willed to be born of you. With what love you and Joseph pronounced this most charming of all names, when you addressed the Son of God.

On the fortieth day you and Joseph brought the Child to Jerusalem *to present Him to the Lord* according to the law of Moses. Who will understand the anguish of your heart when Simeon reminded you that your gentle Child, who was to bring salvation and peace to men, would be an occasion for the fall even of many of His brethren in Israel and that your heart would be pierced by a sword of sorrow? Henceforth there would hardly be an hour of joy unmixed with sadness for you. This was like the Offertory of your life, when you offered to the Heavenly Father your little Son as a victim for the redemption of the world.

But what happiness filled your heart when you witnessed *the adoration of your Child by the three learned kings of the East* as they narrated to you, with beautiful simplicity, their account of the mysterious star that had led them to Christ! Having adored their God, they paid reverence to you, His Mother, but you referred their homage to your Son, with Whom you were one in the redemption of souls. You were grateful to God for having revealed Him to the pagan nations of the world.

Your faith was severely tried by the command of the angel *to flee into Egypt.* Your Son was the Son of the Most High; yet you, His Mother, had to defend Him, the King of kings, from the hatred of an earthly king by flight into a pagan land. You obeyed at once and started in the darkness of the night on your long journey with your Divine Child and Joseph. Though your stay in the pagan land must have been very unpleasant, you awaited a sign from heaven before returning to your own country.

MARY, MY MOTHER, words cannot describe the sorrow of your motherly heart when *you lost your twelve-year-old Son.* You expressed your grief in the gentle complaint: "Son, why hast thou done so to us? Behold, thy father and I have sought thee sorrowing." After doing what He regarded as His Father's will, Jesus went down with you and Joseph and came to Nazareth and was subject to you. Help me to learn from your hidden life with Jesus, that no matter how heavy my cross, I have nothing to fear as long as God is with me. As Jesus withdrew from you, so He may often withdraw from me to prove the sincerity of my love for Him. Teach me to surrender myself to the Divine Will with the childlike confidence which you had in the Providence of God.

(2) MARY, MOTHER OF GOD, your life at Nazareth was a hidden *life of prayer and work.* Your whole day's work was done for God alone because prayer, simple and sublime, filled it completely. A charming simplicity dominated each of your domestic duties. Your disposition was always serene because the thought of God absorbed you. Your heart was in your home, and hence you could not be carried away on the stream of the world. You lived in retirement and poverty, being satisfied with only the necessities of life. Familiar only with God, you wished to pass as the lowliest of His creatures. Sanctity was carefully concealed beneath the quiet simplicity of your daily life so that people did not realize the Son of God and His Virgin Mother dwelt among them.

MARY, MY MOTHER, how reverently you and Joseph admired the beautiful example of Jesus! What food for thought was the obedience of Jesus! His practice of this difficult virtue gave to the hidden life of Nazareth its sweetness, peace, and majesty. Though He was the Son of God, He was subject to His creatures for thirty years. Grant that the example of your Son's obedience to you may ever help me to obey, for I cannot die to myself and become like Jesus and you unless I obey.

I cannot, therefore, measure your growth in holiness. Grace poured constantly from Christ, its source, into your soul, and you were the channel through which it was imparted to His foster father. While your hands were busy, Jesus absorbed your thoughts and affections and thrilled your hearts with the purest love for Him. Divine love united you all in a holy and happy family.

(3) MARY, MOTHER OF GOD, *the imitation of your Divine Son was the great occupation of your life. Jesus became Man not only to die for us, but to teach us how to live by His word and example.* It thrilled you with the purest joy to have so perfect a Model ever before you; to talk freely and often with Him; to be so close an

observer of His conduct. You filled your mind unceasingly with thoughts of His virtues. You pondered over all His words and recorded them in your heart. You were absorbed in acquiring His spirit. You spent yourself and were spent in learning the practical knowledge of Jesus Christ, and in so doing, you became the holiest creature that ever walked this earth—the Vessel of Singular Devotion.

If I am to be a child worthy of so wonderful a Mother, I must burn with the same desire to imitate my Lord and Master. The practical imitation of Christ is my highest duty. I know that you can best teach me to imitate Him because you are the Mirror of Justice who reflects the spirit of Jesus most powerfully and most faithfully. Help me to study my Divine Model with earnestness and perseverance, as you did, and thus gain the knowledge that will be for me eternal life, as Jesus said, "This is eternal life, that they may know Thee, the only true God, and Jesus Christ Whom Thou hast sent" (John 17:3).

MARY, MY MOTHER, help me to copy your example and to see in a hidden life of prayer, work, and daily fidelity to the commonplace, the surest steppingstone to sainthood. *I desire to lead a hidden life with Jesus in the Holy Eucharist.* Through Holy Mass I wish to offer myself through your hands as a sacrifice with Jesus; at Holy Communion I want to be changed into Jesus by divine grace so that I may live His life; by my frequent visits to the tabernacle I want to enjoy His friendship. There may I discover His presence and see His veiled glory with eyes of faith. May the divine silence of Jesus in His school of love, the tabernacle, breathe into my soul the peace of God and make my burdens light. Like you, may I with reverent familiarity speak to my God and ask Him to enlighten me about His providence in my regard and strengthen me to bear the crosses He sends me.

O highest Hope of mortals,
Blest Light of saints above,
O Jesus, on whose boyhood
Home smiled with kindly love.

And thou whose bosom nursed Him,
O Mary, highly graced,
Whose breast gave milk to Jesus,
Whose arms thy God embraced.

And thou of all men chosen
To guard the Virgin's fame,
To whom God's Son refused not
A father's gracious name.

Born for the nation's healing,
Of Jesse's lineage high,
Behold the suppliants kneeling,
O hear the sinners' cry!

The sun, returned to evening,
Dusks all the twilight air:
We, lingering here before You,
Pour out our heartfelt prayer.

Your home was as a garden
Made glad with fairest flowers;
May life thus blossom sweetly
In every home of ours.

Jesus, to Thee be glory
The Maiden-Mother's Son,
With Father and with Spirit
While endless ages run.

† † †

O Lord Jesus Christ, Who, by Your obedience to Mary and Joseph,
sanctified family life with splendid virtues, grant that by their help we may
be instructed by the example of Your Holy Family and become partakers
of their eternal happiness, Who live and reign forever. Amen.

Our Lady of Prompt Succor

Background:

Mother Michel Gensoul, a nun of the Ursuline Order in France, wrote to Pope Pius VII and asked whether she and a group of exiled nuns might go to the Ursuline convent in New Orleans. She prayed to the Blessed Mother in these words: "O most holy Virgin Mary, if you obtain a prompt and favorable answer to my letter, I promise to have you honored in New Orleans under the title: Our Lady of Prompt Succor."

Pope Pius VII was imprisoned by Napoleon and was not permitted to communicate with anyone. Mother Michel mailed her letter on March 19, 1809. The favorable reply was dated April 28, 1809. This would have been considered prompt even in peacetime. Consequently, Mother Michel had a statue carved and blessed. On December 30, 1810, it was placed in the chapel of the convent in New Orleans under the title "Our Lady of Prompt Succor."

After defeating Napoleon in 1814, the British were ready to concentrate on their war against the United States. New Orleans was the gateway to the Mississippi Valley, hence a city worth fighting for. The capture of New Orleans would mean the possession of the vast territory of Louisiana, bought from the French a few years before. This would confine the United States to the area between the Mississippi and the Atlantic.

The Battle of New Orleans was fought after the treaty of peace had been signed. "Never was a city so defenseless, so exposed, so weak, so prostrate as New Orleans in the fall of 1814," says one historian. A force of 20,000 men and a fleet of fifty ships carrying a thousand guns, the elite of England's army and navy, were to face General Andrew Jackson and about 6,000 poorly trained and poorly armed soldiers. The British were so sure of victory that their ships carried a full staff of civil officials ready to administer the province of Louisiana.

The people of New Orleans filled the churches and begged heaven to help them. The Ursuline Sisters promised Our Lady of Prompt Succor that if the Americans won the battle a Solemn High Mass would be offered in her honor every year on January 8th.

37

In just twenty-five minutes the battle was over. The British suffered tremendous casualties. Only about half of the American force came into battle and they suffered few casualties. The British withdrew and made no further attempt to capture the city. New Orleans was saved. Louisiana still belonged to the United States and our country was free to expand to the west. General Jackson visited the Ursuline Sisters after the battle and acknowledged that his victory was due to God's help.

Rome officially approved devotion to Our Lady of Prompt Succor at different times. On September 27, 1851, Pope Pius IX authorized the celebration of the feast of Our Lady of Prompt Succor. On June 21, 1894, Pope Leo XIII granted the privilege of the solemn coronation of the miraculous statue, exposed to public veneration in the Chapel of the Ursuline Convent in New Orleans. In 1924 a new shrine was dedicated. Finally, on June 13, 1928, the Holy See confirmed the choice of Our Lady of Prompt Succor as the Principal Patroness of the City of New Orleans and of the State of Louisiana, and decreed that the Patronal Feast be celebrated on the fifteenth day of January with proper Mass and Office.

Prayer

(1) MARY, MOTHER OF GOD, *you are, after Jesus, our only hope.* As the Mother of the Word Incarnate, your merits have raised you high above the angels and saints to the very throne of the Eternal God. Devotion to you is a God-given means of grace and an important part of Christianity. You are, as it were, the neck of the Mystical Body of the Church, uniting all her members with Jesus Christ, her Head. You are the channel and instrument through which all graces are distributed. Placed between God and His Church, you are our most kind and loving Mediatrix. Hasten, then, to our help. As you once saved a city of our country from ravaging flames because of the earnest prayers of the faithful at your shrine, and our country from her foes, have pity on us in our needs. Your virginal foot crushed the head of the infernal serpent. You are strong against the enemies of our salvation. Deliver us from the wiles of Satan and assist us in the many trials which beset our path in this vale of tears.

MARY, MY MOTHER, Our Lady of Prompt Succor, I consecrate myself to you. Your help is prompt and powerful. I lay at your feet all my cares and sorrows, and place into your hands all my hopes and fears. I entrust to you all my interests, both spiritual and temporal.

Hasten to help me. You offered yourself entirely to God and fulfilled His will perfectly. Make me generous in sacrifice. Because you are the heavenly protectress of souls devoted to your Divine Son, bless me each day of my mortal pilgrimage. Look upon me with eyes of mercy and, after this my exile, show me Jesus, Your Son and our Brother.

(2) MARY, MOTHER OF GOD, *your title of Our Lady of Prompt Succor assures me that I can find in you quick help in my needs.* You are the Queen of the Universe and the advocate of sinners, the haven of safety to the shipwrecked, the health of the sick and infirm, the consolation of the afflicted, the refuge and salvation of all on earth. Even when you lived in this valley of tears, you were most loving and kind toward the afflicted; how much more sympathetic are you now when you reign happily in heaven! Now you realize human misery more fully and, therefore, you show your mercy and give your help more generously. You are our Mother, and a mother cannot forget her children.

MARY, MY MOTHER, Our Lady of Prompt Succor, look upon me with pity, for I turn to you for help. Let me never become discouraged, but have recourse to you in all my needs, being convinced that it is God's Will that you help us in our misery. Heaven and earth shall perish before you are seen to abandon the needy who pray to you sincerely.

(3) MARY, MOTHER OF GOD, *your consoling title of Our Lady of Prompt Succor reminds me of the merciful compassion of your loving heart* which urges you to help those in need as soon as possible. Throughout the ages I can imagine you raising your sinless hands in pleading prayer before the throne of God, causing streams of redeeming grace to flow over the souls of men to regenerate and sanctify them in the Heart of Jesus. Day after day prayers for help burst forth from thousands of lips and hearts as they appeal to you for help. You are so prompt in giving help because your love for your children is so great.

When I look back over my past life, I behold the numberless gifts of your mercy and kindness glittering on the path of my life like so many heavenly diamonds. From my cradle to the present moment, your loving hand has ever showered upon me those heavenly gifts, averted the punishment of God's just anger from me, and repeatedly poured upon my soul the graces merited by the

Precious Blood of Jesus, thus restoring to it, or beautifying, that bright robe of innocence with which I was clothed at baptism.

MARY, MY MOTHER, as I look toward the dim future and fail to see what lies before me, I fondly cherish one hope—that you will never forsake me. I am a sinner and, though I shall henceforth do my utmost to please God, I shall ever stand in need of your heavenly help, which is gently offered to me by your sinless hands. I shall need your prompt help especially at the hour of death. In that dread moment may I, with God's grace and your help, send forth from my heart a cry of loving repentance, and then, with unbounded, childlike confidence, cast myself on the bosom of your mercy, and thus secure the crowning gift of God's mercy—a favorable judgment.

Our Lady of Prompt Succor, this favor I seek above all—the grace of final perseverance in God's grace, a happy death and life everlasting. You are my Mother. You are my hope.

Ave Maria! Blessed Maid!
Lily of Eden's fragrant shade,
    Who can express the love
That nurtured thee so pure and sweet,
Making thy heart a shelter meet
    For Jesus' holy love?

Ave Maria! Mother blest,
To whom caressing and caress'd,
    Clings the Eternal Child;
Favor'd beyond Archangels' dream,
When first on thee with tenderest gleam
    Thy new-born Savior smiled.

Ave Maria! Thou whose name
All but adorning love may claim,
    Yet may we reach thy shrine;
For He, thy Son and Savior, vows
To crown all lowly lofty brows
    With love and joy like thine.

†   †   †

Almighty and Eternal God, You see us surrounded by so many dangers and miseries; grant in Your infinite goodness that the Blessed Virgin Mary,

Mother of Your Divine Son, may defend us from the evil spirit and protect us against all adversities, that always and with prompt succor she may deliver us from every evil of soul and body and safely guide us to the kingdom of heaven, through the same Christ Our Lord. Amen.

The Espousals of the Blessed Virgin Mary

FEAST, January 23 (TRIDUUM, January 20–22)

Background:

It should not surprise us that Joseph sought a wife, for marriage was obligatory for a Jew. An unmarried man was considered to be a man without joy, blessing and well-being. But that Mary, who vowed perpetual virginity, should consent to espousals may seem strange. At the age of about fifteen, she may have yielded to her parents or guardians to conform to the prevailing custom, leaving it to Divine Providence to safeguard her resolution. She may have told Joseph of her vow and persuaded him to consent to a virginal marriage. It is possible, also, that Joseph entertained the same ideals, so that he needed no persuasion to accept the kind of espousals contemplated by Mary.

The man whom God had destined for Mary was worthy. Joseph was a carpenter by trade and, like her, a member of the house of David. Under the inspiration of the Holy Spirit he resolved to lead, like Mary, a pure life within the bonds of marriage. The espousals took place. With the Jews, espousals conferred many of the rights of marriage. Generally the two espoused resided in their own homes until the marriage ceremony. At the period of her life in which the Gospel account opens, Mary was living at Nazareth with her parents, or, if they no longer lived, with her relatives. Joseph also lived at Nazareth.

The Fathers of the Church give several reasons why Mary and Joseph became man and wife. They were not to raise up children to God. Mary, overshadowed by the power of the Holy Spirit, was to conceive and bear the Messias, and at the same time remain a Virgin. But, through Joseph would be known Mary's lineal descent from David. If she had no husband, the unbelieving Jews would stone her as a sinner. In her Motherhood, Mary would need protection, and so would the Child in His infancy. Surely, such a husband had to be a man of faith, of character, of purity—"a just man." And so they were betrothed.

When Joseph noticed that Mary was with child, he planned to put her away privately. Mary was unwilling to reveal her secret to him but resigned herself to the Providence of God, trusting that He would guard her reputation. An angel assured Joseph that he should marry his betrothed bride: she was without sin, and the Son to be born of her would be holiness itself. Joseph submitted without hesitation and arranged with Mary to hasten the celebration of their chaste nuptials. On the appointed day, at nightfall, accompanied by friends, Joseph went in procession to the home of Mary's parents, to conduct her, dressed in her finest clothes and surrounded by her closest friends, to his own house, by the light of lamps and torches, to the joyous sound of flutes and timbrels. The solemn introduction of the bride into the new home which she was to adorn and in which she was to be the queen, was the chief and official marriage ceremony among the Jews. However, as Mary and Joseph were poor, everything was conducted simply.

It is certain that a real marriage was contracted by Joseph and Mary. Still Mary is called "espoused" to Joseph because the marriage was never consummated. The term "spouse" is applied to married people until their marriage is consummated.

In an Encyclical Letter of 1903, Pope Leo XIII wrote: "Marriage is the most intimate of all unions, which from its essence imparts a community of gifts between those joined together by it. Thus, in giving Joseph the Blessed Virgin as spouse, God appointed him to be, not only her life's companion, but also, by virtue of the conjugal tie, a participator in her sublime dignity."

Mary and Joseph were deeply devoted to each other. Each was a source of joy and edification to the other; hence they were true models for husbands and wives, mothers and fathers.

The Feast of the Espousals of Our Lady with St. Joseph originated with the Friars Minor and is observed mainly by the Order. The feast was celebrated in the beginning of the fifteenth century at Chartres, France. It seems to have arisen from popular devotion. In 1913 the feast was removed from the Church Calendar, but in 1928 the Franciscans were again permitted to celebrate it on the 23rd of January. It was eventually extended to several other groups.

Prayer

(1) MARY, MOTHER OF GOD, though marriage and motherhood were the cherished ideals of every Jewish maiden, *you vowed your virginity to God,* under the inspiration of the Holy Spirit. The Lord being your portion, you renounced all else—the honors, the pleasures, and the rewards of marriage—and joyously chose the life of a virgin. In consecrating your virginity to God, you had given up all hope of becoming the Mother of the Messias because you considered yourself unworthy of the highest honor of the

Divine Maternity. No one after Christ was humbler than you were,
yet no one after Christ gave God greater glory. This humility was
richly rewarded. God would work a miracle so that you might remain a virgin, and yet become the Mother of God.

Teach me to imitate your humility by acknowledging my nothingness and seeking the glory of God in everything.

MARY, MY MOTHER, to conceal the miraculous conception and
birth of His Divine Son, *the Eternal Father inspired Joseph to
marry you* before the Annunciation by the archangel Gabriel. The
husband whom God had destined for you was a man of faith, of
character, of purity, "a just man." Like you, he was of the tribe of
Juda and the family of David.

Though Joseph planned to put you away privately when he recognized that you were with child, you still were unwilling to reveal your secret to him, lest you might seem to boast of your gifts.
How great was your trust in God! You resigned yourself to the
care of God, in the fullest confidence that He would guard your
innocence and reputation. Thus an angel appeared to Joseph and
said, "Do not be afraid, Joseph, son of David, to take to thee Mary
thy wife, for that which is begotten in her is of the Holy Spirit. And
she shall bring forth a son, and thou shalt call his name Jesus; for
he shall save his people from their sins" (Matt. 1:20). Joseph
could rest assured and marry you, his betrothed bride. He was
obedient and immediately arranged with you the celebration of
your chaste nuptials. On the appointed day, at nightfall, accompanied by friends, he went in procession to your parents' house, to
conduct you to his own home. You were dressed in your finest
clothes and surrounded by your friends as you joined the procession
by the light of lamps and the sound of music. This introduction
into the new home in which you were to live was your official
marriage ceremony. Joseph, so humble, so pure, so loving, respected
your consecration to God, and he was willing to live with you a
life of spotless virginity. You were indeed two of one heart and one
soul.

(2) MARY, MOTHER OF GOD, *God had a purpose in wanting you
and Joseph to become man and wife.* You were not to raise up
children unto God—not ordinary offspring, but a Child, the Son
of God! Overshadowed by the power of the Holy Spirit, you were
to conceive and bear the Messias, and at the same time remain a

Virgin in every respect. Through Joseph your descent from David
would be known. If you had no husband, the unbelieving Jews
would have stoned you as a sinner.

In your motherhood you would need protection and so would
the Child in His infancy. Your union with Joseph was ordained
in the designs of God for the education of Jesus. You could not of
yourself provide the protection and training the Child needed.
Joseph was chosen by God the Father to take His own place, in
regard to His Divine Son, during the early years of that Son's life
on earth. He was endowed by God with all a father's tenderness
and love for Him Who was confided to him as his Child.

MARY, MY MOTHER, your Son Jesus came to enlighten the world
with His teaching and example. He sanctified your marriage with
St. Joseph so that it might be an example for all Christian marriages.
Be pleased to intercede with Jesus, your Son, for Christian families.
Protect, guard, and keep them in holy fear, in peace, and in the
harmony of Christian charity. By conforming themselves to the
divine model of your Family, may they attain to eternal happiness.

(3) MARY, MOTHER OF GOD, *I believe that the dignity, holiness,
and glory of Joseph rests on the fact that he was your spouse and
that he was the foster father of Jesus Christ.* Your dignity as Mother
of God is so lofty that nothing created can rank above it. But as
Joseph had been united to you by the ties of marriage, he approached nearer than anyone else to your eminent dignity. In
giving you to Joseph as spouse, God appointed him to be not only
your life's companion, but also a sharer of your dignity. Joseph
was a virgin for your sake, that a Virgin Son might be born of a
virginal marriage.

The Scriptures refer to you and Joseph as "the parents of Jesus."
After the prophecy of Simeon, the Scriptures mention that "His
father and mother" were wondering at those things which were
spoken concerning Him. As your true and lawful spouse, St. Joseph
was meant by God to have the privilege of exercising as his right,
in virtue of his virginal marriage, the parental office in regard to
your Child.

MARY, MY MOTHER, you and good St. Joseph were married to
become the models of family life. May your holy marriage be an
inspiration to Christian husbands and wives so that they may always
live in sincere love and peace and be obedient to the command-

ments of God. Through your prayers may they and their children
honor God by a virtuous life so as to be worthy of a heavenly reward. May the love and peace and happiness of your Holy Family
reign in the Christian families of all times.

> Wife did she live, yet virgin die,
> Untouched by man, yet Mother of a Son;
> To save herself and Child from fatal lie,
> To end the web whereof the thread was spun,
> In marriage knot to Joseph she was tied,
> Unwonted works with wonted veils to hide.
>
> God lent His paradise to Joseph's care,
> Wherein He was to plant the tree of life;
> His Son, of Joseph's child the title bare,
> Just cause to make the Mother Joseph's wife.
> Oh blessed man! betrothed to such a spouse,
> More blessed to live with such a Child in house!
>
> No carnal love this sacred league procured,
> All vain delights were far from their assent;
> Though both in wedlock bans themselves assured,
> Yet straight by vow they sealed their chaste intent.
> Thus had she virgin's, wife's, and widow's crown,
> And by chaste childbirth doubled her renown.
>   —BLESSED ROBERT SOUTHWELL, S.J., Martyr, 1595

† † †

Bestow on Your servants, we beg You, O Lord, the gift of Your heavenly
grace, that we for whom the motherhood of the Blessed Virgin was the
beginning of salvation, may be blessed with peace on the solemn feast day
of her espousals. Through Christ our Lord. Amen.

Purification of the Blessed Virgin Mary

Background:

In remembrance of the day on which God struck the first-born among the Egyptians and spared those of the Israelites, *the Law of Moses* ordained that every first-born son should be presented in the temple of Jerusalem and should be redeemed by the payment of five shekels ($1.40). Also, every woman, after the birth of a male child, should offer for her legal purification a lamb and a turtledove. A poor woman might offer a second turtledove instead of the lamb. Accordingly, Mary and Joseph, taking the Child, went up to the Temple in Jerusalem from Bethlehem and carried out the prescriptions of the Law. Mary's was entirely an external redeeming, for she knew well that she was buying Jesus back only to sacrifice Him more completely on the cross.

While in the Temple, they met a devout man named Simeon, to whom the Holy Spirit had revealed that he would not die before seeing the Messias. Prompted by the Holy Spirit, he recognized the long-awaited Savior in Jesus. Mary allowed him to take Jesus in his arms. As he did so, he exclaimed: "Now thou dost dismiss thy servant, O Lord, according to thy word, in peace because my eyes have seen thy salvation, which thou hast prepared before the face of all peoples: A light of revelation to the Gentile, and a glory for thy people Israel" (Luke 2:29).

The prophecy brought home to the parents the fact that the mission of Jesus would extend to all nations and that this mission would entail suffering not only for the Savior but also for His Mother, for Simeon continued: "Behold, this child is destined for the fall and for the rise of many in Israel, and for a sign that shall be contradicted. And thy own soul a sword shall pierce" (Luke 2:34).

The Feast of Our Lady's Purification is probably one of the most ancient of all her feasts, although not until the sixth century was it fixed for February 2nd. Mary has her Child in her arms again, but it is to offer Him in sacrifice. The Light of the World entered into His Temple at Jerusalem, and to celebrate this entry, the Church has prescribed a procession with lighted candles. That Temple built by Herod, beautiful though it was,

47

did not equal the magnificence of Solomon's Temple, yet it had a greater magnificence because Christ entered it. The Prophet Aggeus said: "The Desired of all nations shall come into it and I will fill this house with glory. Great shall be the glory of the house, more than of the first; and in this place I will give peace, saith the Lord of Hosts" (Agg. 2:8–10). The house was filled with glory, and the Lord of Hosts gave peace—His peace—to the world, when Mary carried her Son up the Temple steps at Jerusalem to present Him to the Lord.

Prayer

(1) MARY, MOTHER OF GOD, *I admire your obedience and humility in submitting to the law of purification* by presenting yourself in the temple, like every other Jewish Mother, forty days after the birth of Jesus. You were not bound by the Law, because you were a virgin as well as a mother. You hid your miraculous virginity under the mantle of humility. But the same spirit of humility which had induced Jesus to obey the law of circumcision, made you also submit to the law of purification. The God of holiness, having come upon the earth to take away the sins of the world, chose to appear among us as a sinner. It was, therefore, befitting that you, His Immaculate Mother, destined to cooperate with Him in the work of Redemption, should teach the world, by your submission to the law of purification, this great truth, that humility is the beginning of our salvation, as pride has been the root of our ruin.

MARY, MY MOTHER, you were not obliged by the Law of Moses to present and ransom your first-born Son. In order to free yourself from legal uncleanness and to give us an example of obedience to God's law, you submitted to the ceremony of the purification and made the offering demanded of the poor—two pigeons or turtledoves. In the fulfillment of the law you gave an example of the most perfect obedience and zeal for the edification of others; for since the real nature of your motherhood was not known to your Jewish neighbors, you might have been the cause of scandal to them if you had failed to comply with the law.

(2) MARY, MOTHER OF GOD, *the offering of Jesus was presented by your virginal hands.* Thus you associated yourself yet more directly and intimately with our salvation. You were the first to offer to the Eternal Father His Divine Son as the Victim for the world's Redemption. Here there was a sacrifice, and Jesus was the

Victim. The victim had to belong to the person who offered it. But no child ever belonged to its mother as Jesus belonged to you. In this mystery Jesus is plainly a Victim, and not so plainly a Priest; He could not better communicate His spirit of priesthood than by allowing you, His Mother, to present His outward offering. He could find no worthier altar on which to offer Himself than your immaculate hands. You really had the right to offer Jesus to His Heavenly Father in this mystery.

The Eternal Father once gave you the most precious treasure that heaven possessed—His own Divine Son. In the temple, you returned to Him His gift by consecrating your Child to His honor and glory. For your generosity the Eternal Father made you, through Christ, the dispenser of the riches of God. In presenting your only Son, you present your all. For He was everything to you, and all else was nothing without Him.

MARY, MY MOTHER, your love for Jesus made this sacrifice very great in the eyes of God. In Jesus there was wrapped up the double love of a mother for her only Child and of the holiest creature for her God. And for our sake, you were ready to devote this Child to a life of suffering, persecution, and scorn, even to a shameful death on the Cross.

(3) MARY, MOTHER OF GOD, *by your offering you sacrificed your own heart.* The holy old man Simeon took your Son in his arms. It was in your arms that he found the Savior, to remind me that he who desires to find Jesus will not find Him otherwise than through you. You heard Simeon's words as if they had been spoken to you by God Himself, "Behold, this child is destined for the fall and for the rise of many in Israel, and for a sign that shall be contradicted. And thy own soul a sword shall pierce." Since you were enlightened by the Scriptures, you realized that your Child would be contradicted and utterly rejected by the Jews, who had, for forty centuries, unceasingly sighed for Him as a Savior. You knew that thousands even of His faithful followers throughout the world would turn from Him and would make His coming the occasion of their eternal ruin. You, who were yourself the Queen of Prophets, saw that from that moment "the sword of sorrow" would enter your soul and remain there during the rest of your days. You saw clearly the agony you would feel at the crucifixion.

Having heard the prophecy of your Son's suffering, you almost rejoiced to hear that you would share His suffering. Who can describe the anguish of your generous soul when with your Divine Babe in your arms you were willing to sign His death warrant with your own hands? Jesus was a Son to you and a sword to you: a Son on your breast, a sword in your heart. Your Child, becoming the King of Martyrs, would make you their Queen. Your sorrow would be as deep as the sea.

But this prophecy did not disturb your peace of mind because your will was one with the Will of God. What a difference between the woeful prediction of Simeon and the joyous tidings of the archangel Gabriel announcing the greatness of the Redeemer of mankind! You abandoned yourself to God's Will with deep faith and confidence. You did not try to square both predictions. Your faith taught you that the predictions of both were inspired by the Holy Spirit.

MARY, MY MOTHER, *I wish to offer myself as a sacrifice to God in union with Jesus and through your hands.* Help me to sacrifice myself generously for the love of God—to abstain from those many hurtful things that prevent the union of my soul with God. In order to live, not to myself, but to God, I must bear the cross in union with Jesus. You suffered with Jesus and experienced in your soul what He underwent in His Body. Let me never separate my sufferings from the sufferings of your Divine Son. This loving union will sustain me no matter how heavy my cross. Indeed, I will suffer with joy if I realize that Christ is suffering with me and in me and that He sends me the cross only to trace His image in my soul by uniting me closely with Himself. I shall realize that God, in His infinite wisdom, will make all things work together unto my good.

I wonder, Lord, what words Your Mother said
    When You were cradled in her holy arms.
Her smile was love's caress upon Your head;
    Her eyes reflecting all Your baby charms.

Ah, never was there less of need to speak:
    The Word was there enthroned upon her knee.
What joy was left for either one to seek?
    For each shared in the other's destiny.

And both hearts beat in rhythm, each with each,
   Till something made her catch her breath and hold
You closer, something still beyond her reach—
   A sword would pierce her heart, she had been told.
You raised Your lips to kiss away her fear,
   And saw within her shadowed eyes a tear.

Almighty, everlasting God, we humbly beg Your Majesty, that, as Your only-begotten Son was this day presented in the temple in the form of our flesh, so grant that we, too, may be presented to You with hearts made pure. Through the same Christ our lord. Amen.

Apparition of the Blessed Virgin
Mary Immaculate
(*Our Lady of Lourdes*)

FEAST, February 11 (NOVENA, February 2–10)

Background:

Between February 11 and July 16, 1858, the Blessed Virgin came down from heaven eighteen times and showed herself at Lourdes to Bernadette Soubirous, a little shepherdess who was only fourteen years of age. On February 11th, while gathering wood, Bernadette heard a whistle of wind. With astonished eyes the child saw a niche in the upper part of a rock filled with golden light, and there in the midst of it stood a Lady of great beauty. Her robe glowed with the whiteness of snow in the sunshine and swept in majestic folds to the ground. Her head and shoulders were framed by a white veil, which fell the full length of her robe. A blue sash encircled her waist, and its two ends, wide and unornamented, reached down in front almost to her feet. Each of her feet bore a rose of purest gold. A rosary, whose beads were white and whose cross and chain were of gold, hung from her right arm. Her hands were open, and her arms outstretched slightly in front.

In her apparitions Our Lady appealed for penance and prayers for sinners. On March 25th, the day of the Annunciation, the Blessed Mother declared her name to Bernadette and to the world. On that day Bernadette made this request: "My Lady, would you be so kind as to tell me who you are?" This is how Bernadette describes what happened in that last apparition: "Three times I asked the Apparition her name. At the third instance, she stretched out her hands, which until then she had held joined, raised them, and she said: 'I am the Immaculate Conception.'" And having thus completed her great message to the world, the Lady smiled on Bernadette and withdrew without further word of farewell.

Less than four years before these apparitions, on December 8, 1854, Pope Pius IX proclaimed that Mary in the first instant of her conception was preserved free from all stain of original sin through the merits of her Divine Son. At Lourdes the spotless Queen had come to confirm the infallible utterance of God's Vicar on earth and declared herself not only immaculately conceived, but "the Immaculate Conception." Mary's purpose in appearing to Bernadette, who later became a saint, was to warn the child to pray and make sacrifices for sinners. The many miracles performed every year at Lourdes are the proof that this message was an authentic warning from the Queen of the Universe to her children and that she is deeply interested in their welfare.

Pope Pius XI spoke by radio to Lourdes, on April 28, 1935, at the conclusion of the Jubilee Year of the Redemption: "O Mother of pity and mercy, who as Co-sufferer and Co-redemptrix assisted thy most dear Son, as on the altar of the Cross He consummated the Redemption of mankind . . . preserve in us and increase each day, we beg of thee, the precious fruits of the Redemption and of thy Compassion."

Prayer

(1) MARY, MOTHER OF GOD, *God spoke of you as the Woman who would crush the serpent's head.* Faith tells me that the fall of man was the effect of the malice and envy of the devil, who sought in this way to be revenged upon the Creator for having cast him out of paradise in punishment for his rebellion. But God turned the scheme of the evil one back upon its inventor. A man and a woman had both taken part in the degradation of our race; they must both have part in its restoration. Jesus is the new Adam and you are the new Eve.

God said to the serpent: "Because thou hast done this, I will place enmities between thee and the Woman, between thy seed and her Seed: she shall crush thy head, and thou shalt lie in wait for her heel" (Gen. 3:14–15).

MARY, MY MOTHER, as the Immaculate Conception, you are the Woman who appeared as the mortal enemy of the serpent. Your Divine Son was destined to crush the serpent's head by releasing mankind from the slavery of Satan, thus putting an end to the empire of sin. When God pronounced doom against the evil one, He also announced His merciful plan of saving mankind from the effects of the guilt of our first parents. This was the earliest promise of a Redeemer to come, and you were to be His immaculate Mother.

(2) MARY, MOTHER OF GOD, *you are the new Eve.* The early

writers of the Church speak of you as a second Eve, who fulfilled in
the restoration of mankind a role closely corresponding to that of
Eve in the ruin of our race. You are a second and more blessed Eve.
Eve was unbelieving and disobedient; you were believing and
obedient. Eve listened to the voice of the serpent and brought
death to the human race; you became a source of salvation to all
mankind by receiving with humility the word of God brought to
you by the angel Gabriel.

A woman, the tree, and death symbolize our defeat. Yet these three
have become for us a principle of life. You are the woman, the new
Eve; the wood of the cross is the new tree of life; the death of Jesus,
the new Adam, takes away the sting of the death of Adam. Eve was
the mother of the dead, for all of us, her children, were doomed
to enter this world under sentence of death, the slaves and children
of Satan. But you are the Mother of the living, for by your fidelity
to your Maker you deserved to give to mankind a Redeemer Who
by His death has destroyed the reign of death and has thrown open
to us the gates of everlasting life. You are truly our immaculate
Mother for it is to you, after Jesus, that we are indebted for the
supernatural life of grace and the hope of eternal life.

MARY, MY MOTHER, the beloved disciple, St. John, tells us that
"a great sign appeared in heaven: a Woman clothed with the sun,
and the moon under her feet, and on her head a crown of twelve
stars" (Apoc. 12:1). The Woman is a striking image of you, the
Immaculate Conception. The attitude of the Church toward you,
symbolized by the moon under your feet, is that of a suppliant who
is forever entreating you to use your power in favor of your children.
She is forever imploring you to intercede in their behalf with Him
Who has clothed you with His light and His glory, and has poured
out upon you the fullness of His grace. As our immaculate Mediatrix before your Son you have appeared at Lourdes to encourage
us to amend our lives and to make sacrifices and offer prayers for
sinners. In the spirit of loving confidence we have recourse to you.
We recommend to you our hopes and our fears. Our eyes are up-
raised to you in sorrow and in joy. Immaculate Mother, you are
the hope of a sinful race.

(3) MARY, MOTHER OF GOD, *I firmly believe in the doctrine of
Holy Mother Church concerning your Immaculate Conception;*
namely, that you were, in the first instant of your conception, by

the singular grace and privilege of God, in view of the merits of Jesus Christ, the Savior of the human race, preserved immune from all stain of original sin.

It was fitting that the God of all purity should spring from the greatest purity. Alone of all the children of Adam, you were gifted with the fullness of sanctifying grace which made you the object of a very special love on the part of God. How wonderful were the workings of Divine Power to make you a fitting dwelling for the Redeemer of the world! With no tendency to evil, but with a deep yearning for the highest virtue, you glorified God more than all His other creatures. Never did you yield to the least imperfection, let alone sin. At the very instant of your conception your mind was filled with the light of God, and your will was entirely conformed to the Divine Will. Your extreme hatred of sin was the measure of your supreme love of virtue. Aided by God's wondrous graces you surrendered yourself entirely to God in the smallest details of your life. Forgetting yourself completely, you were most intimately united with God.

MARY, MY MOTHER, help me to imitate your holiness to some degree. My imitation of both Jesus and you depends upon my response to the amount of grace that God sees fit to give me. Your holiness was not the result of the privilege of your Immaculate Conception and sanctifying grace alone, but followed from your gift of yourself to God and your constant cooperation with His graces. Help me to be generous with God by turning to good account the graces that He ever bestows on me, and by rising promptly when I fall, with renewed confidence in His mercy. Aid me through your influence with your Divine Son, to be a true child of yours and to grow daily into your likeness. Help me to imitate your virtues that I may be made worthy of the promises of Christ.

> Seraph of Heaven! too gentle to be human,
> Veiling beneath that radiant form of woman
> All that is insupportable in thee
> Of light and love and immortality;
> Sweet Benediction in the eternal curse;
> Veiled glory of this lampless universe;
> Thou Moon beyond the clouds; thou living Form
> Among the dead; Thou Star above the storm;
> Thou Wonder, and Thou Beauty, and Thou Terror,

Thou Harmony of Nature's Art, Thou Mirror
In whom, as in the splendor of the sun,
All shapes look glorious which Thou gazest on;
Aye, even the dim words which obscure thee now
Flash lightning like, with unaccustomed glow.

✝   ✝   ✝

O God, Who by the Immaculate Conception of the Virgin Mary have
prepared a worthy dwelling for Your Son, we humbly beg of You that we
who celebrate the Apparition of the same Virgin may obtain health of
mind and body. Through the same Christ our Lord. Amen.

The Annunciation of the Blessed
Virgin Mary

FEAST, March 25 (NOVENA, March 16–24)

Background:

About the time of the espousals of Mary and Joseph, the angel Gabriel was sent to Mary at Nazareth and greeted her: "Hail, full of grace, the Lord is with thee" (Luke 1:28). Mary was disturbed by this greeting and wondered what it could mean, but the angel reassured her that she had found grace before God; that is, she was the object of a very special privilege in His eyes. "Thou shalt conceive in thy womb and bring forth a son; and thou shalt call His name Jesus." The angel clearly foretold the Messias who had been yearned for during centuries by all pious Jews. Now Mary was invited to become His mother. She asked how this could happen since she had resolved to remain a virgin. The angel told her that He Who would be born of her was the Son of God, and that is why He would be born of her virginally, by a miracle of God. She would have only to consent to the action of the Holy Spirit Who would make her fruitful. "The Holy Spirit shall come upon thee and the power of the Most High shall overshadow thee." Then, to give further proof, he told of the conception of John, likewise contrary to the ordinary laws of nature.

This was the most solemn instant in the history of mankind. The salvation or the loss of innumerable souls depended on her answer. And Mary said calmly, "Behold the handmaid of the Lord, be it done unto me according to thy word." "And the word was made flesh and dwelt among us."

The Divine Motherhood was *the source of all her dignity and privileges*, for in the words of Pius XII, "from this sublime office of the Mother of God seem to flow, as it were from a most limpid hidden source, all the privileges and graces with which her soul and life were adorned in such extraordinary manner and measure."

Pope Leo XIII in his encyclical on the Rosary tells how *we have access to the Son through the Mother*: "Although the Eternal Son of God willed for the redemption and glory of man to assume the nature of man, and thereby to enter into a kind of mystical marriage with the whole human race, yet

57

He did not do so until the absolutely free consent of His Mother-to-be was given. As Aquinas expresses it so strikingly and truly, Mary acted as it were in the person of the whole human race: 'Through the Annunciation, the consent of the Virgin given in place of the whole human race was awaited.' Therefore, we may with no less propriety and truth affirm that we can receive absolutely nothing from that treasury of all grace which the Lord has brought forth—since 'grace and truth came through Jesus Christ' (John 1:17)—nothing, unless, God so willing, it is bestowed on us through Mary. So that, just as no one can have access to the Father Most High except through the Son, so, in almost the same way, no one can have access to the Son except through the Mother."

As a feast, the Annunciation belongs both to Christ and to His Blessed Mother, since the Word was made incarnate at the very instant of Mary's consent. This feast, prepared by that of St. Gabriel (March 24th), recalls the greatest event in history, the Incarnation of Our Lord in the womb of a Virgin. On this day the Word was made flesh, and united to Itself forever the humanity of Jesus. March 25th is indeed the anniversary of the ordination of Christ as a Priest, for it is by the anointing of the Divinity that He has become Supreme Pontiff, Mediator between God and man. The mystery of the Incarnation has earned for Mary her most glorious title, that of "Mother of God." March 25th will correspond with December 25th, the day on which will be manifested to the world the miracle as yet only known to Heaven and to the humble Virgin. Since the title of Mother of God makes Mary all powerful with her Son, we should have recourse to her intercession with Him for the sanctification and salvation of our souls.

Prayer

(1) MARY, MOTHER OF GOD, *how great was the honor given to you* at the Annunciation! Within your humble home in the little town of Nazareth, the Holy Spirit willed to perform a miracle that was the masterpiece of infinite power—the Incarnation of the Son of God. God sent Gabriel, one of His glorious archangels, to deliver the most important message in the history of mankind, announcing the coming of the Savior of the world and the selection of you to be His Mother. Thus was fulfilled the prophecy that Christ would be born of the family of David.

With heavenly homage the angelic messenger greeted you: "Hail, full of grace, the Lord is with thee; blessed art thou among women" (Luke 1:28) . Never before did angel greet man with the words, "Hail, full of grace." In all humility you attributed this holiness to God alone, working wondrously within you. When the Triune God destined and elevated you, a mortal Virgin, to the dignity of Mother of the Redeemer, *the Father* had to endow you with a fullness of perfection suitable for such a dignity. *The Son,* the Eternal Wisdom of God, in choosing you for His Mother, bestowed on you a certain fullness of grace, so that as you gave Christ His human nature, Christ, in a certain sense, raised you as close to God as a mere creature can come. And *the Holy Spirit,* who descended upon you in the Incarnation with all His fullness, must have conferred upon you such treasures of sanctity as would prepare you to receive the Son of God in your most pure womb. You possessed, according to the words of the archangel, such a fullness of grace that you were worthy to become the Mother of God.

"The Lord is with thee." He was with you in a manner more intimate, more perfect, and more divine than He ever was or will be with any other creature. He was with you not only by His essence, His presence, and His power, as He is with all His creatures. He was with you not only with His actual grace, touching your heart and enlightening your understanding. He was with you not only by His sanctifying grace, making you pleasing in His sight, as He is present with all the just. He was with you not only by a special protection guiding you in His ways and leading you securely to salvation. He was with you, and with you alone, in an unspeakable manner by bodily presence. In you, and of your substance, was this day formed His adorable Body. In you He reposed for nine months, with His whole Divinity and humanity.

MARY, MY MOTHER, the angel said to you, "Blessed art thou among women." Your blessedness was due to your unexcelled sanctity. You would be hailed by all generations as blessed above all other women because you are the Mother of God and at the same time a spotless Virgin. You are blessed because of the fullness of grace you received; blessed because of the greatness of the mercy to be bestowed on you; blessed because of the Majesty of the Person Who was to take flesh of you; blessed because of the glory which would become yours.

(2) MARY, MOTHER OF GOD, *how pleasing to God was your humility!* You were troubled not at the appearance of the angel, but at what he said. Your fear arose entirely from your humility, which was disturbed at the sound of praises far exceeding your own lowly

estimate of yourself. Had the angel said you were the most wicked
sinner in the world, your wonder would not have been so great as
it was at the sound of his praises.

But Gabriel comforted you, "Do not be afraid, Mary, for thou
hast found grace with God." As Christ was pleased to be comforted
by an angel, so was it necessary that you should be encouraged by
one. Do not be afraid, Mary, for you have found, not taken, grace,
as Lucifer tried to take it. You have not lost grace, as Adam lost
it, but you have found it because you have desired and sought it.
You have found uncreated grace; that is, God Himself became your
Son; and with that grace you have found and obtained every created
good.

The more your humility was tried, the more lowly you became
in your own estimation. Your humility was rewarded with the
greatest privilege ever given to a creature. "Behold, thou shalt
conceive in thy womb and shalt bring forth a son; and thou shalt
call His name Jesus. He shall be great, and shall be called the Son
of the Most High." By your humility you have found such great
grace with God that you were chosen to co-operate with His Divine
Son in restoring man to a dignity far superior to that which he
had lost by sin. What greater wonder could the world behold than
a woman become the Mother of God, and a God clothed in human
flesh? Mary, by your humility, you became the Mother of your
Creator. The Creator, in His goodness, became the Son of His own
creature.

The Holy Spirit would work in you the greatest work of His
omnipotence: "The Holy Spirit shall come upon thee and the power
of the Most High shall overshadow thee." By His almighty power
He would form the body of the Savior of the world, and the Divine
Son would unite it to Himself forever. How God rewarded your
humble and deep faith! "And, therefore, the Holy One to be born
shall be called the Son of God." Though you did not know the
meaning of the archangel's inspired words, you serenely submitted
to the Will of God. In doing so, you uttered the most gracious act
of humility that ever fell from human lips: "Behold the handmaid
of the Lord; be it done to me according to thy word." With a "fiat"
God created light, heaven, earth; but with your "fiat" God became
Man. O powerful answer, which rejoiced Heaven and brought an

immense sea of graces and blessings into the world! It was an answer which had scarcely fallen from your lips, before it drew the only-begotten Son of God from the bosom of His Eternal Father, to become Man in your most pure womb!

MARY, MY MOTHER, *the Divine Motherhood meant for you deepest suffering.* To become the Mother of God meant for you a knowledge of and a share in the Passion of Christ that would plunge you into the depths of a sea of lonely desolation. You became a victim and holocaust to the Divine Will, the Queen of Martyrs, the most perfect imitator of the Victim of Calvary. Since suffering is the measure and the very law of love, I cannot imagine the greatness of your love for us, your children. The moment of your exaltation, the highest to which God could raise a creature, finds you sunk in the abyss of your own nothingness. Fully acknowledging your unworthiness to be the Mother of Christ, you accepted the exalted privilege only in obedience to the Divine Will. You called yourself the servant of Him Who for thirty years would be subject to you.

How wondrous you are in your humility! Like you, let me realize my own nothingness. I cannot advance in the path of sanctity without humility which is the heart and soul of virtue. If I have humility, God may flood my soul with grace here and exalt it eternally in heaven.

(3) MARY, MY MOTHER, the instant that you gave your consent to the archangel, *the Holy Spirit overshadowed you and wrought in your most chaste womb the Incarnation of the Son of God.* "The Word was made flesh and dwelt among us." How consistent with the infinite tenderness of God that His Christ, the Immortal Child, should be conceived by the power of the Holy Spirit in the body of a young virgin and that a virgin should bear a Child to redeem the world! In that moment the mystery of love and mercy, promised to mankind thousands of years earlier, foretold by so many prophets, desired by so many saints, was accomplished upon earth. In that instant the Word of God became forever united to humanity; the human soul of Jesus Christ, produced from nothing, began to enjoy God and to know all things past, present, and to come. From your pure blood the Holy Spirit formed the pure Body of Jesus. At that moment God began to have an Adorer Who was

infinite, and the world a Mediator Who was all-powerful. To the
working of this great mystery you also were chosen to co-operate
by your free consent.

You are truly the Seat of Wisdom because you were the living
Tabernacle of the God of Infinite Wisdom. Not only were you full
of grace, but you also bore the Author of grace. You were entirely
under the influence of Christ's divinity. In return for the natural
strength that you gave Him, He gave you His divine strength. What
a divine impression Jesus left upon you, His Mother! You were
united with Him as closely as a Mother is united with her child,
and your thoughts and desires were those of your Divine Son. Your
heart beat in unison with His Heart. I cannot rise to the heights of
your holiness because I cannot grasp the intimacy of your union
with Christ when you became His Mother.

MARY, MY MOTHER, I rejoice with you that you are so privileged,
so exalted as to become the worthy Mother of God. We all rejoice
because all the graces and spiritual benefits we have received and
shall receive, all our future glory comes from this exalted mystery
of the Incarnation. God could not have created a more beautiful
throne for Himself than you, His Mother! I thank God for the great
glory He has bestowed upon you for which all generations shall
call you blessed.

I thank you for the motherly compassion with which you came to
the aid of a helpless race by consenting to be the Mother of Our
Savior.

> Since that Word of Wisdom was
> Announced by Gabriel, and because
> He rested in thy womb a while
> Of Spirit-shadowed days, we style
>   Thee Mother of God.

> Because thy hallowed flesh was one
> With Emmanuel, Jehovah's Son,
> When Love inspired the singing flame
> Of thy canticle, all peoples name
>   Thee Mother of God.

> Since thou wert the maiden who,
> Still virgin as the angels knew

Came vested in a boding veil
To Bethlehem, all nations hail
    Thee Mother of God.

Because, while night was big with earth
And heaven with star, thy flesh gave birth
To Jesus Christ within a stall;
Our little ones, thy children, call
    Thee Mother of God.

Since that the Child Himself Who was
Of thee, His creature yet thy Cause,
Did ever call thee Mother, lo!
From Truth whose Word is Love we know
    Thee Mother of God.

Who yet would sing thy canticle.
Oh! may the Holy Spirit's Will,
Being one with ours as with thine own,
O'ershadow soul and flesh and bone,
    Dear Mother of God.

So our Annunciation Day
Be made our soul's own Christmas: yea,
So that our Guardian speak the word
As Gabriel: "Hail, thou hast the Lord!"
    O Mother of God,

Thus to conceive our Christ! Ah me
What mystic conceptivity:
At once both to conceive and give
Him birth Who died that we might live!
    True Mother of God.

We ask thou intercede with prayer,
So that we may receive thy care
In worthy bosoms, thou to whom
He came by way of virgin womb.
    Ah, Mother of God.

Do thou, as His hand-maiden, spin
That seamless robe of grace wherein

The Living Presence, vested thus,
Shall know thy care, as well as us
        Bemothering God!
                    —FRANCIS CARLIN

† † †

O God, Who wanted Your Word to take flesh in the womb of the Blessed Virgin Mary at the message of an angel, grant that we, Your humble servants, who believe her to be truly the Mother of God, may be helped by her intercession with You. Through the same Christ Our Lord. Amen.

The Seven Sorrows of the Blessed Virgin Mary

FEASTS, Friday of Passion Week and September 15
(NOVENA, Wednesday after the Fourth Sunday
of Lent; also September 6–14)

Background:

Mary's sorrow on Calvary was deeper than any sorrow ever felt on earth, for no mother in all the world had a heart as tender as the heart of the Mother of God. As there was no love like her love, there was no sorrow like her sorrow. She bore her sufferings for you that you might enjoy the graces of Redemption. She suffered willingly in order to prove her great love for you, for true love is proved by sacrifice.

Holy Church honors Our Lady's Sorrows by two feasts—one observed on the Friday of Passion Week, and the other on the 15th of September. The first recalls especially her sufferings during the Passion of Our Lord; the second is dedicated more particularly to her lifelong sorrows.

The Feast of the Seven Sorrows of the Blessed Virgin, the Friday of Passion Week, dates from the beginning of the fifteenth century. It was inaugurated by the Archbishop of Cologne in 1423, as an honorable reparation for the outrages of the Hussites against the images of the Mother of God, particularly the *Pietà.* At the end of the same century Pope Sixtus IV extended the feast to the whole Church. In 1725 Pope Benedict XIII raised it to the rank of a double major, giving it a fixed place in the liturgical calendar.

The second Feast of the Sorrows of Mary is solemnized on the 15th of September. Pope Pius VII, in gratitude to Our Lady for having consoled him during the captivity to which the Emperor Napoleon had subjected him, established it on the occasion of his deliverance, September 15, 1814.

St. Pius X, in his encyclical *Ad Diem,* speaks of Mary's part in the Redemption: "In order that we might live by Him, the most holy Mother of God has not only the honor of having given the substance of her flesh to the only-begotten God about to be born of the human race, whereby a victim was prepared for men's salvation; hers was the task, as well, of caring for and nourishing this same Victim and even of placing It near the altar at the appointed hour. . . . Nor was she merely engaged in witnessing the cruel spectacle; rather, she rejoiced utterly that her Only-Begotten was being offered for the salvation of the human race, although her compassion was so intense that, if it were possible, she herself would have embraced even more eagerly all the sufferings that her Son endured. Now it is because of this community of pain and will between Mary and Christ that she merited to become in a most worthy manner the Reparatrix of the lost world, and, therefore, the Dispenser of the totality of gifts which Jesus by His death and blood has acquired for us."

And Pope Pius XII in his encyclical on the Mystical Body (1943) describes Mary's role in the Redemption and speaks of her sorrows: "Free from all sin, original and personal, always most intimately united with her Son, as another Eve she offered Him on Golgotha to the Eternal Father for all the children of Adam sin-stained by his fall, and her mother's rights and mother's love were included in the holocaust. Thus she who corporally was the Mother of our Head, through the added title of pain and glory became spiritually the Mother of all His members. . . . Bearing with courage and confidence the tremendous burden of her sorrows and desolation, truly the Queen of martyrs, she more than all the faithful 'filled up those things that are wanting of the sufferings of Christ . . . for his body, which is the Church' (Col. 1:24); and she continued to show for the Mystical Body of Christ, born from the pierced Heart of the Savior, the same mother's care and ardent love with which she clasped the Infant Jesus to her warm and nourishing breast."

Devotion to the Sorrows of Mary is the source of great graces because it leads into the depths of the Sacred Heart of Jesus. If you think frequently of the Sorrows of Mary, you will lose ever more and more a desire for the false pleasures of this world, you will embrace patiently the sorrows and sufferings of this life, and you will be penetrated with an abiding sorrow for sin. A religion which would represent Mary with her living Child in her arms and would not give us Mary with the torn Body of her dead Son on her lap would not be the religion to which we could turn when all else has failed. Give yourself over to her love completely and bear your cross patiently in union with your Mother of Sorrows.

Prayer

(1) MARY, MOTHER OF GOD, your sorrows are not merely the sorrows of an earthly mother grieving over the death of an only child. Rather, *your sorrows were ordained by God from all eternity*

as part of the penalty to be paid for sin and were to mingle with the sufferings of your Son in that great sacrifice which was to redeem the world.

The Gospel speaks of you as *standing* beneath the cross. This posture is not the one usually describing a mourner who is affected with only human grief. You would have shown your grief as mothers do by sobs and tears. But though your soul was filled with grief, you bravely stood beneath the cross. You did not abandon Jesus as the apostles did; you remained with Him until He expired. You did not go to a distance, but drew nearer to the cross—the hard bed on which Jesus had to die. You stood by its side, never turning your eyes from Him. You beheld Him suspended by iron nails. You stood there silently fulfilling a part assigned you by Providence.

MARY, MY MOTHER, you were to complete the offering of your Son, which you had begun on the day of His presentation in the temple. You presented Him in sacrifice to the Father as your God and the Son of Man, as your offering and the offering of humanity for the redemption of the world. You so loved the world as to give your only Son for our redemption. It was your duty to represent the whole of mankind and to offer those acts of adoration, faith, hatred of sin, love and prayer, which were due from those who shared in this sacrifice.

At the same time you had to offer the most intense human suffering, in union with the Passion of your Son. You saw in the cross an altar, in your Son a Priest, and in His Blood the price of our redemption. You suffered in your soul what Jesus suffered in His Body, and in union with Him you offered yourself as a victim for our sins. There were two great altars on Calvary: one in the Body of Jesus, the other in your heart; for on that mount, at the same time that your Son sacrificed His Body by death, you sacrificed your soul by compassion. What merits did not your perfect immolation gain! Thereby you sanctified all our afflictions and united them with those of Jesus. I can never fully understand the depth of those sorrows that filled your heart as you begot us to the spiritual life, while standing by the cross on Calvary. The words of the prophet are applied to you: "O all you that pass by the way, attend, and see if there be sorrow like unto my sorrow."

(2) MARY, MOTHER OF GOD, *your life, like that of your Divine Son, was a daily crucifixion and martyrdom.* You found the cross

very heavy during the three years of His public life, for then He had to leave your side that He might be "about His Father's business"—the sanctification and salvation of souls. Though deprived of the joy of His actual presence, you were more intimately united with Him than ever through your sacrificial love, since your will was one with His. He was preparing you for your final separation from Him at the foot of the cross.

Because you freely consented to become the Mother of God, you experienced mentally all the bitterness of your Son's Passion and death. At the very beginning of His public ministry, you observed the hatred and jealousy of His enemies and the false accusations which would bring about His death. Each event of the sorrowful drama of His sufferings was a sword that pierced your motherly heart.

The Apostles, who had abandoned their Master, informed you of your Son's betrayal by Judas and of His brutal capture after His agony. The beloved disciple told you what he had seen in the houses of Annas and Caiphas: how Jesus had been accused as a blasphemer for stating that He was the Son of God. With your own eyes you saw Him brought first to Pilate, then to Herod and then again to Pilate. You were in the judgment hall and heard it ring with lies. You saw Barabbas preferred to Jesus when the Roman governor showed the Man of Sorrows to the angry mob. What grief filled your heart as you gazed upon your Son with His flesh torn, His head encircled with long, sharp thorns, His whole body covered with blood—a mock King with a reed in His hand and a cast-off cloak over His bleeding shoulders!

You heard the mob, led by the chief priests, clamoring for His crucifixion. You saw the heavy cross placed on His bent shoulders. Your heart sank each time He fell beneath its weight. You saw His virginal flesh torn open again when the soldiers pitilessly stripped Him of His garments. You beheld His arms and feet roughly extended on the hard wood of the cross. What must have been your anguish when you looked at the sacred body of Jesus as the long nails were being driven into His hands and feet! You saw the cross raised and heard the mob, not yet satisfied with their bloody work, continue to torment their dying victim.

Though worn with sorrow, you at once took your place at the foot of the cross. There you stood bravely, your eyes fastened on your Divine Son. How generously you offered Jesus, you dearest treasure, as a Victim to the justice of His offended Father! How courageously you united the oblation of your own suffering and grief with the offering of Jesus, thus proving yourself worthy not only to share but also to be one with Him in the redemption of souls.

Parting with your dying Son was the height of your sorrow. But with the same humility with which you had conceived Him, you consented to the supreme loss of your God. Jesus had delivered Himself in His Passion to the Will of His Father, and before His sacrifice for sinners could be perfect He had to be forsaken by that Father. In the same way you, who freely delivered your son to a cruel death, parted with your Son. Only thus could you become one with your God in the salvation of souls.

MARY, MY MOTHER, more courageous than the martyrs, you stood at the foot of the cross. The suffering of Jesus in His dereliction was the most difficult test of your faith. In union with Him you also did the Will of God perfectly as He exclaimed, "Father, into thy hands I commend my spirit."

When you heard Jesus utter these words and saw Him bow His head and die, you died a spiritual death. Gazing sorrowfully on His lifeless Body, you watched the soldier drive the spear into His Heart. The words of Simeon were then fulfilled. "And thy own soul a sword shall pierce." Filled with grief, you saw how the disciples removed the nails from the Redeemer's hands and feet, extracted the thorns from His head, and took Him down from the cross. What a sight met your tear-dimmed eyes when you beheld the Body of your Son bruised and mangled and covered with open bloody wounds! Your soul filled with love and sorrow, you embraced your Son now pale in death, a victim for the sins of mankind.

(3) MARY, MOTHER OF GOD, *you are our spiritual Mother.* The Crucifixion was not only the sacrifice for sin; it was also *the new birth of mankind to the spiritual life,* lost by the sin of Adam. It was the great vital act that completed the work of God in the world. You had a share in that work; it was part of your life work. The Nativity and the Crucifixion were as one action. The sacrifice of the cross began at Bethlehem. The new birth of mankind was completed on Calvary. You were concerned in both, and on each occasion you were present as Mother of the human race.

Your dying Son declared this in His words to you from the cross, "Woman, behold thy Son." Those words include us all. You were declared to be the spiritual "Mother of all the living." On this occasion you bore your share of the penalty allotted to woman: "In sorrow thou shalt bring forth children."

When Jesus said to John, "Behold thy Mother," He wanted John to respect and to love you as His Mother. John took my place on Calvary and you became, in his person, my Mother. Jesus could give me—after the gift of Himself—nothing more precious than you. With your heart breaking with sorrow, you had to die a spiritual death in order to become my spiritual Mother. In becoming my Mother, you became the Queen of Martyrs!

MARY, MY MOTHER, what a truly marvelous *privilege* is mine! Since you are my Mother, I share in the love you have for your Divine Son. Jesus gave me your own dear self, His dearest possession, whom He loved so much that He, in a sense, exhausted His power to exalt you above all other creatures. Jesus exhausted His love for man also. It was not enough for the Infinite Lover of souls to free us from the slavery of hell by His Passion and death and to bestow upon us His Body and Blood, Soul and Divinity. He had to crown the gift of His love with the gift of you, His Mother.

I can best thank Jesus for His dying bequest by striving daily to become like John in his love and imitation of you. It means imitating your humility, your purity, your detachment from the world, and your unselfish resignation to the Will of God in every event of life. It also means unlimited confidence in your motherly intercession if I should have the misfortune of straying from Jesus by sin.

How precious is your love, my Mother! I give you my love by consecrating myself entirely to you, in joy and in sorrow, by complete abandonment to the Divine Will. May I remember always your sorrows on Calvary, through which you begot us to God and became the co-redemptrix of our race. May this remembrance fill me with love and gratitude to you, and be the reason for my trust in your powerful protection and in your prayers in heaven, where you plead with your Divine Son for the salvation of us all.

Do not forsake me, sweet Mother of Sorrows, because you are my spiritual Mother. If I confide my salvation to your loving care and

faithfully imitate your virtues, I know you will keep me in your immaculate Heart both now and at the hour of my death.

"STABAT MATER"

At the Cross her station keeping,
Stood the mournful Mother weeping,
Close to Jesus to the last.
Through her heart, His sorrow sharing,
All His bitter anguish bearing,
Now at length the sword has passed.

Oh, how sad and sore distressed,
Was that Mother highly blest,
Of the sole-begotten One!
Christ above in torment hangs,
She beneath beholds the pangs
Of her dying glorious Son.

Is there one who would not weep,
Whelm'd in miseries so deep,
Christ's dear Mother to behold?
Can the human heart refrain
From partaking in her pain,
In that Mother's pain untold?

Bruised, derided, cursed, defiled,
She beheld her tender Child,
All with bloody scourges rent.
For the sins of His own nation,
Saw Him hang in desolation,
Till His spirit forth He sent.

O thou Mother, fount of love!
Touch my spirit from above;
Make my heart with thine accord.
Make me feel as thou hast felt;
Make my soul to glow and melt
With the love of Christ our Lord.

Holy Mother, pierce me through;
In my heart each wound renew,

Of my Savior crucified!
Let me share with thee His pain,
Who for all my sins was slain,
Who for me in torments died.

Let me mingle tears with thee,
Mourning Him who mourned for me,
All the days that I may live.
By the Cross with thee to stay,
There with thee to weep and pray,
Is all I ask of thee to give.

Virgin of all virgins best,
Listen to my fond request:
Let me share thy grief divine.
Let me, to my latest breath,
In my body bear the death
Of that dying Son of thine.

Wounded with His every wound,
Steep my soul till it has swooned
In His very Blood away.
Be to me, O Virgin, nigh,
Lest in flames I burn and die,
In His awful Judgment Day.

Christ, when Thou shalt call me hence,
Be Thy Mother my defense,
Be Thy Cross my victory.
While my body here decays,
May my soul Thy goodness praise,
Safe in paradise with Thee. Amen.

7 years (378)*

Note: The indulgenced prayers used in this book are taken from the *Enchiridion Indulgentiarum*, the latest official edition of prayers and devotions enriched with indulgences and published by the authority of the Holy See (1950). The numbers in parentheses indicate the number under which the prayer is given in this official collection. Anyone who recites daily for a month the prayers marked with an asterisk (*) can gain a plenary indulgence under the usual conditions (Confession, Communion, visit to a church and prayers for the Pope's intentions. One Our Father, Hail Mary, and Glory be to the Father suffices.)

† † †

O God, in Whose Passion, as Simeon had foretold, the most sweet soul of Mary, Your glorious Virgin-Mother, was pierced through by a sword of sorrow, mercifully grant that we who reverently meditate upon her transfixion and her sufferings, may obtain the blessed fruits of Your Passion through the glorious merits and prayers of all the saints standing at the cross interceding for us. Who live and reign forever. Amen.

Easter

(Octave prayers)

Background:

The Church celebrates the triumph of Jesus during Paschal time; thus *the Solemnity of Easter marks the climax of the liturgical year.* After the hard struggle against the powers of evil, the victorious Christ takes possession of the glorious life, which He will communicate to all those who by baptism are united with Him in faith and love.

Scripture is silent about Mary's share in the burial of Jesus. She probably spent the days between the Crucifixion and the Resurrection recalling the sorrowful scenes of the Passion and death of her loving Son. Yet at the same time Mary must have looked hopefully to the moment of His glorious Resurrection. She did not accompany the holy women who went to the tomb on Sunday morning to anoint Jesus. Since she was absolutely convinced of His Resurrection, she considered this visit unnecessary. *Great saints and scholars consider it almost self-evident that the Risen Christ appeared first to His Mother,* although no apparition of this kind is narrated in the Gospels. Everything in the life of Christ was in accordance with what is fitting, and bore the mark of delicate consideration. So we can read much between the lines of Holy Scripture that is not actually expressed.

Our Lady prepared herself for her Son's appearance. Her faith was firm and lively. There was no wavering or doubt with her, as was the case with the holy women and the Apostles. To her Christ's words were perfectly clear, and she expected the Resurrection on the third day. She must have awaited the Resurrection with great longing. One needs only to know the heart of a mother, and such a Mother, to understand this.

One can hardly imagine the joy in the Heart of Jesus to be able to let His Mother know that her Son lived, was happy, and loved her dearly. He revealed the splendor of His glorious state to no one so fully and so tenderly as He did to her. He must have imparted to her a new and deeper knowledge concerning Himself and His glory so that she might the better share in His triumph and joy. Probably He also revealed to her His reasons for remaining on earth for a little while longer, and all that He meant to do

74

for His Church before He ascended to heaven, and expressed His desire that she share in this glorious work as the Mother of the infant Church and the Queen of the Apostles.

It was fitting that Mary share in the triumph and joy of her Son! He had received from her the life that was now so glorious. She had a share in all His sorrows through life, and she had suffered very generously. The appearance of Jesus filled Mary with consolation and joy—a joy so great as only a soul so gifted by God could experience. She could not rejoice enough over His glory, honor, and happiness. But that joy was quiet and interior. She was ever the same in her modesty, following her Son so faithfully, keeping and pondering everything in her heart, and never pushing herself forward, except where she would be able to share His suffering. Mary was happy also for our sake; she rejoiced at all the great and glorious benefits that the Resurrection brought us. She took the deepest interest in every token of her Son's goodness and graciousness to His friends; for Mary Magdalen, the Apostles, and others to whom Jesus appeared, must have given her glowing accounts of the glory of her Son.

This was the way that Mary kept her Eastertide. We should imitate her in the joy she feels at the triumph of her Son and beg her to help us attain to true holiness, through a hatred of sin, detachment from the things of this world, and a perfect love for God and neighbor, all of which is the foundation of true peace and happiness.

Prayer

(1) MARY, MOTHER OF GOD, *it was fitting that Jesus appeared first to you after His Resurrection.* You are His nearest and dearest in the order of nature and of grace. He has received from you the life that is now so glorious. You had the most intimate share in His mysteries of which this glory was the exceedingly great reward. As you shared more than anyone else in the sorrow and bitterness of His Passion, so also you shared more than all others in the glory of His triumph. Your joy was spiritual, quiet, interior, noble and perfect.

What joy Jesus felt when He saw you, His Mother, so happy! You followed Him through His suffering and stood beneath the cross as He bowed His head in death; and after His death you were immersed in a new ocean of suffering, for your love for Him was immeasurably great. All the more was He now overjoyed that you were no longer suffering. He rejoiced in being able to let you share in His happiness which you experienced at the sight of Him, gloriously risen. How fully He realized by His Resurrection every promise made by the archangel Gabriel when he announced to you that you were to be the Mother of God! His Resurrection was the beginning of that kingdom which was to last forever: "Of his kingdom there shall be no end" (Luke 1:33). I unite myself with the love which Jesus bears you, His holy Mother, and with the joy He experienced on beholding you after His Resurrection. Beg Jesus to increase my love for you, that I may share your joy.

Glorious Mother of Jesus, I rejoice in your Easter joy and I congratulate you with all my heart. How happy you were to see your Risen Son! With firm faith and earnest longing you awaited His appearance. He rewarded you generously for the share you had in the sorrows and sufferings of His life by revealing to you the splendor of His glorious state and by giving you a new and deeper knowledge concerning Himself and His glory. How well you deserved to be the first to share in His glory!

MARY, MY MOTHER, forty days after the Resurrection of Jesus, you were with Him as He bade farewell to His apostles and disciples before *He ascended into heaven.* You saw His sacred body, immortal and glorified, raised on high and dazzling His disciples with its resplendent glory. How you longed for eternal union with Him! You ascended with Him spiritually. In beholding Jesus, the King of Martyrs, ascending to heaven to take possession of His glory, you realized that, as Queen of Martyrs, as Christ's most perfect follower, you would one day share in His eternal reward. Your heart was now in heaven with your Son and your God. But although deprived of His visible presence, you were content to do His will by remaining on earth. You would still have Him really and truly present in the Blessed Sacrament, and that was enough for you.

(2) MARY, MOTHER OF GOD, *you had every reason to be joyful because of the Resurrection of your Son.* His Body, which you had given Him by the overshadowing of the Holy Spirit, was glorified by being united again to His glorified Soul. He rose triumphantly by His own power. His body took on spiritual qualities: immortality, beauty, freedom and the power to move about swiftly and unhindered. The Divinity shone forth through His glorified Body, and floods of joy poured into His Soul and Sacred Heart. His Resurrection was the crown of His life and work as God-Man because it

was His glorification. This was the beginning of the glorious life that was due to Him as the Son of God; it was also the reward of His life of suffering. His Sacred Humanity received an eternal kingdom of power, joy, and glory. His Resurrection was the strongest proof of His Divinity. If He is the Son of God, His teaching must be true, and the Church which He founded is the Church of the living God whose sacraments afford us the means of salvation by imparting divine grace.

MARY, MY MOTHER, you are now no longer the Mother of Sorrows, but the happy Queen of Heaven—Queen of honor, power, and joy. You have now reached the highest joy of Divine Motherhood. With Holy Mother Church I sing: "O Queen of Heaven, rejoice. Alleluia. For He Whom thou didst merit to bear, alleluia, has arisen, as He said. Alleluia." All the joy of the Easter feast is peculiarly your own. You are the Mother of the Risen Savior. You gave Him birth and bore all His sorrows and sufferings with Him till His death.

Rejoice, Mary, for by His Resurrection your Son has confirmed everything: His doctrine, His word, and His Divinity. All is gloriously completed. So pray for us, your children, as you then did for the Apostles and the whole Church. Obtain for Christ's kingdom by your glorious intercession an increase of faith, hope, and love, and for the whole world a share in the true Easter joy in Christ, here below and in a blissful eternity. "Pray for us to God. Alleluia!"

(3) MARY, MOTHER OF GOD, *help me to learn from your example that the object of my joy must be our Savior and spiritual things* and that the manner of it must be quiet, interior and prayerful. The mystery of the Resurrection is called holy because in it Jesus especially fulfills the conditions of holiness; namely, detachment from every creature and sin, and complete surrender to God. Pray for me that I may share in these graces of the Resurrection. Your Son came forth triumphant from the tomb. In Him there was freedom, light, strength, beauty, life. His Divine life is the model of ours, and He has merited for us the grace of living for God as He did. Through the sacraments may my soul be enriched with an ever greater degree of sanctifying grace, the principle of Divine life, that I may live for God alone. Keep me from mortal and venial sin so that my soul, being free, may act only under the inspiration of

grace and for God alone through faith and love. Thus may Christ's
life blossom forth in my soul; as St. Paul says, "It is now no longer
I that live, but Christ lives in me" (Gal. 2:20).

Mother most joyful, remember your children, and through your
prayers obtain for us the real spirit of Easter, the Paschal grace:
detachment from all that is human, earthly, created; and the full
gift of ourselves to God, through Christ, your glorious Son.

O Maria, wondrous fair!
Bright you are, Morning Star,
More than sun or moon by far;
Sweet in truth your virgin face,
Peerless woman of our race!
Seraphim, Cherubim,
You entrance them by your grace.

O Maria, pre-ordained!
Maiden mild,
Favored child,
Ever pure and undefiled,
God the Son the highest Good,
Sought you out for motherhood;
Thrice He blest
That pure breast,
Whence He took His flesh and blood.

O Maria, our delight!
Noblest Queen
Ever seen,
Reigning e'er in joy serene,
Shield us from the crafty foe
With revenge and hate aglow;
By our side
O abide,
Free us from eternal woe.

† † †

O God, Who, through the Resurrection of Your Son, Our Lord Jesus
Christ, filled the world with joy, grant, we beg of You, that through His
Virgin-Mother, Mary, we may obtain the joys of everlasting life. Through
the same Christ Our Lord. Amen.

Our Lady of Good Counsel

FEAST, April 26 (TRIDUUM, April 23–25)

Background:

Genazzano is a busy little town about thirty miles southeast of Rome. A church dedicated to Our Lady of Good Counsel was built there in the fifth century. In 1356 this ancient church was given into the care of the friars of the Order of St. Augustine. In 1467 a local widow, Patruccia de Geneo, felt inspired by Our Lady to rebuild it. When the project had to be stopped for lack of funds, people scoffed at the widow. But she said, "The work will be completed before I die . . . and a great Lady will come to take possession of it."

On St. Mark's Day, 1467, during a grand public fiesta, a number of people standing in the main square saw a fleecy cloud float across the clear sky, descend and affix itself to the face of one of the walls of Petruccia's unfinished church. The cloud divided and displayed in the midst a beautiful small picture of the Madonna and Child which was set against the wall on a narrow ledge, a few feet from the ground, where no picture had been before. At the same moment all the church bells of the town began to ring. Petruccia, who had been saying her prayers in another place, came running forth and threw herself upon her knees, crying with joy and proclaiming that this was the Great Lady come to take possession of her house. Alarmed by the ringing of the bells, other people in outlying villages began to gather and to pray in front of this wonderful picture of Our Lady, and instantly began a marvelous shower of graces and cures which were recorded by an appointed notary. The record, still preserved, dates from April 27 to August 14, 1467, and contains the description of 171 reputed miracles. The townsfolk called the picture the "Miraculous Madonna"; others, unable to explain its origin, called it the "Madonna of Paradise," brought to Genazzano by the angels.

A few days later, two strangers arrived, one of them an Albanian, the other a Slav; both claimed they had seen the same picture a few weeks previously in a church on a hillside outside Scutari, in Albania. They and some of their Albanian friends, refugees from the Turks who ravaged their country, took up residence in Genazzano to be near their Madonna.

Pope Paul II sent two bishops to examine the circumstances surrounding

79

this new shrine and devotion. The details of the findings are preserved in their original texts which are supported by other contemporary records in the Papal Archives.

The painting was done upon a thin layer of plaster of porcelain texture the thickness of an eggshell. No one could have detached it uncracked from another wall. This wafer-like sheet of plaster, although enshrined in marvelous golden framework and adorned with a king's precious stones, stood upright with no support of any kind except the narrow ledge on which it rested for five hundred years. It was possible for the commission to pass a thread of wire around and behind the picture from top to bottom. These careful investigations convinced the commissioners and the Pope himself that this was the picture of Our Lady of Good Counsel that had been venerated for centuries in Scutari. It was proved that the church from which it was believed to have been borne away retained an empty space of the exact dimensions of the picture. All this authentic evidence has been preserved.

In 1630 Pope Urban VIII made a pilgrimage to the shrine in person. In 1777 the Sacred Congregation of Rites approved a proper Office commemorating the history of the shrine, to be used by the Augustinian Order who to this day serve the shrine of "Our Lady of Good Counsel." The picture has survived wars and bombing, though the church was struck and its high altar demolished. The golden shrine shows scars of the late war, but the picture is intact. Devotion to Our Lady of Good Counsel became popular in England, since the English College in Rome has a villa near Genazzano. An excellent reproduction of the picture is enshrined in the Priory Church of St. Augustine in Hammersmith, England.

By a decree of April 22, 1903, Pope Leo XIII added to the Litany of Loreto the invocation, "Mother of Good Counsel, pray for us." He concluded his decree with the prayer that in the midst of disaster and darkness, that loving Mother whom the Fathers called the treasurer of divine grace and counselor of all power might manifest herself to the world as the Mother of Good Counsel and obtain for her children the gift of holy counsel, that grace of the Holy Spirit that illumines minds and hearts.

You are in need of advice in the serious problems of life. Remember that Jesus gave you a Counselor who will never fail you. Go to your Heavenly Mother with childlike confidence and abandonment. Entrust yourself to her prudent guidance, for she is your Mother of Good Counsel.

Prayer

(1) MARY, MOTHER OF GOD, *you are Our Lady of Good Counsel because of the divine wisdom and prudence which you received*

from the Holy Spirit. This wisdom and prudence showed itself at a very early age, when you willed to devote yourself entirely to God and were presented by your saintly parents, at your own request, for the temple service. You remained there working for God, meditating on His holy Law, praying and praising His Divine Goodness.

The virtue of holy prudence guides man in his choice of purposes and in the best means to attain them. You showed singular prudence during your life. You treasured up all the words spoken by the holy angels concerning your Divine Son, as well as those pronounced by the prophetess Anna and by holy Simeon when you presented your Son in the temple, and you prudently pondered them in your heart. During your Son's public ministry you seldom appeared, because this was the prudent thing to do because of your close relationship to the Redeemer.

MARY, MY MOTHER, how perfectly you have followed the inspirations of the Holy Spirit and acted on Divine Wisdom! No one ever carried out the teaching of your Son with greater exactness than you; hence His words refer to you perfectly: "Everyone, therefore, who hears these my words and acts upon them, shall be likened to a wise man who built his house on rock" (Matt. 7:24). Wherefore, the Church applies to you the words Jesus spoke of that other Mary who sat at His sacred feet, drinking in the words of Divine Wisdom flowing from His blessed lips: "Mary has chosen the best part, and it will not be taken away from her" (Luke 10:42). Teach me to imitate your prudence and listen to your counsel in all walks of life. Tell me how to embrace whatever is best that I may attain the great purpose of my life—heaven and the possession of God—and how to reject whatever is opposed to it or likely to make this attainment difficult. Let me never be influenced by temporal considerations—wealth, honors, and pleasures—that I may always follow the counsel of Jesus: "Seek first the kingdom of God, and his justice, and all these things shall be given you besides" (Luke 12:31).

(2) MARY, MOTHER OF GOD, *you are Our Lady of Good Counsel because you are the Seat of Wisdom.* You are the Mother of the Uncreated Wisdom, Jesus Christ, the Son of God. You shared more in this wisdom than did any other creature, because you approached nearer to the Source from which it came—Jesus, the Eternal Wisdom. For thirty-three years you enjoyed the company of the only-begotten Son of God in the intimate relation of Mother and Son; and under

your care, according to the Evangelist, He "advanced in wisdom, and age, and grace, before God and man" (Luke 2:52).

In all your deeds you showed the fruits of the Divine Wisdom which had made you the dwelling-place of God. "The fear of the Lord is the beginning of wisdom," says the psalmist (110:10). Great must have been the childlike reverence and respect with which you watched over your every action and which preserved you from ever displeasing the Divine Wisdom.

MARY, MY MOTHER, I am the work of the wisdom of God together with all other creatures. Everything inside and outside me should reflect His divine perfections. Like you, let me learn Divine Wisdom and see God in all things so that I may rise from the creature to the great Creator. Help me to esteem the light of my reason as a sharing in the Divine Wisdom, especially when I try to follow the teaching of the Gospel. Let me never esteem worldly wisdom so highly as to pay but little attention to the principles of that wisdom which is from heaven and which alone can make me truly wise and happy. Help me to bear in mind that the wisdom of this world is foolishness with God and that the secrets of Divine Wisdom are imparted only to the humble of heart, while they are hidden from the worldly-wise.

Our Lady of Good Counsel, I beg you to teach me true heavenly wisdom which was the source of every good deed you performed. Keep me humble that I may be able to receive your counsel. How often am I confused in the problems of life! How often I do not know where to turn! Advise me what to do. Give me your good counsel so that, following it humbly, I may ever please God, find true happiness on this earth and eternal life in the world to come.

(3) MARY, MOTHER OF GOD, *Our Lady of Good Counsel, I appeal to you for advice and guidance.* Teach me to desire ardently all that is pleasing to God, to seek after it prudently, to accept it truthfully, and to do it perfectly, for the praise and glory of God. I beg you to pray for me that by the light of the Holy Spirit and your direction, I may see my duty, and that by God's grace and your help I may fulfill it.

Pray to Jesus, the Divine Word and Eternal Wisdom, Who is "the life that is the light of men" (John 1:4), that through you He may teach me His Divine Wisdom. He ordered most perfectly His whole creation, for He is the true fountain and highest source of light and wisdom. Ask Him to favor me with a ray of His brightness to enlighten the darkness of sin and ignorance in which I was born. May He, Who makes little ones to speak Divine Wisdom, direct my tongue and pour out upon my soul the grace I need ever to follow His and your example in my state of life.

MARY, MY MOTHER, through your prayers may I be blessed with a keen understanding of the ways of God. I desire to place under your protection all my efforts in my striving for holiness and all the works of my daily life. I declare that I undertake them only that I may better promote the honor of God and devotion to you. Enlighten the beginning of my efforts, direct my progress, bring my completed work to perfection. Grant that following your good counsel, I may avoid sin, practice virtue, save my soul and attain eternal life. Only in heaven will I realize the wisdom of your motherly guidance which urged me ever to seek God and to find my happiness in doing His holy will.

> O Virgin Mother, Lady of Good Counsel!
> Sweetest picture artist ever drew,
> In all doubts I fly to you for guidance;
> Mother, tell me, what am I to do?
>
> By your face to Jesus' face inclining,
> Sheltered safely in your mantle blue;
> By His little arms around you twining,
> Mother, tell me, what am I to do?
>
> By the light within your dear eyes dwelling,
> By the tears that dim their lustre, too,
> By the story that these tears are telling,
> Mother, tell me, what am I to do?
>
> Life, alas! is often dark and dreary,
> Cheating shadows hide the truth from view;
> When my soul is most perplexed and weary,
> Mother, tell me, what am I to do?
>
> Be of all my friends the best and dearest,
> O my counsellor sincere and true;

Let your voice sound always first and clearest,
Mother, tell me, what am I to do?

In your guidance tranquilly reposing,
Now I face my toils and cares anew;
All through life and at its awful closing,
Mother, tell me, what am I to do?

† † †

O God, Who gave her who bore Your beloved Son to be our Mother
and glorified her fair image by a wondrous apparition, grant, we beg of
You, that by always following her counsels we may be able to live after
Your own Heart and arrive happily in our heavenly fatherland. Through
the same Christ Our Lord. Amen.

Our Lady, Queen of the Apostles

FEAST, Saturday after the Feast of the Ascension
(TRIDUUM, Wednesday before the Feast of the Ascension)

Background:

Our Lady, Queen of Apostles, is no mere empty title. It brings to our minds the picture of the Blessed Mother surrounded by the faithful company of Jesus in the Cenacle at the moment of the descent of the Holy Spirit. Together with the Apostles themselves, Mary participated in the birth of the infant Church. The Pentecostal fire, which enlightened their minds and gave ardor to their speech, communicated itself also to Mary, and to her fullness of graces there were now added new dignities, new privileges, and new powers which were apostolic in their nature and effects.

Peter was the Prince of the Apostles, their visible chief, the Vicar of their Christ. But Mary, too, enjoyed a primacy all her own. She was the Queen of Apostles, their heart, the Mother of Christ and, therefore, in a sense, the channel of their apostolic graces as well as the graces of their redemption.

Mary was in the midst of the Apostles in Jerusalem in the first days of Christianity as their counseling Mother. There is no doubt that Mary very effectively assisted the Evangelists in writing or compiling the Gospels. It is generally held that the Apostles enjoyed Mary's help, instruction, and direction for the first twelve years after the Ascension of Jesus. Down through the ages Mary accompanied in spirit and assisted the missionaries in their apostolic work because, as co-Redemptress with her Divine Son, she would cooperate in the salvation of souls. As she was Queen of the Apostles in the Church's infancy, so she is Queen of the Apostles of our own day, of the priests, brothers, and sisters who are working for the salvation of souls in home and foreign missions.

Mary is Queen, too, of all others who in any sense share the apostolate of Christ and His Church. That means that she is the Queen of our lay apostles, of those who in every walk of life, within each social class, defend the rights of God, proclaim His Truth, preach His eternal Will. As Queen of these lay apostles, Mary is at once a channel of the grace by which they accomplish their apostolate and an example of the virtues needed in order for them to do so. Those virtues are joyous zeal for God and for souls and a warm love for divine learning.

The best expression of your love and devotion to Our Blessed Mother is to bring her souls, souls from the darkness of sin to the light of grace, from the darkness of paganism to the light of faith. Pray to her for the priests and missionaries the world over so that she may sanctify them and aid them in their labors. Pray for an increase of missionary vocations.

Pope Leo XIII wrote: "It is no exaggeration to say that it is chiefly under Mary's patronage and by her aid that the doctrine and laws of the Gospel have spread so rapidly in spite of immense obstacles and difficulties, amongst all nations and across continents, inaugurating everywhere a new order of justice and peace . . . she has always unceasingly worked to maintain firm, wholesome and fruitful the Catholic Faith."

Pope Pius XI in his encyclical letter *Rerum Ecclesiae* had this to say: "May Mary, the most holy Queen of Apostles, kindly smile on all and prosper the work undertaken, for since on Calvary all men were entrusted to her motherly care, she does not less cherish and love those who are ignorant of the fact that they are redeemed by Jesus Christ, than she does those who happily enjoy the benefits of that Redemption."

Prayer

(1) MARY, MOTHER OF GOD, at Pentecost you were with the Apostles, preparing for the Holy Spirit, the promised Gift of your Son. Prayer was the soul of your preparation, and the Apostles were inspired by your example. *When the Holy Spirit descended, you received the richest outpouring of His graces.* Your holiness was due to this Spirit of Love, to Whose guidance you abandoned yourself. All that He could give He bestowed upon you, His Immaculate Bride. On the day of Pentecost the Apostles' worldly views about the Kingdom of God on earth were banished by the Spirit of God, and holiness replaced their imperfections, but no taint of the slightest sin had to be removed from your virginal soul. He overshadowed you at the Annunciation, and on Pentecost He made your heart a furnace of divine love.

Not only did the Holy Spirit pour into your soul a fullness of grace, but He entrusted to you, the Mother of the human family, the distribution of all grace. What was true of the effusion of the Holy Spirit on that day is equally true of every outpouring of grace:

God gives nothing to earth without causing the gift to pass through your hands.

MARY, MY MOTHER, you always lived under the divine influence of the Holy Spirit and in the closest possible union with Him. Teach me to understand something of your love for the Holy Spirit and His love for you in keeping your soul beautiful and holy. Teach me to love Him with some of the love that glowed in your own heart so that my heart may always be His pleasing temple. Protect me from losing the Holy Spirit by sin. Make me ever attentive to His inspirations that I may grow in holiness and may merit to see this Divine Guest of my soul in the glory of His heavenly kingdom.

(2) MARY, MOTHER OF GOD, *you are the Queen of the Apostles because you were the source of their inspiration and zeal.* By your love of God and of His adopted sons, you aided the Apostles in the spread of Christ's Kingdom on earth. You could not accompany the Apostles while they fulfilled the duties of their ministry, but in silence and solitude, by the power of your prayers and the fervor of your charity, you were the master missionary of them all.

The part that you have played in the spread of the Church and in its struggles and triumphs clearly shows the Divine Plan in your regard. You have given to the world the Savior Whom the Apostles have proclaimed. From you all missionaries have received the salvation which they bring to the nations. God has made you Queen and Protectress of the Church. You have the charge of keeping faith intact and love unimpaired in the Church founded by Our Lord, and of spreading through the nations and over continents the knowledge of the Kingdom of God. Thanks to you, the grace and the sanctifying gifts of the Holy Spirit are scattered abroad over the Church and its members.

(3) MARY, MOTHER OF GOD, *Queen of the Apostles, pray for the triumph of God's Kingdom upon earth.* Through your powerful intercession promote the propagation of the faith. Give strength and courage to those who work for the salvation of souls as apostles of our own times that, following the example of the Divine Missionary, Jesus Christ, they may labor zealously for the spread of God's kingdom. Give them zeal that by prayer and sacrifice they may cooperate in the great work of the Redemption.

May your glorious example be imitated by countless youths and maidens who will give themselves to the Lord to carry on His work throughout the world. Increase the number of vocations to the priesthood and the religious life and awaken in many young hearts a zeal for the salvation of pagans and sinners.

Pray for more lay apostles, who in every walk of life will defend the rights of God, proclaim His Truth, and preach His holy Will by word and example. Fill their hearts with the virtues of joyous zeal for God and for souls and a warm love for divine learning.

MARY, MY MOTHER, give me the same virtues in my state of life— a will inflamed with the desire that God's Will be done and a mind steeped in the knowledge of what that Will is. Give me enthusiasm and joy in the knowledge, the love and the service of the Lord.

Implore the grace of conversion for many pagans that they may come to the knowledge of the true faith and one day be united with the saints in heaven, there to love you and praise your mercy for all eternity. Bless our prayers and labors for the conversion of the world and support them by your powerful intercession with your Son, Jesus, that His Kingdom of Truth and Life, Holiness and Grace, Justice, Love and Peace, may be spread among men.

> Mother Mary, we revere you,
> As our glorious Mission Queen,
> Deign to harken to our asking,
> Turn to us your glance serene.
> Kindly Mission Queen, remember,
> All your children in the night,
> All those souls which Satan's keeping,
> Far from Jesus and His Light.
> Take our hearts and keep them kindled,
> With a love for souls most true.
> Help us lead those souls, dear Mother,
> Safe to Jesus and to you!
>
> Dearest Mother, hear our pleading,
> For our priests in lands afar,
> Who are gathering in the harvest;
> Be to them a guiding Star.
> Kindly aid them when they're toiling,
> Cheer them when they're sad and lone.
> When you find their zeal is waning,
> Mother fill them with your own.
> Take our hearts and keep them kindled,

With a love for souls most true.
Help us lead those souls, dear Mother,
Safe to Jesus and to you!

Bless our mission fields in China,
In Japan and Philippines,
Those at home and far-off India,
And the Isles of Southern Seas.
Bless our mission fields in Africa.
May they win your special care.
One and all, dear Mother Mary,
Bless our missions everywhere.
Take our hearts and keep them kindled,
With a love for souls most true.
Help us lead those souls, dear Mother,
Safe to Jesus and to you!
—THE REV. LAWRENCE G. LOVASIK, S.V.D.

† † †

Through Your mercy, O Lord, and the intercession of the Blessed Virgin Mary, may Your Church increase in the number of the faithful and ever shine forth in the manifold light of virtue. Through Christ Our Lord. Amen.

Feast of Pentecost

(NOVENA, Friday after the Ascension)
(Our Lady, the Immaculate Bride of the Holy Spirit)

Background:

The Blessed Virgin Mary accompanied her Son to Mount Olivet and witnessed the glory of the Ascension. The great joy which filled the disciples on this occasion must have been hers also, but in greater measure.

After the Ascension Mary was present in the upper room, persevering unitedly in prayer with the Apostles, the holy women, and the brethren of the Lord: "All these with one mind continued steadfastly in prayer with the women and Mary, the mother of Jesus, and with his brethren" (Acts 1:14).

They remained together in the Upper Room or Cenacle, the place where Jesus had appeared to them and which may well be called the first Christian church. About 120 persons were assembled there. They chose Matthias as an apostle in place of Judas; they prayed and waited for the Paraclete, as Jesus had commanded them: "And while eating with them, he charged them not to depart from Jerusalem, but to wait for the promise of the Father, 'of which you have heard,' said he, 'by my mouth, for John indeed baptized with water, but you shall be baptized with the Holy Spirit not many days hence" (Acts 1:4).

Ten days had passed. On the seventh Sunday after the resurrection, at about nine o'clock in the morning, as they were together praying fervently, the Holy Spirit descended upon them. A mighty roar, like the onrush of a violent wind, came suddenly from heaven and filled the room where Our Lady and the disciples were gathered. Tongues of fire descended upon each one present—visible evidence that the Holy Spirit had descended upon them.

After the roar of wind many of Jerusalem's pilgrims hurried to the Cenacle. Now the Apostles, who so shortly before had hidden in fear behind locked doors, came forth and courageously walked among the multitude speaking to each in his native tongue.

Since she was united in prayer with the Apostles, who can describe or even faintly understand the wealth of grace and glory with which that

Divine Spirit has adorned and enriched His beloved and immaculate Bride! Mary must have witnessed stirring events which accompanied the spread of the new Church. Though nothing further is related about her in the Scriptures, by her dignity as the Mother of the Lord, by her holy life, her prayers, and her encouragement, she must have exerted a very great influence upon the infant Church. The part that the Blessed Virgin has played in the birth, infancy, and struggles of the Catholic Faith clearly shows the Divine Plan in her regard. God has made her Queen and Protectress of the Church. She has the charge of keeping faith intact and love unimpaired in the Society founded by Jesus Christ and of spreading through the nations the knowledge of the Kingdom of God. Thanks to her prayers and merits, the grace and the sanctifying gifts of the Holy Spirit are scattered abroad over the Church and Its members.

Pope Pius XII in his encyclical on the Mystical Body wrote: "Thus she who corporally was the Mother of our Head, through the added title of pain and glory became spiritually the Mother of all His members. She it was who through her powerful prayers obtained the grace that the Spirit of our Divine Redeemer, already given to the Church on the Cross, should be bestowed through miraculous gifts on the newly founded hierarchy on Pentecost. . . . She continued to show for the Mystical Body of Christ, born from the pierced Heart of the Savior, the same mother's care and ardent love with which she clasped the Infant Jesus to her warm and nourishing breast."

Ask Our Lady of the Cenacle for a deep personal love for the Holy Spirit. Ask her to help you understand and appreciate the many gifts of grace which this Spirit of Love has bestowed upon your soul. Your imitation of Mary would be imperfect without a personal devotion to the Holy Spirit who made her His Bride and to Whom she owes all her beauty and holiness.

Prayer

(1) MARY, MOTHER OF GOD, *all your natural and supernatural privileges and riches were the gifts of the Holy Spirit to you, His Immaculate Bride*. I believe that, after Jesus became man, no one on earth was closer to the Son of God than you were. Through your Divine Motherhood the Holy Spirit united you most intimately with the Son of God. He chose you from all eternity for this unparalleled greatness. You alone of all the children of men were conceived immaculate, were born full of grace, and are blessed among women. The Holy Spirit graciously prepared your body and soul to be a worthy dwelling place for the Son of God.

In the sacred hour of the Annunciation the Holy Spirit performed in you the great mystery of the Incarnation, as the angel spoke to her, "The Holy Spirit shall come upon thee and the power of the Most High shall overshadow thee; and, therefore, the Holy One to be born shall be called the Son of God" (Luke 1:35).

As the same Divine Spirit, the Finger of God's right hand, formed in you and out of you the human nature of the eternal Word, He also formed you into the most perfect image of your Son. Through grace He took possession of you, adorned you with spiritual beauty, made you His holy temple, and by His indwelling prepared you to be a worthy sanctuary for the Son of God. You are, therefore, next to Christ, the most perfect likeness and image of God, the clearest mirror of His beauty and goodness, the first-born of creation, the most cherished of all God's children, in possession of the highest fullness of all the divine and moral virtues as well as of the seven Gifts of the Holy Spirit. All these wonderful adornments—your Immaculate Conception, your perfect sinlessness, your perpetual virginity, your fullness of grace—were the gifts of the Holy Spirit to you, for you are His Immaculate Bride.

MARY, MY MOTHER, *how you must love the Holy Spirit for having given you all this beauty and glory* which is but a revelation of His infinite love for you! You surrendered yourself to Him in loving devotedness. What a wealth of graces bloomed in the mysterious stillness and depths of your soul because of your union with the Son of God and with the Divine Spirit! Would that I could descend into this silent sanctuary and understand the tenderness of His guiding love and the warmth of devotion in your soul as you abandoned yourself entirely to His divine guidance. Never was a human soul blessed more abundantly with His presence than you, and never was a soul more devoted to Him. You were always full of attention: the gaze of your soul was ever resting on your Divine Spouse. You were ever full of bridal willingness to listen to His inspirations, ready to follow every breath of His grace. You were always full of deepest gratitude for His love.

(2) MARY, MOTHER OF GOD, *you were present when the Holy Spirit descended on the Feast of Pentecost.* His coming was glorious: the rushing and roaring as of a mighty wind signified His proceeding from the Father and the Son by love; the flaming tongues of fire were symbols of the spirituality, holiness, and purifying power

of God. He came upon you and the Apostles and disciples laden with rich graces, and you were "filled with the Holy Spirit"—a fullness that included not merely the gifts of grace, but the Giver of graces Himself.

The Holy Spirit came to you and the Apostles graciously, for He is the God of love, mercy, and peace. He came to save the whole world, to comfort and gladden it by a new presence, to remain with the Church with blessings of truth and grace till the end of time.

MARY, MY MOTHER, you received the largest and the richest outpouring of the graces of the Holy Spirit. On Pentecost, the Apostles' worldly views about the Kingdom of God on earth were banished by the Spirit of God under the influence of the Holy Spirit, and holiness of the highest order replaced their imperfections. But no taint of the slightest sin or the least shadow of imperfection had to be removed from your virginal soul. You were in the midst of the Apostles in Jerusalem in the first days of Christianity, as their counseling Mother. You had an important part in the spread of Christ's Kingdom on earth. In silence, by the power of your prayers and the fervor of your charity you spread the Faith that it cost both you and your Son so much to give to mankind.

(3) MARY, MOTHER OF GOD, *pray that the Holy Spirit may also come to me and overshadow me with His power so that Christ may be formed in me.* May this sweet Guest of my soul unite me closely and forever to the Father and the Divine Word. He overshadowed you with the power of the Most High in your Immaculate Conception, in the Incarnation, and on Pentecost Day. Help me to love Him in union with that love with which Jesus loved Him in the Father from all eternity and with which you love Him, knowing Him to be the God of fair and spotless love.

I venerate you as the immaculate Bride of the Holy Spirit. You are the glory of Jerusalem, the joy of Israel, the honor of all nations! As the valiant woman you crushed the head of the serpent when you offered your Divine Son to the heavenly Father in the love of the Holy Spirit for the salvation of the world. Through the sufferings of your Son, obtain for me the Gifts of the Holy Spirit.

I thank the Holy Spirit for having chosen you as His Bride and made you the dispenser of His graces. Look upon me with your compassionate eyes. Behold my distress and my needs. Help me that I may never lose the grace of God nor defile the temple of the

Holy Spirit and that my heart may ever remain His holy dwelling.
May I become His faithful child on earth, as you were, so that I
may share His eternal glory in heaven.

MARY, MY MOTHER, above all creatures you were disposed
to receive the Holy Spirit, and you received Him with greater fullness than all others. Dispose, I beg you, by your gracious aid, my
cold heart for the graces of the Holy Spirit. Obtain for me a heart-
felt contrition for my sins so that I may receive His many graces as
a true penitent. Grant this not for my merits, for I have none, but
out of your own exceeding goodness and that great love which you
bear to the same Holy Spirit, Who has chosen you to be His Spouse.

Purest and holiest Heart of Mary, in whom Jesus lives through
the Holy Spirit, implore for me from this Holy Spirit that the
Sacred Heart of Jesus, through Him, may live in my heart and in
the hearts of all men.

The Holy Spirit chose thee for His Bride,
His favored Spouse immaculate to be.
By Him thy soul was made and beautified,
A spotless temple for the Trinity.
What veiled magnificence in thee I see:
No earthly pomp and fleeting greatness thine,
But from all stain of sin thy soul is free,
And bright within thy countless virtues shine,
For in thy heart there reigns a Spouse Who is divine.

Within the realms of God's eternal thought,
Thou wast ordained the hope of paradise.
And in thy soul the Holy Spirit brought
The spendor which devotion glorifies.
He made thee pure and spotless in His eyes,
A spouse like to no other spouse on earth;
Salvation's Sun from thee could nobly rise,
O Queen of Saints, before thy blessed birth!
What feeble mortal tongue can fully praise thy worth!

O gentle Queen, the Spirit's chaste abode,
Help us prepare for Him a worthy throne.
The way is dark and life a weary road;
Our will is weak, 'neath sorrow's sting we groan.
To thee we turn in exile and alone,

To see His presence shining in thy heart.
Our consecration to His love we own;
As thou thyself His tabernacle art,
His temples we shall be, and ne'er from **Him** depart.

O God, Who sent the Holy Spirit to Your Apostles, who were united in prayer with Mary, the Mother of Jesus, grant us that, protected by the same Mother of ours and Queen of Apostles, we may be made worthy to serve Your Divine Majesty faithfully and proclaim Your glory by word and example. Through the same Christ Our Lord. Amen.

Our Lady of the Most Blessed Sacrament

Background:

The Blessed Virgin Mary rightly deserves the title of Our Lady of the Blessed Sacrament not only because she gave us the Sacred Humanity of Jesus, Which is the essence of this Sacrament, but also because of her intense devotion to this Mystery of Love. It is to Mary, after God, that we owe the hidden "Gift of God," in the Eucharist, for Jesus is the "blessed fruit of her womb." She has given us the human form of Him, Who, dwelling upon our altars in the Blessed Sacrament, makes heaven of earth. It was from her that He assumed the Flesh and Blood with which He nourishes us.

It is the Eucharistic work of Mary to draw souls to Jesus in the Blessed Sacrament. Devotion to the Holy Eucharist is surely the greatest means to make us more interior, more Christlike, because the Eucharist is the Source from which the graces of Redemption continually flow to mankind. Since this is so, what an ardent longing must burn in the Heart of the Blessed Virgin Mary for the flourishing of devotion to the Blessed Sacrament! How earnestly she must stand at the side of the priest at the altar, encouraging him with devotion; how her loving hand guides her children to the Communion rail! The more the love and veneration of Mary is fostered, the more does devotion to the Eucharist flourish.

The forces of divine grace by which Our Lord raises the souls of men to the supernatural life and brings them to an ever greater perfection in that life center around the sacramental system in the Church. All of these forces, in their turn, center around and find their expression in the Eucharist Sacrifice. Hence the salutary power of Mary's intercession at the throne of God is joined with the effectiveness of the Blessed Sacrament.

Through her we receive every grace, and consequently those graces contained in the Most Holy Sacrament of the Altar. The graces which come to us through the intercession of Our Lady are such as to move men toward the fruitful reception of the Blessed Eucharist. Dwelling now and forever in the glory of heaven, she draws those for whom Christ died on the cross to the Eucharist and disposes them to live ever more perfectly with the

Eucharistic life. She was the first to practice the duties of a truly Eucharistic life, showing us by her example how we ought to assist at Mass, receive Holy Communion, and visit the Most Blessed Sacrament. Consequently, the Church of God delights in hailing her as Our Lady of the Blessed Sacrament.

Prayer

(1) MARY, MOTHER OF GOD, *you are called Our Lady of the Most Blessed Sacrament because you are associated in a special way with the presence of Jesus in the Eucharist.*

From all eternity God chose you to be His Mother, and in time He adorned you with every spiritual charm. He preserved you from original sin and the sway of the devil; He filled you with grace. He made you immaculate in view of the fact that Jesus Christ, the God-Man, was to take His Flesh and Blood from you.

Our Lady of the Blessed Sacrament, I see you in Bethlehem lovingly pressing to your heart your Child, your God, the future Eucharistic Christ. I see you offering Him to the heavenly Father in the temple for our salvation. That very same Christ is mine in the Holy Eucharist when I look upon Him as a Victim on our altars; when I kneel before Him as my Friend in the Tabernacle; when I receive Him into my soul as my Guest in Holy Communion. He is all mine—and all because you gave your consent to become His Mother.

Though it was out of sheer goodness that God decreed to give us His very Son in the Blessed Sacrament, I believe that your prayers had much to do with the carrying out of that plan; for you, too, must have prayed, "Give us this day our daily bread." And when Jesus instituted this Holy Sacrament, He surely thought especially of you.

But I see the relation between you and the Blessed Sacrament above all in your life after Good Friday when you began your new motherhood at the feet of Jesus in the Eucharist. If to live of the Eucharist and by the Eucharist was the very special spirit of the early Church—"And they continued steadfastly in the communion of the breaking of the bread" (Acts 2: 42) —it must have been the summary of your last years on earth. I can easily picture St. John, the Apostle of love, saying Mass each day in his own home and daily giving you the consecrated bread and wine of the Eucharist. There

before the tabernacle you relived in memory all the happy and
sorrowful events of your life with Jesus. In your heart and life
the Eucharist took the place of His former presence in the flesh.
Your ardent faith and intense love pierced that thin veil which
separated you from your loving Son. Your heart and His burned
with one flame of love to the glory of the Father there at the altar.
How happy Jesus must have been to receive the homage that you
paid Him! What joy He must have felt at the thought that His
Sacramental Presence brought you such consolation!

MARY, MY MOTHER, I have every reason to honor you under the
title of Our Lady of the Most Blessed Sacrament, because you have
given me the Eucharistic Christ. It is your Son Who abides with me
in the tabernacle as the best Friend I have in this world, Who offers
Himself to the Father for me as the Victim of Calvary at Holy Mass,
Who gives Himself to me as Food in Holy Communion.

(2) MARY, MOTHER OF GOD, *Jesus in the Holy Eucharist is your
Gift to us.* Jesus, not satisfied with having given Himself to all mankind in the Incarnation, wished to become united with each of us
in a most intimate manner by means of the Holy Eucharist, for by
an unceasing act of love He gives Himself to us in each Consecration
and in each Communion. Your Heart, Blessed Mother, is always
conformable to Our Lord's will. Having loved your sinful children
so much as to sacrifice for them your only Son in His Passion, you
loved them to the end by giving them the Holy Eucharist. This gift
of your heart entitles you to be called the Mother of the Holy
Eucharist. Every day you renew your gift generously, because to
each Sacrifice of your Son you give your consent; each Consecration
is your gift to us. Each Communion is a mystery of your love for us
and a grace which you obtain and bestow on us.

MARY, MY MOTHER, *your whole life was like a Mass.* The presentation of the Child Jesus in the temple was like the *Offertory,* for you
offered to the Heavenly Father this "material" for the sacrifice—
the Body and Blood of your little Son. You offered to the Father
in Heaven the Body and Blood of the Lamb you bore and sacrificed
Him with the knife of your will on the altar of your heart. You were
willing to offer Him at this tender age, for the salvation of the
world.

The *Consecration* took place on Calvary where you shared in the
offering of the bloody sacrifice of the New Testament. You stood

close to Jesus, your head raised to drink the bitter chalice offered, your arms stretched out and reaching upward, like a priest at the altar. You offered Him on the altar of the Cross—the future Eucharistic Christ—in perfect adoration to the insulted majesty of God, in thanksgiving for all the blessings showered on mankind, in reparation for our sins, and in petition for sinners. This Body, given to us at Christmas and immolated on Good Friday, was flesh of your flesh, bone of your bone. It died that we might never die, that It might nourish us unto eternal life.

The *Communion* was your life of union with Jesus in the Eucharist after His Ascension. The offering of your Son was continued in each Holy Mass ever to be offered, in each Holy Communion ever to be received, in each act of adoration and prayer before the Sacred Host.

You were the first Chalice of the Blood of Jesus, for Our Lord dwelt in you during the nine months of expectation as in a kind of ciborium. How much more precious you were than any chalice of richest gold! At the crib you were the first ostensorium of your Son, showing Him to the shepherds, to the Magi, and to the world. After the Ascension you found the past under another form: the consecrated Bread the Apostle John placed on your lips was Jesus, Who was formed from your own flesh and with Whom your body was again united.

(3) MARY, MOTHER OF GOD, *I choose you as my model of Eucharistic devotion.* I wish to attend Holy Mass, receive Holy Communion, and visit Jesus in the tabernacle in union with you, in the spirit in which you yourself did so. Just as in my tenderest years I learned to love God at my mother's knee, so now I desire to learn to love my Eucharistic God, as it were, *at your knee,* for I firmly believe that you are the shortest and surest way to the Heart of the Eucharistic Christ.

Your offering of the bloody sacrifice of Calvary is the perfect model for my offering Holy Mass. You suffered with your Divine Son. Never did a mother love her son as you loved Jesus; and so never did a mother share in her son's agony so deeply as you shared the Passion. Jesus died because He willed to die. You must have willed your Son's death, because, hard as it was to make this sacrifice, it would have been quite impossible for your will to be the least separated from His. He died out of love for us; this was His final proof of love. Aside from the Sacred Heart of Jesus, no human heart ever loved mankind so deeply as your Heart, and, therefore, you wanted to unite your will to His, offering to Almighty God this Holy Sacrifice out of pure charity for the human race.

Help me to share actively in Holy Mass by sharing in your spirit. Teach me to imitate you by accepting willingly all the suffering which my service of God involves, my struggles against temptation, my difficult acts of virtue, my little penances—in union with the Victim Jesus on the altar out of love for God and mankind. You are truly my model in offering Holy Mass. Each time Jesus becomes present in the hands of the priest, the Life given to us by the words of consecration comes originally from you. Surely it is through your special influence as Mediatrix of Graces that this Life is shared with me. Therefore, I offer Jesus to the Father through your hands, and in Holy Communion I ask for graces through you.

How earnestly you invite me to come and partake of this Bread of Life! It is through you that I am able to eat the Bread of Heaven even every day. It is through your prayers that God inspires me to receive It and grants me the grace to receive It worthily. As Eve induced Adam to eat of the forbidden fruit which brought death upon us, so you prompt us to eat the Bread which gives us life. Help me to receive Holy Communion frequently, at least each week, if not daily.

MARY, MY MOTHER, from your early years you adored the one true God in the Temple at Jerusalem. You adored your God Incarnate within your chaste womb from the time of the Incarnation to His birth. In Bethlehem you first adored Him in His visible presence as He lay in all His helplessness before your joyful eyes. From that time forward until His Ascension into Heaven, you were the constant adorer of the Word-Made-Flesh in all the mysteries of His earthly life. The early Christians, all lovers of the Eucharist, who visited you frequently during your hidden life of adoration, must have taken away with them the spirit of your Eucharistic devotion. As you knelt before the Sacred Species, you truly influenced the First Christians to be ardent lovers of your loving Son in the Blessed Sacrament. Teach me to prove my love for Jesus by visiting Him frequently in His tabernacle home, where He lives as the best Friend I have upon earth, ready to console and strengthen me in my trials, for His Sacred Heart invites me, "Come to Me, all you who labor and are burdened, and I will give you rest."

Mary, I beg you to lead me to my Sacramental Jesus! Make me a fervent apostle of the Eucharist. Make me Eucharist-minded to the extent that my very life may be the Eucharist—in union with you, Our Lady of the Most Blessed Sacrament.

Our Lady *

Lady of ladies, Queen of all the queens
That have been or shall be, through thee the word
"Lady," that from our lips so oft is heard,
Glows with the glory of the truth it means:
Truth known to that small band of Nazarenes,
The first disciples, whose weak wills were stirred
When He, the Lord of life, on them conferred
Through bread *Himself*, on Whom creation leans!
"Lady" means "bread-giver,"—how true of thee,
"Our Lady," Mother of our joys to be,
When earth's dominions from thrones are hurled!
True "Lady" thou, who gavest birth to Him,
The Food of wonder to the seraphim,
The Bread of life unto a dying world.
—GEORGE BENSON HEWETSON

† † †

We beg of You, O Lord, our God, by the intercession of the Blessed Virgin Mary, to make the Most Holy Mysteries, which You have given us for the preservation of our spiritual life, a remedy for us both for the present and for the future. Through Christ Our Lord. Amen.

* The word *lady* is derived from the Anglo-Saxon "laef-da," which means "loaf-giver" or "bread-giver."

Mary, Help of Christians

FEAST, May 24 (TRIDUUM, May 21-23)

Background:

The title of "Help of Christians" was given to Mary by the faith and devotion of innumerable Christians who have felt the effects of her motherly intercession down through the ages. It has been the constant tradition of the Church that John represented the whole human race and especially those who are joined with Him by faith as Christians. When Mary heard His voice from the cross: "Behold thy son," she was officially appointed Help of Christians because her duties were to be those of a mother. With a generous heart Mary undertook and discharged those duties, the beginnings of which were consecrated in the Cenacle, when the infant Church awaited the coming of the Holy Spirit. With wonderful care she nurtured the first Christians by her holy example, her wise counsel, her sweet consolation, her fruitful prayers. She was the Mother of the Church, the Help of Christians.

Pope Leo XIII wrote in an encyclical letter of 1889: "From the very fact that the most Holy Virgin is the Mother of Jesus Christ, she is the Mother of all Christians, whom she bore on Mount Calvary amid the supreme throes of the Redemption; Jesus Christ is, in a manner, the First-born of Christians, we by adoption and Redemption are His brothers."

Take Mary for your example, if you see bad examples among Christians, or hear critical words concerning the human frailty found in the Catholic religion. The ocean remains beautiful, although there is wreckage on its shores. The Church and religion likewise remain the beautiful work of God, although human misery and sin are found among the body of believers.

Just as in the order of nature you need a mother's love and tender care, so, too, you need a mother's help in your struggle against the temptations of the world, the flesh, and the devil. Jesus gave you the Mother He chose for Himself so that she might be your help in leading a good Christian life. As the Mother of mankind she understands your needs, and as your Mother she is anxious to help you. When you are in need of assistance for soul or body, call upon your Mother Mary, the Help of Christians.

Prayer

(1) MARY, MOTHER OF GOD, *you are the Mother of mankind and, therefore, the Help of Christians, the all-powerful suppliant.* You abound in divine life for yourself; for us you abound in grace. Your part in distributing God's grace is a result of the part you played in obtaining it. Although it is true that Jesus in glory, by means of His Divine Wounds, is our intercessor before the Father and all God's gifts come to us through His merits, *you are the all-powerful suppliant,* through whom every prayer reaches up to Him and every grace comes down. From the moment you said, "Be it done to me according to thy word," the Father in heaven made Jesus and you, as it were, a redemptive pair; you, of course, have always been dependent on Him. In all of the mysteries of Jesus, in every part of His life, the Father always thought of You two together; together You labored to save men.

You were charged with dispensing the supernatural life to men because this was fitting. But you help Christians also by your prayers. You express your wishes to God, those wishes which have to do with our needs—needs of body and needs of soul. Because of your dignity, you reach to the borders of the divine. He Who gives grace takes your prayers for commands.

How earnestly you wish God's grace for us! How earnestly, too, you want to help us in all our needs! When the Persons of the Blessed Trinity gaze on you, the Immaculate One, most pure, most beautiful, supremely pleasing to Eternal Love, what can They refuse you? They see Jesus Christ in you, the treasure house of all Their blessings. Everything which Jesus may claim in justice is yours by friendship's title. Through your prayers and dignity the power and the fruits of the Passion of Jesus are applied to men. No intercession, neither yours nor that of any saint, is of value except through Him, through His blessed wounds. But, if it is true that in the task of redemption you cooperated with Him in everything, in His joys and sorrows, in His winning our salvation, then it is also true that you do the same in the dispensing of all the graces, material and spiritual, necessary for our salvation.

MARY, MY MOTHER, I could go directly to God and ask Him for His grace without your help and that of the saints, but God has not

willed it so. Having once given us Jesus Christ by you, God does
not change His way of helping us. Through you we have received
Jesus Christ, the Universal Source of Grace, so through your intercession we still continue to receive the various actual graces suited
to our state of life. Jesus continues ceaselessly to pray for us, offering for us to His heavenly Father His infinite merits and atonement,
and causing the floods of grace to descend upon us to save us. Since
you had your place beside Jesus when there was question of ransoming us and meriting for us all the graces necessary for our salvation, you must in like manner have your place beside Him now,
when there is question of securing for us by your prayers in heaven
the graces prepared for us in view of the merits of Christ.

(2) MARY, MOTHER OF GOD, *when I consider your compassion for
mankind and your influence with God, I am urged to give my wholehearted and unlimited confidence to you, Help of Christians.* Your
motherly interest in my needs and the salvation of my soul encourage me to make a prompt appeal to you in all my needs and
dangers.

When I address the Almighty, I am frequently fearful because
of my sinfulness in the presence of His infinite majesty and holiness. Jesus is my Savior, and I have confidence in His infinite merits.
Even in the Son of God I sometimes fear the Divine Majesty because, although He became Man, He did not cease to be God. But
because of my sinfulness, I also have need of an intercessor with
Him. I need an advocate with God, and, therefore, I turn to you,
the Mother of God. You are a human creature, but free from even
the slightest sin or guilt, and absolutely pure by reason of the
singular excellence of your nature. The Son will listen to you, His
Mother, and the Father will listen to His Son.

MARY, MY MOTHER, the word which best summarizes your whole
career is "mother." Mother you are, and that doubly in the terms
of our Catholic belief: human Mother of Jesus, supernatural
Mother of every Christian. You brought forth Jesus, your First-born,
without pain; but in giving birth to your second-born, what agony
did you not have to endure? May I weigh well at what price you became the Mother of the human race, so that I may remember how
much you love me and how eager you are to help me and all
Christians. For from the moment when Jesus told you to see Him,
in John, you saw Jesus in all Christians. You took your only Son

(8)

(8)

to heart in all men born. Then for His sake be our Help! You are, indeed, the ladder by which Christians may ascend to heaven; you are their greatest hope, and the whole ground of their hope. Surely the Son cannot refuse her who gave Him birth, the one who never denied Him anything. This thought wonderfully strengthens my confidence in you, Help of Christians.

(3) MARY, MOTHER OF GOD, *you are the Help of Christians because you are the Mother of the Mystical Body of Christ.* As you were the Mother of Jesus in the Incarnation, when He assumed a physical Body, so also you are the Mother of Jesus in His Mystical Body, and of all those who, as members of that Body, are the brothers and sisters of Christ by divine adoption. Jesus, your First-born, was brought forth in joy at Bethlehem, but His brethren, your spiritual children, were brought forth in anguish of spirit at the foot of the cross.

As you cradled the new-born Savior and nourished and cared for Him, so at Pentecost you cradled the new-born Church, watched over its frail, delicate body and fostered and nourished it with motherly care.

As you were called to cooperate with your Divine Son on Calvary in acquiring the treasure of His infinite merits, so now in Heaven you cooperate with Him in dispensing those merits to His Mystical Body. I believe that all graces and heavenly favors flow to the Mystical Body of Christ as from the Head, but you are the channel, through which, by God's will, all graces come to humanity.

Since you are the Mother of men, God gave you a special knowledge of the needs of every Christian that you might help us to save our souls. You would not be completely happy in heaven if you did not know the interests of those souls redeemed at the cost of so much pain to Jesus and you. I cannot for a moment suspect, all good and all powerful as you are, that you are unwilling to implore for me the graces which I need so much. Moreover, I am confident that you will obtain them for me.

MARY, MY MOTHER, all the saints have prayed to you for help: the prophets, the evangelists, the Apostles, the martyrs, the confessors, the heroic virgins and chaste widows. All those whose Queen you are have learnt of Jesus that they must call you Mother and ask your help. Following their example and striving to attain to their faith, joining in their admiration, in their intense pleading,

I, a poor sinner, who am so in need of help and pity, in need of your mercy, cry out to you: Mary, Help of Christians, pray for us . . . pray for me! Pray for us, you who are so powerful; be all powerful in our behalf! You know all our needs—needs of body and needs of soul—infinitely better than a mother. Pray for us Christians who sigh to you in this vale of tears so that we may be comforted, enlightened, strengthened, guided, and finally saved!

> Bless, O Mother Mary, bless thy loving child,
> With thy hands so gentle, pure and undefiled;
> Bless all that I ever think or do or say,
> That my life resemble thine own more each day.

> Bless, O Mother Mary, all hearts dear to me,
> Shield them 'neath thy mantle, from adversity;
> Help them in their struggles, as they sadly roam,
> Bless their pray'r and labor, bless their hearth and home.

> Bless, O Mother Mary, all thy children here,
> Whisper words of comfort, when the end is near;
> Let thy mother blessing e'er our solace be,
> Both in this our exile and eternity.

† † †

Almighty and merciful God, Who in the person of the Blessed Virgin Mary provided never ending assistance for the defense of the Christian people; grant, we beg of You, that, strengthened by such help, we may do battle during life and be able to obtain victory over the treacherous foe in death. Through Christ Our Lord. Amen.

Mary, Mediatrix of All Graces

Background:

A mediator is one who stands between two persons in order to unite them, either to make peace between them or to obtain a favor. The closer the mediator is to both parties, the more successful will his mediation be. In the supernatural order the two parties to be united were God and man, whom sin had caused to be separated.

Jesus as the God-Man is the perfect mediator between God and man. He is one with God, and the spiritual head of the human race. He alone could in all justice merit our reconciliation with God as well as the graces which God would grant after peace had been declared.

The faithful attribute to Mary a certain kind of mediation. As Mother of God and Mother of men she also serves as a bond between God and men. Yet her mediation does not detract from that of Christ, but rather results from it; it is exercised in union with Christ from Whom her mediation draws all its power. The mediatorship of Jesus is one of justice, belonging exclusively to Him by way of just merit; to Mary is granted a mediatorship of grace, entirely dependent upon the merits of Christ and exercised by way of intercessory prayer.

The mediation of Mary is twofold: (1) as Co-Redemptrix with Jesus she has contributed to our redemption; and (2) as a Dispenser of grace she obtains all graces for men with Christ.

In calling Mary the *Mediatrix of All Graces* we mean that the gaining and the bestowal of all supernatural favors depend in some measure upon her sharing with her Divine Son in the work of saving mankind. As all grace was merited for us by Christ, so all grace is distributed to us from Christ by the Holy Spirit through Mary as the Mediatrix between Him and mankind. It has been taught by saints and doctors of the Church and approved by several Popes that the Blessed Virgin prays for all the graces which are bestowed upon man by God through the merits of His Son. She who is the Second Eve in this manner cooperates with the Second Adam in securing to us the fruits of Redemption, even as the first Eve cooperated with the first Adam in our fall. "We may affirm," declares Leo XIII, "that by the will of God, nothing is given to us without Mary's mediation, in such a way that just as no one can approach the Almighty Father but through His Son, so no one, so to speak, can approach Christ but through His Mother."

The belief that Mary is the Mediatrix of All Graces is not yet an article of faith, but it is the fervent hope of many Catholic hearts that the day is not far distant when the voice of the infallible Church will proclaim it as such. Significantly, a special Mass and Office for May 31st in honor of Mary Mediatrix was granted in January, 1921, by Pope Benedict XV at the request of the Belgian Hierarchy to the dioceses of Belgium and to all other dioceses which should ask for it.

The doctrine about Our Lady, Mediatrix of All Graces, is clearly stated in the pronouncements of recent Supreme Pontiffs, which are an invitation to deepen and extend our sense of dependence on Mary for our spiritual life.

After saying that Mary "may justly be said to have redeemed together with Christ the human race," Pope Benedict XV continues, "for this very reason, every grace we receive from the treasury of the Redemption is given to us as by the hands of the same sorrowing Virgin."

St. Pius X, in his encyclical *Ad Diem* on Mary, Mediatrix of All Graces, writes: "It is clear, then, that we are very far from attributing to the Mother of God the power of producing supernatural grace, a power which belongs to God alone. Because, however, she transcends all others in holiness and in the intimacy of her union with Christ, and because she has been drawn by Christ into association with the work of human salvation, she merits for us congruously (out of fitness), as they say, what Christ merited for us condignly (out of justice), and she is the principal Minister of the graces to be distributed. He 'has taken his seat at the right hand of the Majesty on high' (Heb. 1:3). But Mary as Queen stands at His right hand, 'the safest Refuge and the most reliable Helper of all who are in danger, so that nothing need be feared, nothing need be despaired of, so long as she is our guide, she our patroness, so long as she is propitious, she our protectress.' "

Prayer

(1) MARY, MOTHER OF GOD, *you are our Mediatrix*. I believe, according to the inspired teaching of St. Paul, that there is but *one Mediator between God and man*—your Son Jesus. His role in our salvation is absolutely necessary. He saved us by offering to the justice of God perfect atonement for our sins. He alone has paid

the full price of our ransom, and to this price no one else has contributed.

And yet, in the whole work of the Redemption, your Son wanted to associate you with Himself. Though you did not pay even the smallest part of our debt, you cooperated in His work by the entire union of your will with His. Although He might have wrought our salvation alone, without inviting you to share in His work, He did not choose to do so. He willed that (1) *you should be present at each stage of His mortal career*—renewing, continuing, completing what you had done at the Incarnation. He also willed that (2) everywhere *the offering of Himself should be presented to the Father through your hands.* This is what took place at His entrance into the world; and again when He took upon Himself the office of Savior in the mystery of the Circumcision and received from you the Holy Name of Jesus. Once more He renewed His offering at the Presentation in the Temple. And finally, when the sacrifice was completed by His death upon the cross, you had your place beside Him. Your will was one with His, faithful to your promise made at the Incarnation.

MARY, MY MOTHER, *your mediation is in reality one with that of Jesus, Who had seen fit to give Himself to us only through you.* He made His taking of the role of Mediator dependent on your consent, and it was your motherly care, shown toward Him through life, which made Him ready for the sacrifice that reconciled the world to God. Truly then, you are entitled to be called our Mediatrix.

(2) MARY, MOTHER OF GOD, *you are the Mediatrix of All Graces.* By this title I understand: (1) upon your mediation and intercession depends the distribution of the riches of the treasury which Jesus acquired for the salvation of men; (2) consequently, no grace comes to all of us as a body or to any of us in particular which you have not asked for in our behalf; (3) according to the order of things established by God, you have become, under Jesus Christ, after Jesus Christ, and through Jesus Christ—from Whom you can never be separated—the source and principle for us of all supernatural life.

Your Son won a treasure of grace for us by the life and death He offered up to the heavenly Father. I cannot secure my salvation without these graces, for it is the grace of God which gives me light and strength to do good deeds. Through the sacraments, prayer, and good deeds, I can make my own the merit of the atonement of Jesus. *You took part in this offering of the life and death of Jesus.* (1) You prepared in your virginal womb a fit temple for the union of the Son of God—the Divine Word—with our human nature. (2) You took part in this offering also by the consent which you gave to the whole plan of the Redemption, and by your union of will with that of your Divine Son even to the point of His sacrifice on the cross. *If you had part in the work of the Redemption, then you also had part in all those graces which were prepared for us in view of the merits of Jesus for our salvation.* You truly deserve to be called the Mediatrix of Grace.

MARY, MY MOTHER, God has willed that you should distribute His graces because you far surpass all other creatures in holiness: you are the masterpiece of His creation, who more than all the others honored and loved Him during your life; because you are the one whom He has chosen to be the Mother of His Son; and because you have been, according to the Divine Plan, associated with Jesus in the work of Redemption.

Jesus is the only Mediator of justice, and by His merits He obtains for us all graces and salvation; but you are the Mediatrix of grace. You have merited by a merit of fitness all that Jesus has merited by a merit of justice. You receive all graces through Jesus Christ because you pray and ask for them in the Name of Jesus Christ. Whatever graces we receive come to us through your intercession.

(3) MARY, MOTHER OF GOD, *as Mediatrix of All Graces you have entered into the highest state of power and glory in heaven in order that you may help us on our difficult journey to the heavenly City of God.* All good things come to us through your hands. At every moment you interest yourself in our behalf in heaven, and obtain for us by your prayers all the graces we need to reach salvation. You are the channel by which all the favors of Jesus descend upon us, even as it was through you and in union with you that during His mortal life He won for us whatever title we have to His gifts and graces.

Jesus is the Head of the Church, and you are its neck. I believe that all graces, all heavenly blessings descend from Jesus—as from the Head—by means of you—as the neck—to the body of the

Church. You were united with Jesus when He bestowed special favors. Jesus caused the wonderful effects of grace in the soul of John the Baptist, but at the sound of your voice his sanctification was effected, and both he and his mother Elizabeth were filled with the Holy Spirit. You were the instrument used by your Son. At your prayer Jesus changed the water into wine in Cana.

And so it is even now in heaven. While no gift is bestowed on us by God except in virtue of the Passion and death of your Divine Son, the Precious Blood and the sacred wounds of Jesus are presented to God by you. Apart from your cooperation no grace descends to earth.

MARY, MY MOTHER, since it is the will of God that we should obtain all through you, teach me to turn to you in all my needs. You are all-powerful because your Divine Son instantly fulfills all your desires in order to honor you. At the marriage feast of Cana He worked His first miracle because you asked Him for this favor. Show the same compassion toward me, for I am in need of grace to fight temptation, to avoid sin, and to lead a holy life. For the sake of Jesus be mindful of me as you stand near Him Who granted you the fullness of grace. Bestow on me gifts from the riches of that fullness. You are the channel of all good things after the Trinity, Mediatrix of the world after the Mediator. Through you I hope to reach the heavenly Kingdom. I come to you with confidence, knowing that through you all glory, honor, and holiness given to the human race from the first Adam to the last ages has been granted, is being granted, and will be granted to Apostles, prophets, martyrs and all the just. You "found grace with God" to restore salvation to all men. Save me, a poor sinner who confidently invokes your intercession, through the graces merited for me on the cross by the Precious Blood of your Son.

Gracious Queen of earth and heaven,
Shining star on life's dark sea,
All His grace thy Son has given,
Loving Mother unto thee.

Life is filled with pain and sorrows,
Years are fraught with bitter grief;
In uncertain, dread tomorrows,
Thy fond love will bring relief.

Far removed are heaven's portals
From the weary road we plod;
Thou wilt bring poor banished mortals
To the mercy seat of God.

Lord Jesus Christ, our Mediator with the Father, since You made Your
Mother, the Most Blessed Virgin, our Mother also and Mediatrix with You,
mercifully grant that everyone who comes to You asking for favors may be
gladdened for having received all through her intercession. Who live and
reign forever. Amen.

The Queenship of Mary

Background:

According to ancient tradition and the sacred liturgy, *the main principle on which the royal dignity of Mary rests is her Divine Motherhood.* The Archangel spoke to Mary concerning the Son Whom she would conceive: "He shall be called the Son of the most High, and the Lord God will give him the throne of David his father, and he shall be king over the house of Jacob forever; and of his kingdom there shall be no end" (Luke 1:32). St. Elizabeth calls her "the Mother of my Lord" (Luke 1:43). Hence Mary is a Queen, since she bore a Son Who, at the very moment of His conception, because of the hypostatic union of the human nature with the Word, was also as man King and Lord of all things. The heavenly voice of the archangel was the first to proclaim Mary's royal office.

Furthermore, *God has willed Mary to have an exceptional role in the work of our eternal salvation.* Now, in the accomplishing of this work of redemption, the Blessed Virgin Mary was most closely associated with Christ. Just as Jesus, because He redeemed us, is our King by a special title, so the Blessed Virgin also is our Queen on account of the unique manner in which she assisted in our redemption, by giving of her own substance, by freely offering Him for us, by her singular desire and petition for, and active interest in, our salvation.

Mary is the new Eve. A Virgin was instrumental in the salvation of the human race, just as Eve was closely associated with its death. As Christ, the new Adam, must be called a King not only because He is Son of God, but also because He is our Redeemer, so the Blessed Virgin is Queen not only because she is Mother of God, but also because, as the new Eve, she was associated with the new Adam, for she had been chosen Mother of Christ in order that she might become a partner in the redemption of the human race.

Pope Pius XII published an encyclical letter, *Ad Caeli Reginam,* on the Royal Dignity of the Blessed Virgin Mary and on the Institution of Her Feast, on October 11, 1954. From ancient Christian documents, from prayers of the Liturgy, from the innate piety of the Christian people, from works of art, he gathered proofs of the queenly dignity of the Blessed Virgin Mary. He likewise showed that the arguments deduced by Sacred Theology confirm this truth. The new feast was decreed in these words: "Since We are convinced, after long and serious reflection, that great good will accrue to the Church if this solidly established truth shines forth more clearly to all, like a luminous lamp raised aloft, by our Apostolic authority We decree and establish the feast of Mary's Queenship, which is to be celebrated every year in the whole world on the 31st of May. We likewise ordain that on the same day the consecration of the human race to the Immaculate Heart of the Blessed Virgin Mary be renewed, cherishing the hope that through such consecration a new era may begin, joyous in Christian peace and in the triumph of religion."

Thus, Mary, as Mother of the Divine Christ, as His associate in the Redemption, in His struggle with His enemies and His final victory over them, has a share, though in a limited way, in His royal dignity. From her union with Christ she attains a radiant eminence surpassing that of any other creature. From her union with Christ she receives the royal right to dispose of the treasures of the Divine Redeemer's Kingdom, from her union with Christ is derived the power of her maternal intercession before the Son and His Father.

The sublime dignity of the Mother of God over all creatures can be better understood if we recall that Mary was, at the very moment of her Immaculate Conception, so filled with grace as to surpass the grace of all the saints. Besides, the Blessed Virgin possessed, after Christ, not only the highest degree of excellence and perfection, but also a share in that influence by which He, her Son and our Redeemer, is rightly said to reign over the minds and wills of men. For if through His Humanity the Divine Word performs miracles and gives graces, if He uses His Sacraments and saints as instruments for the salvation of men, why should He not make use of the role and work of His most holy Mother in imparting to us the fruits of redemption? *Mary intercedes powerfully for us with a mother's prayers;* she obtains what she seeks, and cannot be refused, for almost immeasurable power has been given to her in the distribution of graces. We should glory in being subjects of the Virgin Mother of God, who, while wielding royal power, is on fire with a mother's love.

In a radio broadcast addressed to the Catholic pilgrims gathered at Fátima on May 13, 1946, Pope Pius XII said: "He, the Son of God, reflects on His heavenly Mother the glory, the majesty and the dominion of His kingship; for, having been associated to the King of Martyrs in the ineffable work of human Redemption as Mother and co-operatrix, she remains forever associated to Him, with an almost unlimited power, in the distribution of the graces which flow from the Redemption. Jesus is King throughout all eternity by nature and by right of conquest; through Him, with Him and subordinate to Him, Mary is Queen by grace, by divine relationship, by right of conquest and by singular election. And her kingdom is as vast as that of her Son and God, since nothing is excluded from her dominion."

Prayer

(1) MARY, MOTHER OF GOD, I believe that as Mediatrix with Jesus you share also in His sovereign dominion over the universe. *You are Queen because you are the Mother of the Word Incarnate.* Christ is universal King because He rules all creatures by His personal union with the divinity. You brought Him into the world that He might be King, according to the words of the archangel: "And of His kingdom there shall be no end." By consenting to His birth, you made Him King.

MARY, MY MOTHER, you are Queen also *because you are Co-Redemptrix.* Jesus reigns over us not only by natural right, but also by the right of redemption. As cooperator with your Son in that work of redemption, you also acquired the right to reign with Him. God chose you to be His Mother and by that very choice has associated you with Himself in the work of the salvation of men. Since you had your place beside Jesus when there was question of ransoming us and meriting for us all the graces necessary for our salvation, you must in like manner have your place beside Him now, when there is question of securing for us by your prayers in heaven the graces prepared for us in view of the merits of Christ. This is my hope that you will be a Mother to me and obtain for me the grace I need to save my soul.

(2) MARY, MOTHER OF GOD, yours is *a queenship of goodness.* You add a degree of motherly sweetness to the joy of the angels and saints and to the blessed of the Church triumphant. To the Church suffering you bring consolation, relief, deliverance; to the Church militant you offer aid, confidence, victory.

Yours is *a queenship of dominion.* You exercise your queenly dominion over the minds, the hearts, the wills, and even over the bodies of your subjects. You rule over their minds by making them understand better the teaching of Christ; over their hearts, by turning them to Jesus through the charm of your motherly affection; over their wills, by gently inclining them to observe all the commandments of your Son; over their bodies, by teaching men

to subject their members to the law of God through the practice
of temperance and chastity. The more fully you are Queen in a soul,
the more does Jesus reign there as King. Reign over my mind and
heart and will and body so that I may belong completely to Jesus
through you.

MARY, MY MOTHER, yours is *a queenship of conquest.* How many
souls have still to be brought under the rule of Christ the King!
Fulfill your apostolic mission of winning the world for Christ. As
formerly the shepherds and the magi found Jesus close to you, so
now may all sinners, unbelievers, and pagans find Jesus through
you, His Mother. Hasten the reign of Christ by ruling over all of us,
your children.

(3) MARY, MOTHER OF GOD, *the apostolic mission confided to you
as Queen by your Son is to help Him to the end of time in the sanctification and the salvation of all the souls that come into the world.*
This apostolic mission is a consequence of your office as Mother,
as Co-Redemptrix, and as Dispenser of all graces.

As Mother, it is your mission to preserve your children from sin
and to make them live the supernatural life. You are the first apostle
of your children not only because you are the most perfect of
mothers, but especially because you are our spiritual Mother. Your
apostolic work—to snatch souls from Satan and from sin to make
them live the supernatural life—is the very reason for your motherhood.

As Co-Redemptrix, you must finish your work by applying the
grace of Redemption to each individual soul, for only then the
redemption is achieved. This is the very heart of your apostolate.
No apostolic act bears fruit without grace. But all graces come
through you. Through your prayers all graces have come to the
apostle and to the souls converted or sanctified. By granting them
these graces you have performed a work of the apostolate. Your
apostolate is universal because you are the spiritual Mother of all
men and the universal Co-Redemptrix. All other apostles and
workers for the salvation of souls depend upon you for blessing
upon their missionary work. Bless the work of those who spend
themselves to bring souls to your loving Son. Through your powerful intercession obtain for them the graces they need. Sanctify them
first, so that they may then more effectively sanctify others.

MARY, MY MOTHER, as *Dispenser of all graces,* you make the

world share in the infinite merits of the Redemption. You are the
Mediatrix of our peace with God and the Giver of heavenly graces.
You have entered into the highest state of power and glory in
Heaven in order that you may help us in our journey through so
many dangers to the Kingdom of Heaven. I believe with the Church
that from the great treasury of graces that Jesus has merited for us,
nothing comes to us, by the will of God, except through you. Hence,
it is through you that we must go to Christ, almost in the same way
as through Christ we approach our Heavenly Father. You are our
Mediatrix with our Mediator.

We do not attribute to you the power of producing supernatural
grace, even though you are the Mother of God, for this power belongs to God alone. But, because you surpass all other creatures
in holiness and in the closeness of your union with Jesus, and
because you have been, according to the Divine Plan, associated
with Jesus in the work of Redemption, you have merited by a merit
of fitness all that Christ has merited by a merit of justice, and God
has made you the Giver of His graces.

You are Queen of the universe, not by force, but by the power of
love. You embrace the universe in the realm of your love and enrich it through your unfailing intercession. You are "Suppliant
Omnipotence" because your prayer obtains all graces from the
infinite treasures of God.

From your heart we hope to obtain the love of God that He ex-
pects from His creatures, and also the pardon that guilty but repentant creatures ask from their merciful Creator. All souls belong
to you and your Son. He is King and you are Queen of all hearts.
Rule over us by the queenly power of your love that the Kingdom
of your Son—the Kingdom of Truth and Life, Holiness and Grace,
Justice, Love and Peace—may come upon earth.

> Mary, Queen of Heaven, star on life's dark sea,
> All our hearts are given, Virgin pure, to thee.
> Life and land and nation at thy feet today
> All in consecration joyfully we lay.
>
> Queen of God's creation, Spouse of God's fair love,
> Peerless is thy station with thy Son above.
> In thy pure maternal hands our own we press;
> Lead us to eternal heaven's happiness.

Well we know the kindness, shining in thy eyes,
From our sinful blindness thou wilt help us rise.
Earth can claim no other, Virgin, like to thee;
Ever blessed Mother, hear thy children's plea!

† † †

Grant, we beg of You, O Lord, that we who celebrate the feast day of the Blessed Virgin Mary, our Queen, may merit, under her loving protection, to attain peace on this earth and glory in heaven. Through Christ Our Lord. Amen.

Prayer of Pope Pius XII

From the depths of this tearful earth where sorrowing humanity makes weary progress—through the surges of this sea of ours endlessly buffeted by the winds of passion—we raise our eyes to you, O Most Beloved Mother Mary, to be comforted by the contemplation of your glory and to hail you as Queen of heaven and earth, Queen of mankind.

With legitimate filial pride, we wish to exalt your Queenship and to recognize it as due to the sovereign excellence of your whole being, O dearest One, truly Mother of Him Who is King by right, by inheritance, and by conquest.

Reign, O Mother and Queen, by showing us the path of holiness and by guiding and assisting us that we may never stray from it.

In the heights of heaven you exercise your primacy over the choirs of angels who acclaim you as their Sovereign, and over the legions of saints who delight in beholding your dazzling beauty. So, too, reign over the entire human race, above all by opening the path of faith to those who do not yet know your Divine Son.

Reign over the Church, which acknowledges and extols your gentle dominion and has recourse to you as a safe refuge amid the calamities of our day. Reign especially over that part of the Church which is persecuted and oppressed; give it strength to bear adversity, constancy never to yield under unjust compulsion, light to avoid falling into enemy snares, firmness to resist public attack, and at every moment unwavering faithfulness to your kingdom.

Reign over men's minds that they may seek only what is true; over their wills that they may follow solely what is good; over their hearts that they may love nothing but what you yourself love.

Reign over individuals and over families, as well as over societies and nations; over the assemblies of the powerful, the counsels of the wise, the simple aspirations of the humble.

Reign in the streets and the squares, in the cities and the villages, in the valleys and the mountains, in the air, on land and on the sea; and hear the pious prayer of all those who recognize that yours is a reign of mercy, in which every petition is heard, every sorrow comforted, every misfortune relieved, every infirmity healed. Yours is a reign in which, at a gesture from your gentle hands, from death itself there arises smiling life.

Obtain for us that all who now in every corner of the world acclaim and hail you Queen and Lady, may one day in heaven enjoy the fullness of your kingdom in the vision of your Divine Son, Who with the Father and the Holy Ghost, lives and reigns forever and ever. Amen.

Mary, Virgin Mother of Grace

FEAST, June 9 (TRIDUUM, June 6–8)

Background:

By the beautiful title "Mother of Grace" we understand (1) *that upon Mary's mediation and intercession depends the distribution of the riches of the treasure acquired by Jesus for the salvation of men;* (2) that, consequently, no grace comes to all of us as a body or to any of us in particular which Mary has not asked for in our behalf; (3) that, according to the order of things established by God, she has become, under Jesus Christ, after Jesus Christ, and through Jesus Christ, from whom she can never be separated, the source and principle for us of all supernatural life.

In this title we find but *another expression of Mary's spiritual motherhood* of men; for, as she was the physical Mother of the Redeemer, the Author of Divine Grace, so by grace she is the spiritual Mother of the redeemed. Grace is the highest gift that man can receive from God. As Mary was destined to become the Mother of the Author of Grace, she was enriched with grace more than any other creature. She became the object of God's delight, for in her He saw the purest reflection of the goodness of His Son. Mary is full of grace not only for herself, but on our account as well, for by her intercession the gifts of God's grace are bestowed upon men. In all your needs go to the Mother of Grace with confidence.

Where Christ is, there is Mary, and where Christ acts, there Mary acts, too, not by title of equality with Him, but as assistant providentially assigned. A number of striking incidents in the lives of Jesus and His Mother disclose the enduring union between them; consequently, *the supernatural life of the Mystical Body depends, of course, in a subsidiary way, on Mary, our Mother.*

God prepared Mary for her divine and spiritual motherhood by sanctifying her in fullness. She was conceived immaculate and was perfected, to a degree never duplicated in any creature, by sanctifying grace and its accompaniment of infused virtues and gifts of the Holy Spirit. Before Mary could be our spiritual Mother she had to have the supernatural life of grace in such abundance that it not only perfected her individually, but equipped her to share that life with her future children. St. Thomas

Aquinas says, "God gives grace according to the purpose for which He has chosen a person. . . . The Blessed Virgin received such a fullness of grace that she was nearest of all to the Author of grace, because she received within herself Him Who is full of all grace; and then, by bringing Him forth, she did her part in conveying grace to all."

Mary's spiritual motherhood is a prolongation of her divine mother-hood; she could not give birth to Jesus without becoming at the same time Mother of His members. God's plans do not change. Mary still continues in heaven to exercise her maternal activity in all the graces that come to us from God. Our birth to the life of grace and our supernatural growth require the continued action of the Mother who bears us and who bears Christ in us.

Prayer

(1) MARY, MOTHER OF GOD, *since you are the Mother of Jesus Christ, you are the Mother of Grace as well.* God prepared you for this exalted dignity by an extraordinary abundance of His graces, when He chose you to be the instrument of His mercy by making you the Mother of His Divine Son. This is why you were greeted by the angel in the words, "Hail, full of grace." According to earthly standards, nothing could be added to your fullness of grace. According to God's eternal standards, the sanctity proclaimed by Gabriel when he called you "full of grace" was but the beginning of your wonderful growth in holiness. When Jesus was conceived in your womb by the infinite power of the Holy Spirit, you possessed the Author of grace, and He so adorned your soul with the richness of His heavenly gifts that you won the admiration of men and angels. After the birth of your Divine Son, this grace grew in splendor within you as it daily united you more closely with your God. Even your earthly sufferings were to deepen your sanctity. How many and how great, then, were the graces you received in order to reach the eminent virtue that was yours when, on Calvary, you became the Queen of Martyrs!

MARY, MY MOTHER, as I cannot grasp the depth of your sanctity, I cannot understand the measure of your grace. The gift that God conferred upon you when He chose you to be the Mother of His Divine Son, and the grace that was in proportion to that gift, are beyond the understanding of men and even of angels. All that God could give He bestowed on you. The Holy Spirit overshadowed you

at the Annunciation, and on Pentecost He made your Heart a
furnace of divine love.

(2) MARY, MOTHER OF GOD, *you are Mother of Grace, because
we are begotten of you to the life of grace* and are indebted to you
after Jesus, for our supernatural life. God, having once given us
Jesus Christ by you, Holy Virgin, does not change His way of
blessing us with His gifts. As we have received through you the
Universal Source of Grace, Jesus your Son, so we still continue to
receive, by your intercession, the various actual graces suited to our
state and calling in Christ. Your motherly love contributed so
much to our salvation in the Incarnation of the Son of God, Who
is the Universal Source of Grace, that you will eternally contribute
as much to all the works of grace, which come to us because of the
Incarnation.

God is the source of every good and the absolute Master of all
graces. You are only a pure creature, who receives whatever you obtain as a pure favor from God. But it is most reasonable and proper
to say that God, who honored and loved You more than all others
during your life, and whom He had chosen to be the Mother of
His Son and our Redeemer, wills that all graces that are granted
to those whom He has redeemed should pass through your hands
and be distributed by you in order to exalt you. Jesus is the only
Mediator of justice, and by His merits He obtains for us all graces
and salvation; but you are the Mediatrix of Grace. Though receiving all you obtain through Jesus Christ, because you pray and ask
for it in the Name of Jesus, yet whatever graces we receive come
to us through your intercession.

MARY, MY MOTHER, I firmly believe that the saints and blessed
in Heaven can aid us by interceding for us with God. The holier a
person is and the greater the intimacy of his union with God, the
greater also is the power of his prayers. But your holiness is so great
that the power of your intercession is greater than that of all the
other saints. The prayers of the saints avail only in a limited way.
The power of your intercession has no such limits, for the saints
teach me that our Savior can refuse nothing to His Mother. You
are indeed all-powerful in Heaven, but your omnipotence is not
one of authority and command, but of intercession. We can certainly
call you "Suppliant Omnipotence."

(3) MARY, MOTHER OF GOD, *I believe that divine grace is absolutely necessary for the performing of any act that is meritorious for eternal life.* I am grateful to your Divine Son for this priceless gift of God, for by His Passion and death He not only reinstated us in the friendship of His heavenly Father, but also purchased for us all the graces we stand in need of to attain eternal life.

I also believe that grace is a free gift of God, and I have no claim to it except as a member of His holy Church, which is the Mystical Body of Christ. Whoever abides in this Church will bring forth much salutary fruit; whereas, they who willingly separate themselves from it must wither away spiritually. How strongly Jesus reminded me of this: "As the branch cannot bear fruit of itself unless it remain on the vine, so neither can you, unless you abide in Me. I am the vine, you are the branches" (John 15:4).

Help me to be deeply grateful for God's generosity toward me. I have been specially blessed as a Catholic, for God has given me graces which He has not given to everyone else. The Catholic Church, the Gospels, the sacraments, the Mother of Divine Grace as my advocate—these are among the special blessings with which I am favored. I know that much will be required from those to whom much is given. Help me to make good use of the graces given me by God. May my faith influence my conduct. May the instructions I receive increase the love of God in me and strengthen my determination to serve Him with greater zeal. May I derive all the beneficial results the holy sacraments are to produce in my soul.

MARY, MY MOTHER, I realize that I have not always corresponded faithfully with these graces. I will not be discouraged, but rather go with confidence to you, the throne of grace. Even though my past sinfulness may have made me unworthy to appear before God, I trust that you will appeal to God in my behalf as the Mother of Divine Grace. Through your prayers you will obtain forgiveness for my past negligence. You will obtain for me grace to be faithful to God during the rest of my life.

Above all, I beg of you to secure for me in the hour of death the grace of final perseverance: that triumphant grace which crowns the measure of God's gifts here below and which is followed by the possession of God in heaven.

Suppliant Omnipotence,
Hear thy children's pleading call,
Life's hard battle grows intense,
All about the vanquished fall!
Mary Star on life's great surging sea!
In death's bitter pain our Mother be!

Next to God's own throne on high
Thou art Mistress of His grace,
All our needs thou canst supply,
All our woes thou canst efface!
Mary Star on life's great surging sea!
In death's bitter pain our Mother be!

Love of God great gifts has won,
Love of man shall gifts dispense.
Thou art earth's life-giving sun,
Suppliant Omnipotence.
Mary Star on life's great surging sea!
In death's bitter pain our Mother be!

† † †

O God, Who gave the human race the grace of forgiveness through the virginal motherhood of the Blessed Virgin Mary, grant that we who call her the Mother of Grace on earth may enjoy her happy presence in heaven. Through Christ Our Lord. Amen.

Our Lady of Perpetual Help

Background:

In the middle of the fifteenth century, a wonderful picture of Our Lady, in the Byzantine style, was highly honored in a church on the island of Crete. It had been painted, possibly by the master Andreas Rico de Candia, after the model of an older icon, and was regarded with much devotion because of numerous favors granted at its shrine.

One day, toward the close of the century, the picture was stolen by a merchant who took it to Rome, where he was taken ill and died. He confessed the theft on his deathbed to a Roman friend in whose house he was lying and begged him to present the icon to some suitable church. But the Roman's wife persuaded her husband to keep it himself, and so it hung in the bedroom for some time. After the death of the Roman, his six-year-old daughter had a vision in which Our Lady told her to go to her mother and grandfather and say, "Holy Mary of Perpetual Help bids you to remove her picture from your house." In a second vision the child was told to have her mother place the painting in the care of Augustinian Friars in the church of St. Matthew, between the basilicas of St. Mary Major and St. John Lateran. It was carried there in solemn procession on the 27th of March, 1499. When the procession passed by, a man who had long been paralyzed was cured.

For three hundred years the picture hung in St. Matthew's and was venerated there. So many favors were granted that it was called the shrine of "Our Lady of Perpetual Help." But during the wars of 1798, under orders from Bonaparte, some thirty churches were destroyed, St. Matthew's included. The friars removed the picture and set it up in a side chapel of the church of St. Mary in Posterula, which was given them by Pope Pius VII in 1819. In that church a picture of Our Lady of Grace was already enshrined. There, in an obscure corner, the picture hung for sixty-seven years, ignored and neglected. However, an aged lay brother, Augustine Orsini, often served Mass at that altar and often told the story of the wonderful picture to a young server, Michael Marchi.

In 1853 Pope Pius IX requested the Redemptorists to found a house in

Rome. There, one day in 1862, while the Fathers were at recreation, Father Edward Schwindenhammer mentioned that he had discovered from an ancient reference that their new church stood on the spot where once had been venerated a wonderful picture of Our Lady of Perpetual Help. No one seemed to know what had become of it. At these words, another Father, the same Michael Marchi, said he knew where the picture was and told the story of Brother Augustine. The Redemptorist General gave this information to Pope Pius IX, who as a boy visited the miraculous picture. At once he ordered that the picture be brought to the Redemptorist Church of St. Alphonsus in a magnificent procession on April 26, 1866. Two cures were reported on the occasion.

On June 23, 1867, the Church approved the devotion to Our Lady of Perpetual Help, and an official coronation was made in the name of the Pope by the Latin Patriarch of Constantinople in view of the popularity of this icon among the Eastern Rite Christians. Confraternities were formed, all bound together into one Archconfraternity of Our Lady of Perpetual Help and St. Alphonsus, which today numbers at least five million members.

Our Lady of Perpetual Help is unique in the fact that it is regarded with veneration alike in the East and West, by Catholics and by Greek schismatics with their 125,000,000 adherents. It becomes a meeting place for prayers from both sides for unity.

Of all heavenly patrons, Mary is your most powerful helper before the throne of God. Her dignity of Mother of God, her ardent charity, and the fact that Jesus gave her to you as Mother, enable her to obtain for you through her intercession more graces and blessings from God than all the angels and saints can obtain. Besides, Her loving Son has entrusted to her the distribution of the graces He merited for us on Calvary, for Mary was intimately associated with Him in His work of Redemption. When you are in need, remember you have a kind Mother to help you. Since she will always help, she is rightly called the Mother of Perpetual Help.

Prayer

(1) MARY, MOTHER OF GOD, *you are the Mother of Perpetual Help because of the graces you have at your disposal.* God has willed that by your intercession we should obtain the graces Jesus has merited for us. Your intimate union with your Divine Son is the reason for your power with Him. All-powerful though He is, God could not bestow upon a creature a degree of honor higher than that conferred on you as the Mother of His Son. He could not make you divine by nature, but He has made you inseparable from Jesus in the salvation of souls through the grace which He has so

abundantly poured out upon you because of the Divine Motherhood. The angel said to you, "Hail, full of grace, the Lord is with thee: blessed art thou among women" (Luke 1:28). Your fullness of grace brought you to a most intimate union with the Author of grace. It was fitting that you receive into your holy womb the One Who contained all graces. Thus you became in some way the source of that grace which Jesus would pour forth over all mankind.

MARY, MY MOTHER, give me a rich share in the graces merited for me by your Son. Let not my sinfulness and human weakness stand in the way of my receiving the graces I need for the sanctification and salvation of my soul. Through your prayers be always my powerful helper.

(2) MARY, MOTHER OF GOD, *you are my Mother of Perpetual Help because of your love for me.* No creature loved Jesus more than you, and, consequently, no one loves the souls redeemed by His Blood more than you. Jesus purchased me at the cost of His own life, and you offered that life to God for me.

You love Jesus because you are His Mother; and you love me because you are my Mother. By offering your Divine Son on Calvary you brought me forth to a life of grace and thus became my spiritual Mother. When Jesus said, "Woman, behold thy son. . . . Son, behold thy Mother," He gave you to me to be my Mother, for all Christians form one body with Christ, and St. John represented them all beneath the cross. After your Divine Son, you are God's most precious gift to man. Therefore, no one could ever love me more, after Christ, than you do.

MARY, MY MOTHER, help me to realize that the closer my union with you, the more intimate is my union with your Son. I cannot have Jesus for my Brother if I do not have you for my Mother. Help me to love Jesus with all my heart and to show my love for Him by loving you whom He has loved so dearly. I know that He wants you ever to be my Mother of Perpetual Help so that the graces He has merited for me may effect the salvation of my soul.

(3) MARY, MOTHER OF GOD, *in your own lifetime you showed that you are truly our Mother of Perpetual Help.* At the marriage feast of Cana you asked your Son to perform a miracle for the distressed bride and groom. At your request He worked the first miracle of His public life. He was pleased to help others for your sake. Your direction to the waiters, "Do whatever He tells you"

(John 2:5), show that you regard your Son's answer as a striking sign of His special love for you.

Furthermore, Jesus made the revelation of His divinity and the strengthening of the faith of His disciples the effect of your intercession. When He changed the water to wine, He did your bidding as God, since as man He could not perform miracles. Thus He clearly revealed that in His kingdom you were to be the dispenser of His riches.

What a striking lesson you give me by this unlimited confidence in the power and goodness of your Divine Son! Enlightened by God, you knew that He would grant your request. I should learn from your conduct never to oppose the Divine Will, even though conformity to it may mean a severe test of my faith. Your example teaches me that Jesus will work miracles for persevering prayer that springs from confidence and humility.

MARY, MY MOTHER, give me an absolute trust in your help. How truly can the words of Holy Scripture be applied to you: "In me is all grace of the way and of the truth, in me is all hope of life and of virtue" (Ecclus. 24, 25)! How consoling to know that I have Christ, my elder Brother, always living to make intercession for me, and you, my Mother, ever pleading for me before the throne of God. I can pray to you with full confidence because you are loved by the Father as the Mother of His Son, loved by the Son as His own Mother, loved by the Holy Spirit as His Immaculate Bride.

Since Jesus has given you charge of the dispensing of His graces, I know that you are most eager to use this power to help me. You want to give me help every time I need it. I beg you to take care of me, for I am a poor sinful child. Mother of Perpetual Help, pray for me!

> Queen of Heaven, pray, remember,
> Never has it been averred
> That a client turning toward thee
> Ever left thy throne unheard.

> Queen, behold a weary pilgrim
> Bowing low before thy shrine,
> Bent beneath the cares of exile,
> And withal a child of thine.

Hast thou e'er refused a favor
Which thy children humbly sought?
Has the poor repentant sinner
Ever shed his tears for naught?

Mother kind and Virgin fair,
All thy children love and laud thee;
May they find thine aid and care
When they turn to thee in prayer.

Lord Jesus Christ, Who gave us Your Mother Mary that she might be our Mother of Perpetual Help and whose beloved image we venerate, grant, we beg of You, that by earnestly imploring her motherly help we may deserve to enjoy at all times the blessings of Your Redemption. Who live and reign forever. Amen.

Visitation of the Blessed Virgin Mary

FEAST, July 2 (NOVENA, June 23–July 1)

Background:

The archangel Gabriel revealed to Mary the miraculous motherhood of her cousin Elizabeth and invited her to visit her home. Charity urged her to make this *visit* at once to the hill country to a town of Judea. Christ, Whom she was now carrying, prompted her to begin her mission of bringing Him to souls. The trip must have lasted about four days, for the little village to which she was going was located a few miles beyond Jerusalem.

Mary entered the house of Zachary and greeted Elizabeth. As soon as Elizabeth heard the greeting, the child in her womb gave a start. Filled with the Holy Spirit, she exclaimed, "Blessed art thou among women, and blessed is the fruit of thy womb." She asked herself why she was so honored that the Mother of her Lord should come to her. Now that the Holy Spirit Himself had revealed the mystery of her Divine Motherhood to her cousin, Mary spoke her thanksgiving prayer, the Magnificat. She sang of the marvelous goodness of God to her in spite of her nothingness. She praised God for His mercy to mankind in sending a Savior.

Mary remained with her relatives about three months, till John the Baptist was born. They were months of great happiness for her and of blessings for Elizabeth and her son. The aged priest Zachary suddenly recovered his power of speech, which he had lost because he did not believe the angel in the temple who announced that his wife would give him a son who would prepare the way for the Messias. In the inspired canticle, the Benedictus, he began to praise God for having come to redeem His people.

The feast of the Visitation commemorates Our Lady's visit to her cousin St. Elizabeth, the sanctification of St. John the Baptist in his mother's womb, and the occasion on which the Blessed Virgin uttered her hymn of thanksgiving, the Magnificat. This feast was instituted for the whole world in 1389 by Pope Urban VI, in order to obtain the end of the great Western schism. It was later on raised to the rite of double of the second class by Pius IX, for on this feast was completed at Rome in 1849 the victory of the Church over the revolution.

Notice in this mystery of Our Lady's life how God wished to show us that Mary is the instrument and means by which He imparts to us His graces. Our Lady's motherly interest in our sanctification and salvation is expressed in these words of Pope Benedict XV, written in March, 1918: "It is clear, too, that this most sorrowful Virgin, since appointed by Jesus Christ, as the Mother of all men, received them as a testament of infinite charity left to her, and fulfills with motherly kindness the task of forwarding their spiritual life; nor can she fail more especially to assist those most dear adopted children in that hour when it is a question of confirming unto eternity their salvation and sanctity."

Admire, too, the consideration Mary showed for Elizabeth. Your Heavenly Mother is your model in carrying out the second great commandment of charity. Through her intercession ask Jesus for the graces you need, especially that of being charitable.

Prayer

(1) MARY, MOTHER OF GOD, *your charity is strikingly shown forth in the Visitation.* When you learned from the angel that your cousin Elizabeth was with child and needed your help, you set out to care for her. Neither your long absence from home, nor the inconvenience of a difficult and dangerous journey to the mountain country, kept you from making this mission of love. You thought only of the good you could do in Elizabeth's home. Your sincere love made you hasten to be of service. As you entered the house of Zachary and greeted your aged cousin, you offered kind words of comfort and congratulation. You lovingly served her till you saw her happily delivered of the child of promise with which God had blessed her.

How humble you were! Though you were the Mother of the Most High, you wanted to become the nurse of Elizabeth and the infant John. Though declared blessed among women, you considered yourself the servant of two of God's beloved children.

Help me to strive to imitate your wonderful charity by aiding those who are in need, by sympathizing with those who are afflicted, by opening my heart and applying my hands to relieve every form of distress. Give me charity like yours, which recognized in every human being a brother or sister in Jesus Christ, to be treated with respect and tenderness and to be aided according to the measure of my power. Teach me that the test of my following of your Divine

Son is practical charity. Help me, above all, so that by my good example I may enrich and ennoble every human being whose life I touch.

MARY, MY MOTHER, may the thought of your tenderness and charity increase my confidence in you and make me look up to you in all the dangers that surround me in life. I am sure that you, who are all-powerful as my advocate, will not desert me but will bring to my poor afflicted soul grace and sanctification.

(2) MARY, MOTHER OF GOD, *the results of your visit to Elizabeth were wonderful.* Scarcely had you greeted your aged cousin, when mother and son felt at once the sanctifying effects of your loving presence. The child in the womb of Elizabeth was sanctified and exulted for joy at the presence of Jesus. At the sound of your voice Elizabeth was filled with the Holy Spirit and began to prophesy: "Blessed art thou among women, and blessed is the fruit of thy womb." She humbly exclaimed, "How have I deserved this happiness that the Mother of my Lord should come to me?" God freed His future messenger from original sin and enriched him with grace. Elizabeth proclaimed that you were the Mother of Christ and declared you blessed among women because you were the most holy dwelling of the Eternal God.

The effects of the presence of Jesus and you are still the same. Grace comes to us from Jesus and reaches us through you. St. Elizabeth received the Holy Spirit through your intervention, in order to teach us that we must make use of you as our Mediatrix with your Divine Son, if we wish to obtain the Holy Spirit. It is true that we could go directly to God and ask Him for His grace without your help, but God has not willed it so.

MARY, MY MOTHER, in the mystery of the Visitation you began your high office of bringing Jesus into the souls of men. With joy you must have foreseen the millions of souls who by your presence in their lives would cast off the bonds of sin. Through the mystery of your Visitation enlighten my mind with divine truth; warm my heart with heavenly love; strengthen me to win the victory over my evil inclinations and the power of evil.

(3) MARY, MOTHER OF GOD, *how beautifully you expressed your gratitude and humility!* Unmindful of your dignity and greatness, you thought only of returning thanks to God, to Whom you attributed all your greatness and privileges. God had exalted you above

all creatures. You thought only of praising Him as your greatest Benefactor when you exclaimed, "My soul praises the Lord and my spirit rejoices in God my Savior. . . . For He who is mighty has done great things for me." In your humility you looked upon yourself as His lowly handmaid. Though you prophesied that all generations would call you blessed, you attributed all holiness to God. The glory of the great things that had been done in you you attributed to God's mercy and power and love. God had raised you to the highest dignity in His power in choosing you to be the Mother of His Son. The whole human race rejoices in you as Queen and Mother.

MARY, MY MOTHER, teach me ever to seek the glory of God and to render to Him what is His divine right. God looks for gratitude and humility which draw down upon us His favor and His gifts. God wants His gifts recognized. Whereas pride and ingratitude repel grace from our souls, gratitude and humility, like golden keys, unlock the treasury of heaven. Help me to return unceasing thanks to God for His many favors, and keep me humble in possessing and using them. May I be found worthy of your frequent visits with Jesus to my heart in this life and of the invitation to come and live with You both for all eternity in heaven.

> Hail, bright Star of ocean,
> God's own Mother blest,
> Ever sinless Virgin
> Gate of heavenly rest!
>
> Taking that sweet Ave,
> Which from Gabriel came,
> Peace confirm within us,
> Changing Eva's name.
>
> Break the captive's fetters,
> Light on blindness pour:
> All our ills expelling,
> Every bliss implore.
>
> Show thyself a Mother;
> May the Word Divine,
> Born for us thine Infant,
> Hear our prayers through thine.

Virgin all excelling,
Mildest of the mild,
Freed from guilt, preserve us
Meek and undefiled.

Keep our life all spotless,
Make our way secure,
Till we find in Jesus
Joy forevermore.

Through the highest heaven
To the Almighty Three,
Father, Son, and Spirit,
One same glory be. Amen.

3 years (321)*

† † †

Bestow on Your servants, we beg You, O Lord, the gift of Your heavenly grace, that we, for whom the motherhood of the Blessed Virgin was the beginning of salvation, may be blessed with peace on the solemn feast day of her Visitation. Through Christ Our Lord. Amen.

Our Lady of Mount Carmel

FEAST, July 16 (NOVENA, July 7–15)

Background:

The feast of the scapular is that of Our Lady of Mount Carmel. The Scapular of Our Lady of Mount Carmel is the best known, most celebrated, and most widespread of the small scapulars. It is also probably the oldest scapular.

According to tradition, a number of men who embraced the Christian faith on Pentecost Day erected a church to the Blessed Virgin on Mount Carmel. They were called Brethren of Blessed Mary of Mount Carmel. These religious came to Europe in the thirteenth century, when Mary appeared to their General, Simon Stock, at Cambridge, England, on Sunday, July 16, 1251. In answer to his appeal for help for his oppressed order, she appeared to him with a scapular in her hand and said, "Take, beloved son, this scapular of thy order as a badge of my confraternity and for thee and all Carmelites a special sign of grace; whoever dies in this garment, will not suffer everlasting fire. It is the sign of salvation, a safeguard in dangers, a pledge of peace and of the covenant." Indirectly the promise is extended to all who from devotion to the Mother of God wear her habit until death and are thus, as it were, affiliated with the Carmelite Order.

After the promise of salvation attached to the scapular, the greatest reward of this devotion is the Sabbatine Privilege, the privilege which enables a scapular wearer, by the fulfillment of two simple conditions, to assure his liberation from Purgatory on the first Saturday after death. The two conditions are the recitation of the Little Office and abstinence on Wednesday and Saturday. The abstinence can be substituted for, at the discretion of a priest with the proper faculties, by any other pious work, usually seven Our Fathers, Hail Marys, and Glory bes.

The Scapular Devotion is one of the oldest devotions to Our Lady. It has been widespread in the Church for nearly seven centuries. It is blessed with many indulgences. Confraternity members share in the good works of the Carmelite Order. Pope St. Pius X officially decreed that in place of the cloth scapular one might wear a scapular medal, though the Church prefers that we use the cloth.

Leo XIII wrote: "Its nobility of origin, its venerable antiquity, its extraordinary spread in the Church, the spiritualizing effects produced by it and the outstanding miracles worked in virtue of it, render the Scapular of Carmel commendable to a wondrous degree." And Benedict XV wrote: "Let all of you have a common language and a common armor; the language, the sayings of the Gospel; the common armor, the Scapular of the Virgin of Carmel, which you all ought to wear and which enjoys the singular privilege of protection even after death."

The scapular is the sign of devotedness to the Blessed Virgin, just as the carrying of your mother's picture would be a sign of your devotedness to her. Do you wear a scapular, or at least a medal, as a keepsake of your Heavenly Mother? It should remind you that you belong entirely to her and that through her you can best give yourself to God.

Prayer

(1) MARY, MOTHER OF GOD, *you are our true Mother because you have given us supernatural life.* The supernatural life is the life of Jesus in us through grace. You have given us Christ that He may make us live of His life.

At *Nazareth,* you knew that by saying Yes or No to Gabriel, you would be giving us life or leaving us in spiritual death. You said Yes so that we might live. By consenting to give natural life to Jesus, you consented to give us supernatural life. In becoming His Mother, you became ours. From that hour, we were members of the Mystical Body of Christ. I thank you for consenting to become my spiritual Mother by giving me Jesus. Through your prayers, may Jesus make me live of His life through sanctifying and actual grace. May these graces become most fruitful in my soul till I become like you, another Christ.

On *Calvary* our redemption was accomplished; by His death Jesus merited for us the grace to live His life. Jesus did this in union with you. You conceived Him as victim; you prepared Him for this sacrifice; beneath the cross you offered Him to the Father for our salvation. Though you felt joy in the birth of your first-born Son, you brought us forth in sorrow at the death of that same Son. Jesus proclaimed your motherhood from the cross by entrusting you to John and John to you when He said, "Woman, behold thy son. . . . Son, behold thy mother."

MARY, MY MOTHER, at my *baptism* you gave me life at the moment when sanctifying grace was infused into my soul at the baptismal font. You obtained that grace for me. I became a child of God. You brought me forth to the divine life.

(2) MARY, MOTHER OF GOD, *you are more truly our Mother than any other mother by the way in which you have given us life.* To bring us forth, you gave much more than our earthly mothers gave. You bore unspeakable sufferings and offered the life of Him Who was dearer to you than your own life.

You love me with a love that is greater than the love of my own mother; you love me with the very love with which you love Jesus, since all your children form but one Body with Him.

MARY, MY MOTHER, you are Mother in a higher degree because of the kind of life which you have imparted to me. You have given me life without end, a life of happiness for all eternity; not a created life, but a share in uncreated life, in the very life of God. I thank you for all you mean to me as my spiritual Mother. During my whole life you continue to take care of me until Christ be formed in me. If unfortunately I should lose this life by sin, you can bring me back to supernatural life. May I always be most grateful by striving to grow in this divine life. Only then can I really love you as you desire—when Jesus is formed in me so that I can love you as Jesus does.

(3) MARY, MOTHER OF GOD, *how consoling it is for me to venerate you under the title of Our Lady of Mount Carmel!* It takes me back to the days of the prophet Elias, when you were prefigured on Mount Carmel under the form of the little cloud from which, as it grew larger, there fell a kindly rain, a symbol of the sanctifying graces that come to us from you. Even from the days of the Apostles you were honored under this mystical title. Today I am filled with joy at the thought that we are united with those first clients of yours, and in union with them we greet you, saying: O beauty of Carmel, glory of Libanus, purest of lilies, mystical rose in the flowering garden of the Church.

Virgin of virgins, remember me in my needs, and show yourself my Mother. Shed upon me more and more the living light of that faith which made you blessed. Inflame me with that heavenly love with which you loved your dear Son, Jesus Christ. I am filled with miseries both spiritual and temporal. I am afflicted with many sorrows in body and soul, and I take refuge, like a child, in the embrace of your motherly protection.

MARY, MY MOTHER, you have very great power. Obtain for me from Jesus the heavenly gifts of humility, chastity, and meekness, which were the fairest adornments of your immaculate soul. Make me strong in the midst of the temptations and bitterness which so often trouble my soul. And when the days of my earthly pilgrimage are over, according to God's holy will, grant that my soul may obtain the glory of heaven, through the merits of Christ and through your intercession. Amen.

> Hail, O Queen of heaven enthroned,
> Hail, by angels Mistress own'd,
> Root of Jesse, Gate of morn,
> Whence the world's true Light was born.

> Glorious Virgin, joy to thee,
> Loveliest whom in heaven they see,
> Fairest thou where all are fair,
> Plead that Christ us sinners spare.

5 years (324)

† † †

O God, Who honored the Order of Carmel by the singular title of Your most Blessed Mother, Mary ever Virgin, grant, we beg of You, that she whose memory we solemnly venerate today may favor us with her protection so that we may be found worthy to share in eternal happiness. Who live and reign forever. Amen.

Humility of the Blessed Virgin Mary

FEAST, July 17 (TRIDUUM, July 14–16)

Background:

Humility is one of the outstanding virtues in the life of the Blessed Virgin. She never exalted herself because of her heavenly gifts: as she became more and more acquainted with heavenly mysteries, she fixed her mind more firmly in humility. Saints tell us that God chose her to be His Mother more on account of her humility than on account of all her other sublime virtues. She was nothing in her own eyes, yet sufficiently great for the Divinity! Among all Heaven's saints she is the most humble; yet she excels them all in the splendor of her grace and in the fire of her love.

Jesus willed that the life of His Mother should be simple and hidden, because she was to be our model. He did not spare her from the cross, from persecution, nor from sorrow of heart. He willed to make her the Mother of Sorrows, the most tried of all creatures, so that in our pain and troubles of life, we might have a model of perfect submission and abandonment. This humility was the basis of Mary's holiness; she had a sense of utter dependence on God.

Mary seldom appears in the Gospel narratives. All through the intense activity of Christ's public life, it is almost as if Mary has ceased to exist. She is lost in the shadows cast by the light of her Son. Only when He is in shadow does she rush to Him. She is with Him in the shadows of Bethlehem's cave and in the simplicity of the hidden life; she is with Him in His moments of suffering and disgrace on the cross when the sun is obscured over Calvary. But she would never have ascended far above all the choirs of angels if on earth she had not lowered herself by humility below all men. She was one with Jesus in His greatest sufferings; she is now one with Him in His highest glory.

You cannot be a true child of Mary unless you try to imitate your Heavenly Mother's humility. If pride plays an important part in your life, pray to the humble "Handmaid of the Lord" for the virtue of humility and ever keep her beautiful example before you.

Prayer

(1) MARY, MOTHER OF GOD, *humility is the virtue you especially practiced from childhood.* The saints tell me that it is the foundation and guard of all virtues, since without humility a soul can possess no other virtue. Your loving Son came to teach this virtue to mankind by His example, and He desired that we should especially strive to imitate Him, for He said, "Learn from me, for I am meek and humble of heart; and you will find rest for your souls" (Matt. 11:29). As you were the first and most perfect disciple of Jesus in all the virtues, you were the first and most perfect disciple also in humility. First of all, because of your humility you merited to be exalted above all creatures.

The first characteristic of humility of heart is a humble opinion of oneself. You always had so lowly an opinion of yourself that, although you realized how many more graces and favors were bestowed upon you than upon others, you still preferred all others before yourself. Of course, you never thought of yourself as a sinner, for humility is truth, and you knew that you had never offended God.

MARY, MY MOTHER, you did acknowledge having received greater graces from God than had any other creature, for a humble heart always acknowledges the special favors of God that it may humble itself the more. But by the greater light you possessed for recognizing the infinite greatness and goodness of God, you recognized also your own littleness, and, therefore, you humbled yourself more than all others: you ever had before your eyes the majesty of God against your nothingness as His creature. The more you beheld yourself enriched, the more humble did you become, remembering that all came to you from the infinite generosity of your Maker. No creature in the world has been more exalted than you, because no creature in the world has ever humbled itself more.

(2) MARY, MOTHER OF GOD, *your humility was expressed especially in the Annunciation.* You were fully enlightened as to the greatness of the dignity of a Mother of God. Though you had already been assured by the angel that you were this happy Mother chosen by the Lord, you did not stop to rejoice in your exaltation. Seeing your own nothingness as compared with the infinite majesty of God, Who chose you for His Mother, you acknowledged

how unworthy you were of so great honor, but you did not oppose His Will in the least thing. Filled with deep humility, and yet on fire with desire to unite yourself still more closely to God, you abandoned yourself entirely to the Divine Will and answered, "Behold the handmaid of the Lord; be it done to me according to thy word" (Luke 1:38).

MARY, MY MOTHER, *you showed your humility by striving to conceal from others the gifts you received from God.* You concealed even from your beloved spouse, St. Joseph, the important fact that you were the chosen Mother of God, and you awaited God's good pleasure to reveal the great mystery to him.

In your humility you refused praise, giving all the praise and glory to God. When your cousin St. Elizabeth greeted you as blessed among women, you answered, "My soul magnifies the Lord, and my spirit rejoices in God my Savior because he has regarded the lowliness of his handmaid" (Luke 1:46). You humbled yourself so deeply because you knew that of and by yourself you were nothing and had nothing. Therefore, you gave your praise to the Creator and Giver of every good and perfect gift.

In your humility you wished to serve others rather than to be served. You visited the house of Zachary to serve your cousin Elizabeth for three months. Later, in the public life of Jesus, you sought no attention. At one time when you wanted to speak with Jesus, your humility forbade you to enter the house where He was preaching until you were asked to do so.

In your humility you gladly suffered contempt with Jesus. We do not find you in Jerusalem on Palm Sunday, when your Divine Son was received with so much honor by the people. But we do find you standing beneath the cross on Calvary, when your Son was derided and mocked. You did not shrink from the disgrace of being recognized as the Mother of one condemned to die a shameful death.

(3) MARY, MOTHER OF GOD, *teach me to be truly humble.* Since I sincerely love you, I want to follow your example; this is the greatest honor I can pay you. For my proud nature, humility is most difficult to practice. But I can never be your true child if I am not humble. You invite none to come to you but the lowly of spirit. It is under the mantle of humility that you will protect me. Clothe me with your own humility.

Teach me the real kind of ambition, that is, greatness in God's eyes. Only childlike humility entitles me to the first place in God's estimation and, consequently, in heaven also. The degree of childlike humility I have attained in life will be the degree of my greatness in heaven. Help me to see that humility is nothing more nor less than a just and equal judgment of myself, my talents, my opportunities and the use I make of them.

Humility is not belittling myself, but taking the place which rightly belongs to me, not a higher place, nor a lower, but the true and just place where God wants me. For if I have any ability, any worth or goodness, the glory is not mine, but God's. Without God I can do nothing. All that I am or have He has given me. This is truly your spirit, as you expressed it at the Visitation: "Behold, henceforth all generations shall call me blessed; because he who is mighty has done great things for me, and holy is his name" (Luke 1:48).

MARY, MY MOTHER, I beg you for this humility which is so necessary for me that without it I cannot enter God's kingdom. As Jesus reminded His disciples, "Unless you turn and become like little children, you will not enter into the kingdom of heaven" (Matt. 18:3). I beg you for this humility which is loved both by God and men, for in it lies something sublime—a living resemblance to Jesus and to you.

Blessed Mother, teach me humility. Help me to become a child in your school. Let me know nothing else except this entire surrender of myself to God, this simple childlike act of the heart, as I cast myself into the Arms of Jesus and promise Him my fidelity. To love Jesus, to do His will, to accept all from His hands—let this be my humility, as it was yours!

> I cast myself into the ocean of Mary,
> And there, in that sea of deep blue,
> I seek pardon, and refuge, and guidance:
> I belong, dearest Mother, to you.

> I cast myself into the ocean of Mary,
> And there, in that Heart of true blue,
> I surrender my life and my service:
> I give myself, Mary, to you.

I cast myself into the ocean of Mary,
And there, in that deep sunlit sea
Of ruby, and sapphire, and silver,
I'll hide myself, Mary, from *me!*

O God, since You stoop to the humble and dislike the proud, help Your servants to imitate with a pure heart the humility of the Blessed Virgin Mary, who was pleasing to You in her virginity, and because of her humility conceived our Lord Jesus Christ, Your Son, Who lives and reigns with You forever. Amen.

Our Lady of the Snows

FEAST, August 5 (TRIDUUM, August 2-4)

Background:

Devotion to Our Blessed Mother was as intense among Catholics in the sixth century as it is today. A large number of new churches built then were dedicated to her. Into all of them was introduced a beautiful picture of Our Lady, likely to inspire devotion in the hearts of the faithful. One such painting, supposed to have been painted by St. Luke and brought from Palestine by St. Helena, is still the center of the most celebrated Shrine of Our Lady in Rome and the most important church of Our Lady in the Eternal City, that of the Major Basilica of Saint Mary Major, which has its own feast day under the title of Our Lady of the Snows.

The Basilica was built on the Esquiline Hill by a wealthy Roman and his wife during the pontificate of Pope Liberius (352-356). They were guided in their choice of a site at the command of Our Lady, who appeared to them in a dream, and the subsequent miraculous fall of snow in mid-summer confined to this particular hilltop. The snow is said to have covered a piece of ground of the form and size of a large church.

Later, on the occasion of the General Council of Ephesus, at which the Blessed Virgin was declared to be truly the Mother of God, Pope Sixtus III (432-440) rebuilt this Basilica and greatly enriched it in honor of the event. Thus the Basilica of Saint Mary Major became one of the four chief basilicas of the Eternal City.

A few years later the same church was enriched with a famous relic, the manger from the stable at Bethlehem; hence it is also called St. Mary at the Crib. No other shrine of Our Lady has been visited by so many Popes, Princes, and prelates in the history of the Church. It was the favorite shrine of Pope St. Gregory the Great.

It was not until 1613 that the painting, believed to be the most authentic portrait of Our Lady, was removed from its original shrine behind the high altar and put into a magnificent Lady Chapel built by Pope Paul V on the north side of the church. It was at this shrine that Eugenio Pacelli said his first Mass. Forty years later, in 1939, he returned as Pope Pius XII,

144

to kneel in prayer at this beloved shrine and then to pontificate at the Solemn Mass which followed.

This feast is a reminder that you should do all you possibly can to contribute to the honor of Our Lady. She is honored by the little things you do for her out of childlike love, and she will repay you most generously.

Prayer

(1) MARY, MOTHER OF GOD, *you are also the Mother of men.* You conceived Jesus as the Head of regenerated mankind, the Head of a Mystical Body whose members we are. You also conceived His members who have been born again and are called to incorporation with Him. When you became the Mother of Jesus according to the flesh, you became the Mother of men according to the spirit. This truth was confirmed on Calvary, when at the very moment our redemption was to be completed by the death of Jesus, He said to you: "Behold thy son," then to St. John, who took our place beneath the cross, "Behold thy mother." This was a declaration that all Christians are your spiritual children.

MARY, MY MOTHER, I am happy to be your child. As the surest refuge for a child is the heart of its mother, so your Immaculate Heart is my refuge. In His infancy Jesus depended upon your loving care, and in death when He was abandoned by all, even by His Father, He still had your Heart. The last beat of His Heart was to be one with yours just as the first had been.

It is the will of God that His aid should reach me through your Heart, because you are my Mother, and motherliness means willingness to help. He wished to adapt Himself to our nature by giving us life and aid through the heart of a mother, having placed in your Heart some of His own love for mankind to make you the spiritual Mother of the redeemed. He renders it possible to give greater expression to His own love and mercy through your Heart. Therefore, with childlike confidence I appeal to your motherly Heart for help. I trust that through you I shall obtain the help I need to keep the commandments, avoid sin, receive the Sacraments frequently, pray much, and save my soul.

(2) MARY, MOTHER OF GOD, *you are my model of perfect dedication to God.* Holiness is union with God through love. Through love you consecrated yourself with all your powers to God, the

highest form of beauty and goodness. You knew nothing but God
and His love; you wished for nothing but Him and His holy Will;
you sought nothing but His greater honor. This intimacy with God
was the soul of your soul—your very life.

God enriched your soul with such a love above all other creatures
that in you alone He found His fullest delights. Your soul was most
beautiful, lovable, and immaculate, rich in graces and virtues. The
Holy Spirit, Who in virtue of Your Son's merits lived in you, made
you a living image of Jesus. Never were you guilty of the least fault;
never did you offer the least resistance to grace. You are the model
of all virtues. As I gaze upon you—the ideal of perfection and
sanctity, may a similar longing for God and complete dedication of
myself to Him awaken in my soul. God's grace can also do wonders
in me if only I do not refuse to co-operate with it. May looking upon
your Immaculate Heart inspire confidence in me which will make
me more eager to grow in holiness. And I am sure there is nothing
you want more than to see me perfectly dedicated to God even as
you are. Since this is the mission of your life, to bring souls to God
through Jesus, lead me to your loving Son. Only give me the grace
to abandon myself completely to your motherly guidance.

MARY, MY MOTHER, the saints have taught me that the best
veneration of you is always imitation. Teach me to admire your
virtues that I may be constantly reminded to imitate them and become like you. I trust that you will lovingly bow down to help my
efforts. You are a model easy to imitate because you sanctified yourself in the ordinary, everyday life common to most of us, by fulfilling those lowly household duties of a young woman, a mother,
and by leading a hidden, retired life both in joy and in sorrow.
I realize that imitating you is the best way of imitating Jesus and of
obtaining your all-powerful intercession. I unite myself with your
Heart so that everything I have to do or suffer may become a pure
sacrifice of love in the sight of God.

(3) MARY, MOTHER OF GOD, *I consecrate myself to your Immaculate Heart*. Teach me to understand that personal consecration to
you does not mean only to place myself under your special protection, but rather to live for God in union with you by avoiding
every sin and by practicing virtue.

I want to be devoted to you by giving myself entirely to you and
through you to God. In so doing I simply imitate God Who gave

Himself and His Son to us through you. I give you my intellect by holding you in loving reverence because of your dignity as Mother of God. I give you my will by an absolute confidence in you, a confidence founded on your power and your goodness. I give you my heart by the gift of a tender and childlike love, because you are my Mother and you love me more than my own mother could ever think of loving me. I give you my whole being by copying as far as possible all your virtues, by performing each of my actions through you, with you and in you. This is the most pleasing homage I can render to you.

MARY, MY MOTHER, help me to perform all my actions through you—to ask through your intercession the graces I need in order to imitate you and to go through you to Jesus. Help me to perform all my actions with you—to look upon you as a model and helper. Help me to perform all my actions in you—to be entirely dependent upon you, taking your point of view, doing all things as you did them for God's honor and glory.

> Tender arms of Mary,
>   Soft and warm and true!
> All my soul is crying
>   In the dark to you,
> As a little baby
>   Lost upon the stair,
> Mother's outstretched arms
>   Seek to help me there—
> So my soul all frightened
>   In the dark of sin,
> Runs to your embrace,
>   Mother—let me in.
> Tender arms of Mary,
>   Soft and warm and true—
> All my soul is crying
>   In the dark to you.

Grant us, Your servants, we beg of You, O Lord God, that we may be blessed with health of soul and body, and by the glorious intercession of the Blessed Virgin Mary be freed from the sorrows of this present life and enjoy everlasting bliss. Through Christ Our Lord. Amen.

Our Lady, Refuge of Sinners

FEAST, August 13 (TRIDUUM, August 10–12)

Background:

The worst evil that can befall man is sin. God, in His infinite Goodness, Who has procured remedies for bodily ailments, has also provided the means to heal our spiritual sickness. With the sacraments instituted by Jesus Christ to restore our souls to grace or to increase it within us, *God has also been pleased to grant us, in Mary's aid, a powerful remedy for our spiritual infirmities.* Since it was her privilege to be exempt from all sin, the principal grace she obtains for her clients is to preserve them from sin. In fact, Mary has not only given us Jesus Christ, the Shepherd and Physician of our souls, but she also watches over us as a tender mother watches by the cradle of her ailing child. It seems that she was raised to the dignity of Mother of God more for sinners than for the just, since Jesus Christ declares that He came to call not the just, but sinners. Unceasingly praying for sinners, she now stands before her Son.

Pope Pius IX, whose cause for beatification has been approved by Pope Pius XII, wrote in his encyclical concerning devotion to our Lady's Rosary (1891): "Now it is impossible to think of any individual who has ever contributed or ever will contribute as much service toward the reconciliation of men with God as has Mary. It was she, surely, who brought the Savior to men when they were rushing on to their eternal destruction, at the very time, that is, when, 'in the place of the whole human race,' she received and wondrously consented to the message which the Angel brought to earth announcing the mystery of reconciliation. She it is 'of whom was born Jesus' (Matt. 1:16), she who is His true Mother and for this reason is justly regarded as Mediatrix to the Mediator."

What a consolation to know that our Blessed Mother excludes none of her children, not even the most wayward, from her protection and motherly care! Holy Mother Church assures us of this by invoking her as the "Refuge of Sinners." Since she is the Mother of Him Who redeemed man from sin, she is, therefore, ever ready to aid sinners to save their immortal souls. She who is the Mother of God is an intercessor with her divine Son for the guilty children of Eve, the Mother of mankind. If Jesus could say,

148

"There shall be joy in heaven upon one sinner that does penance, more than upon ninety-nine just who need not penance," how great must be the joy of our heavenly Mother when, through her intercession, sinners return to God! How earnest must be her desire for their conversion since the blood of her Son redeemed them, and she had an intimate share in the sufferings of Jesus.

St. Augustine wrote of the Refuge of Sinners in these words: "Through thee do the miserable obtain mercy, the ungracious, grace; sinners, pardon; the weak, strength; the worldly, heavenly things; mortals, life; and pilgrims, their country."

But Mary is the Refuge of Sinners only for such as are earnestly resolved to fly to her for aid and are determined to do penance. We cannot please her while we displease God. Yet through her prayers she has often obtained the grace of perfect conversion for sinners who outwardly appear most unworthy of her help.

At Lourdes the Refuge of Sinners cried out: "Penance! Penance!" At Fátima, she repeated the same call. Mary wished to reawaken a sense of sin in a world that thinks lightly of it or ignores it. She wished to inspire a profound horror for it and to show us its dangers. How often at Fátima that word passed her lips! "Men must not continue to offend our Lord, already so deeply offended." But counsels were accompanied by a promise of the blessing of God. Conversion is the first condition of eternal salvation. But it will also have its reward here below: "If men amend their lives, the war will soon cease."

If you should have the misfortune of falling into sin, go to your Heavenly Mother and beg her for the grace of true contrition. Ask her to help you make atonement for the sins of your past life. Pray especially for souls who are weighed down by sin, so that they may not despair but find a refuge in the loving arms of their Heavenly Mother.

Prayer

(1) MARY, MOTHER OF GOD, *you are the Mother of the Judge; you are also the Mother of the sinners.* You are the Mother of mercy and kindness not only to the just, but also to the despairing sinners so that no sooner do you see them coming to you, and seeking your help, than you aid them; you welcome them and obtain their pardon from your Son. You have such a desire to save sinners that you look for them in order to help them. As the devil goes about seeking whom he may devour, you go about seeking whom you may save. There is no sinner so spoiled and so mired in vice that

you would deny him aid. It is impossible for anyone to perish who sincerely and humbly cultivates devotion to you. But you are Mother only of penitent sinners who have left their evil ways before death. You are certainly the refuge of sinners, but you wish what your Son wishes. If the sinner dies in his sins, you cannot desire to save him, because Jesus will not save him.

From all eternity God chose you to be His Mother that those who could not be saved according to the rigor of Divine Justice might be saved with the help of your sweet mercy and powerful intercession. Unceasingly praying for sinners, You stand before your Son.

How many sinners, after losing hope, have found refuge in you, and, under your protection, returned to God's grace! God has made you so kind to sinners that your goodness restores us to hope. Heaven and earth shall perish before you are seen to abandon the miserable who pray to you sincerely.

MARY, MY MOTHER, when my heart is oppressed with guilt and fear, let me look to you. In every struggle I am sure to find in you both help and consolation because you are the Mediatrix between sinners and your Divine Son. You have never turned away your eyes from souls in need. Look with pity on me, for in you is my hope.

(2) MARY, MOTHER OF GOD, *as Refuge of sinners, you will never turn away those who have recourse to your compassion.* There are some who are far from their Father's house who even refuse to turn to you. But many of these straying children are ignorant and not fully responsible. You love them still, in spite of their sins, and you follow them with your motherly gaze and your prayers. Your heart watches over them tenderly. All these souls were given to you by Jesus on the cross—they are your children. You are not only the Mother of the guilty, but also Mother of Jesus, their Judge.

I plead for these sinners and I beg you to help them to break their chains, to shake off their human respect, to hope in the mercy of your Son. Help those of our faith to throw themselves at the feet of a priest and confess their sins and ask pardon for them. Obtain for them that deep conviction of faith, that unwavering hope, that Jesus, Infinite Love, Who died for them, will be completely ready to welcome them, to take them in His arms, press them to His Heart and once again say, "Father, forgive them . . ." Grant that all these, men and women alike, may be freed from sin, to repose on His Heart of merciful love.

MARY, MY MOTHER, you alone never knew shipwreck in the deep ocean of humanity's crimes. You alone know how to triumph over the old serpent and to crush his head under your heel. Your great lover, St. Bernard, along with many other saints and writers, reminds me: "Through you, Mary, heaven has been filled; through you hell has beheld itself robbed of an army of souls; in a word, through you eternal life was imparted to multitudes of wretched ones, who had made themselves unworthy of it." Refuge of sinners, do not turn us away when we entreat you. Have pity on the sinners of the world.

(3) MARY, MOTHER OF GOD, *you are the hope of sinners; you are my hope!* I, too, am a sinner. I am deeply conscious that I am unable to do good. I need you desperately. Like other men, I bear in my heart the original wound; that wound has opened other wounds which are hard to close and heal.

In fallen man there is, as St. John reminds us, "the lust of the flesh, and the lust of the eyes, and the pride of life" (1 John 2:16). I feel this threefold inclination to evil. It urges my senses to lower desires, because I seek sensible pleasure in its every degree. Because I am arrogant, it makes me rebel against God's law, the law forbidding me that abuse of liberty which insults Him. It impels my mind to self-exaltation, because I am proud. I feel myself consumed by original sin and its dread consequences. Wicked lust, the source and occasion of sin, flowing directly from original sin and inclining to evil, drags me along in spite of myself—although always voluntarily—to personal sins, sins that I know only too well are my own.

I was false to God's trust; I refused to obey my Maker. How often has mortal sin, destroying in me the beautiful image of the Blessed Trinity, brought death to my soul, delivered me to God's wrath and condemned me to everlasting hell-fire!

MARY, MY MOTHER, I am one of the murderers who slew your beloved Son, for it was my sins, together with the malice and cruelty of the Jews, which crucified Him. And I did this, not under the sudden influence of passion, but deliberately, with full knowledge of the act, of its horrible malice in the sight of God and of the terrible consequences in which it involved me. I did it not once or twice, but numberless times. For as often as I offended God by mortal sin, so often have I crucified the Son of God and made a mockery of Him.

And yet, Refuge of Sinners, you are my refuge, if I but have recourse to you, and you will extend your loving hands to receive me, to shelter me from the divine anger I so justly deserve. Your charity for the souls redeemed by the Precious Blood of your Divine Son is so great that you ask mercy for those who flee to you for refuge, with all the earnest tenderness of a mother pleading for her only child. Behold I come to you to show you the wounds sin has inflicted on me. Place your gentle motherly hands on those wounds of my soul and grant that through the grace of the Sacraments and prayer they may be healed. With sincere contrition for my sins I cry to you for help. Be a Mother to me and save me. Obtain for me the grace of true conversion. Give me a deep sorrow for my sins which have hurt God so very much. I earnestly wish to make atonement for all of them. Through your all-powerful prayers, obtain for me not only God's forgiveness, but also the grace to amend my life and to save my soul.

Intercede for us on high,
  Maria, Stella Maris.

Speedily all sin remove,
That the prayers of all may prove
Worthy of thy gracious love,
  Maria, Stella Maris.

Blest, as once the Angel said,
Of God, indeed thou art, Sweet Maid,
Thy holiness for heav'n displayed,
  Maria, Stella Maris.

Limpid stream all undefiled,
Queen of Angels, Mother mild,
Hear the prayer of those beguiled,
  Maria, Stella Maris.

Thou, in truth, art love all fair,
Beautiful beyond compare,
Favors flow from thee most rare,
  Maria, Stella Maris.

The just find thee a pattern bright,
Sinners shield them 'neath thy might,
The blessed praise thee with delight,
  Maria, Stella Maris.

> Turn, O Gracious One, thine eyes,
> Where with Christ beyond the skies
> Thou reignest, Advocate most wise,
> Maria, Stella Maris.
>
> Make all pestilence to cease,
> From every evil bring release;
> Grant us now and always peace.
> Maria, Stella Maris.
> —Fra Girolamo Savonarola (1498)

† † †

O almighty and merciful God, Who in the Blessed Virgin Mary gave sinners a refuge and a help, grant us, who are protected by her, the forgiveness of all our sins and the blessings of Your mercy. Through Christ Our Lord. Amen.

The Assumption of the Blessed
Virgin Mary

FEAST, August 15 (NOVENA, August 6–14)

Background:

The Assumption is the most ancient and solemn of all the feasts which Holy Church celebrates in honor of the Mother of God. It is the fulfillment of all the other great mysteries by which her life was made most wonderful.

The term *Assumption* means three things; namely, the death of the Blessed Virgin, her resurrection soon after death, and her entrance—body and soul—into heaven. At the present time the word Assumption is used exclusively to designate the Blessed Virgin's entrance into heaven, body and soul. It is used in direct contrast to Ascension, which signifies our Lord's bodily entrance into heaven of His own Divine Power. His Mother's Assumption was due solely to the power of Almighty God.

This is the belief of Catholics, founded, not on popular legends, but on authentic and authoritative teaching, dating back certainly to the sixth century and, some think, as early as to the year 58. This teaching is clearer in the West, less outspoken in the East. Its arguments are drawn from tradition, authority, Scriptural comparisons, and the sense of what was fitting for the Mother who gave to Christ His adorable Body and Precious Blood.

One of the earliest feasts we know of in memory of the Virgin Mary was kept at Antioch about the year 380. It commemorated the death of the Blessed Mother. In the sixth century there is mention of a solemn feast of Mary which is believed to have been the Assumption. Proof that the feast dates back at least to the time of the Council of Ephesus (431) and that of Chalcedon (451) is drawn from the fact that it is observed even by those schismatical bodies, such as the Nestorians and Eutychians, which were separated from Rome as early as the fifth or sixth century. In the East the feast was certainly older than the sixth century. In the seventh century it was one of the chief Roman solemnities.

A doctrine, universally held for over thirteen hundred years, could only have originated in a special revelation of Our Lord and His Apostles. The Assumption of Our Lady was defined at Rome, November 1, 1950, by Pope

Pius XII, in the year of the great Jubilee: "By the authority of Our Lord Jesus Christ, of the Blessed Apostles Peter and Paul, and by Our own authority, We pronounce, declare, and define it to be a divinely revealed dogma: that the Immaculate Mother of God, the ever Virgin Mary, having completed the course of her earthly life, was assumed body and soul into heavenly glory."

In this encyclical, *Munificentissimus Deus,* Pope Pius XII gives a survey of the belief in the Assumption through the ages, both in the liturgy and in the writings of the Fathers of the Church and theologians. The Assumption is compared with the Immaculate Conception; with Mary's association in her Son's victory over the devil, sin, and death; with her virginity in the birth of Christ. The common fountainhead of all Mary's privileges is the divine motherhood. At the close of the encyclical, the Holy Father expresses his confidence "That this solemn proclamation and definition of the Assumption will contribute in no small way to the advantage of human society, since it redounds to the glory of the Most Blessed Trinity, to which the Blessed Mother of God was bound by such singular bonds. It is to be hoped that all the faithful will be stirred up to a stronger piety toward their heavenly Mother, and that the souls of all those who glory in the Christian name may be moved by the desire of sharing in the unity of Christ's Mystical Body and of increasing their love for her who in all things shows her motherly heart to the members of this august Body. . . . In this magnificent way all may see clearly to what a lofty goal our bodies and souls are destined. Finally it is our hope that belief in Mary's bodily Assumption into heaven will make our belief in our own resurrection stronger and render it more effective."

The Holy Father's conclusion is expressed thus: "All these arguments and considerations of the Holy Fathers and theologians are based on the Sacred Scriptures as on their ultimate foundation. Indeed, the Scriptures set before our eyes, as it were, God's gracious Mother in most intimate association with her Divine Son, and ever sharing in His destiny. Therefore, it seems all but impossible to see her who conceived, who bore, who nursed Him with her own milk, who held Him in her embrace and pressed Him to her breast, now, after her life on earth, separated from Him, if not in soul, yet in body. Since our Redeemer is the Son of Mary, surely He Who observed the divine Law most perfectly could hardly fail to honor, besides His Eternal Father, His most beloved Mother. And since it was within His power to adorn her with the great honor of keeping her untouched by the corruption of the grave, we must believe that He did so."

Unite your joy and gratitude with that of the angels and saints in heaven as well as that of the Church upon earth, for it is your Heavenly Mother's Coronation Day. How well did she deserve this immortal crown! She crushed the serpent's head. She offered herself and her beloved Son unto

death for the redemption of mankind. She triumphed over the world and
the devil. Pray that Mary may reign as Queen in your heart and in the
hearts of all people. Pray to her for the grace of final perseverance in a
good and a happy death.

Prayer

(1) MARY, MOTHER OF GOD, your death was entirely free from
whatever might make death bitter: attachment to the world, re-
morse for sins, and the uncertainty of salvation. Rather, *your death
was accompanied by three graces that made it precious and full of
joy.* You died as you had lived, entirely detached from the things
of the world; you died in the most perfect peace and in the cer-
tainty of eternal glory.

Your Son, though He was Life itself, did not exempt Himself
from death. So, as daughter of Adam you submitted to the sentence
passed in the garden of Eden. You died of no infirmity. Little by
little, the links between your body and soul were dissolved by the
resistless force of love. Intense love for the Infinite God withdrew
your soul from this earthly life, and caused your death.

MARY, MY MOTHER, though your body was separated from your
soul in death, *your soul was reunited in your incorrupt body, and
you were taken up into heaven by angels.* The bodies of even the
just are corrupted after death, and only on the last day will they be
joined, each to its own glorious soul. But God has willed that you
should be exempted from this general rule because, by an entirely
singular privilege, you completely overcame sin by your Immaculate
Conception. Corruption is a consequence of sin, but you were sinless. You did not have to wait until the end of time for the resurrection of your body. As the body of your Divine Son was preserved
from the corruption of the grave, so you, from whom He took flesh,
were also free from the power of earthly decay. Your body, which
was the living tabernacle of the Eternal God and the temple of the
Adorable Trinity, was not meant to crumble into dust.

(2) MARY, MOTHER OF GOD, *I believe that it is a divinely revealed
dogma that you, Immaculate Mother of God, having completed
the course of your earthly life, were assumed body and soul into
heavenly glory.* Jesus ascended to Heaven by His own power as
Lord and Creator, accompanied by angels who paid Him homage.

You were taken to Heaven by the power of God, accompanied and upheld by the angels, raised aloft by grace, not by nature. Jesus ascended to Heaven before you not only that He might prepare a throne for you in that Kingdom, but also that He might Himself accompany you with all the blessed spirits and thus render your entry into Heaven more glorious and worthy of His Mother. At the Annunciation you received Jesus on earth; it was proper that He should receive you in Heaven. Having deigned to come down to you, He wished to raise you up to Himself in order that you might enter into glory.

MARY, MY MOTHER, *the day of your Assumption was the great day of your triumph.* After the triumph of your Divine Son on the day of His Ascension, there never was, and there never will be, a triumph like that which you enjoyed on this day. When He had finished the work of our Redemption by His labors, suffering, and death, the Eternal Word, clothed in our nature, entered into His glory and was seated on the right hand of the Eternal Father. He became Sovereign Master of the universe and Supreme Judge of the living and the dead. In your triumph, as the Mother of the same Word Incarnate, having perfectly followed out the great designs of God upon you, having acquired immense merits by the practice of all the virtues, and having reached the highest holiness, you were assumed body and soul, into Heaven. Angels came to escort you. You were borne aloft to the palace of your Beloved.

You passed amid the different choirs of the blessed, above all the heavenly spirits, and approached the throne of light prepared for you. Your loving Son welcomed you with joy. What songs of gladness by the elect as you were crowned by the Blessed Trinity and made Queen of Heaven, advocate of the human race, and dispenser of the graces of the Redemption!

(3) MARY, MOTHER OF GOD, *you reign in splendor for all eternity with your Divine Son.* Your kingdom, like His, is a kingdom of imperishable glory, because yours is a throne of clemency, mercy, and pardon. All your trials and sufferings are now transformed into jewels that decorate your triumphal throne in Heaven. In God there are no disappointments, no false promises. Eternity is real; Heaven is eternal happiness, the final reward for loyalty to God. Through you my own goal becomes more real, more attainable, for the lessons of your life are the doors to eternal peace and happiness.

I can only faintly imagine with what tenderness the Eternal Father received you, His loving daughter; the Divine Son, His chosen Mother; and the Holy Spirit, His immaculate Bride. The Father crowned you by making you a sharer in His power; the Son, by making you partaker of His wisdom; the Holy Spirit, by making you partaker of His love. The three Divine Persons declared you Queen of heaven and earth and assigned to you a place at the right hand of Jesus. You received from the Adorable Trinity the crown and scepter, which made you Queen of all the angels and saints and the all-powerful Mediatrix between God and men. You became the treasurer of God's graces, the channel through which He dispenses His gifts upon earth.

Your Assumption was for you not only the crowning of a holy life, but also a cause of joy and triumph for the human race. Just as the patriarchs in Limbo had beheld your birth as the breaking of that dawn which announced to them their near deliverance, so, too, your Assumption, together with the Ascension of Jesus, became for mortal man a sure pledge of resurrection and immortality.

MARY, MY MOTHER, I wish to recall this triumph and to share in your greatness and glory. If the honor of parents descends upon their children, what glory and joy for all of us, your children, to see you raised to such heights of glory! Confidence fills my soul, for you were raised to this glory not for your own advantage only, but for that of your children also, in order to make us feel the effects of your powerful protection and intercession. One of your greatest delights is to lavish these treasures upon your faithful children. With your arms outstretched—those arms in which the Eternal God delighted to rest when He became our Brother—plead our cause. Pray to Him for us, your children, that in our exile we may resemble you, His most devoted follower, and at last may glorify Him in union with you forever.

> When for me the sun is setting
> At the close of life's brief day;
> When my little ship is nearing
> Port in yonder crystal bay;
> Then, O my beloved Mother,
> Stretch thy kind hand out to me,
> Shield me, till my feet have touch'd the
> Shore sand of eternity.

When my strength begins to vanish,
And earth's memories to fade;
When my friends stand sad and silent,
Powerless to give me aid;
Then, my beloved Mother,
Hold my trembling hand in thine,
Till my eyes shall see the steeples
Of the Holy City shine.

When at last my weary spirit
Seeks admission to thy throne,
When my lips in anxious longing
For thy gracious blessing moan!
Then, O thrice beloved Mother,
Open wide thy home and heart,
And let me, thy child, dwell ever,
Where thou Queen and Mother art.

† † †

May the prayer of the Mother of God help Your people, O Lord, and though we know that she passed from this life as every mortal must, may we feel her intercession for us before You in heavenly glory. Through Christ Our Lord. Amen.

The Immaculate Heart of Mary

FEAST, August 22, Octave of the Assumption
(NOVENA, August 13–21)

Background:

The object of the devotion to the Immaculate Heart of Mary is to love Jesus better by uniting ourselves to Mary and by imitating her virtues. Her Immaculate Heart is the model of virtue and sanctity. The recent Popes say much in praise of Our Lady's sanctity. Pius IX will serve as a good example: "He [God], therefore, filled her, far more than all the angelic spirits and all the saints, with an abundance of all heavenly gifts from the treasure of His divinity, in such a wonderful manner that she would always be free from absolutely every stain of sin, and that, all beautiful and perfect, she might display such fullness of innocence and holiness that under God none greater is known, and which, God excepted, no one can attain even in thought." Just as devotion to the Sacred Heart of Jesus is a form of devotion to the adorable Person of Jesus, so also is devotion to the Immaculate Heart of Mary a special form of devotion to Mary.

Slight indications of a regular devotion to the Immaculate Heart of Mary are found in a sermon by St. Bernard in the twelfth century. St. Anselm, Mechtilde, Bernardine of Siena and Francis de Sales speak of the perfection of this Heart. It was reserved to St. Jean Eudes (1681) to propagate the devotion, to make it public, and to have a feast celebrated in honor of the Heart of Mary in a number of French dioceses. In 1805 Pius VII made a new concession, thanks to which the feast was soon widely observed. The devotion was further spread by the revelations of the "Miraculous Medal" in 1830 and by the establishment of the Archconfraternity of the Immaculate Heart of Mary in France. On July 21, 1855, the Congregation of Rites finally approved the office and Mass without, however, imposing them upon the Universal Church. In 1945 a decree of the Sacred Congregation of Rites fixed August 22nd, Octave Day of the Assumption, as the permanent date for the universal Feast of the Immaculate Heart of Mary.

The great love and care that the Immaculate Heart of Mary has for all of us was shown by her apparitions at Fátima in May to October of 1917.

Six times did she deign to appear to the three shepherd children—Lucia, Jacinta, and Francesco—to convey to them her great concern for the spiritual welfare of mankind and to request that ungrateful mankind stop offending Jesus. The means she suggested were reparation to her Immaculate Heart through the daily Rosary and the devotion of the first Saturdays.

Our Lady stated that her Heart is the hope of the world. She expressly requested the practice and spread of devotion to her Immaculate Heart, saying that it is in the designs of the Divine Mercy to help the world through this Heart.

"The war [World War I] is going to end. But if they do not stop offending God, another and worse one will begin in the reign of Pius XI. When you shall see a night illumined by an unknown light, know that it is the great sign that God gives you that He is going to punish the world for its crimes by means of war, hunger, and of persecution of the Church and of the Holy Father. To save souls God wishes to establish in the world the devotion of my Immaculate Heart. If they do what I will tell you, many souls will be saved, and there will be peace. I come to ask the consecration of Russia to my Immaculate Heart and the Communion of Reparation of the [five] first Saturdays. If they listen to my requests, Russia will be converted and there will be peace. If not, she will scatter her errors through the world, provoking wars and persecutions of the Church. The good will be persecuted, the Holy Father will have much to suffer, various nations will be destroyed. In the end my Immaculate Heart will triumph. The Holy Father will consecrate Russia to me, and a certain period of peace will be granted to the world."

As the heart of a mother triumphs over the anger of a father in an earthly family, so the Heart of Mary will triumph by averting the full force of God's justice upon a sinful world. Our Holy Father, Pope Pius XII, fulfilled the first desire of Our Lady by the consecration of the world to her Immaculate Heart on October 31, 1942. Following his example the Bishops of Mexico consecrated their country to the Immaculate Heart. In our own country fourteen dioceses were so consecrated during 1943, and since then all bishops were encouraged to consecrate their dioceses to Mary.

The similarity of Mary's language at Fátima to that used by her Divine Son in His apparitions to St. Margaret Mary inspires the belief that the devotion to her Immaculate Heart is to run parallel to that honoring the Sacred Heart. Of course, it is unnecessary to remind Catholics that adoration is paid to the Sacred Heart and veneration to the Immaculate Heart of Mary.

The apparitions of Our Lady at Fátima are a confirmation of the words spoken over two hundred years ago by St. Grignon de Montfort: "It is in the Heart of Mary that the world will find again true fraternity; it is by the Heart of Mary that it will obtain pardon and mercy of God; it is with the Heart of Mary that the New City will be built in truth, justice, charity; it is for the Heart of Mary, for its honor and glory, that humanity, grateful and free, will, in the near future, increase its manifestations of love and filial gratitude."

In his definition of the dogma of the Immaculate Conception, on December 8, 1854, Pope Pius IX, whose cause of beatification had been approved by Pope Pius XII on the eve of the feast of the Immaculate Conception, December 7, 1954, and of the centenary of the definition of the dogma, wrote: "We have the surest hope and the most utter confidence that the most Blessed Virgin, who, all fair and immaculate, has crushed the poisonous head of the cruel serpent and brought salvation to the world . . . who is the safest Refuge and the most reliable Helper of all who are in danger, and the most influential Mediatrix and Conciliatrix of the whole world with her only-begotten Son . . . who has ever destroyed all heresies and delivered faithful nations and peoples from the greatest and most varied calamities . . . will through her most influential patronage graciously bring it about . . . that the guilty obtain pardon, the sick healing, the weak of heart courage, the afflicted consolation, and those in danger assistance; and that all who are in error, may, with the removal of all blindness of spirit, return to the path of truth and justice, and that there may be one flock and one shepherd."

The portrait of the Immaculate Heart of Mary as Mediatrix and her role in the Redemption is beautifully summarized by Pope Pius XII in the concluding prayer of his encyclical on the Mystical Body, 1943: "May she, then, the most holy Mother of all Christ's members, to whose Immaculate Heart We have trustingly consecrated all men, her body and soul refulgent with the glory of heaven where she reigns with her Son—may she never cease to beg from Him that a continuous flow of graces may pass from its glorious Head into all the members of the Mystical Body. May she throw about the Church today, as in times gone by, the mantle of her protection and obtain from God that now at last the Church and all mankind may enjoy more peaceful days."

The month of August is traditionally dedicated to devotion to the Immaculate Heart of Mary, and the Church has granted an indulgence of five years to the faithful who devoutly recite prayers in honor of the most pure Heart of Mary on any day during the month of August, and a plenary indulgence if the prayers are said throughout the entire month. The same indulgence is granted for a Novena in her honor at any time of the year.

In May of 1943, Pope Pius XII urged Catholics to invoke the intercession of the Blessed Virgin, especially by reciting the Rosary, for the needs of humanity and the attainment of a just peace, and asked them to consecrate themselves to her Immaculate Heart.

The object of the Feast of the Immaculate Heart of Mary, instituted by

Pope Pius XII in 1945, is to promote devotion to the Immaculate Heart of Mary so that through her intercession all nations may enjoy peace and religious liberty, sinners may be converted and all the faithful may advance in virtue.

Prayer

(1) MARY, MOTHER OF GOD, your Heart is a *shrine of holiness,* into which the demon of sin has never entered; whose sanctuary was never once defiled by the least touch of evil; whose altar was the chosen resting place of the Holy Spirit. After the Sacred Heart of Jesus, never was there a Heart more pure and more holy.

The Eternal Father takes pleasure in looking upon your Heart as the masterpiece of His Divine Power. The Son takes pleasure in it as the Heart of His Mother, the source from which He drew the blood that ransomed us. The Holy Spirit dwells in you as in a temple.

When still a child you consecrated yourself entirely to God, the Lover of chaste souls; and afterward you would rather be deprived of the great dignity of Divine Motherhood than to lose your virginity. Your Heart remained spotless as a lily, and you are, therefore, justly called the "Queen of Virgins."

Your Heart is a *shrine of peace,* for it is the Heart of the Mother of the Prince of Peace, a Heart never for a moment disturbed by evil passions, a Heart whose gifts to mankind are mercy, love, and peace. To all of us your Immaculate Heart after that of Jesus is most loving and most merciful. How many afflicted hearts are consoled in you! How many frail hearts are strengthened by you! How many are now in heaven because of the protection given them by your merciful Heart! We obtain everything for our peace of soul in time and eternity from the Father through the Heart of Jesus and everything from Jesus through your Heart. You are truly the "Queen of Peace."

Your Heart is a *shrine adorned with all the skill of the Divine Creator,* Who has lavished upon it the riches of His treasure house —sanctifying grace, greater in worth than all the riches of the world.

MARY, MY MOTHER, your Heart is the masterpiece of the Holy Trinity. The Eternal Father unfolded His Omnipotence in order to form in you a Heart full of sweetness and obedience to your Creator. The Divine Son gave you a mother's heart, in which, as in a sanctuary, He wished to dwell. The Holy Spirit gave you the heart of a bride, all burning with a love pure and ardent. Your Heart is truly a mirror of all the virtues, a vivid image and a faithful copy of the Sacred Heart of Jesus; hence you are called the "Mirror of Justice."

(2) MARY, MOTHER OF GOD, *your Heart is a counterpart of the Heart of Jesus.* His Heart is a *loving* Heart, and that love is symbolized by the flames which St. Margaret Mary saw coming forth from it. Your Heart is also the most affectionate of hearts after that of Jesus. You love us as a mother loves her children. Your eyes ever watch over us; your ears ever listen to our cries; your hands are ever extended over us to help us and impart heavenly gifts to us; above all, your Heart is full of tenderest care for us.

You had a *Heart of love* from which in the course of time was to be formed the Sacred Heart of the loving Christ. Even before His coming your Heart was filled with love for those whom later He was to love with a tremendous love. Aside from the Sacred Heart of Jesus, no human heart ever loved mankind as deeply as your Heart. There the poor find aid; the sick and needy, remedy; the afflicted, consolation; the doubting, counsel; the distressed, help.

But your love for God was even greater. God inflamed no other heart, after that of the Heart of His Son, with His love so much as yours. Free from all attachment to earthly things, you were most capable of being filled with divine love. Such love set your heart on fire with love for your Divine Son, not only as your Son, but also as your God and Savior, since you had shared in advance in the merits of His Passion and death.

The Heart of Jesus was a *suffering* Heart, symbolized by the thorns encircling it, the cross above it, and the gash opened in its side. Your Heart was also a suffering Heart. Its martyrdom began with holy Simeon's prophecy in the temple and was completed on Calvary. When the hands and feet of Jesus were pierced with nails, the sound of each blow of the hammer inflicted a wound in your Heart. When His head was crowned with thorns, another crown of thorns encircled your Heart. When His side was opened with a lance, a sword of anguish also pierced your Heart. When His lips were tortured with gall and vinegar, a sea of bitterness was poured into your Heart.

The Heart of Jesus was a *pure* Heart, symbolized by the light that

St. Margaret Mary saw streaming round it. Your Heart was also a pure Heart, pure as the light, purer than the snow, free from the stain of original sin, from the least taint of actual sin, from the least evil tendency of our fallen nature—a heart full of light and beauty reflecting to the full the radiance of the Sacred Heart of your Divine Son.

Your Heart is pure and spotless because sanctified beyond all other hearts by the indwelling of the Holy Spirit, making it worthy to be the dwelling place of the Sacred Heart of Jesus. You are the spotless tabernacle, the earthly resting place prepared for the Son of God; hence the Church pays loving respect to your Immaculate Heart.

Mary, my Mother, the Heart of Jesus was a *generous* Heart, symbolized by the wound in His side from which came forth the last drops of His Heart's Blood shed for us, and by which we can reach the treasures of that Divine Heart. Your Heart is also a generous Heart, full of love, abounding in mercy. All mankind may find a place there as your children, if they only choose to listen to your loving appeal. Your Heart is a refuge for sinners, for you are the Mother of Mercy, who has never been known to turn away anyone who came to seek your aid.

(3) Mary, Mother of God, *your Immaculate Heart is the Hope of the world*. In your apparitions at Fátima you revealed that it is the designs of the Divine Mercy to cure the world through your Heart. As the heart of a mother triumphs over the just anger of a father in an earthly family, so your Heart will triumph by averting the force of God's justice upon this sinful world. In your six apparitions at Fátima you made repeated demands for penance and reparation.

Grant that we all may heed your warning, for only through penance and reparation can we blot out sin and the insult it afflicts on God. Penance and reparation are ways of winning God's love and blessing for a misguided and sinful world. In the past you have expressed your willingness to help and made your requests in your personal apparitions. Be pleased to lead mankind securely to certain victory over Communism through the triumph of your Immaculate Heart as you promised at Fátima: "In the end my Immaculate Heart will triumph and an era of peace will be conceded to humanity."

MARY, MY MOTHER, help me to take your requests at Fátima to heart. I wish to do penance by giving up sin and amending my life, by asking pardon and making reparation to the Heart of Jesus and to your Immaculate Heart, so grievously offended by our sins. I wish to make reparation by offering sacrifices to atone for sin by fulfilling my daily duties well, by accepting the crosses of life with resignation and love, by obeying the commandments, by going to Mass, confession, and Communion frequently, above all on the first Saturday of each month, and by praying much, especially your holy Rosary.

I consecrate myself entirely to your Immaculate Heart. I consecrate to you my very being and my whole life: all that I have, all that I love, all that I am. To you I give my body, my heart, and my soul. I desire that all that is in me and around me may belong to you and may share in the benefits of your motherly blessing. I promise to devote myself wholeheartedly to the spreading of devotion to your Immaculate Heart so that the Kingdom of the Sacred Heart may come and He may reign with you in my heart and in the hearts of all men.

> Virgin, Jesus' Mother mild,
> Keep me ever as thy child:
> Thine in life and thine in death,
> Thine in sorrow, gloom, and dread,
> Thine in pain and crosses sore,
> Thine today and evermore.

> Mother, on thee my soul relies;
> Mother, to thee it calls and sighs.
> Mother most gentle, aid me still;
> Mother most mighty, strengthen my will.

> Dear Mother, O come and help me pray;
> Dear Mother, O come in the weary fray.
> Dear Mother, O come and comfort me;
> Dear Mother, O come and take me to thee.

> Thou canst give aid, O mightiest Queen;
> Thou lov'st to give aid, O gentlest Queen;
> Thou must give aid, O most faithful Queen;
> Thou wilt give aid, O most merciful Queen.

Mother of grace, bright dawn of the day,
Refuge of sinners, salvation's true way,
Hope of the world and Heaven's delight,
Balm to the sorrowing, star of the night.

Who ever invoked thee, sweet Mother, in vain:
When hast thou forgotten thy children in pain?
Unceasing my cry under burdens of grief;
Mary is ever my soul's one relief.

Come life or come death, still will I cry;
Mary helps ever to live and to die.
Virgin and Mother of beautiful love,
Mary, O help me to heaven above.

† † †

Almighty and eternal God, Who in the Heart of the Blessed Virgin Mary prepared a worthy dwelling for the Holy Spirit, mercifully grant that, devoutly celebrating the feast day of this most pure Heart, we may be enabled to live according to Your own Heart. Through Christ Our Lord. Amen.

Our Lady, Health of the Sick

FEAST, Saturday before the last Sunday in August
(TRIDUUM, Wednesday before the last Sunday in August)

Background:

Perhaps the greatest tragedy in the world, after sin, is wasted pain. The reason so many people find suffering too difficult to bear is that they lose sight of its purpose or fail to use the God-given means of bearing it patiently. God has given us not only His grace and the Sacraments to aid us in our spiritual sickness, which is a result of original sin, but, in addition, the care of a loving Mother. The devotion of the faithful has also chosen Mary as the healer of bodily ailments.

Because of the Blessed Virgin Mary's power of intercession in obtaining remedies for soul and body, the Church calls her "Health of the Sick." As much as her compassionate maternal heart sympathizes with man's sufferings from bodily infirmities, she certainly experiences a greater sense of responsibility and care in regard to the spiritual maladies and weaknesses under which we labor. In all sickness of body and of soul, the Blessed Mother is a sure refuge and relief. Who can number those who have recovered health, corporal or spiritual, through her intercession? The many shrines everywhere in the world, which have been built in her honor, are a proof of mankind's deepest gratitude for material and spiritual blessings received. Here thousands of cures were wrought. As her loving Son "went about doing good" in His lifetime, so now in heaven Mary continues His work of healing souls and bodies throughout the whole world. Her children turn to her as to their dearest Mother in all their needs. She never fails them, because it was for this purpose that she was given to us as a Mother by her dying Son.

Even the favors for which we thank the other saints come through the Queen of All Saints. Thus Pius XI in his encyclical on the Rosary mentions his gratitude for the recovery of his health: "This grace . . . We attribute to the special intercession of the virgin of Lisieux, St. Thérèse of the Child Jesus, but we know nonetheless that all things are given to us by the great and Good God through the hands of His Mother."

Recommend to Mary all the sick throughout the world. If God has sent you sickness, or if He should do so, have recourse to your Heavenly Mother, the Health of the Sick.

Prayer

(1) MARY, MOTHER OF GOD, *help me to understand as clearly as God wishes to let me do so, the value of suffering and sickness.* God has created nature and all the wondrous functions of the human body. He is the Master of His creation. He can and does suspend the laws of nature for those who have faith in His goodness and entreat Him in fervent prayer. He promised that my prayers would be heard when He said, "Ask, and it shall be given you" (Matt. 7:7).

During His lifetime Jesus cured sickness and disease and even raised the dead to life, because people asked Him to do so in prayer. I firmly believe that He will hear my prayer also, if this should be the Will of God.

Help me to realize that it is only through the cross that I can attain to its glory and that it is only through suffering that I can possess the kingdom of heaven. Before you were crowned Queen of Heaven, you became the Mother of Sorrows. All the saints suffered during their lifetime, but you are the Queen of them all as Queen of Martyrs. If I have been blessed with suffering, let me remember that this is the only way I can follow Jesus and you, for He said, "If any one wishes to come after Me, let him deny himself, and take up his cross and follow Me" (Matt. 16:24).

(2) MARY, MOTHER OF GOD, *because of your influence in obtaining helpful remedies against spiritual and bodily maladies, the Church calls you the "Health of the Sick."* Your power and motherly care not only embrace spiritual miseries but also extend to the ills of the body. How often do we see you restoring health to the sick, who have recourse to you with childlike confidence? But much as your compassionate heart sympathizes with man's sufferings from bodily sickness, you certainly show greater care to relieve the spiritual sickness and weaknesses under which we labor.

How much I worry about my physical health! But how careless I am about my spiritual health! I realize that it is the command of God that I take ordinary care to ensure bodily health. However, my sick soul is entitled to more vigilant care, for Jesus reminded me, "What does it profit a man, if he gain the whole world, but suffer the loss of his own soul?" (Matt. 16:26).

MARY, MY MOTHER, in all infirmities of body and soul you are a sure refuge and relief. Down through the ages numberless people have recovered health of body and of spirit through your intercession! You lighten our sufferings, you obtain for us bodily health when it is conducive to our salvation and you help the soul to conquer its spiritual enemies. Teach me to be more earnest about seeking health of soul: to overcome my ruling passion, to free myself from the occasions of sin. I ask this with special earnestness from you who are the Health of the Sick.

How unimportant are the infirmities of the body compared to the infirmities of the soul! Infirmities of the body, patiently endured, may become the occasion of great merit. May the infirmities of my soul be my chief concern. Let me fear such sickness of soul as avarice, lust, luxury, ambition, hatred, anger—because, unless these are cured, they may bring about the eternal death of my soul.

(3) MARY, MOTHER OF GOD, *sincere devotion to you is a sign of perseverance in doing good till death.* Infirmities of the body are nature's warning voice concerning the approach of death, which I cannot finally escape. The Church teaches that final perseverance in good and in a happy death is a grace so great that no one can obtain it by his own merits or without special help from God. But saints and writers of the Church speak of devotion to you as a sign of perseverance in good and in a happy death. They apply these words of Scripture to you: "He that shall find me, shall find life, and shall have salvation from the Lord" (Prov. 8:35).

Jesus gave you to me to be my Mother that you may enable me at my death to say as He did with a sense of humble gratitude to God for His graces: "It is finished"—"I have done the work God placed me upon this earth to do. I have loved and followed Jesus to the end. I have carried my cross patiently which He gave me to carry. I have saved my soul."

MARY, MY MOTHER, I turn to you rather for health of soul than of body. Keep my soul in good health so that when my body fails, my soul may be prepared to meet its Maker and Judge. I am in need of forgiveness of sin, of strength in temptation. I need virtues, especially charity and humility and purity. Help me to overcome the enemies of my salvation and to persevere to the end in the friendship of God.

For vain joys or small profits people sacrifice much. For the small sacrifice of being devoted to you I can obtain a happy death and eternal life. I want to take devotion to you seriously. If I put my trust in you, I shall be saved. If you receive me under your care, I shall fear nothing because devotion to you is an unfailing sign of salvation. Your aid at the hour of my death will be for me a guarantee of salvation if through life I have sought to imitate the beautiful example of your life. How fortunate I will be, if at death I am bound with the sweet chains of love to you! These chains are chains of salvation for me, and they will make me enjoy in death that blessed peace which will be the beginning of my eternal peace and rest. I look to you for the grace of final perseverance and a happy death. Thus you will be for me not only the Health of the Sick but also the Gate of Heaven.

> Still thy love is glowing,
> Mother, in my heart;
> Keep it ever growing,
> Never more to part.

> Life's short years are fleeting
> On time's rapid wings,
> Still my heart is beating,
> Still my spirit sings.

> Thou alone, dear Mother,
> Canst my love enthrall;
> Time shall find no other,
> Thou surpassest all.

> Death shall come to grasp me
> When life's span is o'er,
> ·To thy heart then clasp me,
> Safe forevermore.

† † †

Grant us, Your servants, we beg of You, O Lord God, that we may be blessed with health of soul and body, and by the glorious intercession of the Blessed Virgin Mary, be freed from the sorrows of this present life and enjoy everlasting bliss. Through Christ Our Lord. Amen.

Our Lady of Consolation

FEAST, Saturday after the Feast of St. Augustine (Aug. 28)
(TRIDUUM, Wednesday nearest the Feast of St. Augustine)

Background:

The Blessed Virgin Mary knows by actual experience what sorrow is, since she herself drained a most bitter cup of sorrow. Therefore, she knows how to console and help suffering mankind. The Church invokes her as the "Comforter of the Afflicted." The greatness and holiness of God's Mother certainly impress man with deep respect and admiration. But the sympathy she has with man in his suffering and her great desire to assist him in all his difficulties should call forth our sincerest gratitude and love. Although raised above man and even the angels, she does not forget those from whose ranks she has been so exalted, and who are exposed to the wickedness of the enemies of God and souls. Thus St. Peter Damian asks her: "Do you, O Blessed Virgin, therefore, forget our lowliness, because you are so highly exalted? No! Such mercy as yours could not forget such misery as ours."

Amid the sorrows of this earthly pilgrimage God has prepared for you in the continual help of your Heavenly Mother a rich source of consolation. She has taught you by her example never to despair of God's help in time of suffering, but to value at the proper worth the crosses He sends you. In all your pains and disappointments do not seek relief in worldly pleasures, which soon pass away; rather unite your sufferings with those of Jesus and His sorrowful Mother, in whom alone, after God, the afflicted can find true consolation.

Prayer

(1) MARY, MOTHER OF GOD, *you are the Comforter of the Afflicted because in your lifetime you bore every sort of affliction and you can now sympathize with me in my sufferings.* You willingly became the Mother of Jesus when you answered the message of the archangel Gabriel with the words, "Behold the handmaid of the Lord, be it done to me according to thy word" (Luke 1:38).

This marked the beginning of your life of suffering together with Jesus. Simeon prophesied it when you offered the little Victim-Savior to the Heavenly Father for the first time in the temple: "And thy own soul a sword shall pierce" (Luke 2:35). You confidently accepted whatever God willed. You bore your sorrows bravely because you received them from God's hands.

Three swords brought anguish to you while Jesus was yet a young child; four swords pierced your soul in His Holy Passion. Yet no selfish thought, no bitter resentment marred your beauty. From the knowledge of the Will of God you gathered the strength that was to uphold you at the foot of the Cross on which your Son hung, dying. Through thirty-three years of Jesus' life on earth you suffered in silence. The climax of that sorrow came when the innocent Victim for the sins of mankind was given, dead, into your arms. Your loving submission to the Divine Will could not dry your tears, but it quieted the agony of your mother heart.

MARY, MY MOTHER, you associated yourself with the suffering and crucifixion of Jesus in order that you might share in His glorification. You had to become the Mother of Sorrows before you were raised above the angels as heaven's Queen. In life's dark hours you always remembered that you were God's handmaid, and you always wanted everything to be done according to His holy Will. Your heart was visited with seven swords of sorrow before you became the Comforter of the Afflicted and the Cause of our Joy.

(2) MARY, MOTHER OF GOD, *I pour out to you the sorrows of my own troubled heart.* In your greater sorrow may my own be lost, and in calm resignation may my anguished soul find peace and strength. Through the sorrow which you felt during your whole life, but especially when you saw Jesus led to His death and then crucified, obtain for me the grace that I may patiently bear the sufferings which God has seen fit to send me, even as you bore your sufferings. Let this be my consolation to know that I am doing God's Will. I shall be blessed if I imitate you in bearing my cross till death. Since you bore a much heavier one together with your innocent Son, should not I, a sinner deserving of eternal punishments, carry mine patiently? Let me find consolation and strength in your favorite devotion—the rosary.

When you lived in this valley of tears, you were ever loving and merciful toward the afflicted. How much more compassionate are you now since you reign happily in heaven? Now you realize human misery more fully and, therefore, show your mercy and compassion and help more generously. You are, indeed, our Mother; and a mother can never forget her children.

MARY, MY MOTHER, I thank you for having suffered and wept for love of me that you might become my consolation in affliction. I entrust to you all my anxieties and needs so that through the merits of your sorrows I may bear the trials and sufferings of life with the same love and resignation to God's Will with which you bore yours. I beg you to make me strong enough to bear my trials for the love of God so that I may become like you in suffering. Help me to cling tightly to Jesus and to you. May each pain and disappointment of my life become a perfect act of love of God because I offer all to God through your immaculate hands.

To you I entrust my soul for which Jesus died, and I beg you to help me to save it. Protect me from the snares of the world, the flesh, and the devil. And grant that after having suffered with you and your loving Son in this life, I may be glorified with You both in His Kingdom beyond the stars.

(3) MARY, MOTHER OF GOD, *I thank you for being my companion in suffering.* You love me with a Heart human like my own—a Heart that can understand my sorrows and problems because you experienced all that I must bear; a Heart that can sympathize with me and befriend me in my hour of need. Not all the affection you pour out upon countless other souls lessens your love for me. Even when I forget you and begin to complain in my sufferings and crosses, you try to console me. Even when I disappoint you by doing my best to shake off the cross God has placed upon my shoulders, you pray for me. When I have pain, you are ready to comfort and strengthen me.

I am most grateful for such devoted love and sympathy. You are indeed the most wonderful Mother that has ever walked this earth. Teach me to answer such love with childlike confidence. I want to turn to you in all my pressing needs and difficulties as to a most sure refuge, imploring the help of your protection, choosing you as my advocate, wholeheartedly entrusting my cause to you who are the Consoler of the Afflicted. But that my devotion may be acceptable and my homage pleasing, let me endeavor to maintain within my soul, as much as possible, the spotlessness of your purity and try to walk in your footsteps humbly and gently.

MARY, MY MOTHER, I unite myself with you in the spirit in which you offered yourself as a sacrifice of love during your lifetime. Through your hands I offer myself with Jesus during the Holy Sacrifice of the Mass. Give my heart sentiments like His and your own so that, through frequent Holy Communion and prayer, I may become a worthy co-victim with Jesus, holy and pleasing to God, and so that all the actions, sufferings, tears, and disappointments of my life may be thus consecrated to God as a sacrifice for His glory and the salvation of souls, especially my own. Everything that God may send me, or permit in my life, whether favorable or unfavorable, sweet or bitter—even illness, is acceptable to me, for I have resolved, after your example, to conform myself to the Divine Will in all things. Jesus invites me to do so, for He said, "Take my yoke upon you. . . . My yoke is easy and My burden light" (Matt. 11:29).

> In the midst of all my trials,
> Mary, be forever near;
> I can hear you gently speaking,
> "Courage, child, and have no fear."

> Working with you, working for you,
> I can tread as Jesus trod;
> 'Tis the secret to be holy
> And to do the Will of God.

> When the path seems hard to nature,
> Deign to watch with anxious care;
> Your sweet smile will lighten labor,
> And your love will strengthen prayer.

> Through you I to Jesus offer
> All my life and all my love;
> Then you'll weave my crown of glory
> In our endless home above.

† † †

Lord Jesus Christ, Father of mercies and God of all consolation, grant in Your loving kindness that we who joyfully venerate on earth Mary, Your most pure Mother, as our comforter, may deserve to enjoy with her the unending happiness of heaven. Who live and reign forever. Amen.

Our Lady, Mother of the Good Shepherd

FEAST, September 3 (TRIDUUM, August 31–September 2)

Background:

Jesus once said: "I am the good shepherd. The good shepherd lays down his life for his sheep. . . . I am the good shepherd, and I know mine and mine know me, even as the Father knows me and I know the Father; and I lay down my life for my sheep. And other sheep I have that are not of this fold. Them also I must bring, and they shall hear my voice, and there shall be one fold and one shepherd" (John 10:11–16).

The reason for the pastoral care and love of Jesus is the fact that He is the Only-Begotten Son of the Heavenly Father. Sharing the same nature, He recognizes and loves His Father in His whole Fatherhood, since He is not only His Father, but also the Father of all men. Since His Father regards and loves all men as His adopted children, through sanctifying grace, and wills that His Son regard and love us as His brethren, Jesus claims us as His own and loves us as His sheep with the love with which He loves the Father and Himself. He even delivered Himself up to death of His own free will to show His love for us and to bring His other sheep into the true fold.

Pope Benedict XV in an apostolic letter of 1918 describes Our Lady's role in the redemption: when Jesus, as a Good Shepherd, laid down His life for His sheep, she, as Mother of the Good Shepherd, immolated her Son: "Thus, Mary suffered and all but died along with her Son suffering and dying; thus, for the salvation of men she abdicated the rights of a mother towards her Son, and insofar as it was hers to do, she immolated the Son to placate God's justice, so that she herself may justly be said to have redeemed together with Christ the human race."

Pope Pius XII, in a radio address to the Marian Congress at Ottawa, Canada, June 21, 1947, said: "When the little Maid of Nazareth uttered her 'fiat' to the message of the angel and the Word was made flesh in her womb, she became not only the Mother of God in the physical order of nature but also in the supernatural order of grace she became the Mother of all, who through the Holy Spirit would be made one under the headship of her Divine Son. The Mother of the Head would be the Mother of the members. The Mother of the Vine would be the Mother of the branches."

On Calvary the Good Shepherd entrusted His sheep to the keeping of His Blessed Mother. Like her beloved Son, she, too, is filled with a burning love for souls. She does all in her power to bring them to His Sacred Heart and to save them from eternal death. Pray to the Mother of the Good Shepherd for the souls who are still outside His fold, as well as for yourself, that you may faithfully follow Jesus, the Shepherd of your soul.

Prayer

(1) MARY, MOTHER OF GOD, *you are the Mother of the Good Shepherd Who came to lay down His life for His sheep.* From the very beginning, God the Father endowed you with all that would make you worthy to bear His only Son at the moment of His Incarnation. God the Son, eternally honoring you as His Mother, prepared you for this dignity. And the Holy Spirit, looking upon you as His most perfect sanctuary after the holy humanity of the Savior, was pleased to enrich you with the fullness of His treasures.

MARY, MY MOTHER, you have a real title to respect from Jesus, to His love and, upon earth, even to His obedience. By giving Him His Body and Blood—the instruments of our Redemption—and by sharing in His mysteries, you were the secondary but true agent, the co-worker with your Son in effecting the sanctification and salvation of men. By your generous assent to the Angel's message, you became at once the well beloved daughter of the Heavenly Father, the Mother of the Only-Begotten Son and the sanctuary and Immaculate Bride of the Holy Spirit. You were elevated to a dignity and office never accorded to any human being and far surpassing the angels in majesty.

(2) MARY, MOTHER OF GOD, *by your prayers as Mother of the Good Shepherd, you obtain for us all kinds of graces.* Your intercession is all-powerful. Your slightest wish is like a command, because your Son has made you the dispenser of all His treasures.

In view of the merits of your Son the Heavenly Father is willing to be reconciled to mankind, to forgive our sins, to pour out His grace abundantly upon us. When He beholds the Divine Victim that has been slain for us, sees His wounds, and hears the voice of His Blood crying out for pardon for us, His fatherly Heart is moved, the gates of His mercy are unlocked, and the streams of grace flow downward to fill our souls.

But the Lamb of God, immolated on Calvary, was offered up through your hands, because you are the Mother of the Good Shepherd. He did indeed offer Himself as the principal agent, even as in Holy Mass it is He Who is High Priest no less than Victim. But as in the Eucharistic Sacrifice He is pleased to use as His instrument a mortal man, so, too, it was His Will that you should be present at His side as He hung upon the cross and that by the union of your will with His you might cooperate with Him in His saving sacrifice.

MARY, MY MOTHER, even now in heaven, since no gift is bestowed on us by God except in virtue of the Passion and death of His Divine Son, the Precious Blood and the sacred wounds of Jesus are presented to God by you. Then turn to us and help us in our needs. Mother of the Good Shepherd, obtain for us, for whom your Divine Son was willing to suffer and die, the graces we need to save our souls.

(3) MARY, MOTHER OF GOD, *teach me to know and love Jesus, the Good Shepherd of my soul.* How generous is His love for us, His sheep! He strengthens the weak, heals the sick, binds up that which is broken, seeks that which is lost, and rules over His flock with tenderness and love. He knows His sheep by name, so that at the sound of His voice they follow Him. He watches over them with a care which knows no fatigue, with a love which considers no sacrifice. For their safety, that they may enter into life everlasting, He willingly laid down His life. He died for all men, thereby opening to all who make use of His grace the door to His sheepfold, which is eternal life. His life's last concern was that the Apostles and the priests and missionaries who would follow them would be enabled by God's grace and their own word and example to lead His scattered sheep into the one true fold.

Sweet Mother of Jesus, thank the Good Shepherd for the tender care He gives me: for seeking after me when I have strayed, for healing the wounds caused by sin in the Sacrament of Penance, for feeding my hungry soul in the Sacrament of the Holy Eucharist, for permitting me to enjoy all the privileges of being a Catholic in His sheepfold, the one true Church.

In return for such generous love, help me to be a good sheep of the flock of the Good Shepherd. Help me to know Jesus by His word and example; to find joy in all that concerns Him; to follow Him by permitting myself to be guided in the path of virtue, when

He wishes to hold me back from the poisonous pastures of worldly joys and from the dangerous wild beasts of evil.

MARY, MY MOTHER, give me your aid that I may be a true follower of the Good Shepherd and make His interests mine. There is no interest closer to His loving Heart than that of spreading the light of divine faith and love to the souls of men. Through prayers and good works, may the power of God's grace touch the hearts of men that many souls may be brought to the sheepfold of your Son.

> Queen of the Angels, Mary, thou whose smile
> Adorns the heavens with their brightest ray,
> Calm star that over sea directs the way
> Of wandering barks unto their homing isle;
> By all thy glory, Virgin without guile,
> Relieve me of my grievous woes, I pray!
> Protect me, save me from the snares that stay
> Beyond to misdirect me and defile!
>
> I trust in thee with that same trust of old,
> Fixed in the ancient love and reverence
> Which now I tell as I have always told.
> Guide thou my journey, strengthen my pretense
> To reach with thee at last the blessed fold
> Thy Son prepares His flock in recompense.
> —GIOVANNI BOCCACCIO (1375)

† † †

Lord Jesus Christ, Good Shepherd, Who gave Your life for Your sheep, and Who when dying on the Cross entrusted to the Virgin Mary the sheep of Your pasture, grant that through her intercession we may on earth follow You, our Shepherd, and so be led to the heavenly pastures of life everlasting. Who live and reign forever. Amen.

Nativity of the Blessed Virgin Mary

FEAST, September 8 (NOVENA, August 30–September 7)

Background:

According to an *ancient tradition* the parents of the Blessed Virgin were Joachim and Anna. Nothing historically trustworthy is known about Joachim and Anna, but they must have been persons of superior sanctity, for they have been virtually canonized by the Church. We may rest assured that God would have chosen parents worthy to educate a child of such high destiny and singular holiness. For a long time they were without children. God rewarded their prayers and granted them a daughter. There cannot be the least doubt that Mary was of Davidic lineage, at least through Joachim, and perhaps through Anna as well. The bodily origin of the Messias from David had been predicted by Isaias (11:1). Joachim and Anna named their daughter Miriam, after the valiant sister of Moses.

Because the Annunciation took place in Nazareth and because most of Mary's relatives resided there, she was most probably born in that village, situated in the hill country of southern Galilee. According to tradition, the house where Mary was born was located on the site where the Basilica of the Annunciation now stands. This is built over some caves, one of which is venerated as the scene of the Annunciation. Even today Nazareth contains homes consisting of two parts: a small wooden flat-topped house fronting the street and an adjoining cave hollowed out by human hands or by nature. A home of this type may well have been the place of Mary's birth.

Mary was chosen from all eternity to give us the Savior; hence she was eternally in God's plan of Redemption. In time she was immaculately conceived and her birth brought salvation to mankind. *Next to Christmas, there is no other birthday so happy and so important as the birthday of Mary the Mother of God.* Today there is born unto us a child who is unlike other infants, for the world sees for the first time since Paradise was lost, a human being who is free of every stain of sin from the beginning of her existence.

The birthday of Our Lady brings to our minds the sanctity of the Mother God has prepared for Himself. Recent Popes have said much in praise of that sanctity. Pius IX will serve as a good example: "He [God], therefore, filled her, far more than all the angelic spirits and all the saints, with an abundance of all heavenly gifts from the treasury of His divinity, in such a wonderful manner that she would always be free from absolutely every stain of sin, and that, all beautiful and perfect, she might display such fullness of innocence and holiness that under God none greater is known, and which, God excepted, no one can attain even in thought."

Mary's nativity carried with it a *fourfold joy:* joy to the Blessed Trinity, for she was to cooperate in the Incarnation; joy to the Angels, for she was to be their Queen; joy to the saints in Limbo, for she was to be the Mother of their Deliverer; joy to all Mankind, for Redemption was at hand. Thus Holy Mother Church sets the keynote of joy for this feast, exulting in the first steps of the long-awaited fulfillment of God's promise; for the Virgin's birth was the coming forth of the rod out of the root of Jesse, as Isaias had foretold. Over and over again the Church rejoices in her Liturgy: "Thy Nativity, O Mother of God, was the cause of universal joy. . . . Let us keep with rejoicing the birthday of the Blessed Virgin Mary."

To this *very ancient feast,* already solemnized in the seventh century, Pope Innocent IV gave an Octave at the first Council of Lyons in 1245. This date, September 8th, served to fix that of the Immaculate Conception on December 8th. Mary is inseparable from Jesus in the Divine Plan; wherefore, the Epistle (Wisdom 7:22–25) applies to her what Holy Scripture says of the Eternal Wisdom.

Let your desire to honor and love the Blessed Virgin prove itself by the imitation of her virtues. A child learns best at its mother's knee, for nobody understands a child better than its mother, and nobody can help more readily and patiently. It is quite the same in your spiritual life. She is truly your spiritual Mother. Being the Mother of the Head of the Mystical Body, Jesus her Son, she is also the Mother of its members. On the cross Jesus entrusted you to her care, and it is His will that all the graces He has merited for you by His Passion and death should reach you through her hands. This double title of Mother of God and Mother of men is the foundation of the part which Mary holds in your spiritual life. Therefore, unite yourself with Mary, for then you will be united with Jesus.

The more frequently and the more trustingly you turn to Mary in prayer, the more abundantly will you experience her motherly kindness. She is not only the Mother of God and your Mother, but also the Mediatrix of all grace for you. How much help, security, and comfort can be found in the thought that you are able to take refuge in the Heart of a Mother who is so close to God and so powerful with Him that He has placed the fullness of His graces in her hands! The most precious fruit of veneration of our Lady is this: if you are united with Mary, you are also united with Jesus; then His Heart will live in your heart as It does in hers.

Thank God for having created this most beautiful of creatures and for having given her to you as a Mother. Thank Him for all the mercies He has shown to mankind through Mary. Let your birthday gift to your Heavenly Mother be the wholehearted consecration of yourself to her.

Prayer

(1) MARY, MOTHER OF GOD, *you are the Virgin who was promised as the Mother of the Savior.* After the fall of our First Parents, earth, which was to be paradise, was changed into a valley of tears on which the curse of God fell. People became the poor banished children of Eve. They roamed about in the darkness of sin and despair. In His infinite mercy God chose Abraham who was to be the Father of a Chosen Nation. You were descended from the most renowned men of that nation and counted among your ancestors patriarchs, prophets, leaders of the people of God, and kings of the ancient law. Your birth was represented beforehand by many figures, announced by prophets, desired for many ages by the human race.

Prophets foretold the coming of the Savior and the manner in which the Redemption would take place. They spoke of you as His Virgin Mother and of the part you would play in the Redemption of mankind. Balaam referred to you as a star: "The star which shall arise from Jacob." Isaias called you a Virgin: "Behold, a virgin shall conceive and bear a son, and His name shall be Emmanuel." King Solomon described your beauty: "Thou art all fair, my beloved, beautiful as the moon, brilliant as the sun."

MARY, MY MOTHER, your birth was awaited as the near sign of the deliverance of the human race. The Church regards you as the rising dawn. As the dawn precedes and announces the coming of the sun, makes the darkness of the night disappear, consoles the sick and rejoices all nature, so you went before and announced Jesus, "The Sun of Justice," who made the darkness of the world disappear by the light of His Gospel, consoled and cured the sick in soul and body, and brought an abundance of graces and blessings to the whole world.

(2) MARY, MOTHER OF GOD, at the very beginning of your existence *you received grace exceeding in greatness that of all the saints together* because you were destined to be the Mother of the Redeemer and the Mediatrix of the world. From the first instant

of your existence your mind was filled by the supernatural light of faith and your soul with love of God. You used most perfectly every actual grace given you by God in acts of virtue. What untold merit you must have laid up for eternity during the nine months that preceded your Nativity. Who can describe the merits and graces that adorned your soul at the glorious instant of your Nativity at a period when all other children have no merit!

How delightful a sight must your beautiful soul have been to heaven! The angels saw a soul which had never been touched by original sin. They had seen Adam created in grace, and John the Baptist, spotless from his birth, because he had been cleansed from original sin before birth. In his soul they saw no more than they see in each little soul as it leaves the baptismal font, grace having taken the place of original sin. But in you they saw a soul whose sanctity surpassed that of angels and of men, a soul which would glorify God more perfectly than any other creature ever had glorified Him, or ever would glorify Him. No wonder the angels were lost in admiration! They beheld the dwelling place prepared for the Son of God.

Mary, my Mother, your little life held a mystery immeasurably deeper than that of any other human life, since no mind could measure the distance that lay between the chosen Maiden who was not only the servant of the Lord but also His true Mother, and the rest of mankind who were His servants and no more. You were one of us, and yet you stood above us! With my whole heart I thank God for all He has done for you and for all mankind through you!

(3) Mary, Mother of God, *your dear parents, St. Joachim and St. Anna, rejoiced at your birth.* I admire the holiness of their lives and the nobility of their family. Joachim was of the royal house of David, and Anna of the priestly family of Aaron. They observed the Law of God most diligently and spent their days in prayer and in works of mercy.

Though they had both vowed to consecrate their first-born child to the service of the Lord, they remained childless, a condition considered a disgrace among the Jews and a mark of heavenly disfavor. Only after many years of fervent prayers did God reward them. You were born into the world in the humble city of Nazareth. Your birth was a miracle of the power of God because both of your parents were far advanced in years. Who could tell the great joy which filled their hearts when they held you in their arms?

But all heaven rejoiced at your birth, because you were destined one day to bring the Savior into the world; you were to become God's Mother and the Queen of heaven and earth.

MARY, MY MOTHER, I rejoice with the Blessed Trinity on your birthday because you were to take part in the Incarnation and Redemption of the world. I rejoice with all mankind because you became the Mother of our Redeemer. I rejoice with the whole Church because you are our life: you bore Jesus, Who is the Way and the Truth and the Life, and Who was to restore to mankind that supernatural life which had been lost. I have every reason to rejoice, for as the Mother of Jesus and my Mother, you are my hope of salvation. Through your prayers and the prayers of your holy parents may I learn to know and love you more and ever remain your faithful child. This is my sure way of reaching heaven and my God.

Daughter of the mighty Father,
Maiden, heaven's brightest ray,
Angel forms around thee gather,
Dawn of earth's Eternal Day!

Mother of the Son and Savior
Of the Truth, the Life, the Way,
Guide our footsteps, calm our passions,
Dawn of earth's Eternal Day!

Spouse of the Eternal Spirit,
Blossom which will ne'er decay,
Let us but thy love inherit,
Dawn of earth's Eternal Day!

Daughter, Mother, Spouse of Heaven,
Hearken to our earnest lay,
Sweetest gift to man e'er given,
Dawn of earth's Eternal Day!

† † †

Bestow on Your servants, we beg of You, O Lord, the gift of heavenly grace, that we, for whom the Blessed Virgin's motherhood was the beginning of salvation, may be blessed with peace on the sacred feast day of her Nativity. Through Christ Our Lord. Amen.

The Most Holy Name of Mary

FEAST, September 12 (TRIDUUM, September 9–11)

Background:

Ave Maria! This name was inserted into the Hail Mary, not by the Angel, but by the devotion of the faithful. The Evangelist Luke says significantly, "And the name of the Virgin was Mary." This most holy, sweet, and worthy name was eminently fitting to so holy, sweet, and worthy a virgin.

If many of God's servants received their names from God, the Mother of the Redeemer, surpassing them all in dignity, surely received her name directly from God. He was supremely interested in the name of His Daughter, Mother, and Spouse. There can be no doubt that *the name of Mary must possess, as much as the name of the Redeemer, a meaning by virtue of divine inspiration,* which corresponds to the dignity and position of her who bears it. The ancients considered the Hebrew "Mirjam" as a compound of two words: *jam* (more) and *marah* (to be bitter). The best and richest explanation is the one that St. Jerome gives; namely, "enlightening." It characterizes Mary's own position and activity, that is, her Divine Motherhood. In virtue of this privilege, according to the expression of the Church, she reflects as a spotless mirror the Eternal Light of the World, which is first poured into herself and illuminates her; as Mother of the spiritual and heavenly life she is the mediatrix of the light of grace to mankind. In this way the meaning of "stella maris" (star of the sea) is also associated with the name "Mary." Mary is the "woman clothed with the sun" of the Apocalypse. Others have interpreted it to mean "Lady." As we call Jesus "Our Lord," we call Mary "Our Lady."

The most holy names of Jesus and Mary possess a hidden power which puts to flight the demon and fills the soul of him who utters them in loving faith with consolation and hope. It is certain that God has attached a wonderful power of sanctification and life to the devout uttering of these two names by the faithful, because Jesus and Mary are the desired objects of His love.

The saints derived much consolation from the name of Mary. St. Francis of Assisi exclaimed: "When I pray 'Hail Mary,' the heavens smile, the

angels rejoice, the earth is happy and the devils tremble." St. Bernard
writes: "O great, O holy, O ineffable Virgin, thy name is so sweet and
lovely that it cannot be pronounced without our becoming inflamed with
love for thee and for God Who gave this name to thee!"

Eight days after the birth of Mary, according to the custom of the Jews,
her parents, Joachim and Anna, gave her the name of Mary. Wherefore,
during the Octave of her Nativity, the liturgy keeps a *feast* in honor of this
holy name. Spain with the approval of Rome, in 1513, was the first to
celebrate it; in 1683 it was extended to the whole Church by Innocent XI
to thank Mary for the victory which John Sobieski, King of Poland, had
just gained against the Turks who besieged Vienna.

The Name of Mary is a source of power, consolation and hope. Prove
your love for your heavenly Mother by often uttering her holy name with
loving confidence. If you do so frequently in life, you will surely do so at the
hour of your death, when you will need her most. After receiving the Last
Sacraments of the Church, you cannot be better prepared to meet your
Divine Judge than with the names of Jesus and Mary upon your lips.

Prayer

(1) MARY, MOTHER OF GOD, *your name is most glorious and
most powerful.* After the most holy and adorable name of Jesus,
there is no name more glorious and more powerful than yours. At
the mention of it, the angels rejoice and the devils tremble; through
the invocation of your name sinners obtain grace and pardon.

Your name is the name of the one I love. At the same time your
name brings before me your virtues, your merits, your beauty. Merit
and glory attend your name. How I long to repeat it unceasingly
so as to spread its fame, to carry that fame to every shore, to im-
print it on every mind. Teach me to utter your name with deep
respect because, after the name of Jesus, it is most sacred and revered
above all others.

When I say, "Hail Mary!" I breathe the name of one who is
virgin and mother, Mother of God and Mother of men, my Mother.
I need not see you appear, as you did to so many others. I am unworthy of that. But when I say, "Mary," in an instant you are there
before me, and I feel in my heart a stirring of joy and comfort.
You see me, smile on me, listen to me, stretch your arms out to me,
because you hear my prayer and, like a mother, you are anxious to
help your child. After the name of Jesus, neither heaven nor earth

can utter a name by which my faith and love receive more abundant grace, and reassuring hope, and lasting sweetness.

MARY, MY MOTHER, as often as your sweet name comes to my lips, you appear to me as a masterpiece of God's power, so perfect and so sublime that even the hand of Almighty God could not produce anything more perfect in the form of a pure creature. May my soul always find comfort in your holy name! A mother, as she hears her child lisping her name, is thrilled beyond all telling, at all times; and better than she, you will understand me when I say, *"Hail, Mary!"*

(2) MARY, MOTHER OF GOD, *your name means Lady and Queen.* If Jesus is Our Lord, so you are Our Lady. You rule in heaven and on earth. You are the Queen of your Son's kingdom. In heaven all your subjects are crowned by the King of kings, and they pay homage to you. Here on earth kings and rulers lay at your feet their crowns, their very selves. Hell is forced to bear the weight of your lasting hatred. Satan is more humiliated at seeing himself under the heel of the lowliest of creatures than at feeling himself crushed by God's almighty arm.

You are my Queen, my Lady. I long for your complete dominion over me—over my body, my soul, my senses, over all that I am and have. I regard that dominion as a shining star lighting and guiding my life.

MARY, MY MOTHER, your name means *Star of the Sea.* You are the morning star—the morning star that announces the arrival of the sun of justice. You are to be our guide toward the haven of salvation. I fix my gaze on that star and wish never to turn from it. I find faith in its light, hope in its help. As a slave of love, I willingly deliver myself to the everlasting service of so wonderful and majestic a Lady.

Your name means *Sea of Bitterness.* You experienced a sea of bitterness in your life so that you might be an example to us in our sufferings and so that we might learn from your own sorrow to sympathize with others in theirs. We know that You are ever ready to be our help in trouble, our solace in affliction, our hope in despair.

(3) MARY, MOTHER OF GOD, *your name means "full of light" and "light-giving."* How well your name gives expression to your position and your mission in life—your Divine Motherhood! In

virtue of this privilege, you reflect as a spotless mirror the eternal Light of the Word, which is first poured into you and illuminates you. Being filled with light from Heaven, you have shed brightness upon the whole world, by giving birth to the Eternal Light, Our Lord Jesus Christ, although still remaining in the glory of your virginity.

As Mother of the spiritual and heavenly you are the mediatrix of the light of grace to mankind. Truly, you are "light-giving" because you have given us Jesus, the Light of the World. Jesus is our Life, and you have given Him to us. He has reconciled us to God. He is for us the source of all grace, the cause of our supernatural life. To you, then, we owe the salvation which Jesus brought to us. To you we owe the life of grace, without which there is no escape from the death of sin. You are our Mother, the Mother of all the living. You are our spiritual Mother in the order of grace. You are our Mother because you have begotten us to the life of grace. It is to you, after God, that we are indebted for our spiritual life, the life of the children of God. As breathing is not only a sign but even a cause of life, so your name, which is constantly found on the lips of your servants, both proves that they are spiritually alive, and at the same time causes and preserves their life, and gives them every help in their needs.

Teach me to utter your most holy name that it may fill my heart with hope and burning love for you and that loving you I might reach the Light of the World.

MARY, MY MOTHER, glorious is your name for those who pronounce it at death, for they need not fear all the powers of hell. As wax melts before fire, so do the devils lose their power against those souls who remember to speak your name and devoutly invoke it. May your name be the last sound that escapes my lips upon this earth and the first I breathe in heaven.

> Mary, the dearest name of all,
> The holiest and the best,
> The first low word that Jesus lisped
> Laid on His Mother's breast.
>
> Mary, the name that Gabriel spoke,
> The name that conquers hell;
> Mary, the name that through high Heaven
> The angels love so well.

Mary, our comfort and our hope,—
Oh, may that name be given
To be the last we sigh on earth,
The first we breathe in Heaven!

Grant, we beg of You, Almighty God, that Your people who rejoice in the name and in the protection of the most holy Virgin Mary may by her intercession be delivered from all evil here on earth and be found worthy to attain to everlasting joys in heaven. Through Christ Our Lord. Amen.

Seven Sorrows of the Blessed Virgin Mary

FEAST, September 15 (NOVENA, September 6–14)

Background:

We have here a case of a liturgical double—two feasts having the same object and using the same formulas. It is possible, however, to differentiate them: the Lenten feast more especially recalls Our Lady's share in the Passion of her Son, her presence at Calvary at the foot of the cross; that of September embraces all the sorrows of Our Lady and, in particular, the seven that have made the strongest appeal to devotion—the prophecy of Simeon, the flight into Egypt, the three days' loss of Jesus, the meeting with Jesus carrying His Cross, His death on Calvary, His deposition from the Cross, and His burial in the tomb.

It was to the Order of Servites, founded in 1233 near Florence, that the feast of the third Sunday in September was first granted, in 1668; and this, too, was extended to the whole Church by Pius VII, in 1814, and given the rite of Double of the second class by Pius X, who fixed September 15 as its date, when he restored the liturgy of the Sunday.

After the joyful welcome of the Redeemer, Simeon foretold to the Mother the opposition He would arouse, and the sword that was to pierce her own heart. Thus the feasts of Our Lady's Sorrows are linked to the Purification. On May 1, 1918, Pope Benedict XV wrote: "The Doctors of the Church are unanimous in affirming that it was by a special design of Divine Providence that the Blessed Virgin Mary, who appears so little in the public life of Jesus, was near Him on His way to death and at His Crucifixion. Nay, the Passion and Death of her Son were in a certain sense her Passion and Death, for she utterly surrendered her motherly rights over Jesus."

It was not because she was the Mother of God that Mary could bear all her sorrows, but because she saw things from His point of view and not from her own—or rather, she had made His point of view hers. Try to do the same, and you will be amazed at the courage, and strength, and power of endurance that you will possess. The Mother of Sorrows will be on hand to help you.

(See the Feast of Seven Sorrows,
Friday of Passion Week, page 65.)

190

Our Lady of Mercy

(*Our Lady of Ransom*)

FEAST, September 24 (TRIDUUM, September 21–23)

Background:

By the special intervention of Mary, St. Peter Nolasco, St. Raymond of Penafort, and King James of Aragon established an Order for the redemption of captives in the thirteenth century under the name of Our Lady of Mercy. Under Mary's protection the Order grew rapidly. These laymen not only devoted themselves to collecting alms for the ransom of Christian captives, but even gave themselves up to voluntary slavery. To return thanks to God and the Blessed Virgin, the Feast of Our Lady of Ransom was instituted. Ask Our Lady of Mercy to ransom sinners from the captivity of Satan and to free the souls in purgatory.

After the fall, man became subject to sin, misery, disease, and death. God, Who is rich in mercy, gave us two persons animated with tenderest sentiments of compassion and mercy—Jesus and Mary. Jesus willed to become like one of us and chose to know sorrow. Mary, the Mother of Sorrows, became the loving Mother of mankind beneath the Cross. She is full of compassionate mercy. During her whole life she attended the school of sorrow. It was needful that the Mother of Mercy should be herself a child of grief. By her own tears she was taught the sympathy which would enable her to comfort the children whom the first Eve had brought forth to weep. Pope Pius IX, in his encyclical on the Immaculate Conception, encouraged the faithful to appeal to the Mother of Mercy: "Let all the children of the Catholic Church who are most dear to Us hear Our words, and with even more ardent zeal for piety, religion and love, continue to cherish, invoke and beseech the Blessed Virgin Mary, Mother of God, conceived without original sin, and let them with entire confidence have recourse to this sweetest Mother of Grace and Mercy in all dangers, difficulties, necessities, doubts and fears."

Pope Leo XIII in *Magnae Dei Matris,* one of his encyclicals on the Rosary, wrote: "When we have recourse to Mary in prayer, we are having

191

recourse to the Mother of Mercy, who is so well disposed toward us that, whatever the necessity that presses upon us, especially in attaining eternal life, she is instantly at our side of her own accord, even though she has not been invoked; and dispenses grace with a generous hand from that treasure with which from the beginning she was divinely endowed in fullest abundance that she might be worthy to be the Mother of God."

Entreat this Mother of Mercy to help suffering mankind. May her example teach you to show sympathy to your fellow men. In your sinfulness and in your sufferings, remember that the heart of the Mother of Mercy is open to you.

Prayer

(1) MARY, MOTHER OF GOD, *you are so filled with compassion that you deserve to be called not only merciful but even mercy itself.* We praise your virginity and admire your humility; but because we are poor sinners, your mercy attracts us more and we embrace it more lovingly. You are the throne of divine mercy in whom we find the solace of mercy. The more holy you are, the greater is your sweetness and compassion toward sinners who have recourse to you with the desire to amend their lives. Your prayers are those of a Mother and, therefore, have a certain maternal authority with Jesus Christ so that you obtain the grace of pardon even for those who, though guilty of grievous crimes, commend themselves to you. Your protection never ceases; your intercession brings hope and life.

MARY, MY MOTHER, you stand in the presence of your Son, interceding for sinners. You are truly the pledge of Divine Mercy. Be merciful to us. Help us that our souls may be cleansed from the stains of sin.

(2) MARY, MOTHER OF GOD, *you are called Mother of Mercy because of the fullness with which mercy is given to those who seek it at your hands.* Mercy proceeds from you as from an abundant, never failing source. Mercy is your special work in this drama of human life.

You are called the Mother of Mercy because God has given you power to deal with every sort of misery to which mankind is subjected. God reserves to Himself the dispensing of justice to all creatures. It was His will that you dispense mercy by helping sinners, healing the sick, relieving the distressed, and comforting the sorrowful everywhere. You are far more than an instrument of God's mercy toward us. You yourself are full of grace, and from the Holy Spirit, your Divine Spouse, you have received in over-flowing measure His boundless love for all mankind. You are ever active in procuring for each one of us, by fervent and ceaseless intercession, all the heavenly gifts we need. Such gifts assure us the everlasting indwelling of the Holy Spirit in our hearts, together with the Father and the Son, and that endless life which is its blessed fruit.

MARY, MY MOTHER, your intercession is all-powerful. No other saint exerts such universal influence in the affair of our salvation as you do. No other has a like understanding of our miseries, or is in a position to render us on all occasions timely and powerful help. I may address myself to the saints for favors of various kinds, but my prayer must always pass through your hands if it is to reach the throne of grace and draw down the divine blessing.

(3) MARY, MOTHER OF GOD, *I turn to you in all my pressing needs and difficulties as to a most sure refuge.* I implore the help of your protection and choose you as my advocate. I entrust my cause to you who are the Mother of Mercy, and I wish to offer you day by day my most reverent love. But that my devotion may be pleasing to you, help me to maintain my soul and body in the spotlessness of your purity; help me to try as best I can to walk in your footsteps, humbly seeking to be like you.

Even if I have committed all possible sins, let me never lose confidence in you, for I know I shall always find your Heart filled with mercy. The Son of God has His justice, but you, the Mother, have only your mercy. You desire more to do good to me than I can desire to receive favors from you, for your Heart is all love and mercy.

MARY, MY MOTHER, how shall I stand before my Judge at the day of judgment? How shall I answer for the wasted days and years which God has given me to serve Him alone? I look to you, Mother of Mercy. You are all-merciful that you may obtain for me pardon and mercy. You are kind and loving, for you have a mother's heart, full of pity for the erring. You are a Mother of Mercy to the sinner and the fallen; have pity on me! Obtain for me the forgiveness of my sins, the grace of final perseverance, and a happy death, that I may praise you eternally for having been a Mother of Mercy to me.

> Mother of Christ,
> Hear thou thy people's cry,
> Star of the deep
> And portal of the sky.
>
> Mother of Him
> Who thee from nothing made,
> Sinking, we strive,
> And call to thee for aid.
>
> Oh, by that joy
> Which Gabriel brought to thee,
> Thou Virgin first and last,
> Let us thy mercy see.

5 years (323)*

O God, Whose compassion is without limit, show us Your mercy on earth through the most holy intercession of Mary, the Mother of Your Son, that we may merit to attain eternal glory. Through the same Christ Our Lord. Amen.

Our Lady of the Holy Rosary

FEAST, October 7 (NOVENA, September 28–October 6)

Background:

One of the most highly indulgenced of all devotions, *the Rosary,* is both vocal and mental prayer. Vocally we recite the Our Fathers, Hail Marys, and Glory bes. Mentally we meditate on the great mysteries of our Faith. The Rosary is a summary of the main events in the life of Jesus and Mary. The Holy Eucharist is the testament of Jesus; the Rosary is the testament of Mary. The Joyful Mysteries contain the foundation of the work of our salvation; the Sorrowful, the accomplishing of it; and the Glorious, the perfecting of it. Many sacred writers have called the Rosary Mary's favorite prayer, and Popes for nearly four hundred years have recommended it as the best remedy for the evils afflicting society.

It was the custom in the Middle Ages for noble personages to wear crowns of flowers called chaplets. The Blessed Virgin, as Queen of Heaven, has a right to the same homage; wherefore, the Church asks us to recognize the title of Mary as Queen of the Holy Rosary and urges us to offer to her three crowns of roses in the joyful, the sorrowful, and the glorious mysteries of the Rosary. While in the meditation of the mysteries Mary's part in the work of Redemption is considered, in the words of the Hail Mary the lips pay honor to her wonderful dignity and holiness. She is brought before us in the Rosary as the Mediatrix of the graces of the Redemption, the Mother of Mercy, eager to use on behalf of the redeemed a power with God that exceeds that of all other creatures combined. The Rosary is the cry of the child which will not stop calling on its mother until it has obtained what it wants; it is the humble voice of the poor man, who will not leave the gate of the wealthy until he has received a generous alms.

The history of the Church bears testimony to the power of the Rosary, for example, the defeat of the Turkish forces which threatened to invade Europe in the naval battle of Lepanto in 1716, and the victories gained over the same enemy in the last century at Temesvár in Hungary. After the victory of Lepanto Pope St. Pius V declared: "By the Rosary the darkness of heresy has been dispelled, and the light of the Catholic Faith shines with all its brilliancy." In order to keep alive the memory of the victory of Lepanto, Gregory XIII (1585) established the Feast of Our Lady of Victories, which Clement XI (1721) later distinguished by the title of Rosary Sunday and commanded it to be celebrated throughout the universal Church. The Feast of the Holy Rosary was changed from the first Sunday of October to October 7th.

In our own day Mary has appeared to the children of Fátima and proclaimed the pressing need for prayer, especially the Rosary, and sacrifice, if the world is to be saved from the threatening horror of an atheistic way of life. It is well to be acquainted with the Communist peril. But it is more important to work and pray that the evils of Communism be overcome. Like all forces of darkness, they can be overcome by the light of Christian living and the intercession of Mary Immaculate. In every age, whether in public or private misfortune, the faithful have turned to Mary. So also in our day will the Blessed Virgin obtain from her Divine Son peace for the world and a victory over the forces which aim to crush Christian civilization if with great faith and fervent piety we pray to Our Lady of the Rosary.

In the encyclical letter of September 1, 1883, Pope Leo XIII wrote: "Urban IV testifies that every day the Rosary obtains fresh boons for Christianity." Sixtus IV declared that this method of prayer redounded to the honor of God and the Blessed Virgin and was well suited to obviate dangers; Leo X, that "it was instituted to oppose pernicious heresiarchs and heresies;" and Julius III called it the "glory of the Church." St. Pius V said that "with the spread of this devotion the meditations of the Faithful have begun to be more ardent and their prayers more fervent." Later, in his apostolic letter dated December 24th of the same year, Pope Leo XIII wrote: "To the honor of Mary, the great Mother of God, for a perpetual remembrance of the prayer for her protection offered among all nations throughout the month of October to her Most Pure Heart; as an enduring testimony of the unbounded trust which we put in our most loving Mother, and in order that we may day by day more and more obtain her favorable aid: we will and decree that in the Litany of Loreto, after the invocation, 'Queen conceived without original sin,' shall be added the suffrage, 'Queen of the most Holy Rosary, pray for us.' " Obeying the wishes of our Holy Father, we should with the simplicity of children turn to Our Lady of the Rosary and a more intense Catholic life.

All Catholics have added to the glory of the Queen of Heaven; and from every corner of this earth today has risen the joyous praise of her who is Queen of the Holy Rosary. On earth she was the lowly handmaid of the Lord, and now all generations proclaim the greatness of her name.

Prayer

(1) MARY, MOTHER OF GOD, the joyful mysteries of your Holy Rosary remind me of the mysteries in which the Word was made flesh and you, the inviolate Virgin and Mother, performed your maternal duties with holy joy. You became the Mother of a Son Who is almighty, eternal, and infinite in all perfections, equal to the Father and to the Holy Spirit. You became the Mother of God without ceasing to be a virgin, and your happy fruitfulness only consecrated and increased your purity. By your Divine Motherhood you formed the closest bond of union with the adorable Trinity: the privileged Daughter of the Father, the loving Mother of the Son and the immaculate Spouse of the Holy Spirit. By your Motherhood you acquired a mother's power over your Divine Son, and you saw yourself raised above all the angels and saints.

When the Angel Gabriel came as a messenger from God, it was not only to ask your consent to become the Mother of the Son of God, but also to treat with you of the salvation of the human race, of the birth of the Savior of the world, of the regeneration of mankind and the setting up of an everlasting kingdom. The repetition of the Hail Marys keep before my mind the importance of the Incarnation and your share in it. When you agreed to the proposal made to you by the Angel, you gave Jesus to us by your own free act. Realizing that your consent had been made a necessary condition for the accomplishment of the great mystery of the Incarnation, you made the supreme act of obedience and faith when you said, "Behold the handmaid of the Lord; be it done to me according to thy word." You spoke in behalf of our human nature, and by your consent sealed forever the union between our human nature and the Son of God. Thus, in consenting to the Incarnation, you cooperated directly in the Redemption of the world, for the Incarnation was the first step in the work of our salvation.

MARY, MY MOTHER, may the faithful recitation of the Rosary help me to remember God's love for me in becoming man for my salvation. May it be given me to understand your own love for me, and your dignity and beauty, that I may love you with a love more like the love that God Himself has for you.

(2) MARY, MOTHER OF GOD, *the sorrowful mysteries of your Holy*

Rosary remind me of the sorrows, the agony, and death of the suffering Christ, the price at which the salvation of our race was accomplished. As Mother of God, you became a co-operator in the Redemption of mankind. It was you who nourished and prepared the holy Victim Who was offered to the Eternal Father in expiation of our sins. From you was derived the Precious Blood which was shed upon the cross for our salvation and the adorable Body which, after having been made the price of our Redemption, has become the food of our souls in the Holy Eucharist.

From the moment of His entering the world, your loving Son Jesus was the price of our salvation. He took to Himself our human flesh and became man in order that He might give Himself up for us to the death of the cross. From the very first, He offered Himself as our ransom and the victim for our sins. He did so through your hands when you presented Him in the Temple, and in union with Him you offered yourself to the Father on Calvary.

From the cross Jesus gave you to me to be my Mother, and I was entrusted to your care as your child. You brought me forth spiritually to a new life of grace. This was your spiritual Motherhood. The pangs of this childbirth were the sufferings you felt on Calvary. Your life, like that of your Divine Son, was a daily crucifixion and martyrdom, but on Good Friday that crucifixion reached its climax. The cross is the measure of God's love for us and the sum total of our love for God. Only when I have understood your martyrdom, will I understand the greatness of the love of Jesus for you and the intensity of your love for your Son. It was your exclusive privilege to be Christ's Mother according to the flesh. Not for this reason alone did He love you. Your willingness to suffer and to bear your cross in imitation of His own resignation to the will of God made you especially dear to Him.

MARY, MY MOTHER, may the faithful recitation of my Rosary show my gratitude to Jesus for having redeemed me on the cross and for having given you to me as my spiritual Mother. Make me your faithful child. Teach me to bear my cross patiently in imitation of Jesus and you so that in this way I may prove how much I really love you. Since you have had such an intimate share in my Redemption, I entrust my soul to your loving care. Help me to use the graces God gives me for my sanctification. May the merits of my crucified Savior never be lost on my soul, but rather may they enable me to reach true holiness and the possession of God in His eternal kingdom.

(3) MARY, MOTHER OF GOD, *the glorious mysteries of the Holy Rosary remind me of the glory of your Son, Jesus Christ,* His triumph over death, His Ascension into Heaven, the sending of the Holy Spirit. *These mysteries remind me also of your own glory,* the Assumption of your soul and body into heaven and your crowning there as Queen of Heaven and Earth. Finally, they remind me of the everlasting glory of all the saints in Heaven united with your own glory and that of your Son. And now as Mother of God and Mother of men, and as Queen of Heaven and Earth, you serve as a bond between God and men. As the God-Man, Jesus is the perfect Mediator between God and man, because He alone could in all justice merit our reconciliation with God as well as the graces which God would impart after the reconciliation. *You are a Mediatrix in union with Christ* from Whom your mediation draws all its power. With Christ you have contributed to our redemption; hence you may be called Co-Redemptrix. You consented to be the Mother of the Redeemer at the Annunciation, and thus you were willing to share in the sufferings of the Redeemer. But you merited the title Co-Redemptrix above all by your union with Christ in His redemptive sacrifice. After Jesus, no one suffered as you did. You share so entirely in His Passion that, if it had been possible, you would gladly have borne all the torments your Son bore.

You are a Mediatrix because since your Assumption, with Christ you obtain all graces for men. This is your role of universal Dispenser of all graces. Your action is above all one of intercession. In your contemplation of God, you behold our needs with our prayers, and you beg God to grant these favors to us. You obtain graces for us even without our asking you for them. It is truly the will of God that all graces should come to us through you. Since with Christ you had helped to merit all graces, it is fitting that you also should help to distribute all graces with Him. It affords Jesus the joy of rewarding you who, with Him, suffered so much for men. Who can understand the joy you feel to be able to give happiness to the whole world? This universal distribution of grace enables you to exercise your spiritual motherhood: to make your children live the divine life by obtaining for them sanctifying grace and all their actual graces.

MARY, MY MOTHER, may the faithful recitation of my Rosary be a sign of my gratitude to Jesus and to you for all you have done for me in bringing about my Redemption. May the Rosary also be a means of obtaining all the graces I need for the sanctification and salvation of my soul.

Queen of the Holy Rosary, in times past, when the enemies of the Church sought to break its unity, you came to the aid of your suffering children. To single nations, to private families, to individual persons, you have always provided help, given solace and rekindled hope, especially when they turned to you with Rosary in hand. More than ever before, we have need of your help today. The dangers facing the Church and the world are grave and evil. Those dangers are to be found in the principles and activities of Communism, the present day Anti-Christ, which tries to penetrate every walk of life, every class of society. In this time of crisis there is need that we hasten to you for aid, strength, and direction. With your foot you crushed the head of the serpent and conquered evil with goodness. Crush the evil which strives to destroy all that is Catholic, all that is Christian, all that is civilized. Help us to heed your message of Fátima so that by penance and prayer, especially the Rosary, we may appease the just anger of God and obtain His forgiveness and blessing. We join you, Queen of the Holy Rosary, in praying for peace in the world.

> Mother and Maid, the praise of thee
> The burden of our song shall be;
> Thy joys, thy sorrows, and the crown
> Of thine eternal bright renown:
>
> The Heavenly tidings brought to earth,
> The visitation and the birth,
> Christ offered, Christ restored to thee—
> Hail, in each Joyful Mystery;
>
> The bloody sweat, the soldier's scorn,
> The scourging and the crown of thorn,
> The burdened way, the bitter tree—
> Hail, in each Woeful Mystery;

The risen and heaven-ascending Lord,
The Pentecostal unction poured,
Thy crown and endless jubilee—
Hail, in each Glorious Mystery.

May age to age forever sing
The Virgin's Son and angels' King,
And praise with the celestial host
The Father, Son, and Holy Ghost.
—FATHER AUGUSTINE RICCHINI, 18th century

† † †

O God, Whose only-begotten Son by His life, death, and resurrection obtained for us the rewards of eternal salvation, grant, we beg of You, that meditating upon these mysteries in the most holy Rosary of the Blessed Virgin Mary, we may both imitate what they contain and obtain what they promise. Through Christ Our Lord. Amen.

Maternity of the Blessed Virgin Mary

FEAST, October 11 (NOVENA, October 2–10)

Background:

Among the titles with which faith and love honor the Blessed Virgin Mary, that of "Mother of God" surpasses all others, for in it we find the source and origin of all others. It comprises such praise and glory that no other can be compared with it. The first step toward a recognition of Jesus Christ as Savior of the world is belief in the Divine Maternity; on the other hand, whosoever refuses to acknowledge Mary as true Mother of God has by the very fact given up his faith.

Our Lady appears in the first pages of the Gospel as the Mother of Jesus. With the same right and clarity her maternal office is mentioned in *the earliest Creeds of the Church.* After the New Testament, no form of early Christian literature is more ancient than the primitive Creeds. By these early symbols catechumens, that is, those to be baptized, committed to memory a brief summary of the principal doctrines of Christianity. The teaching Church, under the guidance of its bishops and Supreme Pastor, presented to the believing faithful a summary of theology in a set of articles of belief. The first symbol listed in the old Roman Creed is: "I believe in God the Father Almighty, and in Christ Jesus His only Son, Our Lord, Who was born from the Holy Spirit and the Virgin Mary, Who was crucified under Pontius Pilate . . ." Although our present Apostles' Creed is not earlier than the sixth century, an ancient Roman Creed appears at the end of the second century, and in its essential content comes from the age of the Apostles.

The Nicaean Symbol was called forth by the need to defend the divinity of the Son of God. In defending the divinity of the Second Person of the Blessed Trinity, *the Council of Nicaea* (325) was implicitly protecting Mary's privilege as Mother of God.

Nestorius, Archbishop of Constantinople, denied that Mary was the Mother of God and, by a necessary consequence, denied that there was a personal union of the two natures of God and Man in Jesus Christ. He thus made void the cross of Christ, since it is only this union which imparts an infinite value to the sufferings endured by Christ in His human nature.

Thus the Maternity of Mary involved the whole question of the Incarnation. The zeal of St. Cyril, Patriarch of Alexandria, was aroused in favor of the honor of Mary, and he condemned the teaching of Nestorius. The case was laid before St. Celestine, the Pope, and in a Council held at Rome in 430 he condemned the heresy and excommunicated and deposed Nestorius unless he retracted his error. This Nestorius refused to do. The Pope then summoned a General Council to meet at Ephesus in 431 and appointed St. Cyril to preside in his name. The Council of Ephesus proclaimed: *If anyone should not confess that Emmanuel is truly God, and that in consequence the Blessed Virgin is the Mother of God—for she brought forth according to the flesh the Word of God made flesh—let him be anathema.*

Pope St. Pius X wrote an encyclical letter in 1904 to commemorate the fiftieth anniversary of the definition of the Immaculate Conception, in which he speaks of the Mother of God as a restorer of mankind: "For who has not discovered that there is no surer or easier way to unite all men to Christ and to obtain through Him that perfect adoption of sons, by which we become holy and immaculate in the sight of God, than through Mary? . . . Does this mean that God could not have given us the Restorer of the human race and the Author of our faith except by way of the Virgin? . . . Rather, it means that, since it pleased God in His eternal providence that we should have the God-Man through Mary, who conceived Him by the Holy Spirit and carried Him in her womb, there is nothing left for us but to receive Christ from the hands of Mary. For this reason, so often as prophecy is made in Holy Scripture 'of the grace that will one day come to us,' almost as often the Savior of men is associated with His most holy Mother. . . . If, then, the most Blessed Virgin is at once the Mother of God and the Mother of men, can anyone doubt that she makes every effort that Christ, 'the head of his body, the Church' (Col. 1:18), should infuse into us, His members, the gifts which are His, in order that we may above all come to know Him and to 'live by him' " (1 John 4:9).

The outstanding document of modern times on the divine motherhood is Pius XI's encyclical commemorating the anniversary of Ephesus, *Lux veritatis*, December 25, 1931. In it is explained the central dogma of the Incarnation—that Christ is true God and true man, the divine and human natures existing unconfused in the hypostatic union (the union of the one divine Person with the human nature). The divine Maternity is shown to result from this doctrine. From this truth the Pope derives also the belief that Mary is our spiritual Mother. He concludes by a double gesture to commemorate the anniversary of Ephesus: the restoration of the mosaic in the basilica of St. Mary Major in Rome of the Mother of God, first placed there after the triumph of Ephesus by Pope St. Sixtus III in 432, and the extension to the universal Church of the feast of the Divine Maternity on October 11th.

From all eternity God thought of the Virgin of Nazareth as the future Mother of His Son. At the Annunciation, Mary became the Mother of God. This is her most exalted title, the source of all her other privileges. On Calvary Christ gave His Mother to all men to be their spiritual Mother, so that through her they might come to God as through her He came to them. It is the will of Jesus that you love His Mother. Love her because she is your very own. How can you fail to love her whom Jesus loved so tenderly?

Prayer

(1) MARY, MOTHER OF GOD, I believe that *the most sublime of your privileges is your divine maternity.* Without that maternity, your other privileges would not exist; you yourself would not exist, for you were created only to be the Mother of God.

Your divine maternity is great also because this privilege is the reason for your other privileges—your Immaculate Conception, miraculous virginity, fullness of grace, Assumption, and the spiritual maternity of all mankind. The divine maternity explains everything in you; without this maternity nothing in you can be explained.

I believe the teaching of the Church concerning the union of the human and divine natures in Christ: that Jesus Christ is God and man, perfect God and perfect man, and that this divinity and humanity are united in only one person so that the actions of the divine nature or the human nature are the actions of one person, the divine Person. Since God was born of you, you are the Mother of God. If we could not say that you are the Mother of God for having given a body to the Son of God, then we could neither adore this Body; nor would we have been redeemed by the sacrifice of this Body on the cross; nor would we be united to the divinity in receiving this Body in the Eucharist.

MARY, MY MOTHER, your divine maternity is such a sublime privilege that no creature, not even you yourself, can understand it fully. To understand your dignity as Mother of God in all its fullness, we would have to understand fully the dignity of the Son of God Whose Mother you are. The dignity of the divine maternity raised you above all the rest of creation. As Mother of God you surpass, in an immeasurable degree, all other creatures, angels and men. They are God's servants, but you are His Mother. We have the sublime dignity of being children of God by adoption; Jesus alone is His Son by nature. But you are not the adoptive Mother of the Son of God; you are His real Mother. We can lose our divine adoption, but you can never lose your divine maternity. God might have created a more beautiful world, more perfect men, more marvelous spirits; He could not have made anything more wonderful than a Mother of God.

(2) MARY, MOTHER OF GOD, *your divine maternity places you in a very wonderful relationship with the three divine Persons.* You are the loving *daughter of the* Father, because, before all creatures, you were predestined to be His daughter at the same moment that He decreed the Incarnation of His Son. He bestowed marvelous privileges upon you and loved you more than all other creatures together. As Mother of the Son of God, you are associated with the Father in the generation of His Son. With the Father you, too, can say, "This is my beloved Son in whom I am well pleased."

You are *the Mother of the Son of God.* You fulfill the duties and enjoy the rights of a true mother. From your own flesh and blood you formed the body of your Son. You nourished Him, clothed Him, educated Him. You commanded Him and He obeyed. How can I ever understand the great love that bound your hearts together!

You are the *spouse of the Holy Spirit* because according to the gospel and the teaching of the Apostles' Creed, you conceived of the Holy Spirit the Son of God, made man. You are also called the temple of the Holy Spirit because, in virtue of your Immaculate Conception and your fullness of grace, He dwells within you in a most singular manner.

MARY, MY MOTHER, through your divine maternity you procure for the three divine Persons a new and singular glory. To the *Father* you present, in your Son, an adorer worthy of Him, and adoration and love of infinite value. To the *Son* you give His human nature which allows Him to make full reparation to the honor of His Father outraged by our sins. You permit Him to draw the hearts of men toward Himself and to be the object of our love and confidence. To the *Holy Spirit* you offer the possibility of giving a new existence to the Son and of making this Son live in the hearts of the faithful through the power of His grace.

(3) MARY, MOTHER OF GOD, *your divine maternity is most cher-*

ished by you because it is a token of God's special love for you.
Though a creature, you gave birth to the Creator. He is your child
and you are His Mother. You were chosen as Mother, predestined
before all creatures, filled with all grace, all virtue, all holiness so
that the Son, infinitely pure, Who in Heaven has an immortal and
eternal Father, on earth has a Mother exempt from all sin. As in
Heaven the Divine Word is like the Father, so on earth the Son,
according to the flesh, is like you, His Mother. Jesus is the Son of
God by His marvelous and eternal birth "in the bosom of His
Father." He is Son of man by His birth, in time, in the bosom of a
woman. You are this woman, and you are a virgin. It is from you
alone that Christ took His human nature. You became the Mother
of God and remained a virgin. How God has loved you by making
you His Mother!

The divine maternity permits you to love God with a very singular kind of love and to be loved by Him with an equally singular
love. There is no closer bond of love among relationships than that
which exists between a mother and her son. All your privileges
increased your power to love God. Your Immaculate Conception
permitted you to love God from the first instant of your existence;
your virginity led you to vow an undivided love to Him; your
fullness of grace made you capable of loving Him with the most
intense love possible. No one could ever love God with the love of
a mother. Only you could love God as your Son; only you could
love your Son as God.

MARY, MY MOTHER, during all eternity it will be one of our greatest joys to admire the infinite love of God for you whose Son He
willed to be, just as He is in all truth the Son of the Father. The
divine maternity itself, more than any particular privilege, is a mark
of God's unequaled love for you. I rejoice with you in the happiness
which filled your heart because of such love. I beg you to ask God
that I return His love with some of the generosity and fervor with
which you loved Him.

> O Queen of all the virgin choir
> Enthroned above the starry sky,
> Who with thy bosom's milk didst feed,
> Thy own Creator, Lord most high.

What man had lost in hapless **Eve**,
Thy sacred womb to man restores;
Thou to the wretched here beneath,
Hast opened heaven's eternal doors.

O hail, resplendent Hall of Light!
Hail, Gate sublime of heaven's high **King!**
Through thee redeemed to endless life,
Thy praise let all the nations sing!

O Jesus, born of Virgin bright,
Immortal glory be to Thee!
Praise to the Father infinite,
And Holy Ghost eternally. Amen.

3 years (321)*

† † †

O God, since by the fruitful virginity of the Blessed **Virgin Mary You** gave to mankind the rewards of eternal salvation, grant, **we** beg of **You**, that we may feel her intercession for us, by whom we received the **Author** of Life, Our Lord Jesus Christ, Your Son, Who with **You and the Holy** Spirit lives and reigns forever. Amen.

Purity of the Blessed Virgin Mary

FEAST, October 16 (TRIDUUM, October 13–15)

Background:

One of the extraordinary privileges of the Blessed Virgin Mary consisted not only in being always free from all actual sin and imperfection, so that she never offended God in any way, however slight, and was ever docile to the inspirations of grace, but also, in being, from her very conception, absolutely free from original sin. She was united with God by the closest and tenderest of ties by which man can conceive the creature approaching the Creator—the tie of motherhood. She, whose perfect purity and holiness were necessary in consequence of this union with God, could never possibly have been in sin.

St. Anselm, that renowned servant of Mary and doctor of the Church, has written: "It was fitting that she, in whose bosom the conception of a Man-God was to take place, should be a mother most pure; it was fitting that from then on she should be resplendent with the most complete holiness that can be conceived after that of God. God the Father decided to give her His only Son, the Son who was equal to Him and whom He loved as Himself, to be her Son also."

Before the definition of the dogma of the Immaculate Conception, *Pope Pius IX* dwelt at some length on the reasons that convinced him that the doctrine could be defined as a truth revealed by God. In his argument from Tradition, he stated: "That Fathers and writers of the Church . . . proclaimed in appropriate and in precise terms that where sin is treated no question whatever is to be raised concerning the holy Virgin Mary. For to her an abundance of grace was given to conquer sin completely. They also declared that the most glorious Virgin was the Reparatrix of her parents, Life-Giver to posterity, chosen before the ages, prepared for Himself by the Most High and foretold by God when He said to the serpent: 'I will place enmity between thee and the woman,' who has undoubtedly crushed the poisonous head of the same serpent. Therefore, they affirm that the same Blessed Virgin was through grace perfectly free from every stain of sin and from all contagion of body and soul and mind; that she was always at home with God and united with Him in an eternal covenant; that she

208

was never in darkness, but always in light; that she was, as a result, a perfectly suitable dwelling place for Christ, not because of her bodily endowments, but because of her original grace."

Mary, your Heavenly Mother, was most pure. The slightest taint of original sin never soiled the lily-white purity of her soul. She was untouched by the imperfections that mar even the holiest lives. No thought, word, or deed of hers ever savored of earth, but everything was centered in God.

The purity of Our Blessed Mother should make you bear in mind that your body is the "temple of the Holy Ghost" (1 Cor. 6:19), and that every principle of right reason and religion imposes on you the obligation of keeping it pure and undefiled. St. Paul said, "But if any man violate the temple of God, him shall God destroy. For the temple of God is holy, which you are" (1 Cor. 3:17).

Prayer

(1) MARY, MOTHER OF GOD, *you are the Virgin most pure because you are the Immaculate Conception*. The closer a soul is to God, the farther it is from sin. God is infinite good; sin, horrible evil. No one could have had a closer approach to God than you, for it is impossible for any creature to be closer to God's Son than His own Mother. From eternity, before anything was, you were united to your Son in the mind of God as His most pure Mother. When God decreed the incarnation of the Word, His very own Son, through you alone, you had a place in the same plan as Jesus. Since the conception of the Son of God is all holy, all pure, infinitely removed from every appearance of sin, it was supremely fitting that your conception should be equally far from sin. For that reason you were conceived by your mother, St. Anna, without even the shadow of sin. You are the Virgin most pure.

Because you were to be the Mother of God, original sin, which like all Eve's daughters you should have contracted, could not touch you. Such a stain would have reflected upon your Son, Who is Holiness itself. Then Satan could boast that he had overcome Jesus in you, His Mother. You are pure and sinless. You expressed this to St. Bernadette at Lourdes when you said, "I am the Immaculate Conception."

MARY, MY MOTHER, there is no sin in you; in you there is only God's grace—His light, His splendor, His love, His unspeakable delight. You are truly His beloved Daughter, the only one in whom there was never a stain. With you all is pure, virginal, immaculate. In you there is no inclination to evil—no impure thoughts or desires. You are God's purest and holiest creature, the one chosen to conceive and bear the Son of God. Who would not love you and endeavor to imitate you, O most beautiful and immaculate Mother of God?

(2) MARY, MOTHER OF GOD, *you are the Virgin most pure because you are full of grace.* You are the most beautiful of creatures, the one in whom there is no spot, God's masterpiece. You are full of grace, the Lord's free gift, and it overflows in you, filling your soul with every virtue and perfection. What marvels of grace possessed your soul! Sanctifying grace made you God's adopted child and the lawful heir to His eternal kingdom, putting you in possession of God's goods and of God Himself forever. That grace made you holy and most pleasing in God's eyes, the special object of His love. Sanctifying grace likened you to God as it did no other pure creature. Because you were full of God's grace and a Virgin most pure, Gabriel could exclaim, "You have found grace with God." No one has found or received such grace as you.

But who can describe the matchless purity and beauty of your soul? Jesus is the most beautiful of men; you were His mold, His mirror; and He, yours. Your soul contained all the marvels of God's grace, for which reason the Church calls you the Singular Vessel of Devotion.

MARY, MY MOTHER, you are all beautiful—beautiful in mind, in body, in soul! In you I behold the charm of the purest of virgins, the majesty of the noblest of mothers. You are beautiful at your presentation in the temple; in prayer before Gabriel as he awaited your answer; in Nazareth's hidden life and later as you followed Jesus and listened to Wisdom speak. You were beautiful when you stood as the brave Queen of Martyrs beneath the cross of your dying Son; in the supper room beneath the fiery tongues of the Divine Spirit; beautiful, above all, in the glory in which you reign with Jesus. If a single soul in the state of grace by far excels in beauty all other earthly beauty, what beauty must you possess, Virgin most pure, who surpassed in holiness all other souls in the state of grace!

(3) MARY, MOTHER OF GOD, *you are the Virgin most pure because you are the holiest of God's creatures.* You are the holiest of God's

creatures because you are the Mother of God. The Prophet tells us that God is "wonderful in His saints" (Ps. 67:36). How wonderful, then, He must be in the Mother of the Saint of saints! In you, to an eminent degree, all the privileges of other saints meet. The Church venerates many holy virgins, martyrs, and other saints, but no one of them has merited or obtained your title of Holy Virgin, Virgin most pure. Whatever of sanctity, of dignity, of merit, of grace and of glory that we can imagine, all is in you.

Holiness is a complete separation from creatures and perfect union with God through love. No one ever belonged to Jesus as completely as you, for you are His Mother. Jesus belonged entirely to you, the holiest among women. Your womb was so pure, so immaculate that it became the Holy of Holies, in which Jesus Christ Our Lord, the Eternal High Priest, alone found entrance.

MARY, MY MOTHER, God raised you so high in Himself that He never has created and never will create a holier person more worthy of Himself, of His greatness, His love, than you, O Virgin most pure. Having carried within you Jesus Christ, the Son of God, you share, as no one else does, in your Divine Son's holiness and purity. You come nearest to the holiness of God.

You are the holiest of women, the Virgin-Mother thrice holy, because you are holy of the Father, holy of the Son, holy of the Holy Spirit of Love. Hence with Holy Church I repeat, "You are all fair, Mary, and the stain of original sin is not in you. You are the Glory of Jerusalem; you are the Joy of Israel; you are the Honor of our people."

Sweet Mother of the Lord most high,
To thee we bow in humble prayer,
To thee from evil powers we fly;
O shield and keep us in thy care.

It was to lift our fallen race
Above the curse of Adam's crime,
The King bestowed on thee all grace
And shaped thy motherhood sublime.

So, Mother, unto thee we pray;
Thou seest our need; thy Son entreat
That He, His anger turned away,
May raise our souls in mercy sweet.

† † †

Grant us, we beg You, Almighty and Eternal God, that solemnly venerating the spotless virginity of the most pure Virgin Mary, we may by her intercession obtain purity of mind and body. Through Christ Our Lord. Amen.

Presentation of the Blessed Virgin Mary

FEAST, November 21 (NOVENA, November 12–20)

Background:

For a long time Mary's parents, St. Joachim and St. Anna, were without children. God rewarded their prayers and granted them a daughter late in life. They may have made a vow before her birth to offer her to God. When Mary was three years old, her parents took her to Jerusalem to present her to God in His temple.

This event in Mary's childhood was recorded for the first time by St. Evodius, perhaps one of the seventy disciples of Our Lord, who was Bishop of Antioch preceding St. Ignatius. St. Jerome, St. Gregory of Nyssa, St. Gregory Nazianzen, and other Church authorities who lived when traditions were still very recent, related the same event and held it as true. Two apocryphal gospels also mention the presentation. Apocryphal gospels contain certain passages derived from primitive tradition which may complete what the inspired Gospels relate. Already in the sixth century the event is commemorated in the East. Pope Gregory XI introduced the feast at Avignon and Sixtus V in Rome in 1585 for November 21st.

According to apostolic tradition, the writings of the Fathers, and the opinion of the Church, Mary spent her early years in the temple, that is, from the time of her presentation at the age of three until her espousals to Joseph. Mary's own immaculate Heart was the temple in which the adorable Trinity delighted to dwell. The Father looked upon her as His beloved Daughter; the Son, as the one chosen to become His Mother; the Holy Spirit, as His Immaculate Bride. The time had come when Mary felt that she could not give herself entirely to God except by the practice of virginity. Divine grace enlightened her that it was the Will of God that she make a vow of chastity, even though this was unknown among the Jews.

Under the patronage of your Heavenly Mother consecrate your whole life to God and serve Him in your state of life with the devotedness and earnestness with which Mary served Him.

Prayer

(1) MARY, MOTHER OF GOD, tradition tells us that *when you were three years of age, your parents, Joachim and Anna, took you to the temple in Jerusalem to fulfill their vow.* The holy couple offered you to God by the ministry of the priest in charge, who invoked the blessing of God upon you and your parents. How fervently your mother and father thanked God for having given you to them and begged Him to accept the offering which they were making! They then left a small offering of silver required by the Law of Moses.

What a beautiful example for parents to imitate! Their children also belong to God, for they are His gift. Teach parents to care for their children as God's sacred trust, to guard them from sin and to lead them in the way of virtue. May they consider it to be the greatest privilege bestowed upon them by God to dedicate their sons and daughters to His holy service. Help them to become worthy of this blessing through their own prayers and good example.

MARY, MY MOTHER, your first presentation to God, made by the hands of your parents, was an offering most acceptable in His sight. Let my consecration of myself to God be made under your patronage and assisted by your intercession and in union with your merits.

(2) MARY, MOTHER OF GOD, *already in your childhood you dedicated yourself to the love and service of God.* Led by divine inspiration to His house, you prepared yourself for your sublime dignity of Divine Motherhood in silence and solitude with God. Though the designs of God were unknown to you, you, nevertheless, detached your heart from the world in order to give all your love to God.

I can picture you alone with your God, following with devotion the life led in common by the virgins of God's house. You were trained there with other girls, under the care of holy women, and with deepest reverence you assisted at the sacred functions. But the true sanctuary in which you dwelt with God was not the palace of worship at Jerusalem but the immaculate temple of your heart.

You may have remained in the temple till the age of twelve. When you later returned to your home, you were under the loving care of your mother, St. Anna. With her you loved to sing the psalms and canticles of the inspired authors of your nation. From Anna you heard the touching story of the chosen people. You learned to read the sacred books by yourself and tried to penetrate their hidden meaning. You often discussed the coming of the Messias, since you knew He would be of your race and family.

I cannot even imagine the heavenly beauty that adorned your innocent soul as you were being prepared by the Eternal Father to be the Mother of His Divine Son and the Spouse of the Holy Spirit. The wisdom and power of God was constructing a living temple for the Savior of the world.

MARY, MY MOTHER, you were laying the foundation of that hidden life in which, by the practice of the highest virtues, you were to reach that sublime degree of holiness to which you were predestined as Mother of the Son of God and Mother of all the souls for whom He was to die. Attentive to the voice of the Holy Spirit, you diligently gathered up all His lessons, preserving them in your soul with zealous care.

(3) MARY, MOTHER OF GOD, *may the perfect gift of yourself to God through love in your presentation in the temple be an inspiration to me.* You loved God with your whole heart and mind and strength. Obtain for me the grace to love God with my whole *heart*—so that all the love my heart is capable of may be consecrated to Him, and all other affection subordinated to the love I owe God.

Help me to love God with my whole *soul*—so that all the faculties of my soul may be consecrated to Him, and that I may make use of them only to make Him known, loved, and served.

Help me to love God with my whole *mind*—so that my mind may be habitually occupied with God and that I may value His good pleasure above everything else—above my convenience, above all earthly treasures, above all knowledge and friendship, above health and life.

Help me to love God with my whole *strength*—so that I may consecrate undividedly, unreservedly, and continually to His service, my life, my health, and all I am and have.

MARY, MY MOTHER, pray that the love of God above all things and detachment from the world and its false pleasures may also make my soul the temple of the living God. After your example, I desire to be known to God and unknown to men, to possess God and to be forgotten by creatures. May God dwell in me and may I live to Him alone through frequent Holy Communion and still more frequent prayer so that God may direct my whole life—my thoughts, words, and actions—to His greater honor and glory.

> O stainless Mother of the Lord,
> While we your glory chant,
> A gracious ear to us accord
> And heavenly favor grant.

> A sad inheritance we own—
> In guilt our lives begin;
> Exempt from Adam's fall alone,
> You never knew a sin.

> Prone on the earth beneath your heel
> The serpent's head remained;
> Alone you do to heaven reveal
> An origin unstained.

> Your matchless glory takes away
> The shame of Mother Eve;
> Accept the tribute that we pay,
> And all our wants relieve.

> From Satan's every dart and snare
> Our weakened souls defend,
> That so your glory we may share,
> In joys that never end.

> To You, O Jesus, glory meet,
> The Virgin Mary's Son;
> To Father and to Paraclete
> Be equal honor done. Amen.

† † †

O God, Who willed that the Blessed Virgin Mary, herself the dwelling place of the Holy Spirit, should this day be presented in the temple, grant, we beg of You, that through her intercession we may be found worthy to be presented in the temple of Your glory. Through Christ Our Lord. Amen.

Mary, Mother of Divine Providence

FEAST, Saturday before the 3rd Sunday of November
(**TRIDUUM**, Wednesday before the 3rd Sunday of November)

Background:

The Blessed Virgin Mary bears a tender love for all mankind, even for the most wretched sinners. Like the best and most loyal of mothers, Mary took the whole posterity of Adam under her protective mantle and cares for all most faithfully. In fact, she cares so much about us that as our enemy, the devil, goes about seeking whom he may devour, Mary looks for those whom she may aid unto salvation. She cannot help loving those who love her, and she does not fail to serve those who serve her. Should they be sinners, she employs all her power of intercession to obtain pardon for them from her Divine Son.

As our great Provider, Mary offers the prayers of her servants to God. As the Son intercedes with the eternal Father, even so Mary intercedes with the Son. She does not cease pleading for our salvation, and for the favors we ask of her, until she is heard. Yet she always seeks God's Will in all things and provides for us whatever is most conducive to the glory of God and the salvation of our souls. As she is the most powerful with God of all the saints in heaven, so she is the most desirous of our welfare. After Jesus Christ, there is no one who has so much care for us and for our salvation.

Through her motherly prayers Mary can influence the designs of Divine Providence in your regard. When Jesus entrusted you to the care of His Mother, He gave her to you to be your very own. She proves her motherly love for you by providing for your spiritual and temporal needs. Appeal to your Mother of Divine Providence, for she both understands your needs and is most willing to help you.

Prayer

(1) MARY, MOTHER OF GOD, *the miracle of the marriage feast of Cana shows that you are the Mother of Divine Providence.* For the first time in the public life of Jesus you appeared in the exalted

character of our Advocate, a character which would be yours as long
as time would last. Filled with motherly compassion, you appealed
to Jesus in behalf of your friends. With greatest confidence in the
mercy and kindness of your Son, you left Him free to give assistance
or withhold it, as He saw fit.

Jesus rewarded your confidence and resignation by working His
first miracle at your request. He wanted the strengthening of the
faith of His disciples and the manifestation of His Divinity to depend upon your prayers. In this I see God's plan that in the Kingdom of Jesus all graces should go through your hands and Heart.
As your prayer brought about His birth as the Sun of Justice, so
also your request decided His rise and shining in His public life.

MARY, MY MOTHER, how kindly you provided for the needs of
this newly married couple! This is but a reminder that you are
equally interested in providing for all your children in all their
needs of soul and body. Teach me to seek all things through your
prayers, for your intercession is most powerful, and Jesus can refuse
you nothing. Help me to imitate your zeal in assisting my neighbor
in his needs.

(2) MARY, MOTHER OF GOD, *as the Mother of Divine Providence
you provide for us in our varied needs through your prayers in the
presence of God.* Your own extraordinary grace and merit, your
own wondrous privileges give to your prayer an irresistible force and
power. As the loving Mother of Jesus, the glorious Daughter of the
Father, the cherished Bride of the Holy Spirit, you can never meet
with a refusal. Your slightest wish carries with it a powerful appeal.
Yet more powerfully still than even your exalted merits does the
Precious Blood render God merciful to the sinner, for all comes to
us through the Passion and death of Christ, your Son.

But it has been the will of God that from first to last, Jesus, as
the Victim of atonement for our sins, should be presented to Him
by you. It was so when you gave your consent to the divine plan of
the Redemption. It was so when you renewed your consent at the
birth of the Savior at Bethlehem, at His presentation in the temple
at Jerusalem, and finally at the foot of the cross on Calvary.

And now in Heaven, when the fruits of the Redemption are
applied to our souls, and the graces won for us by the Passion of
Jesus are distributed to the redeemed, being united to Him by a
close and unbreakable bond, you still continue your part as Media-

trix in the work of our salvation, by offering to the Father the merits of Christ, uniting meanwhile your prayers, and, in a secondary sense, your merits, to the intercession of your Divine Son.

MARY, MY MOTHER, as Mother of Divine Providence, remember your children in need of God's mercy and help. Plead for us in the presence of God and provide for us those graces and blessings especially which will enable us to serve God better and save our souls.

(3) MARY, MOTHER OF GOD, *in the Kingdom of Heaven you are continually employed in deeds of kindness and mercy; therefore, you are truly the Mother of Divine Providence.* You are ever imploring favors for the just, as well as for sinners. Your eyes are the eyes of a good Mother, ever watchful to notice the need of your children, just as you looked out for the young couple at the marriage feast of Cana. Your Son will deny you nothing. God destined you to be a Mother of Mercy, a Refuge of Sinners and an Advocate of the Afflicted, and you fulfill these offices perfectly. You are so tender and compassionate, so watchful to relieve the needy, that it would seem you had no other desire, no other concern except this.

If you showed such compassion for the sufferings of others while on earth, and were so ready to relieve them, how much greater must your compassion be now that you are in heaven and understand so much better the difficulties your children meet with and the sufferings that afflict them? Though you are raised to the high dignity of Queen of Heaven, you have not forgotten man's wretched condition. You show your compassion toward all so that there is no one in this world who does not, if he seeks it, share in the kindness and mercy of your motherly Heart. You have become all things to all men; you have opened your Heart to all that all may receive of your generosity: the imprisoned, freedom; the sick, health; the afflicted, consolation; the sinner, pardon; and God, glory.

MARY, MY MOTHER, your power as Mother of Divine Providence is indeed as great as your compassion and willingness to help. As you are powerful to obtain and provide, you are merciful to pardon. You can as readily obtain for us whatever you will as you can listen to our woes. Then, through your compassion be pleased to send down to us, your poor servants, a rich abundance of your graces and blessing. Provide for our needs of soul and of body. May your title of Mother of Divine Providence ever give us confidence that

you will never fail us, but will provide for all we need in this present
life that we may attain eternal life.

> Advocate of exiled pilgrims,
> Ever calling on your name,
> Mother Mary, Mother Mary!
> Never do we call in vain.

> In my need and hour of darkness,
> I, too, seek your radiant smile;
> Be my tower of strength, O Mary,
> In my God-sent weary trial.

> All but crushed beneath the burden,
> Onward I must struggle still;
> Mother Mary, come to help me—
> You once knew a cross-crowned hill.

> All through life I see you, Mother,
> In all danger, need and fear;
> But above all help me, Mother,
> When my death is drawing near.

† † †

O God, since You never fail us in Your Providence, we humbly beg You,
through the intercession of the Blessed Virgin Mary, the Mother of Your
Son, to remove all evils from us and provide us with that which will profit
our souls. Through the same Christ Our Lord. Amen.

Our Lady of the Miraculous Medal

FEAST, November 27 (TRIDUUM, November 24–26)

Background:

Catherine Laboure was born in France on May 2, 1806, the ninth of eleven children. She joined the Daughters of Charity founded by St. Vincent de Paul. On July 18, 1830, the Blessed Virgin appeared to this humble novice at night in the novitiate chapel of the Motherhouse of the Daughters of Charity in Paris.

Late in the afternoon of November 27, 1830, the Blessed Virgin again appeared to Catherine and on this occasion unfolded the lofty mission to be entrusted to her. Catherine herself has recorded this vision. "As I was absorbed in contemplating the Blessed Virgin, she lowered her eyes to me and said: 'The globe which you see' (I understood her to mean the one she had beneath her feet) 'represents the world and every single person.' And then she added: 'The rays are the symbols of the graces I shed on those who ask me for them.' Then an oval frame was formed about the Blessed Virgin, on which these words were stamped in letters of gold: 'O Mary, conceived without sin, pray for us who have recourse to thee.'

"The inscription was arranged in a semi-circle, beginning from her right hand, and passing over the head, finished at the height of her left hand. Then a voice was heard which said to me: 'Have a medal struck according to this model; those who wear it after being blessed, shall receive great graces, especially if they wear it around their neck. Graces will be abundant for those who have confidence!' At that instant the picture seemed to turn around, and on the reverse, one saw the letter *M* surmounted by a cross, with a big line at the base, and underneath the letter *M* were the Hearts of Jesus and Mary; the first encircled by a crown of thorns; the other transpierced by a sword."

Catherine told her pious director of this vision. Severe though he might be with his penitent, he did not desire to do anything contrary to the wishes of the Blessed Virgin. And yet, he was still undecided when, the following month, Catherine returned to him. She had experienced another vision which was practically the same as that of the preceding month. The Blessed Virgin said, "My daughter, you will not see me any longer, but you shall hear my voice in your meditations."

It was to be a matter of two years before the Miraculous Medal, so called because of the many spiritual and temporal favors it brought, was struck. In June, 1832, her director, Father Aladel, showed Sister Catherine, who by this time had passed from the Novitiate and was stationed at the Hospice at Enghien, a sample of the Medal. She was delighted and grateful, as she said, "Now it must be spread abroad." Her tone was almost commanding.

And so it happened. While Sister Catherine was going about her simple tasks at the Hospice, the Miraculous Medal was being spread abroad by thousands of people.

With the spread of devotion to the Miraculous Medal came great and unusual happenings, proofs of the power of the Blessed Virgin's intercession, which she had promised in a special way to those who devoutly wore the Medal. Alphonse Ratisbonne, a Jew, was converted on January 20, 1842, when he entered a chapel at Rome and beheld the Blessed Virgin exactly as she was represented on his Miraculous Medal.

Immediately after the Feast of the Immaculate Conception in 1876, Sister Catherine had to take to bed. On December 31st she received the last Sacraments and late in the afternoon fell into a gentle sleep from which she awoke in the life of eternity. For forty-six years she had remained at the hospice and for the greater part of that time had cared for the old men who were kept there.

Sister Catherine Labouré was beatified on May 28, 1933, and canonized on July 27, 1947. The ecclesiastical authorities, after two years of rigid investigation, declared the apparitions to be fact and not fiction, and allowed the Medal of the Immaculate Conception to be struck and to be used by the faithful. Marvels of grace and health, peace and prosperity followed in its wake so that before long the people were calling it the "Miraculous" Medal. Largely because of the Medal, the dogma of the Immaculate Conception was defined by Holy Church twenty-four years later. And four years after that, Our Lady appeared at Lourdes as though to confirm the now infallible doctrine of her glorious privilege.

It is not strange that God works miracles through a Medal. He uses water to cleanse the soul of original sin in Baptism and oil to confer His graces in Confirmation and Extreme Unction. Similarly, He uses a Medal, not indeed as a sacrament, but as an instrument, in bringing to pass certain marvelous results. We wear the Medal upon our breasts as a sign to Mary that we need her aid, and Mary has promised to recognize that sign always, for she said, "Persons who wear it indulgenced will receive great graces."

Prayer

(1) MARY, MOTHER OF GOD, *how deeply significant are the symbols of your Miraculous Medal!* The *joyful* side of the Medal shows

you in the glory of your Immaculate Conception. You stand upon the globe, as the Mother and Queen of all mankind. Your feet crush the serpent, to proclaim that Satan and all his associates are helpless before you. From your outstretched hands pour "the graces which you shed on all those who ask for them." Etched about the rim is the invocation you yourself have composed: "O Mary, conceived without sin, pray for us who have recourse to thee."

MARY, MY MOTHER, we are all tainted with original sin when we enter this world; you alone are the exception. Because of your future Divine Motherhood, God preserved you from original sin, and your life was wholly free from every taint of personal sin. The Angel expressed this very clearly: "Full of grace"—there was no room left for sin; "The Lord is with thee"—where God dwells, Satan can have no rights; "Blessed art thou among women"—you were elevated above all other women. Your Son was God and was without sin by nature. You were without sin by grace. You were sinless because God, your Creator, chose to make you so; at the moment of your conception He could say, "Thou art all fair, my beloved, and there is no spot in thee."

(2) MARY, MOTHER OF GOD, the reverse side of your Miraculous Medal is the *sorrowful* side. It bears *your own Heart as well as that of your Son*—His crowned with thorns and yours pierced by a sword. These symbols recall to my mind the union which exists between you and your Son both in suffering and in love. The Heart of Jesus is the model of all sanctity, the source of all grace. Your Heart is the faithful mirror of the divine perfections, the channel through which grace is poured out upon the world. The Heart of Jesus will save us; but we must go to the Heart of Jesus through your Immaculate Heart.

The *cross* placed between these two Hearts signifies that the same love consumes the Heart of the Son and that of His Mother and that the same sacrifice immolates them. Jesus saved the world by His Cross, and you cooperated in the Redemption of the human race by consenting to the death of Jesus and by offering to His heavenly Father the life of your well beloved Son, over which you had rights. The Sacred Heart of Jesus, opened on Calvary, is the inexhaustible fountain of all graces; but the reservoir which receives them, the channel which communicates them to men, is your Immaculate Heart, pierced by the sword of sorrow at the foot of the Cross.

MARY, MY MOTHER, from all eternity before time began, you were intimately united with the Word of God in the plan of Redemption, which, in the designs of Providence, your Son was to accomplish. With the Redeemer you were to be the co-Redemptrix; with your Son, the Mother; with the Author of grace, the Mediatrix of all graces. In adoring this marvelous plan, I thank the mercy of God for uniting your Heart with that of your Son inseparably for time and eternity.

(3) MARY, MOTHER OF GOD, there are no words on the reverse side of your Miraculous Medal because, as you said to Sister Catherine, "*the* M *and the two hearts* express enough." Indeed, they tell us that you are not only Queen and Intercessor, but also Mother of Sorrows and Mother of our Redeemer; you are ever by the side of your sorrowing children, as you were by the side of your Son. For the love of men His Heart wears a crown of thorns; for the love of men yours is pierced with a sword. Beneath the cross we find the letter *M*, because to the end you stood beneath the cross of Christ.

The *twelve stars* refer to the Apostles, the first messengers of salvation, or to the stars in the vision of St. John, in which "a great sign appeared in Heaven, a woman clothed with the sun, and the moon under her feet, and on her head a crown of twelve stars." It is your part to bring your children through the sorrows of earth to the bliss of heaven, where in your crown they will shine like stars for all eternity.

MARY, MY MOTHER, may devotion to your Miraculous Medal be spread throughout the world so that more souls may feel the power of your intercession. Through that medal work marvels of grace and conversion, peace and health for mankind. May that medal inspire me to ever greater love for you, Immaculate Virgin, and to greater generosity in bearing the sufferings of life and the toils of working for God in my state of life in union with the Heart of Jesus and your own most pure Heart, till I, too, have the privilege of seeing the "great sign in Heaven, a woman clothed with the sun, and the moon under her feet, and on her head a crown of twelve stars."

> Guide thou o'er life's dark ocean
> My bark with gentle care.
> Still thou the wild commotion,
> O Mother, hear my prayer.
> When billows rise around me,

Let not their rage confound me,
Immaculate Conception,
O pray, remember me!

Bless all that lie forsaken
In storm and frost and rain.
The souls by grief o'ertaken,
The orphan's weary pain.
When ev'ry joy has vanished,
When hope itself seems banished,
Immaculate Conception,
O pray, remember me!

I beg for true contentment,
For holiness and peace.
O banish all resentment,
And let all anger cease.
Till heart and soul united,
I sing to thee delighted,
Immaculate Conception,
O pray, remember me!

Lord Jesus Christ, Who wanted the Most Blessed Virgin Mary, Your Mother, sinless from the first moment of her conception, to be glorified by countless miracles, grant that we, who never cease imploring her patronage, may obtain eternal happiness. Who live and reign forever. Amen.

Part II

OUR LADY'S TITLES

Meditations on the Litany of Loreto
for each Saturday of the year

The first *Marian litanies* must have been composed to foster private devotion, as it is not at all probable that they were written for use in public by reason of their drawn-out and heavy style. A number of such litanies began to appear in the twelfth century. But once the custom grew up of reciting Marian litanies privately, and of gradually shortening the text, it was not long until the idea occurred of using them for public devotion, especially in cases of public calamities, as had been the practice of the Church with the litanies of the saints.

Despite the fact that, from the seventeenth century onward, *the Litany of Loreto* has been the subject of many ascetical writings, there is a lack of documentary evidence concerning its origin and development into the form under which we know it. The Loreto text had the good fortune to be adopted in the famous shrine of the Holy House of Loreto, the actual house in which Our Lady dwelt and where Our Lord spent the years of His childhood. (See Feast: Transferring of the Holy House, page 12.) Thus the Loreto text became known to the many pilgrims who flocked there during the sixteenth century and was brought home to the various countries of Christendom. The earliest printed copy of the Litany of Loreto so far known is that of Dillingen, which is undated and which seems to belong to the end of 1557. It was probably published and circulated in Germany by St. Peter Canisius. The Loreto text was introduced elsewhere, and even reached Rome, when Sixtus V, who had entertained a singular devotion for Loreto, by the Bull *"Reddituri"* of July 11, 1587, gave formal approval to it, as to the litany of the Holy Name of Jesus, and recommended preachers everywhere to propagate its use among the faithful.

The various titles of the litany are an expression of heart-felt love and admiration of the faithful for the Blessed Virgin and touch on the virtues that make her so pleasing to God and lovable to her children. These invocations to Our Lady are, therefore, a fruitful source of meditation, which, in turn, encourages imitation. The first part of the Litany celebrates the personal perfections of the Blessed Virgin. The second part unfolds her relations to the Church, Militant, Suffering, and Triumphant.

Hail to thee, Mary, full of grace!
The Lord is with thee! In thy place
Beside the King of kings I see
Thee lifted up in majesty
Yet clothed in sweet humility.

Mirror of Justice! Morning Star!
Tower of Ivory! Afar
We know thy beauty, veiled and dim,
Blurred by the clouds of seraphim
Mounting, in splendor, up to Him

Whom thou didst bear a little Child
Who stretched His arms to us, and smiled.
Queen of Angels! Mystical Rose!
O Gate of Heaven never close
Before our prayers that seek repose

In thee! O Mother Undefiled
Who knelt beside that little Child
Laid in a manger filled with hay—
Incline, as then, to Him and pray
For us in Paradise to-day!

Vessel of Honor! House of Gold!
Refuge of sinners manifold!
As we respond "Thy will be done"
In adoration of thy Son,
O Mother, gently, one by one,

Wilt thou present our hearts to Him
In view of saint and seraphim?
Lo! The angelic hosts prostrate
Before the Throne thy words await
Blind with the glory of thy state!

O Flower of our fallen race
Remember us before God's face!
Scatter our prayers like petals where
We pass into His presence there
Along the angel-guarded stair!

                         —MARY DIXON THAYER

1. Holy Mary

Consideration:

Mary is holy because She is the Mother of God's own Son, Who is holiness itself. God prepared her for this sublime dignity. She was conceived without sin, full of grace, the model of all virtues.

Our first and most important task in life is to become holy, as Jesus said, "You therefore are to be perfect, even as your heavenly Father is perfect" (Matt. 5:48). And St. Paul says, "For this is the will of God, your sanctification" (1 Thess. 4:3). Let Mary be your guide and helper that you may reach the degree of holiness God has destined for you in your state of life.

Mary's name means *Mistress,* because, being the Mother of God, authority has been given to her over all the adopted children of God and she wants us to be holy; and *Star of the Sea,* because on this perilous journey across the sea of life we must look up to Mary, the Star of the Sea, ever shining in peaceful radiance, untouched by the fury of the storms, ever pointing to heaven and its eternal peace, that we may not lose our course, become discouraged, and perish in the waves.

Prayer

(1) MARY, your name means *Lady.* As Mother of God you have the highest power in heaven and on earth after God. The Ruler of the whole world is your Son. He raised you above every creature. I pledge my loyalty to you as my Lady and Queen. Let me ever serve you as your faithful subject and devoted child.

Your name means *Star of the Sea.* As the star sheds light without any loss to itself, so as the purest of virgins you brought forth your Son without the loss of your virginity. The sailor looks up to the stars for guidance. Be my Guiding Star in life that I may avoid the dangers of sin, and reach the port of eternity safely in the grace of God.

Your name means *Sea.* Your whole life upon earth was like a sea of bitterness. What sadness must have filled your soul at the prophecy of Simeon in the temple when he said, "Thy own soul a sword shall pierce"! What pain you felt at the flight into Egypt, at the loss of your Son, and at the sight of the Savior mistreated, condemned to death and crucified! But you descended to the depths of sorrow when the lifeless body of Jesus was laid in your arms. You were plunged into a sea of sorrow. Help me to be patient in bearing the sufferings of my life, and ever resigned to God's will, for He knows what is best for me, and He loves me with an infinite love.

(2) MARY, your name is so *lovely* that the angels rejoice when they hear it, and so *sweet* that your children never tire of speaking it. Your name gives consolation to the sick, comfort to the discouraged, strength to the tempted, peace to the dying, and joy to all. After the name of Jesus, no name shall be dearer to me than yours.

Mary, let me bear your lovely and sweet name within my heart and invoke it many times each day, especially in time of temptation and need. May your holy name be a pledge of eternal life for me.

(3) MARY, after the name of Jesus there is no other name so *powerful* to help me and to obtain for me the many graces which I need. In dangers, difficulties, and doubts, let me invoke your name, for then I shall not despair. When you support me, I cannot fall.

Mary, I confide in the power of your name that I may obtain all the graces I need to avoid sin, practice virtue, and save my soul. May your sweet name and that of your Son Jesus be the last words my lips shall speak. O clement, O loving, O sweet Virgin Mary!

Grant, we beg You, Almighty God, that Your people who rejoice in the name and in the protection of the most holy Virgin Mary, may by her intercession be delivered from all evil here on earth, and be found worthy to attain to everlasting joys in heaven. Through Christ Our Lord. Amen. (*Feast of the Holy Name of Mary,* September 12)

Aspiration:

Mary!

300 days (292)*

2. Holy Mother of God

Consideration:

Mary is the Mother of God because *Jesus, the Son of God, assumed human nature in her and was born of her.* Since Jesus is true God, His holy Mother must be the Mother of God.

And since there is but one God, Mary must, in virtue of her Divine Motherhood, enter into a *special relationship with each of the three divine Persons.* She shares the right to call the eternal Father's Son her very own Son. Having given life to the incarnate Word of God, she is associated with Him in His mission of the redemption and sanctification of the world. She is the immaculate Bride of the Holy Spirit because by the overshadowing of His love and by His divine power she conceived and became the Mother of Jesus.

Wonderful acts of God's mercy and love were made possible through the Divine Motherhood and the Incarnation. The heavenly Father could demand obedience and worship from His Son; the Son could work and suffer and offer Himself as a victim for the glory of the Father and the salvation of the world, and the Holy Spirit could sanctify souls by means of the merits of Christ.

Show your gratitude to God by loving the Mother He has prepared for Himself and whom He has given to you that you, too, might call her your own.

Prayer

(1) MARY, you are the Mother of God because *you are the Mother of Jesus Christ, the true Son of God.* You could not be the Mother of His Divine Nature, which has existed before all time and from all eternity, but you brought forth Jesus after He had assumed human nature in you.

The archangel Gabriel recognized this dignity of Divine Motherhood when he said, "The Holy Spirit shall come upon thee and the

power of the Most High shall overshadow thee; and therefore the
Holy One to be born of thee shall be called the Son of God"
(Luke 1:35). And Elizabeth exclaimed, "And how have I deserved
that the Mother of my Lord should come to me?" (Luke 1:43)

Since God was pleased to choose you as His Mother because of
your humility, help me to be truly humble of heart that, like you,
I may be pleasing to God and may deserve to be exalted in heaven.
Banish all pride and vanity from my heart, and let me ever seek
the glory of God in all things.

(2) MARY, to understand *how great you really are as Mother of
God*, I would have to understand the greatness of God Himself. Your
dignity surpasses that of all the saints, for they are only God's servants, while you are His Mother. No angel or saint could ever say
to Jesus, "You are my Son." Your dignity on that account is nearly
infinite, since you are so closely united with the infinite Good.
God could not create a greater Mother than His own. Conscious
of this dignity, you exclaimed, "Henceforth all generations shall
call me blessed" (Luke 1:48).

Sweet Mother of God, I admire your dignity, which was the
greatest ever bestowed upon a human being. Each day of my life
I wish to thank God for the graces and privileges He has bestowed
upon you to make you what you are.

(3) MARY, because you are the Mother of God, *I can pray to you
with full confidence.* Jesus would hardly refuse you any request
that was in keeping with God's will, for if He grants the requests
of the saints, who are only His servants, how can He refuse His own
Mother whom He loves so tenderly? I am sure Jesus is pleased to
have you ask Him for anything, since He wants to be generous to
us for your sake. Is not this in some measure a reward for the
human nature you have given Him?

Mother of God, since God was pleased to choose you as His
Mother, and since He was very generous to you in making you
worthy of this dignity, I confidently hope that He will be generous
to me if you pray for me. I entrust my salvation to your care. Never
let me fail to invoke your intercession in all my needs, for Jesus
will refuse you nothing because we both can call you "Mother."

O God, You willed that Your Word should take flesh in the womb of
the Blessed Virgin Mary at the message of an angel; grant us, Your humble

servants, that we who truly believe her to be the Mother of God may be
helped by her intercession with You. Through the same Christ Our Lord.
Amen. *(Feast of the Annunciation,* March 25)

    Aspiration:

      O Mary, Virgin Mother of God, pray to Jesus for me.

300 days (305)*

3. Holy Virgin of Virgins

Consideration:

Mary is the Virgin of virgins, because she has been chosen to be the *virginal Mother of the Savior,* as Isaias had foretold. "Behold a virgin shall conceive and bear a Son, and His name shall be called Emmanuel" (Isa. 7:14).

Virginal motherhood is *Mary's exclusive privilege*—she alone glories in the joys of motherhood together with the honor of virginity. It was not fitting that Jesus should have a father on earth and enter the world by the way in which original sin is transmitted. The virginal birth of Jesus is a pattern of the spiritual regeneration of men as children of God, as St. John says, "Who were born not of blood, nor of the will of the flesh, nor of the will of men, but of God" (John 1:13).

The Virgin of virgins has become *the inspiration of all those men and women who choose a virginal life* in order to serve God and thereby become the spiritual fathers and mothers of souls. God needs them in His Church, and their number will increase the more Mary is loved and venerated.

Prayer

(1) MARY, you are the Virgin of virgins because *you stand at the head of the long train of Christian virgins.* Though motherhood was far more respected than virginity among the Jews, you resolved to live and die a virgin. God inspired your marriage to Joseph, who respected and defended your virginity. And when you were asked by the archangel Gabriel whether you would accept the dignity of becoming the Mother of God, you were assured that by the power of the Holy Spirit you would become a Mother without sacrificing the purity which you have vowed to God.

Virgin of virgins, teach me to love and strive for virginal purity in my state of life, for there is no virtue more beautiful and more pleasing to God. Help me to preserve at least the chastity of my vocation in life.

(2) MARY, *you are the purest of all virgins,* as the sun surpasses the stars in splendor. Holy Scripture compares you to a lily: "As the lily among thorns, so is my love among the daughters" (Canticles 2:2). Being without the stain of original sin, you were free from all evil desires and inclinations, an angel in human flesh. Your beauty awakened a love for chastity in all who saw you.

Virgin of virgins, I entrust the purity of my soul and body to your care. Keep me from entertaining any unchaste thought, or performing any unchaste deed. Shield me from offending God by my eyes or ears or tongue. And when the demon of impurity troubles me with his vile temptations, let me fervently beg your protection and help.

(3) MARY, *you have a special love for virginal souls.* To be like you, countless virgins in every age and country, rank and condition of life, have consecrated to God the purest affections of their hearts, and have found in their detachment from earthly pleasures the most pure and enduring happiness. You watch over them with zealous care because you consider them spouses of your Divine Son.

Virgin of virgins, I hope to obtain from you the grace to overcome every temptation, and to preserve holy purity all the days of my life, that I may be numbered among your special friends. May I belong to that chaste generation of which the Scriptures speak: "O how beautiful is the chaste generation with glory: for the memory thereof is immortal: because it is known both with God and with men" (Wisdom 4:1).

Grant us, we beg You, Almighty and Eternal God, that, solemnly venerating the spotless virginity of the most pure Virgin Mary, we may by her intercession obtain purity of mind and body. Through Christ Our Lord. Amen. (*Feast of the Purity of the Blessed Virgin Mary,* October 16)

Aspiration:

Virgin before your delivery, pray for us. Hail Mary, etc.

Virgin in your delivery, pray for us. Hail Mary.

Virgin after your delivery, pray for us. Hail Mary.

300 days (295)*

4. Mother of Christ

Consideration:

The word Christ means "the Anointed One." In the Old Testament prophets, kings, and priests were anointed. Since Jesus is the teacher, king, and priest, sent by God, He is eminently the Christ.

Jesus is *the Teacher* Who alone could say, "I am the Way, and the Truth, and the Life" (John 14:6). He is the teacher of truth, and He promises, "If you abide in my word, you shall be my disciples indeed, and you shall know the truth, and the truth shall make you free" (John 8:31).

Jesus is *King*. He said to Pilate, "I am a king. This is why I was born, and why I have come into the world, to bear witness to the truth. Everyone who is of the truth hears my voice" (John 18:37).

Jesus is *the High Priest and Victim* of the sacrifice of our salvation on the cross, and continues to act as Priest in the unbloody sacrifice of the Mass. We, too, share in His priesthood for we must offer ourselves with Him in His sacrifice. The worship of God calls for sacrifice.

The Mother of Christ will help us to be obedient and humble disciples of Christ the Teacher, loyal followers of Christ the King, generous lovers of sacrifice in the spirit of Christ the Priest and Victim.

Prayer

(1) MARY, *you are the Mother of Christ, our Prophet.* The Jews themselves acknowledged Him as such: "This is indeed the Prophet who is to come into the world" (John 6:14). He appeared as the Teacher of truth to enlighten those who were sitting in the darkness and the shadow of death. He imparted the most necessary instruction concerning God and their duties to Him, to themselves, and to their fellow men. Through the Catholic Church He still shows mankind the way and gives them the means by which they can arrive at true holiness and salvation.

Mother of Christ, help me to realize that the privilege of being a Catholic is the greatest grace God could have given me. Help me to show my appreciation by living up to the teaching of the true Church so that I may save my soul.

(2) MARY, *you are the Mother of Christ, our King.* He Himself said to Pilate: "Thou sayest it, I am a king" (John 18:37). But His kingdom is not of this world; it is a spiritual one which extends to all men through faith and grace. His Church in which He rules will exist to the end of time, and the gates of hell shall never prevail against her, because she is the pillar and the ground of truth. The Church Militant on earth will be transformed into the Church Triumphant in heaven, and Christ, your Son, will reign forever.

Mother of Christ, teach me to be subject to Christ, my King. As a citizen of His spiritual kingdom, let me never set my heart upon the world and its deceitful pleasures and goods, but help me to seek with all my heart the "kingdom of God and His justice" in my soul, that at my death I may be admitted into His heavenly kingdom.

(3) MARY, *you are the Mother of Christ our High Priest.* He has offered Himself as a sacrifice to His heavenly Father upon the altar of the cross. In order to apply the fruits of His bloody sacrifice to the people of all times, He offers Himself daily in the Mass in an unbloody manner by the hands of priests. His Sacrifice and priesthood are infinitely exalted above the sacrifices and priesthood of the Old Law and will last till the end of time. As the Mother of the Eternal High Priest you are full of mercy toward sinners and ever intent upon making them partake of the fruit of the sacrificial blood of your priestly Son for the salvation of their souls.

Mother of Christ, I appeal to your mercy, and I beg you to plead my cause with your Divine Son. Let me share in the fruits of His sacrifice of the cross through the Mass. May His mercy reach all poor sinners. Through the merits of Jesus and through your intercession may we all be be truly penitent and save our souls.

Mother of Christ, the Eternal High Priest, you offered Jesus to the Heavenly Father during His sacrifice on the cross, and now you stand before God as our Mediatrix uniting your prayer with that of Your Son, our Divine Mediator. You are truly our hope!

O God, by the fruitful virginity of the Blessed Virgin Mary, You gave to mankind the rewards of eternal salvation, grant, we beg of You, that we may feel her intercession for us, by whom we received the Author of Life, Our Lord Jesus Christ, Your Son. Who with You and the Holy Spirit lives and reigns forever. Amen. (*Feast of the Maternity,* October 11)

Aspiration:

O Mary, Mother of God and Mother of mercy, pray for us and for all who have died in the embrace of the Lord.

300 days (294)

5. Mother of Divine Grace

Consideration:

Mary is the Mother of Divine Grace because no soul was so richly endowed with the grace of God as hers. *Whatever she is and has is a gift of divine grace:* her Immaculate Conception, her Divine Motherhood, her fullness of grace, her growth in holiness.

Mary is *the Co-redemptrix and Mediatrix of all Graces.* Jesus merited graces by His life, sufferings, and death. He now desires that these graces reach men and bear fruit in their souls. Through Mary Our Lord distributes the graces we need for our salvation and sanctification.

Imitate the Mother of Divine Grace by faithfully cooperating with the graces God offers you just as she did. Go to the Mediatrix of All Graces to obtain the graces you need to become holy and to save your soul.

Prayer

(1) MARY, you are the Mother of Divine Grace because *God bestowed upon you the fullness of His graces even before your birth.* Having destined you to be the Mother of His Son, He adorned you with privileges corresponding to that dignity. If John the Baptist was sanctified before his birth, how much more were you to be sanctified and filled with graces before your birth, since you were destined to be not only the forerunner of Jesus, but His Mother!

Because of your intimate union with Jesus as His Mother, and because of His tender love for you, the measure of grace which God gave you in the first instant of your life was greater than that which He imparted to the angels and saints, who were only His servants. In order to merit this fullness of grace for you, Jesus shed His Precious Blood.

(2) MARY, *you continually increased in grace as long as you were*

241

on earth. You did so in a far greater measure than all the saints of God. Not defiled by original sin, and hence free of evil inclinations, you had no obstacle to overcome in the way of sanctity. There was no self-love or love of the world in your Immaculate Heart; you gave all your love to God and dedicated yourself entirely to Him. This love urged you to do whatever you knew was pleasing to God. Since every good work is rewarded by an increase of grace, who can tell how great was the number of graces which you acquired in your lifetime?

Mother of Divine Grace, help me to treasure sanctifying grace more than all the goods of the world because it enables me to possess God Himself by divine love; it makes me His child and an heir to His kingdom. Let me rather die than lose this grace by a willful mortal sin. If this should ever happen to me, help me to recover at once, by sincere contrition and penitence, the grace I have lost. And since every good work is meritorious in the sight of God, and increases sanctifying grace if done for the love of God, aid me in being zealous in doing good.

(3) MARY, *you have conceived and brought forth Jesus Christ,* "in whom are hidden all the treasures of wisdom and knowledge," and "in whom dwells all the fulness of the Godhead bodily" (Col. 2:3, 9). You alone obtained the grace which was given to no other creature; namely, to be filled with God Himself, the Author of grace. Every saint has received graces to help save a certain number of souls, but you have received such a fullness of graces that, as Mediatrix of All Graces you were to co-operate in the salvation of the whole world.

Mother of Divine Grace, I have great confidence in you because God has made you the Mediatrix of All Graces and Mother of Grace for the benefit of your children. Do not refuse my request when I ask you to help me to grow in the love of God to such an extent that I may reach that degree of holiness which God has destined for me.

O God, You gave the human race the grace of forgiveness through the virginal motherhood of the Blessed Virgin Mary; grant that we who call her the Mother of Grace on earth, may enjoy her happy presence forever in heaven. Through Christ Our Lord. Amen. (*Feast of the Virgin Mother of Grace,* June 9)

Aspiration:

    O Mary, Mother of grace and Mother of mercy, protect us from our enemy, and receive us at the hour of our death.

300 days (307)*

FEBRUARY—Second Saturday

6. Mother Most Pure

Consideration:

"Most pure" refers to the innermost fountain of Mary's interior life; her life is pure at the source. She was not only preserved from original sin, but also *free from every imperfection*.

Mary is *most pure in relation to her motherhood*. She accepted her Divine Son from God, raised Him for the purpose of God's service, and offered Him on the cross as a sacrifice with all her mother's love and mother's rights.

She is *the beautiful model of all Christian mothers*. The primary purpose of marriage is the begetting of children. Every child is a most precious gift of God, to be gratefully accepted and brought up in the fear and love of God, so as to be ready to serve God according to His holy Will. Christian mothers should learn from Mary to appreciate the glory and accept generously the responsibility of Christian motherhood.

Prayer

(1) MARY, you are the Mother most pure because *you were perfectly free* from every stain of sin. The words of the Holy Spirit are to be applied to you: "Thou art all fair, O my love, and there is not a spot in thee" (Canticles 4:7). Even the greatest saints in the very instant of conception are tainted with original sin. You alone are an exception; you were conceived and born without original sin.

How could you, who were to crush the serpent's head, have been under the slavery of the devil even for a moment? As the chosen Daughter of the Father, the most holy Mother of the Son, and the immaculate Spouse of the Holy Spirit, you could never have been under the curse of sin. Your dignity as Mother of God demanded such a privilege. It was fitting that the God of all purity should

244

spring from the greatest purity. God was able to grant such a privilege, and He did. And for this I praise you as Mother most pure.

(2) MARY, *you were also preserved from all actual sin and imperfection,* so that you never offended God even by the most trifling
offense. On your deathbed you were as pure as when you were conceived and born. Because God has destined you to be the Mother of
His Son, He gave you extraordinary graces with the help of which
it was possible for you to preserve your soul from even the shadow
of sin. You were ever obedient to the inspirations of grace, and you
never had the least inclination to sin. You detested sin as the greatest
of all evils.

Mother Most Pure, be always my model of purity. Strengthen
me against mortal sin, and help me to use the graces God gives me
to overcome it. Aid me in shunning even willful venial sin and
everything that may lead to it.

(3) MARY, *you had no inclination to whatever was useless or
dangerous to your virtue.* Your heart, being filled with the love of
God, had no room in it for anything that was not God or did not
lead to God. You were so pure that not even a natural imperfection
cast the least shadow upon your soul. Your nature, which had remained untouched by original sin, was completely under the con-
trol of the spirit, and the spirit was subject to the Will of God in all
things. You were the perfect model of sanctity because everything
in your life was well regulated, everything in beautiful harmony.

Mother Most Pure, detach my heart from the perishable goods
of this world, that I may not risk losing the eternal joys of heaven.
May I hereafter have the happiness of beholding your glory in
heaven, since God has promised His kingdom to those who are pure
of heart: "Blessed are the pure of heart, for they shall see God"
(Matt. 5:8).

Almighty and eternal God, Who in the Heart of the Blessed Virgin Mary
prepared a worthy dwelling for the Holy Spirit, mercifully grant that,
devoutly celebrating the feast day of this most pure Heart, we may be
enabled to live according to Your own Heart. Through Christ Our Lord.
Amen. (*Feast of the Immaculate Heart of Mary,* August 22)
  Aspiration:
    Blessed be Jesus Christ and His most pure Mother!

                                              300 days (80)

7. Mother Most Chaste

Consideration:

"Most chaste" can refer to all the consequences of the purity of the innermost source of Mary's life. *Everything in her thoughts, words, and acts was perfectly chaste.*

Chastity is contained in purity. It is the virtue which controls and submits the sexual appetite to the dictates of reason and faith. Conjugal chastity keeps the married mindful of the fact that they have consecrated their bodies to a most sacred purpose: to cooperate with God in the propagation of the human race. In the unmarried chastity excludes all voluntary expression of the sexual appetite for sexual pleasure.

Though free from all evil inclinations and living a virginal life, *Mary practiced all those things which ensure the practice of chastity:* remembrance of the presence of God, fervent prayer, self-sacrifice, modesty, avoidance of the occasion of sin, true love of neighbor.

Purity is Mary's favorite virtue. If you sincerely cultivate Mary's friendship, you will be pure. To be her true child, you must love the things she loves and hate the things she hates. She hates nothing more than sin, for she has crushed the head of the infernal serpent. Call upon her especially in time of temptation. With her help you will triumph over the evil spirit who tempts you. She will give you the necessary help to achieve the ideal to which she inspires you.

Prayer

(1) MARY, you are the Mother Most Chaste because *there has never been a saint who loved chastity as you did.* When the angel appeared and called you blessed among women, you were frightened. His message of the Divine Motherhood confused you because you ardently longed only for the happiness of virginity. Filled with wonder, you replied, "How shall this happen, since I do not know man?" Not for one moment did you think of accepting an honor which you must purchase at the sacrifice of your virginity, till the

246

angel made known to you how you could become a Mother without ceasing to be a virgin. "The Holy Spirit shall come upon thee and the power of the Most High shall overshadow thee; and therefore the Holy One to be born shall be called the Son of God" (Luke 1:35). How highly you esteemed virginal chastity, preferring it even to the dignity of being the Mother of God!

(2) MARY, *you were most careful to preserve chastity.* Knowing well that this tender virtue could fade in worldly soil, you withdrew into solitude as much as you could. You were kneeling in prayer when the angel came with his message. While other virgins enter the state of matrimony to become mothers, you were married to Joseph in order the more securely to remain a virgin. You placed yourself under his protection that you might avert the dangers which might threaten your virginity from the outside world.

Though you were free from all evil desires of the flesh and had no fear of temptation, yet you watched over all your thoughts and every emotion of your heart with the greatest care. Living upon earth like an angel in the flesh, you must have been continually occupied in loving God with all your heart.

(3) MARY, *you love chaste souls as your dearest children.* You take them under your special protection and are most happy to assist them with your prayers. You rejoiced when you received the innocent John as your son, and you were a protection and a model to him as long as you lived upon earth.

You show your love and goodness to all, yet your loving heart reaches out with special tenderness to youths, because they are most in need of your motherly care in their struggle to preserve holy purity, which is tried most in that stage of their lives.

Mother Most Chaste, keep my body pure and my soul holy. Let me imitate your example by avoiding bad company and every occasion of sin that may endanger holy purity. I wish to recommend myself daily to your intercession, especially when temptation strikes. With your help I shall be victorious. Make me pure that I may serve God more faithfully in my state of life, die more peacefully, and attain the glory prepared for the virgins in heaven "who follow the Lamb wherever He goes."

O Lord, we beg You to grant us the grace of true humility through the intercession of the Blessed Virgin Mary, Mother of God. At the same time take from our hearts the desires of the flesh and the eyes, so that, living wisely, justly, and piously, we may obtain eternal rewards. Through Christ Our Lord. Amen. *(Feast of the Humility of Mary,* July 17)

Aspiration:

> O Mary, you entered the world without stain; obtain for me from God, that I may leave it without sin.

300 days (355)

8. Mother Inviolate

Consideration:

By "inviolate" we mean that *the shrine of Mary's soul has never been broken into by that Enemy of Mankind,* who forces himself into our personal sanctuary. Mary's soul has never been violated; it remains forever unsullied without any trace of sin; no flaw nor weakening due to past forgiven sins survives.

Inviolate virginal motherhood is Mary's exclusive privilege. She became the Mother of God and yet remained a virgin. As a virgin she conceived, and as a virgin she brought forth the Son of God. She remained an inviolate virgin after the birth of her Son. Hers were the joys of motherhood and the honor of virginity.

Mary invites you to *Christian heroism.* To remain pure is a big task; it calls for the best that is in you. Alone—without the grace of God—you cannot accomplish this task; with His grace and the help of Our Lady, you are all-powerful. You obtain the grace of God especially through the Sacraments, prayer, and self-denial.

Prayer

(1) MARY, you are the Mother Inviolate because *your virginal purity was not in the least tainted by the conception of your Divine Son,* but you remained a pure, inviolate virgin as before. The prophet Isaias foretold this great miracle of God: "Behold, the virgin shall be with child, and shall bring forth a son; and they shall call his name Emmanuel (God with us) ."

You conceived as a virgin. It was your peculiar privilege to possess both the joys of motherhood and the honor of virginity, as the Gospel relates: "Do not be afraid, Joseph, son of David, to take to thee Mary thy wife, for that which is begotten in her is of the Holy Spirit" (Matt. 1:20).

(2) MARY, *you preserved your virginity also in the birth of*

249

Jesus. As a virgin you conceived, and as a virgin you brought forth the Son of God. As the rays of the sun penetrate glass and yet do not break or injure it in any way, so Jesus, the Sun of Justice, was born of you without violating your virginity.

Mother Inviolate, teach me to cherish holy purity as the most precious treasure of my heart, as you did. Make me modest and retired. Help me to avoid every indecent thought, word, and action. Let me never forget that the more chastely I live, the more quietly I shall die, and the greater will be my confidence when I appear before my Eternal Judge.

(3) MARY, *you remained a pure, inviolate virgin after the birth of the Son of God.* You would have given up the dignity of Divine Motherhood had it been impossible for you to remain a virgin. How chaste was Joseph, who, after you had brought forth the Son of God, lived in perfect continence out of reverence for you and through love for virginal purity!

Mother Inviolate, I cannot practice chastity in my state of life without the aid of God's grace. Help me to pray often, especially in temptation, for God gives His grace to those who ask Him. But, above all, aid me in receiving Holy Communion frequently, which is the most important means I have of preserving holy purity, because there I am united most intimately with your loving Son, Who is a Lover of pure souls.

May all our hope of assistance, O Lord, ever rest upon the loving kindness of Your only-begotten Son! May He, Jesus Christ, Our Lord, Who when born of the Virgin did not detract from the virginity of His Mother but made it sacred, cleanse us of our sins on this solemn feast day of her Nativity, and make our prayers pleasing in Your sight. Through Christ Our Lord. Amen. *(Feast of the Nativity of the Blessed Virgin Mary,* September 8)

Aspiration:

In your Conception, O Virgin Mary, you were immaculate; pray for us to the Father Whose Son Jesus, after He was conceived by the Holy Ghost, you brought forth into the world.

300 days (353)

9. Mother Undefiled

Consideration:

Mary is a Mother undefiled because in her motherhood she did not experience the sad effects of original sin. She conceived the Son of God without sacrificing her virginity, and she brought Him forth without the pains of childbirth.

Mary was never subject to those infirmities of body and soul with which the human race is afflicted: darkness of the mind, weakness of the will, evil inclinations and desires, the rebellion of the flesh against the spirit. By reason of her Immaculate Conception she was free from original sin and from its effects, so that supported by grace her mind was clear, her will strong to do God's Will, her inclinations centered on God alone in complete liberty of spirit.

Mary was *undefiled even in death.* She died of sheer longing for Jesus and of tremendous love for God. Her body knew no corruption either. It was united with her soul shortly after death and was taken to heaven glorified, spiritual, and immortal.

Undefiled in glory as Heaven's Queen and Queen of Mankind, she is the glory of our race, the admiration of the angels, the Advocate of mankind and the giver of the graces merited by her Divine Son. Through her all-powerful intercession you are assured of the help you need to reach God's kingdom and to be glorified with Him eternally.

Prayer

(1) MARY, you are the Mother Undefiled because *in your motherhood you did not experience the sad effects of original sin.* Having conceived of the Holy Spirit, you were exempt from the sufferings of other mothers. You were favored above all women in that you conceived the Son of God without sacrificing your virginity, and brought Him forth without the pains of childbirth.

(2) MARY, *you were not subject to those infirmities of body and*

251

soul with which the whole human race is burdened. As a result of
original sin our understanding is darkened, our will weakened.
Being free from original sin and from its effects, your understanding was clear, your judgment sound, and your knowledge such as
our first parents possessed before their fall. Your will enjoyed the
most complete liberty; no evil desire ever arose in your heart. Supported by grace, you could easily observe the holy law of God, since
you had no interior struggles.

Even external temptations did not afflict you, because in your
nature there was no inclination which the devil and the world could
make use of in order to lead you to evil. You were not subject even
to the weaknesses of the body in so far as they are an effect of original sin. You suffered, but your suffering was not the result of
bodily weakness.

Mother Undefiled, help me to conduct myself as becomes a Christian and live chastely. Though I am weak and very much inclined
to evil, let me not be discouraged, for God will give me the grace
I need, and I know you will help me. Never allow me to be the
slave of wicked passions and low desires. I am sincerely resolved
to abandon my sins, to carry my cross patiently for the love of God
and in atonement for my sins, and to devote the remainder of my
life in serving God in imitation of you.

(3) MARY, *you were the Mother Undefiled also in death.* You
died, but not because of sickness or old age. It was your longing
for Jesus and your ardent love for Him which caused your soul to
escape from your body without the pain or agony of death. Your
death was as calm and peaceful as if you were falling asleep.

Nor did your body see corruption either. A short time after your
burial it rose from the grave, united itself with your soul, and
entered heaven glorified, spiritual, and immortal. There with body
and soul united, you are enthroned as the Queen of Heaven in a
glory and majesty greater than that of the angels and saints.

Mother Undefiled, I give myself to you, and through you to
Jesus. While I have time, I will work for His glory and yours.
Through your powerful prayers may I receive from Him a glorious
crown and see You both in the glory of God's kingdom.

Lord Jesus Christ, You Who wanted the Most Blessed Virgin Mary, Your
Mother, sinless from the first moment of her conception, to be glorified by

countless miracles, grant that we, who never cease imploring her patronage, may obtain eternal happiness. Who live and reign forever. Amen. *(Feast of Our Lady of the Miraculous Medal*, November 27)

Aspiration:

Our Lady of Lourdes, pray for us.

300 days (296)

10. Mother Most Amiable

Consideration:

To be "amiable" means to be deserving of love. God is infinitely amiable; people are amiable in the degree that they share in the perfections of God. Mary is the Mother most amiable because *more than any other created being she possesses the virtue of her Divine Son.*

Spiritual beauty is higher than any natural perfection of feature and grace of body. There is nothing so beautiful and so powerful as virtuous loveliness, and a person possessing it is most amiable. Riches, high position, physical beauty—none of these attracts as do beauty of soul and sinlessness.

In Mary there is the purest reflection of the beauty of God, a beauty ever ancient and ever new. *If you really love Mary you will try to be like her.* Her virtues will make you amiable. If you are like Mary you are like Jesus, because no one ever resembled Him more than His own Mother. Love of Mary is the best preparation for heaven, for you cannot love Jesus without also loving His Mother.

Prayer

(1) MARY, *you are the Mother Most Amiable in the eyes of God.* You are a source of never ending joy to Him, and the object of His most tender love. God *the Father* loves you more than all His other creatures, for you are more than His child—you are the Mother of His only-begotten Son.

You also enjoy the most tender love of the *Son of God,* the Divine Word, for He elevated you alone of all women in the world to the dignity of Divine Motherhood. As the God-Man He showed His love for you in being subject to you for thirty years, in performing His first miracle at your request, and in remembering you with tender pity on the cross when He said to the beloved Apostle John, "Son, behold thy mother."

(2) MARY, *the Holy Spirit gives you all His love,* for you are the Masterpiece of His power. For love of you He worked a miracle

at your conception which preserved you from the stain of original sin and infused into your soul the fullness of grace in the first instant of your existence. He enlightened the Prophets concerning you many centuries before your birth, and bade them announce to the nations of the earth the happiness which would be given to the world through you. After your birth He watched over you with great care in order to preserve you from even the least sin. He worked wonders for you by overshadowing you with the power of His Godhead, and accomplished in your virginal womb the Incarnation of the Son of God. No creature in heaven or on earth was ever loved so much by the Blessed Trinity.

Mother Most Amiable, God loved you so much because you loved Him above all things. Help me to love God above all things all the days of my life, just as you did. Help me to guard against sin and to observe the commandments, for Jesus said, "He who has my commandments and keeps them, he it is who loves me" (John 14:21). Let me prove my love for God by frequent Communion and prayer—the most effective means of strengthening and preserving the love of God in my heart.

(3) MARY, *you are the Mother Most Amiable also to men.* You love us all more than our own mothers can, for you have cherished us all in your heart ever since the day your dying Son entrusted us to your care. Your heart is full of love and mercy toward us, and is always ready to do us good. In fact, you never feel happier than when you find an opportunity of doing us a favor.

On account of your holiness you are so amiable that after God there is nothing on earth that can be compared to you. What the sun is among the stars, you are among the angels and saints. You are a Lady of surpassing mildness, love, and goodness. And since you are most gracious to all, all hearts turn to you in devoted affection.

Mother Most Amiable, obtain for me the grace to cherish a tender love for you, for I can do nothing better than to imitate God in His love for you; and I certainly cannot love you more than He does. Be to me a Mother Most Amiable in life and in death, but above all for all eternity in heaven.

O Lord God, we beg You to forgive the sins of Your servants, that we who are unable to please You by our own deeds may be saved by the intercession of the Mother of Your Son, Our Lord. Who lives and reigns with You forever. Amen. *(Feast of the Assumption,* August 15)

Aspiration:

O Mary, may your children persevere in loving you!

300 days (317)

11. Mother Most Admirable

Consideration:

"Admirable" means, strictly, "to be wondered at." *Mary provokes our wonder;* even our awe. God the Father chose her to be the Mother of His Son. God the Son also chose her for His own Mother and merited for her all the graces that were needed to make her worthy of this highest of all dignities. God the Holy Spirit formed the human nature of the Word of God in her and out of her, and also formed her into the most perfect image of her Son.

How wonderful is the sanctity with which God has adorned her soul! Through grace God took possession of her, adorned her soul with the highest spiritual beauty, made her His holy temple. He gave her a fullness of all the divine and moral virtues as well as of His seven Gifts. All this magnificent adornment, all these natural and supernatural privileges and riches make Mary truly a creature to be wondered at with a kind of reverence and awe.

Even natural motherhood is something admirable and mysterious; infinitely more *admirable is Mary's motherhood,* since her Son is also the Son of God, and she became His Mother without human father. Her motherhood is a priestly motherhood. Jesus is the Priest and Victim of the sacrifice of the New Law by which our redemption was accomplished. Mary joined Him in the offering of His sacrifice on Calvary, but also in every Holy Mass, with all her mother's love and all her mother's rights.

All these blessings bestowed upon Mary were meant not only to make her worthy of being God's Mother, but also our own. She is a Mother Most Admirable for us!

Prayer

(1) MARY, you are the Mother Most Admirable because *God the Father has done great things for you.* From all eternity He chose you to be the Mother of His Son. He spoke of you to our first

parents immediately after the fall, when He cursed the serpent: "I
will put enmities between thee and the woman, and thy seed
and her seed; she shall crush thy head, and thou shalt lie in wait
for her heel" (Gen. 3:15). God announced you four thousand
years before your birth, and pointed to you as the one who, through
your Son, would destroy the power of the devil.

How admirable also was your entrance into this world! In order
to give a worthy Mother to His Son, it was His Will that the law
of nature, according to which the descendants of Adam are all
conceived in sin, should have no effect upon you, and that you
should remain perfectly free from the stain of original sin. You were
holy and full of grace in the very first moment of your life.

The great miracle of the Incarnation was wrought when the
heavenly Father sent the archangel Gabriel to greet you: "Hail,
full of grace, the Lord is with thee. Blessed art thou among
women" (Luke 1:28). Another miracle took place when you
entered the house of your cousin Elizabeth. Enlightened by the
Holy Spirit she recognized you as the Mother of her Lord; and the
infant leaped for joy in her womb.

(2) MARY, *God the Son has done great things for you*. The
Second Person of the most Holy Trinity, the Divine Word, chose
you for His own Mother and merited for you all the graces that
were necessary to make you worthy of the highest dignity ever bestowed upon a creature. Though a mortal being, you brought
forth Him Who is immortal and eternal; though a creature you
are the Mother of your Creator. What greater miracle could be
worked than that of a God confining Himself within the womb of
a virgin?

And how wonderfully is all this done! You become the Mother
of God without ceasing to be a virgin: a Mother because you conceived and brought forth the Son of God, and a virgin because at
the conception and birth of the Son of God you preserved your virginal purity as inviolate as if you had never conceived.

(3) MARY, *God the Holy Spirit has done great things for you*.
As "the Finger of God's right hand," He has formed in you and out
of you the human nature of the eternal Word, and also formed
you into the most perfect image of your Son. Through grace He
took possession of you, adorned you with spiritual beauty, made
you His holy temple, and by His indwelling prepared you to be a

worthy sanctuary for the Son of God. You were in possession of the highest fullness of all the divine and moral virtues as well as of His seven Gifts. All this wonderful adornment, all your natural and supernatural privileges and riches, were the gifts of the Holy Spirit to you, His Immaculate Spouse.

God glorified you by miracles not only in your life, but also after your death. Never has there been a century in which numberless miracles have not been worked. At Lourdes and Fátima and at many other shrines you obtained sight for the blind, hearing for the deaf, speech for the dumb, the use of their limbs for the lame, and help for the afflicted.

Mother Most Admirable, I thank God the Father, the Son, and the Holy Spirit for all the wonderful things They have done for you, which make you a Mother Most Admirable to all your children. Teach me to have recourse to you in every need. The miracles which you worked for others you will work for me because you love me as your child just as you loved your other children for whom you have done wonderful things. If, however, I should not receive what I ask, I know I shall not have invoked you in vain; you will surely obtain for me something of far more benefit to my soul. My most earnest petition is that you make my soul pleasing to God, as yours always was, that I may deserve to admire you in heaven eternally as I have always admired you on earth.

Moved by the pleading of the Blessed Virgin Mary, in answer to whose prayers Jesus Christ, Your Son, wrought the first of His miracles, give us the grace, O Lord God, to prepare a clean heart for the Sacrament of the Body and Blood of Your Son, so as to deserve to sit down to the everlasting banquet of eternity. Through the same Christ Our Lord. Amen. (*Feast of Our Lady of the Miraculous Medal,* November 27)

Aspiration:

Draw us after you, holy Mother.

300 days (313)

12. Mother of Good Counsel

Consideration:

When we say that a man "takes counsel with himself," we mean that he ponders, deliberates, chooses, and determines what he shall do in a particular situation that confronts him. Counsel is very closely allied to prudence. *Counsel directs our particular acts.* When a child comes to his mother for advice, he usually wants to know what he is to do, here and now. No concern of the child is unimportant to her, if it is important to him. She gives him what good counsel she can. And that is the reason why Mary, our Mother, is not only the Seat of Wisdom but also the Mother of Good Counsel.

At Cana the Mother of Good Counsel turned to the servants and said to them, "Do whatever he tells you." The servants followed her advice. On Christ's command they filled the water pots with water, and the water, by His power, turned to wine. In these few words of Our Lady we have the summary of her advice to us as our Mother of Good Counsel: *Do whatever God asks of you,* when He asks it of you, and how He asks it of you. He has given you duties by the very state in life in which He has placed you; He commands certain acts and forbids others by the voice of conscience which He has given you.

But in spite of good intentions and good will, it is often difficult to know exactly what you should do. God's plan for you is not always clear to your mind. That is why Christ gave you on Calvary His own Mother as a Mother of Good Counsel, to whom you can pray and from whom you can ask for counsel and advice. Reflecting on the fact that Mary is filled with the grace of the Holy Spirit and enlightened by His wisdom, St. Bernard wrote, "If you doubt, remember Mary, pray to Mary. If you remember her, you will make no mistake."

Prayer

(1) MARY, *your title, "Mother of Good Counsel," touchingly appeals to every child of Adam.* As a result of original sin, we have

been deprived of that heavenly grace which would ever have enlightened our minds in Paradise. In its stead our minds dwell in darkness. Left to myself, I am feeble in mind, unreliable in judgment, inconstant in decision, and often in danger of taking a false step that would lead me away from God. The road to heaven is not only difficult, but at times dark and dangerous. I need an unfailing guide to direct me along that narrow path. God's sweet Providence has given you to me to be my heavenly guide. The Church impresses upon me this truth when she proclaims you the "Mother of Good Counsel."

When I am called upon to make an important decision which will influence the course of my life, may I seek your guidance. When I want to follow rashly my natural inclinations, instead of seeking light and guidance, may I turn to you who are ever ready to direct me. In all matters of everyday life, which are important to my own welfare and that of others, let me seek your wise counsel.

Mother of Good Counsel, you are my guide on my journey to eternity. I am like a wayfarer in a small vessel on a stormy sea. Be the star that will safely guide me onward until I arrive at the haven of eternal peace.

(2) MARY, *your power and goodness encourage me to put absolute confidence in you.* Your *power* consists in your never failing intercession with God, Who will not turn a deaf ear to you whom He honors and loves above all creatures. You gave Jesus His very flesh, that human nature which made it possible for Him to acquire merit. You co-operated with Him in the work of Redemption by your acts and sufferings. It is most fitting that you should have a share in the distribution of the fruits of Redemption. Jesus will never refuse your request.

Your *goodness* is that of a mother who has for us, the members of Christ, the same love you bear your own Son. Your love is measured by the price of your sacrifice. As our spiritual mother you brought us forth in pain and labor during the anguish of Calvary.

Mother of Good Counsel, give me firm confidence in you in spite of my sins, for you are also the Mother of Mercy, whose concern is not justice, but compassion, kindness, and sympathy. May my confidence in you be complete and extend to all the graces I need for conversion, for spiritual growth, for final perseverance, amid dangers, trials, and difficulties.

(3) MARY, *I give myself entirely to you and through you to God.*
In this way I shall imitate God, Who gives Himself and His Son to
us through you. I give you my *mind* by holding you in deepest
reverence, my *will* by placing an absolute confidence in you, my
heart by offering you the gift of a tender and childlike love, my
whole being by copying as far as possible all your virtues.

You are the living picture of your Son and, therefore, an example
of all virtues. To resemble you is to resemble Jesus. Help me to
strive to imitate you in my own life by performing each of my
actions through you, with you, and in you. I wish to do all things
through you by asking through your intercession all the graces I
need to save my soul. I wish to perform my actions with you as a
model and helper. May I ask myself often what you would do were
you in my place and humbly beg you to help me to do God's Will.
I wish to perform my actions in you, in entire dependence upon
you, taking your point of view, entering into your plans, doing all
things as you did them, for God's honor and glory.

Mother of Good Counsel, I beg you to be my guide in all the
problems of my life. Be my counselor when I am not sure of the
way to take. If my undertakings are in your hands, I am assured of
success, and I shall rest with an easy and joyous mind under your
protection.

O God, Who gave her who bore Your beloved Son to be our Mother and
glorified her fair image by a wondrous apparition, grant, we beg of You,
that by always following her counsels we may be able to live after Your own
Heart and arrive happily in our heavenly fatherland. Through the same
Christ Our Lord. Amen. (*Feast of Our Lady of Good Counsel,* April 26)
    Aspiration:
        My Mother, my hope!

                                                      300 days (302)

13. Mother of Our Creator

Consideration:

Mary is the Mother of our Creator because *she is the Mother of the Son of God, Who is also our Creator.* Since the three Divine Persons are only one God, they possess the same power, the same will, the same goodness.

There are *two creations.* The *first was the creation of man,* through sanctifying grace. Through sin man lost the life of sanctifying grace which raised to the supernatural order; he could destroy but not remake it.

The second creation took place when the Son of God came down to earth to create the world anew and to make it more wonderful than it was in the beginning. In this creation God associated with Himself a Mother, so that a woman might share in the restoration of mankind since a woman had cooperated in its ruin. Mary is that Woman. She assisted in meriting in union with her Divine Son by sharing in the mysteries of His life; she now distributes the graces by which we are born again in baptism and live a new life for God. This second creation cannot be destroyed for the whole human race, though it can be destroyed through sin in the individual. May the Mother of the Creator preserve us from this greatest tragedy—mortal sin!

Prayer

(1) MARY, you are the Mother of our Creator because *you are the Mother of the Son of God, Who is also our Creator.* Of you and in you He assumed human nature. Since the three Divine Persons are only one God, They possess the same power, the same wisdom, the same goodness, the same will. St. John tells us that the Divine Word co-operated in the work of creation: "All things were made through him [the Word], and without him was made nothing that has been made" (John 1:3). Your Creator dwelt in your womb and was born of you, His creature. You can say with truth, "He who created me rested in my tabernacle" (Ecclus. 24:12).

All the works of God—the earth, the heavens, the angels—though great and glorious, are indeed very small compared with Him who created them all. How then can I understand your greatness and dignity as the Mother of this Creator? Your dignity is so great that although God should create a thousand worlds more beautiful than the one we inhabit, He could never create a greater Mother, because your dignity as Mother depends upon the dignity of your Son. None but God can fully understand the perfection of His own nature, and none but God can estimate your greatness as Mother of the Creator.

(2) MARY, *your Son is also our Creator in the spiritual sense,* for He created a new human race. As a result of sin, mankind, groping hopelessly in the black night of ignorance, had lost almost all knowledge of God and His revelation, and the grace of becoming pleasing to God. Your Son came upon earth to free men from this miserable state—to enlighten them as to what they should do to become good and be saved. He raised them up from their spiritual death to the life of grace, blotting out their guilt, justifying and sanctifying them; He conquered even death itself. This new creation is accomplished in holy Baptism and is continued in the other Sacraments, which receive their power to impart grace from the merits of your Son.

Mother of Our Creator, teach me to admire the power, wisdom, and goodness of my Creator, and to adore Him. Since He has created all things for my benefit, help me to show myself grateful to Him and to make use of His gifts according to His will as you have ever done. Let me never offend Him by abusing my body with its senses, my soul with its faculties, my temporal good or anything else by committing sin. Help me to use God's gifts in His holy service and for the benefit of my immortal soul.

(3) MARY, *you are all-powerful in your prayers with our Creator.* The Creator is almighty; otherwise, He could not have created anything; He is infinitely good; otherwise, He would not have been willing to create us; He is infinitely merciful; otherwise, He would not have re-created us. You called this Creator your Son when, after finding Jesus in the temple, you asked Him, "Son, why hast thou done so to us?" Surely, this almighty, this good and merciful Creator cannot refuse you, His Mother, when you intercede for us. The Son is pleased if His Mother makes a request of Him, and He will give

you everything you may ask of Him. How great then should be my confidence in you!

Mother of Our Creator, I put complete confidence in your prayers because you have a Mother's power over the Heart of your Divine Son. Plead then that I may reach my goal in life, the vision of God, Who created me to live with Him and to share in His bliss for all eternity.

O God, You never fail us in Your Providence; we humbly beg You, through the intercession of the Blessed Virgin Mary, the Mother of Your Son, to remove all evils from us and provide us with that which will profit our souls. Through the same Christ Our Lord. Amen. *(Feast of the Mother of Divine Providence,* Saturday before the third Sunday of November)
Aspiration:

Pray for us, O holy Mother of God, that we may be made worthy of the promises of Christ.

300 days (314)*

14. Mother of Our Savior

Consideration:

Mary is the Mother of Our Savior because she brought forth Jesus Christ Who redeemed us. After the fall, the evil spirit had enslaved mankind. In that frightful slavery man turned from revealed truth and was afflicted with moral corruption. In its helplessness mankind, through the chosen people, longed for a Savior and prayed for His coming.

Mary generously offered Jesus for our salvation. To ransom a slave God gave up His Son. Mary made the same sacrifice by becoming the Mother of the Savior. The Savior came; Mary was His Mother. He has merited most precious graces for us and reconciled us with God. These graces are applied to our souls through Holy Mass, the Holy Sacraments, prayer, indulgences, and good works.

Jesus willed to associate Mary in the Redemption so that she might plead for mankind and save it from eternal ruin. As the Mother of the Redeemer she is also the spiritual Mother of the redeemed. Next to Christ, we owe to her the life of grace that makes us children of God. The Mother of Our Savior is our hope, for she made it possible for us to be saved, and no one after God desires to help us attain salvation more than she.

Prayer

(1) MARY, you are the Mother of Our Savior because *you brought forth Jesus Christ Who has redeemed us.* The angel said to Joseph, "And she shall bring forth a son, and thou shalt call his name Jesus; for he shall save his people from their sins" (Matt. 1:21).

What happiness to have Jesus as Our Savior! We were all sinners, burdened with the guilt of original sin and countless actual sins. It was not in our power to free ourselves from this weight of sin, for we were unable to render due atonement to divine justice. Left to ourselves, nothing remained for us but to live and die in sin and to be eternally rejected. Your Son redeemed us from the terrible slavery of Satan and from eternal damnation. What love and veneration we owe you for having given birth to the Savior of the world!

(2) MARY, *your loving Son has acquired for us most precious graces and reconciled us with God.* As sinners we had brought down upon ourselves God's displeasure. Jesus rendered full satisfaction for the injuries we offered to God; now the heavenly Father admits us again to His love and friendship, and we can look up to Him with confidence and say, "Our Father." Your Son has opened for us the gates of heaven that had been closed against us. He has merited for us the graces we need to live a holy life and to save our souls.

In the holy Sacrifice of the Mass the merits of His bloody sacrifice on the cross are applied to my soul; in the Holy Sacraments I am cleansed from sin, justified and sanctified; indulgences blot out my temporal punishments; the rich treasure of the merits of the saints are for my benefit.

Mother of Our Savior, thank my loving Jesus for the great graces He has won for me. Since Jesus redeemed me from sin, obtain for me the grace of forgiveness for them. Make me truly penitent and sincerely determined to amend my life. Never allow me to be overcome by temptation lest I again become the slave of the devil.

(3) MARY, *you cooperated in the work of our redemption.* I could have no Savior if you had not become the Mother of God. You knew what to expect should you assume the responsibility of Divine Motherhood, but you made this sacrifice because you most ardently desired the Redemption of man. You also consented to the death of your own Son for love of us, and this love made you strong enough to stand erect in sorrow which pierced your motherly heart like a sword. Like the heavenly Father you, too, have given your only Son for the Redemption of the world. You are still most active in applying to us the fruits of Redemption. You do all that your power and love can do, in order to gain souls for your Son. Teach me to be a missionary together with you in saving souls through my good example, my prayers, and my sacrifices.

Mother of Our Savior, through your intercession with your Son, Who died for my soul, obtain for me the grace I need to make good use of the Sacraments and prayer, to overcome sin, to fulfill the duties of my state of life, to keep the commandments of God, and to persevere to the end. Mother of my Savior, save me.

Lord Jesus Christ, our Mediator with the Father, You made Your Mother, the Most Blessed Virgin, our Mother also and Mediatrix with You; mercifully grant that everyone who comes to ask You for favors may be gladdened by having received all through her intercession. Who live and reign forever. Amen. *(Feast of Mary, Mediatrix of All Graces,* May 31)

Aspiration:

Most high Queen of the universe, Mary ever Virgin, make intercession for our peace and salvation, you who bore Christ the Lord, the Savior of all mankind.

300 days (312)*

15. Virgin Most Prudent

Consideration:

To be "prudent" means to exercise common sense in everyday affairs and not to be impetuous. Mary managed her home well. The tremendous choices of her life were wise.

To be "prudent" means to be conscientious and thoughtful. Mary treasured words and events that she could not at once understand, and "pondered them in her heart."

To be "prudent" also means to be "provident." Mary looked ahead, was farsighted. Before the Incarnation her eyes had always been fixed upon the distant promises of God; and, in her little Son, she could see that in some mysterious way God was in Jesus. At Cana she told the servants to do whatever Our Lord might tell them, which amounted to some kind of check.

Christian prudence is the first of the four cardinal virtues. It shows us how to choose the right way to attain a given end, which is always the way of the Will of God. Undue love of created things and of self interferes with doing the Will of God. But prudence takes into account the purpose and value of all created things for the attainment of our last end. "What does it profit a man, if he gain the whole world, but suffer the loss of his soul?"

Mary had the prudence of the five prudent virgins mentioned in the Gospel. She made herself, body and soul, an ever burning flame to illuminate the path of the Divine Bridegroom, spending all her energy and time in the service of God. She was prepared to meet the Bridegroom with the lamp of her soul filled with the oil of grace and burning with the love of God.

Prayer

(1) MARY, you are the Virgin Most Prudent because *you possessed in the highest degree the wisdom of always having God before your eyes and of fearing nothing more than to offend Him.*

"The fear of the Lord is the beginning of wisdom" (Ps. 110:10). You loved God above all things and with your whole heart, and you hated sin above every evil.

When the angel greeted you as full of grace and blessed among women, in your humility you feared a trick of the evil spirit to make you offend God. But when an angel appeared to Joseph in sleep and ordered him to flee into Egypt with you and your child, you did not delay a moment in obeying, because God willed it. And when you stood erect under the cross, you bravely offered your Son for the salvation of the world. In all things you willingly did what you recognized to be right and good, because a childlike fear of God filled your heart.

(2) MARY, *God alone was the object of your love and desires.* This is true wisdom, for God made us for Himself, and our hearts are restless until they rest in Him. Never has there been a human being upon earth whose heart was so detached from the goods of this world as yours.

You lived a life of poverty, retirement, and sacrifice. You did not make your appearance in Jerusalem on Palm Sunday when the people received your Son with every mark of honor. But you did not fail to be present on Calvary at the crucifixion of your Son where you were exposed to shame as the Mother of a criminal who was being executed. You followed your poor, despised Jesus on the way of the cross even to His death.

(3) MARY, *the love of God urged you on in the zealous practice of every virtue and good work.* Faith taught you that our love for God is proved by deeds, and that God will reward us according to our zeal in doing good and striving for holiness. The more you advanced in years, the more you increased in virtue, until finally you reached so high a degree of holiness as to surpass all the angels and saints.

Virgin Most Prudent, teach me the true wisdom of giving my entire, undivided love to God and of fearing nothing more than to displease Him in the slightest degree. May the fear of the Lord accompany me in all my ways that I may seek God's will even at the cost of great sacrifices.

Teach me the rules of Christian wisdom and prudence according to your own example: to fear God, preserve a pure heart, and lead a blameless life; to live in peace and friendliness with all; to love what is true and good, but disapprove, condemn, and detest what is sinful and contrary to truth; to be kind and merciful to the needy; to be zealous in the service of God; to practice virtue and good works, and to labor daily at my amendment and perfection until the day I save my soul.

O God, You gave her who bore Your beloved Son, to be our Mother, and glorified her fair image by a wondrous apparition; grant, we beg of You, that by always following her counsels we may be able to live after Your own Heart and arrive happily in our heavenly fatherland. Through the same Christ Our Lord. Amen. *(Feast of Our Lady of Good Counsel,* April 26)

Aspiration:

You are my Mother, O Virgin Mary; keep me safe lest I ever offend your dear Son, and obtain for me the grace to please Him always and in all things.

300 days (310)

16. Virgin Most Venerable

Consideration:

Mary is most venerable for *she is worthy of honor and respect* because of her holiness and because she holds a place of special honor in the plan of our Redemption.

You venerate Mary by praying to her. Jesus delights in having Mary present your petitions to Him for He has made her the Advocate and Mother of mankind. When you pray to Our Lady, you honor the mercy and goodness of God, Who made her a means of our salvation.

But you venerate the Blessed Mother especially by imitating her virtues. You cannot reach her perfection, but you can become more like her and daily advance in holiness. In doing so you do honor to Jesus Who gave her this perfection. He is pleased to see His virtues reflected in you as He saw them reflected in His own Mother.

Prayer

(1) MARY, you are the Virgin Most Venerable because *the Old Testament pays you the greatest veneration and honor.* In the first of all the prophecies you were the woman who was to crush the serpent's head. You are announced and, with Christ, solemnly promised to the world as the Mother of the future Redeemer, as the victorious heroine who shall destroy the power of the devil.

The prophets, too, speak of you in most beautiful comparisons. You are to them that precious bud of the root of Jesse from which comes forth the Savior; the blessed earth of which the Savior is born (Isaias 45:8); the chaste spouse who enjoys the most intimate love of God (Canticles 4:9); the glorious queen upon whom the angels look in amazement, and who sits at the right of God (Ps. 44:10). Isaias speaks of a miracle: a sign which God will give to His people, and in which the full splendor of His power shall be made known. You are this sign; you are to become a Mother and still re-

main a virgin; you shall bring forth a Son Who will be God and
Man at the same time: "Therefore the Lord Himself shall give you
a sign: Behold, the virgin shall be with child, and shall bring forth
and they shall call his name Emmanuel" (Isaias 7:14).

(2) MARY, *in the New Testament you are revered as the Mother
of God and Mediatrix of Grace.* God sends an angel to you, who
greets you, "Hail, full of grace, the Lord is with thee. Blessed art
thou among women" (Luke 1:28). Of the Holy Spirit you conceive the Son of God and become a Mother without ceasing to be
a virgin. Then at your visit to Elizabeth, she is filled with the Holy
Spirit, and her infant is sanctified and leaps in her womb.

In the Apocalypse St. John proclaims your greatness as Mother
of God: "A great sign appeared in heaven: a woman clothed with
the sun, and the moon was under her feet, and upon her head a
crown of twelve stars" (12:1). You are this woman of whom it is
said that she brought forth a male child who was to rule all nations
with an iron rod, because you brought forth the Son of God, the
ruler of heaven and earth.

Virgin Most Venerable, there is no creature in heaven or on
earth worthy of such high honor as you deserve, because you are
the Mother of God. Fill my heart with a tender and childlike love
for you. By venerating you I hope to please your dear Son Jesus,
Who loved you more than anyone else ever could.

(3) MARY, *you are deserving of veneration because of your dignity.* If we honor great people on earth because of their dignity, we
should all the more venerate you who by a special privilege were
chosen to become the Mother of God. Why should we not honor you
who conceived and brought forth a God-Man, carried the true God
in your arms, and by reason of your motherly authority could
command Him? You have seen Him obey your every wish as an
obedient son. You will ever remain the Mother of God, and Jesus
will forever love you as His Mother. Hence you will be honored
forever in heaven by all the angels and saints, even by God Himself. Should not the whole world imitate their example and give
you loving veneration? Why should not I, a poor miserable sinner
who stands so much in need of your mercy and help, venerate and
invoke you as my only hope?

Virgin Most Venerable, I wish to imitate the angels and saints in
heaven, and all the faithful Christians on earth who love and ven-

erate you. Help me in my daily needs. Look kindly upon the efforts I make to do you honor. Reward my life of devotion to you with the greatest of all graces—final perseverance in the grace of God, and the eternal possession of God in His heavenly kingdom.

O God, You have been pleased to bestow upon us unceasing favors by having placed us under the special protection of the Most Blessed Virgin Mary; grant us, Your humble servants, who rejoice in honoring her today upon earth, the happiness of seeing her face to face in heaven. Through Christ Our Lord. Amen. (*Feast of Our Lady of Guadalupe,* December 12)

Aspiration:

Virgin Mary, you are blessed by the Lord God most high, above all women upon earth.

300 days (311)*

APRIL—Fourth Saturday

17. Virgin Most Renowned

Consideration:

Mary is the Virgin most renowned because *she is the Mother of God.*
Angels and saints are worthy of praise and honor. They are God's servants,
but Mary is His Mother. Therefore she is deserving of the highest respect.

No one ever honored Mary more than God Himself. In honoring her
you imitate God. *All the honor given to Mary redounds to the honor of
her Divine Son.* You praise the Maker of the most wonderful creature that
ever graced this earth when you honor the Mother of God. Therefore
through her intercession you can hope to obtain the greatest graces from
God for your happiness and salvation.

No other saint receives as much public veneration as the Blessed Virgin.
There is not a month of the year during which Holy Church does not
celebrate some feasts in her honor. She is mentioned often in the Mass.
Churches are named after her. Her shrines and images are to be found over
the whole earth and in every Christian home. Her rosary is recited and
devotions conducted in her honor. All of this is a fulfillment of her
prophecy: "All generations shall call me blessed."

Prayer

(1) MARY, you are the Virgin Most Renowned because *you are
the Mother of God.* We respect the angels and saints in heaven more
than anyone on earth of high position and power. But angels and
saints are servants of God, while you are His Mother.

You are deserving of the highest respect and veneration. The
Church fervently sings your praises: "Blessed art thou, holy Virgin,
and worthy of all praise, because from thee has come forth the Sun
of Justice, Christ, our God." You are excelled by no one except by
Him Who created you. You yourself humbly attribute to your
Divine Motherhood the praise which would be given you by all
men. Being greeted by your cousin Elizabeth as the Mother of God,

you gratefully exclaimed, "He has regarded the lowliness of his handmaid; for, behold, henceforth all generations shall call me blessed; because he who is mighty has done great things for me" (Luke 1:48).

You inspire all the faithful with a holy zeal; they never grow tired of singing your praise. Writers, poets, painters, sculptors, and musicians of every nation and in every age have combined their efforts to proclaim your praises and to pass down to future generations the sentiments of religious veneration which they themselves felt.

(2) MARY, *you are also renowned because of your sanctity.* Although the dignity of Divine Motherhood is a privilege and grace which you could not merit, yet it was bestowed upon you as a reward for your worthiness. No young maiden during your lifetime served God as zealously as you, and none loved God with such perfect love. Your sanctity made God look upon you with the greatest delight and to choose you to be the Mother of His Son.

Jesus Himself declared that you are to be praised, not alone for being His Mother, but in a far greater degree for being a saint, for faithfully observing what God wills and teaches. When the woman in the Gospel raised her voice and said of Jesus: "Blessed is the womb that bore thee, and the breasts that nursed thee," He replied, "Rather, blessed are they who hear the word of God and keep it" (Luke 11:27–28). Being the Mother of Jesus would not have meant so much if you had not had the great happiness of carrying also in your heart Him Whom you bore in your womb.

Virgin Most Renowned, I join the praise with which the whole Church greets you, and I wish to venerate you daily with the most fervent devotion. Since the imitation of your example is the praise that is most pleasing to you, help me to make every effort to be like you in humility, chastity, contempt of the world, self-denial, obedience, meekness, patience, and love of God and my neighbor.

(3) MARY, *you are renowned on account of the benefits which you have conferred and still confer upon the human race.* Holy Mother Church attributes to you the praise which the Jews gave the pious widow Judith who cut off the head of Holofernes and delivered her city from ruin: "Thou art the glory of Jerusalem, and thou art the joy of Israel, thou art the honor of our people. For thou hast done manfully, and thy heart has been strengthened, be-

cause thou hast loved chastity . . . therefore also the hand of the
Lord has strengthened thee, and therefore thou shalt be blessed
forever" (Judith 15:10–11).

You deserve even greater praise because you delivered your Son
to death in order to make the Redemption of the world possible,
and you saved all nations from eternal ruin. You continue to apply
to us the fruits of Redemption, for you are a most affectionate
Mother, and you never feel happier than when you find an opportunity to give to your children proofs of your motherly goodness
and mercy.

Lord Jesus Christ, You have given us Your Mother Mary that she might
be our Mother of Perpetual Help, whose beloved image we venerate; grant,
we beg of You, that by earnestly imploring her motherly help we may
deserve to enjoy at all times the blessings of Your Redemption. Who live
and reign forever. Amen. (*Feast of Our Lady of Perpetual Help,* June 27)
   Aspiration:
      Holy Mary, Our Lady of Deliverance, pray for us and for the holy
      souls in purgatory.

                                              300 days (425)

18. Virgin Most Powerful

Consideration:

The Mother of the Almighty God must be most powerful because *He has chosen her to have a share in the grandest work of power ever accomplished on earth*—the Redemption of mankind from the slavery of Satan, and the raising of mankind to the dignity of children of God.

Mary is called *"Suppliant Omnipotence"* because there is nothing the Mother of God cannot do through her prayers if it serves the glory of God and the salvation of souls. If saints have shown their great power of intercession in the numberless miracles which they have wrought, how can their Queen be less powerful? The wonderful things that happened at Lourdes and Fátima are but a reminder of that power.

In these times of materialism and vice, *the thought of Mary's power is our comfort and hope and inspiration.* When Satan's forces threaten with enslavement, torture, and death, Almighty God will break their power through the Virgin most powerful as He predicted at the dawn of creation: "I will put enmities between thee and the woman, and thy seed and her seed: she shall crush thy head, and thou shalt lie in wait for her heel" (Gen. 3:15).

In your own struggle with the powers of the world, the flesh, and the devil, you have nothing to fear as long as the Virgin most powerful is on your side. Your fervent and continual devotion to her will keep her on your side.

Prayer

(1) MARY, *you are most powerful in your intercession with God because of your sanctity.* God has all power of Himself, while you, being a creature, receive your power from God. The saints have influence with God because they are His friends; He loves them as a father loves his good children.

278

How much greater must your influence be, since, unlike the saints, you are free from every stain of imperfection and sin! You combine in yourself every virtue which the saints had, and in each virtue you reach the highest perfection. Since God loves the saints according to the degree of sanctity they have attained, He loves you most; and if He loves you most your intercession is more powerful than theirs.

(2) MARY, *you are most powerful because of the dignity of your Divine Motherhood.* Dearly as God loves the saints, they are only His servants; but you are His Mother. All that the best of mothers can be to her child, this and much more you have been to the Divine Child. You served Him in all His needs with tender love and faithfulness. You shared joy and sorrow with Him till the last moment of His life. Jesus in all His glory still has His human nature, and you are still His Mother.

What great confidence I should have in you! If even a sinful man cannot resist the requests of his mother, Jesus, Who is sanctity itself, surely cannot refuse your requests. You refused Him nothing while on earth; He can refuse you nothing in heaven. You are all-powerful in your intercession with God. The saints have called you "Suppliant Omnipotence" because by your prayers you are able to obtain all things that are not contrary to the will of God.

(3) MARY, *you are most powerful in relieving the temporal and spiritual needs of mankind.* You are the compassionate intercessor of sinners, the help of the helpless, the Mother of orphans, the consolation of the sorrowing, the health of the sick, the comfort of the afflicted, and the salvation of mankind. Your power shows itself especially in those cases in which all human help fails. You are truly the Mother of Perpetual Help.

Virgin Most Powerful, let me ever remember that my own prayers will have greater effect if I keep from sin and lead a holy life. God is inclined to answer the prayers of the innocent, whom He loves more deeply and rewards more generously.

I am happy to have a Mother to help me who is so powerful. I place all my confidence in you. Through your prayers I hope to obtain help in my temporal and spiritual needs. Pray for me that I may detest sin, keep the commandments, love God with all my heart and my neighbor for the love of God, lead a life of prayer and virtue, and one day deserve the reward of the just in heaven.

O Lord God Almighty, You willed that all things should be given to us through the Immaculate Mother of Your Son; grant that under the protection of this mighty Mother we may escape all the dangers of these our times, and in the end may come to life everlasting. Through the same Christ Our Lord. Amen. *(Feast of the Miraculous Medal,* November 27)
  Aspiration:

Rejoice, O Virgin Mary; you alone have put down all heresies in the whole world.

300 days (316)

19. Virgin Most Merciful

Consideration:

Being the *chosen daughter of the Father* of all mercies, Mary must be full of mercy. Being the *Mother of the merciful Redeemer,* the Good Shepherd Who laid down His life for His sheep, she must possess some of His compassion. Being the *Immaculate Bride of the Holy Spirit,* Who is Love personified in the Trinity, she must be filled with tremendous sympathy for mankind.

Mercy is the flower of love; it inclines to help in need, to forgive, to return good for evil. As the Virgin most merciful *she is ever eager to help the needy, to plead for the sinner, to stay the hand of Divine Justice through her motherly intercession.* No saint in heaven could be more earnest about leading sinners back to their Savior and their God, but no saint has ever loved them so much and suffered so much for their salvation. Her mercy is even greater in heaven because now she has a clearer understanding of our misery.

Millions of Christians throughout the ages proclaim her as the Virgin most merciful. She has helped them in their spiritual and material needs, rescued them from great dangers, and saved them from eternal death.

Mary's mercy should encourage you to turn to her in your misery and sinfulness that you might find a kind mother and advocate. Her mercy should urge you to be merciful to your neighbor and to assist suffering mankind.

Prayer

(1) MARY, you are most merciful because *you love souls most tenderly.* Your heart is full of compassion for all, and you use your influence with God to relieve the needs of all mankind. When the archangel Gabriel came to announce to you that you were chosen by God to become the Mother of His Son, you could have declined. You accepted even though you knew that untold sufferings would

await you, and that you would become the Queen of Martyrs. You accepted for the love of sinful man. Had you not given your consent, we would have remained without a Redeemer.

At the marriage feast of Cana you noticed how distressed the newly married couple were when the wine began to fail. You immediately brought a request to your Son: "They have no wine" (John 2:3). Jesus heard your prayer and worked His first miracle by changing water into wine because you asked Him.

In heaven you love us even more than you did on earth. Your mercy is also greater because now you have a clearer understanding of our misery.

(2) MARY, *you love us more tenderly and care for us more earnestly in our temporal and spiritual needs than our own mothers can.* Eve was a cruel stepmother to us; through her the infernal serpent breathed into the first man his deadly poison. But you are a true Mother to us; you have prepared for us the remedy against this poison. After the fall, man became subject to sin, misery, disease, and death. God, Who is rich in mercy, gave us Jesus and you. No two persons were more animated with tenderest sentiments of compassion and mercy. Jesus willed to become like one of us and chose to know sorrow. As the Mother of Sorrows you became the loving Mother of mankind beneath the cross. In you there is nothing stern or terrifying; you are full of mildness and mercy. I thank God Who in His great goodness gave me such a gentle, loving, and powerful intercessor before His throne.

(3) MARY, *the history of all ages proves how merciful you are.* Thousands upon thousands of Christians who have found help in their needs through you acknowledge with one voice that you are the merciful Virgin who rescued them from great dangers, saved them from eternal death, and granted them innumerable blessings.

Virgin Most Merciful, may your mercy teach me to be merciful and unselfish. I cannot imitate you if I care only for myself and disregard the misery of others. I entreat your help for suffering mankind and for myself in my miseries. May your great mercy and goodness also encourage me to be kind toward my fellow men, to treat all charitably, to bear patiently with their weaknesses, and to help them in their needs, that you may prove yourself a Mother of Mercy to me.

O God, Whose compassion is without limit, show us Your mercy on earth through the most holy intercession of Mary, the Mother of Your Son, that we may merit to attain eternal glory. Through the same Christ Our Lord. Amen. *(Feast of Mary, Mother of Mercy,* Saturday before the 4th Sunday of July)

    Aspiration:

        Mother of Mercy, pray for us.

300 days (304)

20. Virgin Most Faithful

Consideration:

To be "faithful" means to keep promises made, to fulfill obligations assumed, to render the service owed to God. To be "faithful" means to be loyal. Mary was so loyal to her vow that she was ready to renounce the motherhood of the Messias till it became clear to her how she could become His Mother without violating her word. She was loyal all through Bethlehem and Egypt, loyal in Nazareth and Calvary, loyal to the Apostles afterward, loyal to us. How many a sinner who cannot bring himself to give up sin will trust her fidelity and ask her to pray for him in the very hour of his sin, certain that he will not refuse?

Mary's baptism, so to say, was her immaculate conception; *her baptismal promises* the answer she gave to the angel, "Behold the handmaid of the Lord, be it done to me according to thy word." How faithfully she kept that promise—faithful, though it meant the piercing of her soul with the sword of sorrow! She was loyal unto death.

The work of Satan is sin, treason against God. The pomps of Satan are riches, worldly display, and sensual enjoyment. *In baptism* you renounced Satan and all his works and all his pomps. Are you faithful to these promises? Devotion to Mary will help you to be loyal to God as she always was.

Prayer

(1) MARY, *you were the Virgin Most Faithful to God.* From your infancy to the day of your death, you carefully fulfilled His will in all things. You are said to have made a vow of perpetual virginity in your earliest youth, in order to dedicate yourself entirely to the Lord. Well aware that by becoming the Mother of God your whole life would be filled with sufferings, you, nevertheless, consented to accept this responsibility with as much humility as willingness: "Behold the handmaid of the Lord; be it done to me according to thy

word" (Luke 1:38). Because it was God's Will that you should become the Mother of His Son, you were ready to make every sacrifice, even the greatest.

You were always doing some good deed: you never questioned whether God had commanded it, but only whether it was pleasing to Him. In this spirit you fulfilled all that the Law prescribed for the purification of mothers by taking Jesus to the temple of Jerusalem, though you could have disregarded that Law because you were without sin. How wonderful is the fidelity with which you devoted yourself to God in your childhood, youth, motherhood, and widowhood! You knew no other joy than that found in God; you had no other wish than to please Him in faithful service.

Virgin Most Faithful, help me to overcome my inconstancy in the service of God. Make me fervent in spirit that I may serve God with all my heart and with the most exact faithfulness.

(2) MARY, *you were the Virgin Most Faithful, especially to Jesus.* At the word of the angel you arose with your Child and Joseph to make the long and difficult flight into Egypt. After Herod's death you returned into your own country and dwelt in Nazareth. How patiently you toiled and watched and suffered with your little Son! And when He was lost in Jerusalem at the age of twelve, you sought Him anxiously and prayerfully till you found Him in the temple. With mingled feelings of joy and sorrow, you asked: "Son, why hast thou done so to us? Behold, thy father and I have been seeking thee sorrowing" (Luke 2:48).

You were faithfully at the side of your Son on the day of His greatest humiliation. When His disciples fled in terror and Peter denied Him, you fearlessly went to meet the murderers of your Son. You did not try to rescue Him from their hands, since you well knew that it was His Father's Will, as well as His own, that He should die. But you followed Him and witnessed all His sufferings. Standing beneath the cross, you heard His last words and saw Him complete the sacrifice of Redemption—while you were spiritually crucified with Him. No human being has ever clung to Jesus with such fidelity, such love, such heroism!

Virgin Most Faithful, I vowed fidelity to my Savior in holy Baptism and have renewed this vow often in my lifetime, but I do not always observe it. As long as I meet with no obstacle or suffering, I am a disciple of Christ and act according to His holy will. If, however, my fidelity to Jesus demands courage and sacrifice, I fail my Master. Help me to amend my life and to imitate your fidelity.

(3) MARY, *you are also the Virgin Most Faithful to us, your children.* You protect and assist us in life and in death, for you love us most tenderly, and desire nothing more ardently than that we should serve God and save our souls. You do all in your power to keep us from sin, or to raise us up if we have been so unfortunate as to fall. As the devil goes about seeking whom he may devour, you go about seeking whom you may save. You hasten to help struggling souls at the hour of death: you enlighten, comfort, and strengthen them that they may overcome temptations, preserve the grace of God, and depart from this world in peace.

Virgin Most Faithful, teach me to be faithful in my devotion to you. Be faithful to me now and at the hour of my death.

May the kind intercession of Mary, Your glorious and ever Virgin-Mother, be our help, we beg of You, O Lord, that it may make those whom it has blessed with continual favors ever to know what should be done, and then strengthen them to carry it out faithfully. Who live and reign forever. Amen. (*Feast of Our Lady of Good Counsel,* April 26)

Aspiration:

Help me to praise you, O holy Virgin; give me strength against your enemies.

300 days (293) *

21. Mirror of Justice

Consideration:

In scriptural language "justice" means the perfect observance of the commandments of God. Thus St. Joseph was "a just man." But all such holiness is a reflection of the holiness of God. Mary is called "the mirror" of justice because *God could reflect Himself in Mary's soul without any flaw distorting His image.*

The fulfillment of the great commandment of love is the fulfillment of all commandments. *Mary loved God with her whole heart,* with her whole soul, with her whole mind, and with all her strength. "God is Love," says St. John, "and he who abides in love abides in God, and God in him" (1 John 4:16). The love of God was reflected in Mary's soul. In fact, God, Who is Love, actually lived in her soul.

Be devoted to God's Mother and *study in this mirror of justice all the virtues of a perfect Christian life.* Thus becoming more like Mary, you will be like a mirror reflecting the light of God's truth and holiness into the spiritual darkness of the world about you.

Prayer

(1) MARY, you are called the Mirror of Justice because *you are the most excellent model of the love of God.* The whole Divine Law rests upon the great commandment of charity—love of God, of oneself, and of our neighbor. In your whole life is reflected, as in a mirror, perfect love of God.

The love that burned in the hearts of the saints cannot be compared with yours. No creature was so devoted to God as you were; none observed His commandments as perfectly as you did. Your whole life was a proof that the Will of God was dearer to you than all else, and that you were prepared to die rather than disobey His commands. When a certain woman lifted up her voice from the crowd and said to Jesus, "Blessed is the womb that bore thee, and the breasts that nursed thee," He answered in your praise, "Rather, blessed are they who hear the word of God and keep it" (Luke 11:27–28).

(2) MARY, *your love for yourself was also conformed to God's Will.* You took care of the salvation of your own soul first, as Jesus spoke of the other Mary in the Gospel: "Mary has chosen the best part, and it will not be taken away from her" (Luke 10:42). God was your choice at all times, and serving Him was your daily food, so that you could say with your loving Son, "My food is to do the will of Him who sent me, to accomplish His work" (John 4:34).

How well you understood and practiced His teaching: "What does it profit a man, if he gain the whole world, but suffer the loss of his own soul? Or what will a man give in exchange for his soul?" (Matt. 16:26). "Blessed are they who hunger and thirst for justice, for they shall be satisfied" (Matt. 5:6). No one ever desired self-sanctification as much as you did. You never tired of striving for virtue. God, in return, poured upon your soul the rich fullness of His graces.

All the virtues were reflected in your soul as in a mirror: humility, chastity, meekness, patience, mercy, faith, hope, charity. In order to preserve and increase sanctifying grace, you availed yourself of every means of grace with zeal and earnestness. You are truly blessed because of your hunger and thirst for holiness, for God has given you a fullness of His graces that made you "blessed among women."

(3) MARY, *you are the most excellent model of the love of neighbor.* Since love of neighbor is in proportion to our love of God, and since no creature has ever loved God so much as you loved Him, no one has ever loved his neighbor more than you did. During your life upon earth you used every opportunity to do good; and now that you are enthroned in heaven, your love for us is even greater, and you shower upon us your choicest blessings. You have at heart especially the spiritual welfare of all, even the most unfortunate sinners, and you obtain for us numberless graces for the salvation of our souls.

Mirror of Justice, help me ever to admire and imitate all your virtues, for then I shall be more like Jesus, your Son, Who is the Model of all perfection. You are a perfect image of your Son. Lead me to that degree of holiness which God has destined for me. Give me a hunger and thirst for holiness that I may find my truest joy in God on earth and my everlasting bliss with Him in heaven.

Through Your mercy, O Lord, and the intercession of the Blessed Virgin Mary, may Your Church increase in the number of the faithful and ever shine forth in the manifold light of virtue. Through Christ Our Lord. Amen. (*Feast of Our Lady, Queen of the Apostles,* Saturday after the Ascension)

Aspiration:

Bless us, Mary Maiden mild; bless us, too, her tender Child.

300 days (309)

22. Seat of Wisdom

Consideration:

Mary is called the Seat of Wisdom because, as the Mother of the incarnate Divine Wisdom, *she possessed and practiced wisdom in the highest degree.* She clearly understood that the purpose of all creation is to give glory to God and to do His Will. It was her delight to glorify God in the labors and sufferings of her life. Jesus was praising His own Mother when He said, "Rather, blessed are they who hear the word of God and keep it" (Luke 11:28).

You imitate Mary the Seat of Wisdom when you direct all things to the glory of God as she did, and devote yourself faithfully and cheerfully to His service. This heavenly wisdom will protect you against the false wisdom of the world, which is foolishness in the eyes of God.

Frequently ask the Seat of Wisdom to make you truly wise, that you may love what God commands and, amid the changing conditions of this life, keep your mind and heart set on the things of heaven, where alone true joys abide.

Prayer

(1) MARY, you are the Seat of Wisdom because *the Son of God, the eternal Wisdom, assumed flesh from you, dwelt in your virginal womb, and as an Infant rested in your arms.* As the Son of God, Jesus is called Wisdom. The Father thinks of Himself from eternity. This thought of the Father is a distinct person—the Word, the Wisdom of God.

But the Son of God is also called Wisdom because in the work of Redemption Divine Wisdom shows itself in the highest degree. After becoming Man, Jesus taught us wisdom. He taught us that temporal goods are vain and possess true value only in so far as they are means for obtaining our final destiny. He has reminded us to be most earnest about saving our souls.

Seat of Wisdom, you bore in your womb Him Who is the personal and eternal Wisdom of God, and Whose words and teaching give evidence of wisdom in the highest degree. Obtain for me the grace to embrace wisdom with my whole soul as I see it in the doctrine of your Divine Son.

(2) MARY, *Divine Wisdom showed itself in you in a particular manner.* Evil and ruin were brought upon the human race through a woman, Eve, our first mother. God's wisdom therefore ordained that salvation and grace should be brought to the whole human family through a woman. You are that woman, our second, better Mother. Eve permitted herself to be deceived by a spirit of hell, so that she became disobedient and ate of the forbidden fruit. God's wisdom ordained that you should be obedient to an angel of heaven who announced to you the Will of God, and caused you to say, "Behold the handmaid of the Lord; be it done to me according to thy word." Eve's sin came from unbelief, for she no longer believed what God had told her and Adam; you placed all your faith in the words of the angel Gabriel and thus repaired the sin of Eve. Thus the wisdom of God knew how to create in you a woman who was like our first mother in all things, but who used the privileges and graces received, not as did Eve, for our harm, but for our eternal salvation.

The wisdom of God also showed itself in your marriage, that the birth of the Son of God might not become known before the time, that your reputation might remain free from reproach, and that the Divine Child might have in Joseph a foster father and a protector.

In His divine wisdom God fulfilled His prophecies through you. Though very poor, you were a descendant of the royal house of David; you lived at the very time when the scepter had passed from the descendants of David into the hands of strangers; your home was at Nazareth, but in obedience to a decree of Caesar you went to Bethlehem and there brought forth your Divine Child. After your return from Egypt, you went to Nazareth, where Jesus lived with you up to His thirtieth year. For that reason He was called a Nazarene.

Divine Wisdom made you share in the poverty, the humiliation, and the persecution of Jesus. God kindled in you the fire of divine love, reared you in the school of suffering, bestowed upon you a heart full of compassion and mercy toward men—a heart which knew no greater delight than to comfort the afflicted, to save sinners, and to do good to all. He afforded you opportunities to acquire countless merits, and gave you the grace to attain the highest degree of holiness. Thus you became the Queen of Heaven. "Oh, the depth of the riches of the wisdom and of the knowledge of God! How incomprehensible are his judgments and how unsearchable his ways!" (Rom. 11:33)

(3) MARY, *you teach us true wisdom.* The highest of all wisdom is to know how to live a good life. You possessed this wisdom more than anyone else, for you loved God above all things and sought His holy Will in everything. You faithfully used every grace and means of salvation in order to unite yourself more intimately with God and to become daily more like Him. Help me to imitate you that I may obtain that heavenly wisdom which makes me good and happy here and blessed forever in heaven. Let me be guided by Divine Wisdom as willingly as you were. Everything tends to make me a devoted Christian and to lead me to eternal joy. Never let my wisdom oppose the wisdom of God. Whatever God wishes is always good.

Seat of Wisdom, do not let me be deceived by the false wisdom of the world which teaches me to consider this world as the final aim of man. Help me always to act according to Christian wisdom: to mortify all my inordinate inclinations, and never attach my heart to the vain, perishable goods of the world, to guard against sin, to practice virtue and good works, and to love God above all things and with my whole heart.

Confirm in our minds, we beg of You, O Lord, the mysteries of the true faith, that we who believe Him Who was conceived of a Virgin to be true God and Man may deserve to arrive at eternal joy, by the power of His saving Resurrection. Through the same Christ Our Lord. Amen. (*Mass of the Blessed Virgin on Saturdays*)

Aspiration:

Holy Mary, Virgin Mother of God, intercede for me.

300 days (315) *

23. Cause of Our Joy

Consideration:

Mary is the Cause of Our Joy because *she brought forth the Savior of mankind.* His birth was announced by the angels as news of great joy. She shared in His mission of bringing joy to the world, for through the work of Redemption we received the graces that would bring us holiness and the possession of God in Whom all happiness can be found. He created us that we might share His happiness. He used Mary as a means to enable us to share His eternal bliss.

The joy which Mary offers you has its source in God and in the gifts received from Him: forgiveness of sin, holiness, and heaven. God has made her the distributor of all the graces we need for our salvation. He has deposited in her the fullness of all His blessings, to teach us that all hope, all grace, and salvation come to us through her hands.

Ask Mary to lead you to her Son, for it is in Jesus that she herself finds her greatest joy. *Devotion to Mary is the surest way of finding Jesus; and, having found Jesus and Mary, you are truly happy.* Through prayers and the frequent reception of the Sacraments, you, too, can feel some of the joy that filled her heart when at the visitation she sang her hymn of praise, "My soul magnifies the Lord, and my spirit rejoices in God, my Savior."

Prayer

(1) MARY, we greet you as the Cause of Our Joy because *you brought forth the Redeemer and thereby shared in the work of our Redemption.* Your Son Jesus is the only Cause of Our Joy, for He alone redeemed us from sin and hell, reconciled us with God, and opened for us a pathway to heaven. If our first mother Eve had not consented to the temptation of Satan, sin with all its evil consequences would not have entered into the world. Eve was the cause of sin and perdition.

Having given your consent to become the Mother of God, you

also became the Cause of Our Joy, for you cooperated in the work
of our Redemption. Your great sanctity consists in a perfect conformity of your thoughts and will with the thoughts and Will of God.
You shared with God that wonderful compassion in the sacrifice of
His Son, and you gave and offered for us the Son of God, Who was
also your Son, with the same love and willingness as God did.
Though you loved Jesus with all your heart, it was even your wish
that He should suffer and die for us, because you knew that our
Redemption was only possible through His Passion and death.

You sacrificed your Son, Whom you loved more dearly than
heaven and earth and your own life. And I value my salvation so
little that I will make no sacrifice for it! In order to save my soul,
help me to overcome every evil habit and inordinate desire and to
shun every dangerous occasion of sin.

(2) MARY, *through you God distributes to us all the graces we
need for our salvation.* God made you His treasurer. He filled you
with all graces that through you as through a channel men might
obtain every blessing. God has deposited in you the fullness of all
His blessings, to teach us that all hope, all grace, and salvation come
to us through your hands. For this reason the Church applies to you
the words of the Book of Wisdom: "In me is all hope of life and
virtue"; "in me is all grace of life and of truth"; "he who finds me,
finds life and draws salvation from the Lord."

Cause of Our Joy, how much God desires us to know you! How
I should always have recourse to you and place my confidence in
your help! May I always appeal to you when I desire to obtain a
grace, that it may the more surely be granted to me and be a source
of true joy to my soul. When I appeal to the saints, or to your Son,
I know that the grace I receive from Him will be given to me
through your hands.

(3) MARY, *you take the deepest interest in our welfare and obtain for us pardon and salvation.* You are like the rainbow which
God caused to appear in the sky as a messenger of peace to men
after the deluge and which rejoiced their hearts. As God on beholding the rainbow was reminded of His covenant, so through
your intercession He forgives sinners their offenses against Him
and makes peace with them.

The Church applies to you the words of the Canticle: "Thou
art fair as the moon." As the moon is between heaven and earth,

so you stand between God and man, that you may pacify heaven, enlighten sinners, and lead them back to God. God Himself has given you the power of helping the miserable.

Cause of Our Joy, may my greatest happiness be to possess the love and grace of God; my greatest glory to be a disciple of Jesus and a child of yours. I rejoice in this happiness and exult in this glory. Let not human pride and worldly desires keep me from perfect devotion to you and your Son.

O Lord, we beg You to forgive the sins of Your servants, that we who are unable to pleace You by our deeds may be saved by the intercession of the Mother of Your Son, Our Lord. Who lives and reigns forever. Amen.
(Feast of the Assumption, August 15)
Aspiration:
> O Virgin Mary, Our Lady of the Blessed Sacrament, glory of the Christian people, joy of the universal Church, salvation of the whole world, pray for us, and awaken in all the faithful a lively devotion toward the Most Holy Eucharist, that they may be made worthy to receive It daily.

300 days (418)

24. Spiritual Vessel

Consideration:

Mary can be thought of as a precious shrine containing a great treasure. *She is the Shrine of the Holy Spirit,* Who overshadowed her and dwelt in her. She is the immaculate Bride of the Holy Spirit, for He has chosen her to be the sacred sanctuary which would shelter the Son of God. He adorned her soul with the richest graces ever given to mankind: sanctifying grace, theological virtues of faith, hope and charity; the moral virtues of prudence, justice, temperance, and fortitude; His seven Gifts of wisdom, understanding, counsel, fortitude, knowledge, piety, fear of the Lord, and also His twelve Fruits.

Mary is the spiritual vessel because *all things which are associated with spirituality are found in her more abundantly than in any other saint:* love of God and men, hatred of sin, contempt of the world, the spirit of prayer, the perfect practice of every virtue.

You, too, are a spiritual vessel, since the Holy Spirit has made your soul His dwelling place in Baptism, and has blessed you with many spiritual gifts. But you carry this treasure in a fragile vessel and therefore you need Mary's help and protection. She will make you more spiritual in your outlook on life, in your desires and deeds, so that you may allow yourself to be led by the Spirit and prove yourself a true child of God.

Prayer

(1) MARY, I greet you as a Spiritual Vessel, not only because the Son of God assumed flesh of you and dwelt in you, but also because the Holy Spirit infused into your soul, as into a precious vessel, the fullness of His grace.

The Holy Spirit gave you a rich measure of faith. St. Elizabeth called you blessed on account of your faith: "Blessed is she who has believed, because the things promised her by the Lord shall be accomplished" (Luke 1:45). Eve, believing the serpent rather than

God, brought death; you, believing the words of the angel, brought salvation to the world.

The wonderful extent of your faith, its unwavering firmness and extraordinary activity shone forth in every action of your life. Christ is born in the greatest poverty; He lies a weak babe in a crib; He is subject to all the wants of infancy like any other child; but you do not for a moment doubt His Divinity. You worship in Him the omnipotence of God and recognize Him as the Lord of heaven and earth. You needed no miracle to make you believe; the simple words which the Lord had spoken to you through the angel were enough to strengthen you so firmly in your belief that you never faltered in it during life.

How great is your faith in the time of the Passion and death of Jesus! The Jews rise up against Him and revile Him as a false prophet and a criminal. Even His disciples begin to doubt Him. Though He seems to be forsaken by God and dies on the cross, you adore Him with the same strong conviction of faith as you now adore Him in heaven.

Spiritual Vessel, help me to be firm in the holy Catholic faith. Let nothing make me waver in my faith. Give me three supports for my faith: humility, the fear of God, and fervor in prayer.

(2) MARY, *you were strongly grounded in hope.* God enlightens us by faith that we may understand His goodness and promises, and arouses us by hope that we may cherish an ardent desire to possess Him. You had faith in an extraordinary degree, hence you had firm hope and could say with David: "In God I have put my trust; I will not fear what flesh can do against me" (Ps. 55:5). Your trials were great beyond comparison, but you never lost courage or became weak in faith, because you were sustained by hope.

You did not complain when you had to seek refuge in a stable where you gave birth to Jesus. Later you gave the most beautiful proof of your confidence in God when you set out on your journey into Egypt with your little Child.

At the marriage feast at Cana, in spite of the answer of Jesus, "What wouldst thou have me do, woman? My hour has not yet come," your confidence was not shaken. You told the waiters to do whatever your Son should tell them, for you hoped with confidence that He would grant your request. Jesus rewarded your confidence by working His first miracle.

At the sight of Jesus dying in utmost abandonment on the cross a sword pierced your heart; but you stood immovable as a rock because hope sustained you. You knew you would have your Son again and nothing would separate you from Him.

I hope to obtain heaven and all things necessary for salvation—the forgiveness of my sins and the grace to do good; for God has promised me all this through the merits of your Son. Spiritual Vessel, help me to fear and hope: fear, because I am very weak and liable to fall into grievous sin; hope, because God will never abandon those who sincerely desire their salvation.

(3) MARY, *you were filled with the love of God and your neighbor.* Your heart was not divided between God and creatures; it belonged entirely to God. Knowing that the surest proof of love is to suffer for the beloved, you gladly made use of every occasion which presented itself to sacrifice for the love of God. And as love always tends to a union with the person one loves, your soul was always united with God by prayer.

You were also filled with the most tender love for your neighbor. Like your Divine Son, you loved everybody and fervently desired the salvation of all mankind. Because true love never passes away, you show yourself at all times our most amiable Mother and obtain for us all the graces we need.

Spiritual Vessel, help me to love God above all things and to make every sacrifice for the love of Him, even the sacrifice of my life, if I can no longer preserve it without sin. Aid me in loving my neighbor for the love of God. May my good example shine before men by always conducting myself as a good Catholic.

We beg of You, O Lord, our God, by the intercession of the Blessed Virgin Mary, to make the Most Holy Mysteries, which You have given us for the preservation of our spiritual life, a remedy for us both for the present and for the future. Through Christ Our Lord. Amen. (*Feast of Our Lady of the Most Blessed Sacrament,* May 13)

Aspiration:

O Mary, make me live in God, with God, and for God.

300 days (306)

JUNE—Fourth Saturday

25. Vessel of Honor

Consideration:

The Holy Spirit made Mary "a vessel of honor" *because she was to hold the flesh and blood of the incarnate Son of God, like a living chalice and paten used for the offering of Holy Mass.* This vessel was prepared by the Holy Spirit through her Immaculate Conception and fullness of grace; then He impressed upon her mind and will the form of Christ. He consecrated this living chalice when at the Annunciation He overshadowed her with His power and love and formed in her the sacred humanity of Jesus Christ.

We decorate shrines richly for the sake of what they contain, and behave ourselves respectfully in them. Anyone who came near Mary felt that there was hidden in her something that he could not see, but whose radiating reality made itself unmistakably felt. He would then have wished to do "honor" to her. *This Shrine was indeed "worshipful."*

You, too, are a vessel of honor bearing Christ within your soul; hence, you, too, must become another Christ, not conformed to the standards of the world, but dedicated to the service of God through Baptism. Mary, the Vessel of Honor, will keep you ever mindful of *your Christian consecration and dignity* if you are devoted to her, imitating her virtues, seeking her help, and loving her with all your heart.

Prayer

(1) MARY, we praise you as the Vessel of Honor because *you are the Mother of God.* If everything in any way connected with Christ Our Savior is venerable, what an object of honor you must be to us! As Mother of Christ you stand in closer relationship to Him than any other creature in heaven or on earth.

You are a living tabernacle of God, in whom the only-begotten Son of God dwelt for nine months. He rested in your arms and received nourishment from your hands. But Jesus not only dwelt

299

in you; He even assumed human flesh of you, for you are His Mother. You are more worthy of honor than any creature because you are the Mother of Him Who created and governs the world, and Who is your Creator. You have nourished Him by Whom all living creatures are sustained.

All the angels and saints of heaven pay you homage because of your exalted dignity and unsurpassed glory; all Christians place their confidence in you; and the souls in purgatory look to you for help. You are the brightest adornment of the heavenly kingdom, the delight of the faithful, the honor of mankind. Your prophecy is truly fulfilled: "Henceforth all generations shall call me blessed" (Luke 1:48).

(2) MARY, *your soul resembles a precious vessel filled with graces of every kind.* For this reason the archangel Gabriel greeted you, "Hail, full of grace!"

You are filled with *sanctifying grace,* which makes your soul holy and pleasing to God, a child of God and an heir to the kingdom of heaven. You received sanctifying grace in the first instant of your conception. You were preserved free from original sin and ever remained a child of grace. You received sanctifying grace more abundantly than any angel or human being. To other creatures grace is given partially; but it was poured out upon you in all its fullness. Since you were raised above angels and men by your dignity as Mother of God, it was fitting that God should bestow upon you a greater measure of grace than upon any other person. Even as an infant you excelled all the angels and saints in holiness. In every moment of your life you acquired merits, which increased sanctifying grace in your soul.

Who can number the *gratuitous graces* you received, not so much for your own salvation as for the benefit of mankind, or the numberless miracles to help people which God has worked for you?

You also received *actual graces* by which God enlightened your mind and strengthened your will to avoid evil and to do good. As Mother of God you were to surpass all the saints in sanctity and merits. You were to become the Queen of Angels and Saints, hence a greater measure of grace was required to accomplish this. Your sanctity was never to be marred by the slightest venial sin or fault. Extraordinary graces were necessary for you to preserve the first grace to the close of your life. And since it is certain that God gives graces more abundantly the more we make use of them, you received far more and greater actual graces than any other created being. And you faithfully used every grace!

(3) MARY, *you deserve all the honor I or anyone else on earth can give you.* I wish to honor you as much as I am able, and I am determined to be zealous for your honor in seeking to encourage others to honor you and to have great confidence in your intercession.

Vessel of Honor, I can honor you best by imitating you. My soul is also a vessel of honor, for in Baptism the Holy Spirit purified and sanctified it, infused His grace into it, and made it the image of God and the dwelling place of the Holy Spirit. Help me to esteem sanctifying grace as the most precious treasure on earth, for if I possess it God loves me and promises me heaven with its eternal joys as my glorious reward. In order to merit sanctifying grace for me, your Son has shed His Blood on the cross. Never let me lose that grace by mortal sin.

My body is a vessel of honor, for it is sanctified when I receive in Holy Communion the Body and Blood of Jesus. Never let me profane the temple of the living God by sins of impurity.

Offering the Immaculate Lamb to Your Majesty, O Lord, we beg You to enkindle our hearts with that Divine Fire which unceasingly glowed in the Heart of the Blessed Virgin Mary. Through Christ Our Lord. Amen. (*Feast of the Immaculate Heart of Mary*, August 22)
  Aspiration:
  Holy Mary, make my heart and my body clean.

300 days (713)

26. Singular Vessel of Devotion

Consideration:

"Singular" means "incomparable." "Devotion" means "Devotedness." *Mary is a shrine of incomparable devotedness.* Mary is like that alabaster vase which the penitent woman broke above the feet of the Savior, and scent arose from the spices so that the whole house was made fragrant. From the heart of Mary is breathed a perfume of incomparable holiness so exquisite that the whole Church is fragrant because of her.

"Devotion" means "devotedness to God," full surrender of ourselves to God and His service, the spirit of prayer and recollection, spiritual consolation and joy. Conscious of her dignity as Mother of God, and grateful for the gifts she had received from God, *Mary pledged herself to the fulfillment of her vow of dedication* expressed at the Annunciation: "Behold the handmaid of the Lord, be it done to me according to thy word." Mary kept all these wondrous mysteries of God's mercy and love in her heart, pondering over them in prayerful admiration; the result was a peace and joy which never left her even in her sorrows.

Mary, the Singular Vessel of Devotion, will deepen your spiritual life so that *you may share in her perfect dedication to God* and enjoy the fruits of this union of love. Devotion to her will enable you to serve God with perfect devotedness as she did; that you may give yourself wholeheartedly to Him in all things, and serve Him with a generous and cheerful heart.

Prayer

(1) MARY, you are the Singular Vessel of Devotion because *you consecrated yourself entirely to God.* You knew no more important concern, no greater happiness than to serve Him and to act according to His will. Your heart was constantly turned toward God; He was the only object of all your wishes, your hopes, and your love.

Your life was consecrated to His service. Even in your most tender years, you offered yourself as a sacrifice to God and were ever intent upon walking in His holy fear and love.

Your understanding was constantly occupied in admiring His goodness and holiness; Your memory, in recalling His benefits. In your will you erected an altar upon which the fire of love burned continually, thus fulfilling your words to Elizabeth: "My soul magnifies the Lord, and my spirit rejoices in God my Savior" (Luke 1:46–47). You also consecrated your whole body to God's service with unceasing and fervent devotion.

(2) MARY, your devotion showed itself in love and fervor in prayer. No one has ever more perfectly complied with the words of our Savior that we should pray always and without ceasing.

You practiced *mental prayer,* for the Gospel says of you: "Mary kept in mind all these words, pondering them in her heart" (Luke 2:51). There was scarcely a moment in which you did not think of God and silently offer up some prayer to Him. You had so great a desire to fulfill the will of God that you could say with your Divine Son, "My food is to do the will of him who sent me" (John 4:34).

You also loved *vocal prayer.* To do this more perfectly, you went to the temple when a child and dwelt there among the virgins consecrated to God until your fourteenth year. Each year you made the long journey to Jerusalem in order to pray in the temple. With what fervent devotion you must have said your family prayers! After the Ascension of your Son you were with the Apostles in the upper room of Jerusalem and persevered in one mind with them in prayer until Pentecost. Prayer to your Eucharistic Son was the heart and soul of your life after His Ascension into heaven. Praying, you departed this life; your last breath was the most ardent expression of that devotion which inflamed your loving heart.

(3) MARY, *you communicate to other souls the fervor of devotion which burns in your own heart.* How many prayers are said in your honor throughout the world! Who can number the Rosaries that are recited!

Singular Vessel of Devotion, help me to understand that true devotion does not consist in sweet sentiments or pious actions, but in the perfect love of God and the faithful performance of His holy Will. Help me to make a complete sacrifice of myself to God as

you did; help me to use the faculties of my soul and body only to
do what is right, good, and pleasing to God.

I ask that you help me to raise my heart often to God in prayer
as you did. Let me seek your intercession and venerate you with a
tender affection, that you may take me under your powerful protection in life and in death.

O God, You sent the Holy Spirit to Your Apostles, who were united in
prayer with Mary, the Mother of Jesus; grant us that, protected by this
same Mother of ours, the Queen of Apostles, we may be made worthy
to serve Your Divine Majesty faithfully and proclaim Your glory by word
and example. Through the same Christ Our Lord. Amen. (*Feast of Our
Lady, Queen of the Apostles,* Saturday after the Ascension)
   Aspiration:
      Most pure Heart of the Blessed Virgin Mary, obtain for me from
      Jesus a pure and humble heart.

                                                    300 days (387)*

JULY—Second Saturday

27. Mystical Rose

Consideration:

The saints are often compared to flowers. Since *the rose* is the queen of flowers, Mary, the queen of all saints, has been compared to the rose. She is called the Mystical Rose because of the mysteries contained in her person and her life.

Blessed by the rays of the eternal love of the Holy Spirit, this rose bloomed in the soil of unworldliness and piety. She is like the *white* rose of purity. We think of her as the *red* rose when she stands beneath the cross of Calvary watching the Precious Blood of her Divine Son. We think of her as a rose of *gold* as she rejoices in the bliss and glory of her Son's Resurrection.

But this Mystical Rose also had *thorns*—thorns of a life of trials and sorrows. You, too, must walk the path of thorns to reach heaven. To attain to true beauty of soul you must sacrifice self; only then will you resemble the Mystical Rose.

The *green leaves* of a rose are a sign of hope even in the greatest trials. Mary is your hope. You will obtain from God all the graces and blessing you need through her prayers. Never lose confidence in the Mystical Rose, for in the end you will find God and, like her, you will one day adorn the garden of Paradise.

Prayer

(1) MARY, you are called the Mystical Rose, for in a spiritual sense I see in you everything that is found in a rose: sharp thorns, green leaves, and sweet fragrant flowers.

The thorns of a rose are the trials and sorrows of life. The path of suffering was the path your footsteps trod. I think of the pain you felt because of the danger to your Divine Child through the cruelty of Herod, the arduous flight into Egypt, and your long stay in that country. What bitterness you felt when you lost your Child and sought Him three days. You yourself exclaimed: "Son, why hast thou done so to us? Behold, thy father and I have been seeking thee sorrowing" (Luke 2:48). You shared all the sufferings which the Divine Savior had to suffer during His public life. No mother ever suffered as much as you did: standing beneath the cross, you felt as if you were plunged in a sea of sorrow. Aged Simeon's words were fulfilled: "Thy own soul a sword shall pierce" (Luke 2:35).

Mystical Rose, you and the saints have trod the path of thorns to reach heaven; I cannot avoid this rugged path. Suffering is a sign that God loves me and wishes me to be saved. Let me never forget that suffering, if borne with patience and love, will win great glory for me in heaven.

(2) MARY, *the green leaves of a rose are a symbol of the hope which we place in you.* You are our hope. We place our hope in God as the Fountain of all good, as the Author and Giver of all graces; but we place our confidence in you only in so far as you can and will obtain from God all blessings and graces by your intercession. Jesus will not refuse your petitions because you are His Mother. He owes His very life to you. He loves you most tenderly on account of your sanctity. No creature on earth can obtain for us so many graces as you, our intercessor, whom God has honored with the privilege of being His Mother. Since you are also our Mother, you know no greater delight than to make use of your power with God to procure for us the help of heaven in all our needs.

Mystical Rose, be my hope in life. Turning to you with confidence, I firmly hope that you will help me in every danger and obtain for me the grace to overcome all the enemies of my salvation so that I may remain steadfast in God's grace to the very end. Be my hope in death, when the devil will exert his utmost power to ruin me. Protect and strengthen me that I may be victorious in that last struggle and die a happy death.

(3) MARY, *the red rose is a symbol of your love; the white rose, a symbol of your virginal purity.* God, Who is love, appeared on earth to enkindle in all mankind the fire of His holy love; but He inflamed no heart with His love so intensely as your own. Being entirely free from all desire for earthly things, you were most capable of receiving His holy love. You alone without any imperfection fulfilled the great commandment of charity.

As a white rose you appear in matchless beauty of virginal purity. You are the queen of virgins. Virginal purity was of greater value in your eyes than even the dignity of being the Mother of God. Therefore, you love virginal souls most tenderly, and graciously listen to their prayers.

Mystical Rose, help me to love God with a love that is ready to sacrifice everything, even life, rather than offend Him and lose His grace. Help me to love chastity and to take heed lest I do or permit anything contrary to this holy virtue. Through prayer and frequent Holy Communion aid me in preserving the virtue of purity until death.

May the right hand of Your Immaculate Mother raise up those, O Lord, whom You have nourished richly with food from heaven, that through her help we may come to our everlasting home. Who live and reign forever. Amen. *(Feast of the Apparition of the Blessed Virgin,* February 11)
   Aspiration:
      Sacred Heart of Jesus, I give myself to You through Mary.
                                             300 days (238) *

28. Tower of David

Consideration:

The Tower of David was the strongest tower in the wall of Jerusalem which survived even the destruction of the city. This title proclaims Mary as *a strong fortress* in the defense of the Church and *the armory* where the faithful find all the weapons they need for their warfare against the powers of hell. If we regard the "new Jerusalem" as the Church, as St. John invites us to do, then Mary becomes its strong citadel and watch-tower, and its greatest glory, as the Church has her speak in the liturgy, "And so, in Sion was I established, and in the Holy City made I my rest, and in Jerusalem was my power."

Your warfare is against the spirit of the world and against the evil spirits prowling about the world seeking to destroy souls. Your greatest enemies are the world, the flesh, and the devil.

Mary is your unconquerable defense in the conflict with the powers of darkness. If you face these enemies courageously, you can count on her help as a shield in your hands. Mary will help you to use the right weapons, especially prayer and penance, for which she pleaded at Lourdes and Fátima. With her help you will be victorious.

Prayer

(1) MARY, you are called the Tower of David because the Church applies to you these words of the Canticle: "Thy neck is as the tower of David, which is built with bulwarks; a thousand bucklers hang upon it, all the armor of valiant men" (4:4).

The towers which David built to the walls of Jerusalem rose above all the other buildings. From them one could obtain a clear view of the surrounding country and observe every movement of the enemy. As the Tower of David surpassed all other buildings of Jerusalem, so *you, the daughter of David, excel all angels and men in dignity and sanctity.* The angels and saints are servants and friends of God, but you are the Mother of God. No dignity is higher than this. Consequently, God has endowed you with a higher degree of sanctity than that which all angels and men could possess.

Tower of David, you were the most humble of all; hence the Lord did great things for you. He chose you to become the Mother of His Son and made you the Queen of Heaven. Help me to become daily more humble, that I may be great in the eyes of God.

(2) MARY, the Tower of David was so strong and provided with so many means of defense that it could resist the attacks of the enemy. Greeting you as the Tower of David, I acknowledge that *the devil could not prevail against you* and that you overcame all his attacks. Though he lay in wait for your heel, you crushed his head (Gen. 3:15). By an extraordinary grace God preserved you from the stain of original sin and thereby prevented you from falling into the power of Satan in the very first moment of your life.

The weapons you used in your struggles against Satan were those which your Divine Son recommended to His disciples and to us: "Watch and pray, that you may not enter into temptation" (Matt. 26:41). You were watchful over your heart, over your senses, over your surroundings. Where you could not escape the attacks of the enemy, you met them with courage and confidence in God, with your eyes fixed upon God, and asking His help in prayer.

Let me also be like a Tower of David in the struggle with my spiritual enemies. With the help of divine grace I can conquer evil. Help me to be watchful over myself; for the devil often makes use of the inclinations of my heart and my external senses in order to tempt me to sin. Make me watchful in dealing with the world, so that I may avoid all occasions of temptations. Like you I wish to place my entire confidence in God and to pray frequently, especially in the hour of temptation.

(3) MARY, the Tower of David afforded protection and safety to all on account of its firmness and its powerful means of defense. You are such a tower for me. *You afford me the most powerful protection and will permit no harm to befall me,* if I have recourse to you in my struggle against evil. I hope certainly to be saved, because a firm trust in you is my weapon. I shall face my enemies courageously when I can count on your help as a shield in my hands.

Tower of David, protect my soul from sin. I turn to you for aid when the battle is heaviest. With your help I shall be victorious.

Lord, we beg You, may we be helped by the prayers of Your most holy
Mother, whose Rosary we are honoring, that we may draw strength from
the mysteries which we reverence, and obtain the effect of the Sacraments
which we have received. Who live and reign forever. Amen. (*Feast of the
Most Holy Rosary*, October 7)

    Aspiration:

      O Mary, our hope, have pity on us.

300 days (299)

29. Tower of Ivory

Consideration:

As the Tower of David suggests war, *the tower of ivory suggests peace, wealth, joyous feasting.* Rich people in ancient times used to build palaces in which ivory was so plentiful that they were called ivory palaces.

Mary is like an ivory tower, reaching to the very heavens as a symbol of peace, for through her peace and salvation came to the world because she gave mankind a Savior. *In this tower of ivory there is the wealth of grace, the refinement of perfect virtue, the joy and peace of union with God.* In this tower the jubilant Magnificat, Mary's hymn of thanksgiving, first re-sounded and continues to re-echo through the heavens.

Let Mary's life of virtue serve as *an example* for your imitation. Let her wealth of grace and heavenly joy give you confidence that you can secure true holiness through her prayers. The pure white ivory reminds you of the sinlessness which was hers and the purity that must be yours if you wish to become like Mary and pleasing to God.

Prayer

(1) MARY, the Church greets you as a Tower of Ivory, for under this symbol you appear in Holy Scripture, where it is said of you: "Thy neck is as a tower of ivory" (Canticle 7:4).

In calling you a Tower of Ivory I indicate your beauty. The Church applies the words of the Canticle to you: "Thou art all fair, O my love; and there is not a spot in thee" (4:7). The great beauty of your soul, your angelic innocence, your perfect sanctity so rejoiced the Heart of the Holy Trinity that the Father chose you for His Daughter, the Son for His Mother, and the Holy Spirit for His Spouse. While the saints, too, possess beauty of soul, none of them equals you in holiness. You preserved your original innocence throughout life: not the least stain of sin ever disfigured you; you were entirely free from every imperfection.

Tower of Ivory, help me to recognize the vanity of all earthly things. Bodily beauty without beauty of soul is nothing. I desire above all else a beautiful soul, adorned with innocence and Christian virtues, especially humility, chastity, and the love of God. Give me such a soul that God may love me more and give me heaven as my reward, where I shall see your everlasting beauty.

(2) MARY, a tower of ivory has a shining whiteness and wonderful strength. In a spiritual sense, you are like a strong tower of ivory. *With a pure white soul you cling firmly to God in joy and in sorrow.*

How firm is your *faith!* When the angel reveals to you that you are to conceive the Son of God and become a Mother without ceasing to be a virgin, you believe and consent. How firm is your *confidence* in God! Trials of all kinds come upon you, but you put all your hope in God and submit to His adorable Will. How strong is your *love* for God! Nothing in the world is able to captivate your heart; you know no other delight than to serve God, and you are ready to make any sacrifice for His honor. You practice every virtue all your life with the greatest fidelity. Accepting with perfect *resignation* all that God is pleased to send you, you embrace it with joy for love of Him. Even when you see your Son dragged to execution and crucified, you do not abandon Him. You hide your grief in the depths of your heart. How perfect is your life of *prayer!* After the Ascension of Our Lord you devote yourself to prayer and good works till your very death.

(3) MARY, you are like a tower of ivory because *by your example you make us love virtue, and by your protection you guard us against the attacks of Satan.* After your edifying example I wish to lead a virtuous life. I rely on your protection in every temptation because I know that as Mother of God you possess more power than all the angels and saints, and as my own Mother you are ever ready to help me.

Tower of Ivory, make me like a tower of ivory. Help me to serve God with fervor and faithfulness all the days of my life as you did. I have consecrated myself to my Savior in holy Baptism and promised to be always His follower. Let me never become a traitor and associate myself with His and my enemies, Satan and sin. Never permit anything in the world to cause me to waver in my fidelity to God. Let me be diligent in prayer and in receiving the Sacraments, for by these powerful aids I can persevere to the end and save my soul.

May the prayer of blessed Mary, Your Mother and our Mediatrix, help us, O Lord; that through the bestowal of Your grace we may obtain an increase of eternal redemption. Who live and reign forever. Amen. *(Feast of Mary, Mediatrix of All Graces,* May 31)

Aspiration:

Hail Mary, etc. By your Immaculate Conception, O Mary, make my body pure and my soul holy.

300 days (358)

30. House of Gold

Consideration:

"House of Gold" refers to Sion, Jerusalem, that David fortified, and to *the Temple that Solomon built* there, overlaying its walls and very floor with gold. The Oriental enjoyed grandeur, and the Golden House of the Lord seemed to him supremely suitable. Hence he had lavished on it all he could. And so indeed did God, for the Heart of Mary; for her who would even physically shelter His Son for those first months, and in whose Heart He would always "feel at home." The psalmist says, "Holiness befits Thy House, O Lord, for ever and for ever!"

Gold represents to us the highest in value. *When God made Mary, this House of Gold, He used the gold of His love and grace.* Mary is filled with divine love because she is full of grace, and the Son of God finds His delight in dwelling in her.

Learn from the House of Gold that *true wealth* is not material riches, but riches of the soul—virtue, love, grace, merit. Let your one ambition be to acquire the gold of divine love and grace, so that God may always find His delight in dwelling in your soul as He did in Mary's.

Prayer

(1) MARY, we honor you as the House of Gold because *in you the Blessed Trinity has performed such great and wonderful things.* The temple of Jerusalem which King Solomon built was magnificent. Scripture says, "There was nothing in the temple that was not covered with gold" (3 Kings 6:22). This temple could justly be called the "house of gold." But how much more does that name apply to you, the living Sanctuary, whom the Lord made for Himself!

Even before the Incarnation, you were in a marvelous sense "the House of the Lord, His House of Gold" (Isaias 7:14). God *the Father* worked the greatest miracle at the moment of your concep-

314

tion. He commanded human nature, defiled by sin, to stay its course until you, the child of grace, were conceived and born free from corruption of nature and untouched by original sin. *The Divine Son,* delighted with your beauty, descended from heaven and was made Man in you by assuming flesh from your flesh. God *the Holy Spirit* lovingly looked upon you as His Spouse and poured into your soul the fullness of His graces. He worked in you the tremendous miracle of the Incarnation of the Divine Word, so that you became the Mother of God without ceasing to be the Virgin of virgins.

House of Gold, my soul is also a house of gold because it is sanctified by the presence of the Blessed Trinity. My body is a house of gold because it is a temple of the Holy Spirit and most intimately united with Jesus in Holy Communion. Let me never profane the temple of my soul with wicked desires and sins, for the Apostle says, "If anyone destroys the temple of God, him will God destroy; for holy is the temple of God, and this temple you are" (1 Cor. 3:17). Preserve my body undefiled, and do not permit me to do anything that would be displeasing to God.

(2) MARY, you are adorned with all virtues and especially with the seven Gifts of the Holy Spirit. "Wisdom has built herself a house; she has hewn her out seven pillars" (Prov. 9:1). The Fathers and writers of the Church recognize this house to be you.

You possessed the gift of *Wisdom,* for, being detached from everything earthly, you always had before your eyes the salvation of your soul and earnestly strove to obtain it; the gift of *Understanding,* for your knowledge of divine things was most wonderful, deeper than that of the theologians or even the blessed spirits in heaven; the gift of *Counsel,* for in doubtful affairs you knew what was good and pleasing to God, and you could, therefore, give good counsel to others; the gift of *Fortitude,* for you overcame every obstacle to salvation, and nothing could weaken your virtue, especially when you accepted God's holy Will in the great sufferings of your life; the gift of *Knowledge,* for you had a thorough insight into the mysteries and truths of the Christian religion and were able to lead others to the knowledge of them; the gift of *Piety,* for you recognized and honored God in all things as the infinitely wise, kind, and merciful Father, and you found no greater happiness than to adore and serve Him with all your heart; the gift of the *Fear of the Lord,* for you loved God above all else and feared nothing more than to offend Him.

Immaculate Spouse of the Holy Spirit, House of Gold, obtain for me the seven Gifts of the Holy Spirit. Since prayer is the key to God's Heart and draws down upon us every good and perfect gift, teach me to pray frequently for these gifts. Keep me humble and pure of heart so as to make myself worthy of receiving them.

(3) MARY, *you are for us a House of Gold.* You have borne in your womb and brought forth Him to Whom we owe every blessing, Jesus, our Redeemer, Who has broken the chains of sin, reconciled us with God, and opened heaven for us.

You are the House of Gold, the door of which stands ever invitingly open, and through which we receive treasures far more precious than all the gold in the world. You are a Mother who has a most tender compassion for her children, who looks upon us with eyes of mercy, and who comes to our aid in all our needs. Look upon me with mercy, for I need your aid so very much. Unite me with your loving Son so that I may receive the treasures of His grace in this life and everlasting life in heaven.

O God, Who mercifully sanctified the house of the Blessed Mary ever Virgin through the mystery of the Incarnation, and placed it in the bosom of Your Church in a wonderful manner; grant that we may avoid the dwellings of sinners and someday live in Your holy home. Through Christ Our Lord. Amen. (*Feast of the Transferring of the Holy House of Mary,* December 10)

Aspiration:

My Mother, deliver me from mortal sin. Hail Mary (*three times*).

300 days (297)

31. Ark of the Covenant

Consideration:

We know that God made His earlier covenant or alliance with His People, and that the very symbol of His presence among them was *the Ark.* His glory hovered over the Ark, and the Tables of the Law were preserved in it. The Old Law was graven on tables of stone, but the New Law must be written deep in human hearts. The Covenant now is Christ Himself. He is our Sacrifice and "our Peace" (Eph. 2:14).

Mary is called the Ark of the Covenant because in a true sense *it is within Mary that Jesus is always living.* She bore within herself not the tablets of the Law, but the Lawgiver Himself; not the manna of the desert, but the true Manna and Bread of Life everlasting; not the rod of Aaron, but the divine High Priest.

Through *baptism* you become a partner to this covenant made between God and yourself. Mary, the Ark of the Covenant, will help you to become a worthy partner by helping you to observe the commandments, to receive the Bread of Life frequently, to join the divine High Priest in the offering of His Sacrifice in the Mass.

Prayer

(1) MARY, in the Old Testament *the ark of Noe was a symbol of you.* When God decided to destroy the human race because of its many sins, He ordered Noe to build an ark for himself and his family. After the deluge came, all mankind, except Noe and his family, perished.

You are in a more perfect sense an ark of safety than was Noe's ark, for through you we have received the Redeemer Who saved not only a few persons, but all mankind from destruction. As by the ark of Noe men were rescued from death, so through you all mankind has been rescued from the shipwreck of sin. Under your protecting mantle the just and sinners find refuge.

I take you, a spiritual ark, as my model. The waters of sin have never destroyed your pure soul. Help me to avoid every mortal sin and even those venial sins which I frequently commit. As you receive all, the just and the unjust, and reveal yourself to them as a loving, merciful Mother, help me to be kind toward all, and do good whenever an opportunity presents itself.

(2) MARY, *the ark of the covenant was also a symbol of you.* At the command of God, Moses built the ark of gold and precious wood and put into it the two stone tablets containing the Ten Commandments, the blooming rod of Aaron, and a golden vessel with manna. This ark, the most sacred object of the Mosaic Law, was placed in the Holy of Holies. Afterward it was brought to the temple of Solomon where it remained for over four hundred years till the destruction of the temple.

The ark was made of precious *setim-wood,* which owing to its durability never decays. It is a symbol of the truth that your soul remained untouched by the corruption of sin, and that your body also did not see corruption, but, united with your soul soon after your death, was assumed into heaven. The *gold,* with which the ark of the covenant was overlaid within and without, is a symbol of your virtues, especially your love of God and purity of intention, the foundation of all your actions. In the ark of the covenant, the two stone *tablets of the Law* were deposited; in you, the living ark of the covenant, the Lawgiver and Savior Himself dwelt for nine months. The blooming *rod of Aaron* was a symbol of Christ, the eternal High Priest, who became Man in your womb. The vessel containing *manna* reminds me that you bore under your heart the spiritual Manna, Jesus Christ, Who called Himself "the living bread that has come down from heaven" (John 6:51) .

Help me to be like an ark of the covenant. May my life resemble setim-wood—pure and untouched by the coruption of sin. May my heart be of gold so that divine love may burn in it, and so that I may do all things for the love of God. Make me a living ark: to keep the commandments of God in my heart and have no other desire than that of fulfilling the holy will of God. Keep in my heart a most fervent desire for the heavenly Manna of Holy Communion, so that I may receive this Sacrament frequently and worthily.

(3) MARY, you are the ark of the covenant because *you support us in the struggles against the enemies of our salvation.* The ark of

the covenant was the most sacred object among the Jews. From its golden covering God spoke to them and gave them His blessings. Because of it He worked many miracles to protect them. You not only protect us from evil, but also intercede with God to obtain for us grace and mercy.

Ark of the Covenant, I beg for your protection against the enemies of my soul—the world, the flesh, and the devil. Plead to God in my behalf if I should have the misfortune of offending Him. Ever be to me a Mother of Mercy and the source of all the graces I need to find Jesus and salvation.

O Lord, abide with Your people who are refreshed by receiving Your Body and Blood, that by the help of Your most holy Mother we may be freed from all evil and be protected in every good work. Who live and reign forever. Amen. (*Feast of Our Lady of the Most Blessed Sacrament,* May 13)

Aspiration:

Hail, true Body, born of the Virgin Mary!

500 days (141) *

32. Gate of Heaven

Consideration:

Mary is called the Gate of Heaven because *the Son of God came down from heaven and entered this world through her.* The Church in her liturgy calls her "the gate of the great King, the blessed gate, the gate of light." Mary is the blessed gate through which the King of Heaven entered this world, and she remained an inviolate virgin before, in, and after the birth of Jesus.

Mary is the Gate of Heaven because *through her hands God imparts to us all the graces which we need to enter heaven.* As the Mother of God she shared in the Redemption, therefore she now distributes the graces merited by her Son. It is God's Will that all graces should reach us through her prayers. She is the Mediatrix of Graces.

Mary is the Gate of Heaven *for you,* if only you come to her with child-like confidence. Through her prayers you will obtain all the graces you need to live a holy life and to enter the gates of heaven.

Prayer

(1) MARY, we greet you as the Gate of Heaven because *you are the Mother of the Gate of Heaven, Jesus Christ, our Redeemer.* He said, "I am the Door. If anyone enter by me he shall be safe, and shall go in and out, and shall find pastures. . . . I came that they may have life, and have it more abundantly" (John 10:9). St. Paul says that "there is but one God," and one "Mediator of God and men, the man Christ Jesus; who gave himself a redemption for all."

When the Church calls you the "Gate of Heaven," she is not attributing to you what belongs to the God-Man. But she teaches that all the honor paid to you tends to the glory of Jesus. If you have so much power, it is from Jesus that you derive it, and with Him that you exercise it.

(2) MARY, you are the Gate of Heaven because *through your hands God imparts to us all the graces by means of which we obtain*

heaven. God left it to your own free choice to accept or to refuse the honor of becoming the Mother of His Son. But having become the Mother of God, you share in the work of our Redemption. From the very moment that you conceived the Divine Word in your womb, you obtained, so to speak, power over the gifts which are imparted to us by the Holy Spirit, so that no creature obtains any grace from God without your mediation.

Gate of Heaven, you are the sweetest, the tenderest, the kindest of mothers, constantly watching me with eyes of love as I wend my weary way through this same valley of tears that was once marked by your own blessed footsteps. How surely does devotion to you open the heavenly portals to numberless souls! Be the Gate of Heaven to me by obtaining through your prayers all the graces I need to live a holy life and to enter the gates of heaven.

(3) MARY, *you are all-powerful with God by your intercession.* Your Divine Son is ever ready to listen to your prayers, because He desires so ardently to gladden your heart, so that you seem to command rather than to ask. Therefore, you are all-powerful in heaven and on earth through your prayers, and you are able to raise the hopes even of those who are on the point of despair.

Your loving Son said, "Strive to enter by the narrow gate; for many, I tell you, will seek to enter and will not be able" (Luke 13:24). Banish from my heart all sinful desires, all attachment to the world and its goods and pleasures. Help me to live a mortified life so that I may be able to enter heaven through the narrow gate. Teach me to be humble, and in all things to seek the honor of God and to bear with patience the crosses of life.

Through your prayers, be the Gate of Heaven to me, for you speak in the words of the Scripture: "Blessed is the man that hears me and that watches daily at my gates, and waits at the posts of my doors. He that shall find me shall find life, and shall have salvation from the Lord" (Prov. 8:34).

May the prayer of the Mother of God help Your people, O Lord, and though we know that she passed from this life as every mortal must, may we feel her intercession for us before You in heavenly glory. Through Christ Our Lord. Amen. (*Feast of the Assumption,* August 15)

Aspiration:

My Mother, my hope.

300 days (302)

AUGUST—Fourth Saturday

33. Morning Star

Consideration:

Our Lord is constantly called the "Sun of Justice." *Mary is His forerunner* like the morning star, that planet which in the south shines so strongly that it can actually cast a shadow.

Mary is *the herald of the dawning day of redemption.* She stood in the sky of the Old Testament as the Virgin that would conceive and bear a Son, Whose name would be Emmanuel. That sun began to shine on the day of the Annunciation, for the Word was made flesh and dwelt among us. On Christmas she gave the Sun of Justice to a dark, sad, and sinful world. The day of Redemption had come.

Mary is also the Morning Star that *proclaims the joy and bliss of the eternal day.* Redemption was a preparation for the endless day of eternity. In her Assumption she heralded the hope of our eternal life with God and the enjoyment of the day that will never see a sunset.

We need the cheering light of this Morning Star in the darkness and confusion of our day of materialism and vice. With our gaze fixed on this Star, we shall never lose our course, for Mary will lead us surely to Jesus and we shall reach the harbor of peace on the blissful shores of eternity.

Prayer

(1) MARY, your loving Son Jesus calls Himself the Light of the World: "I am the light of the world. He who follows me does not walk in the darkness, but will have the light of life" (John 8:12). The Church calls Him the Sun of Justice. As the morning star precedes the sun, announcing the dawn of day, so *you precede Christ, the Sun of Justice, announcing the day of salvation.* Through your coming, blessed Morning Star, the whole world was enlightened. You were truly the bright Morning Star of that blissful day when the world saw the Divine Sun of its Redemption arise upon it.

You withdrew during the public life of Jesus, when like the sun

He gave light by word and deed. But when the Sun of Justice went down, you again appeared as the Evening Star, for I behold you on Calvary standing under the cross of your Son. Even now, after our Divine Savior has withdrawn His visible presence and is enthroned in heaven at the right hand of His Father, you shine in the Church as a friendly Star whose radiant light will never more be extinguished till the end of time.

(2) MARY, *you are greater than all the angels and saints, as the morning star excels all other stars in size and beauty.* The saints are friends and servants of God, but you are His Mother. You also surpass the angels and saints in the splendor of your sanctity. Since you possess the highest dignity among all creatures, it is fitting that you should also possess the greatest degree of sanctity. As the morning star receives its light from the sun, you possess your sanctity not of yourself, but from God. God sanctified and preserved you from every stain of sin from the first moment of your conception. It was He Who watched over you through your whole life and preserved you from the least fault. It was He Who strengthened you to overcome every temptation and to walk with perseverance on the path of virtue. You had to acknowledge with the Apostle Paul: "By the grace of God I am what I am, and his grace in me has not been fruitless" (1 Cor. 15:10).

As the morning star shines by the light which it derives from the sun and which it reflects, you eagerly received the graces which God imparted to you so richly, and you faithfully made use of each grace for the salvation of your soul. It was this constant cooperation with grace that enabled you to attain the highest degree of sanctity.

(3) MARY, as the morning star is a welcome sight to those who sail on the sea as well as to those who travel on land, *so also are you a source of hope to those who call upon you* amid the tempests of the heart, the storms of the mind and the senses. I have been saved through the mild splendor of that cherished Star. Help me to honor you by a life pure as the unchanging rays of your light!

Blessed Morning Star, when I find myself tossed about by storms in the current of this world, teach me to turn my eyes to your brightness. When winds of temptation arise, I want to look up to you and call upon you. When I am tossed about on the whisperings of pride or ambition or envy; when anger, avarice, or evil desires trouble my mind, let me turn to you. When frightened at the greatness of my sins, or terrified with the dread of the future judgment, or feel discouraged—in dangers, in difficulties, and in doubts, I want to think of you, lovely Morning Star, and invoke your intercession. Let your name never depart from my mouth or heart. And that I may obtain the benefit of your prayers, let me imitate the example of your life. While you support me, I cannot fall; while you protect me, I cannot fear; while you guide me, I cannot feel tired. And if you are kind to me, I shall arrive in safety at the port of heaven. Grant this, I pray, for the love of your dear Son, Jesus Christ.

Lord Jesus Christ, Good Shepherd, Who gave Your life for Your sheep, and Who when dying on the Cross entrusted to the Virgin Mary the sheep of Your pasture, grant that through her intercession we may on earth follow You, our Shepherd, and so be led to the heavenly pastures of life everlasting. Who live and reign forever. Amen. (*Feast of Our Lady, Mother of the Good Shepherd,* September 3)

Aspiration:

Sweet Heart of Mary, be my salvation.

300 days (386) *

34. Health of the Sick

Consideration:

Mary is called the Health of the Sick because she is the *Mother of the Divine Physician*. In His day, Jesus "went about doing good." The Gospel says that He was "going about all Galilee, teaching in their synagogues and preaching the gospel of the kingdom and healing every disease and every sickness among the people" (Matt. 4:23).

Innumerable cures of the sick are wrought through the intercession of the saints. It would seem strange if their Queen would be without such power of healing. The fact is, *no other saint has wrought more cures of the sick than Mary*. Lourdes, Fátima, and other shrines throughout the world are a silent tribute to her motherly care of the sick and the afflicted.

Mary's cures often come rather for the benefit of the soul than of the body. She knows how to direct the mind of the sufferer to the blessing of suffering and to see in it a proof of God's love. Through her prayers the sick and afflicted find the grace to accept their cross with resignation, patience, and love, just as she did during her lifetime, for she is the **Mother of Sorrows** and the **Health of the Sick**.

Prayer

(1) MARY, *you have learned the meaning of compassion* while you witnessed the long and bitter sufferings of your Son during His holy Passion. At the foot of the cross you received from His lips as an inheritance all the faithful as your children in the person of the beloved disciple John. Your children who invoke you know that your power equals your love. When you were told that Elizabeth was with child, you hastened to her side to help her. If you showed such compassion for the married couple at Cana who were disturbed because the wine failed, how much more will you have pity on the sick whose need is far greater. Who can number all the

miraculous cures of the most terrible diseases of body and soul, which have been wrought through your intercession? When we visit sacred shrines, like Lourdes and Fátima, where great churches have been erected in your honor, we find there inscriptions engraved by gratitude and gifts offered to your altar as trophies of your power over diseases which resisted all human aid.

Therefore, to whom after Jesus can the Christian turn in the crosses and sufferings of life, if not to you, the Health of the Sick? In your motherly compassion, sympathize with the sick throughout the world and give them comfort and help, and even health, if this should be God's will.

(2) MARY, *you comfort the sick with motherly love and alleviate their sufferings.* You take an interest in them lest they lose patience and become discouraged. A mother watches day and night by the bedside of her darling child when it is dangerously ill; lovingly she treats the little one and caresses it. But your love for us is greater than any mother's love. Unseen you stand at the sickbed and serve them with motherly care. You pour strengthening remedies into the hearts of the sick so that they feel their pains soothed; you speak words of peace and consolation to their souls, so as to revive their courage and to strengthen their confidence; you procure for them the forgiveness of their sins and peace of conscience which is such a comfort in suffering. You help them in every temptation and give them grace to gain the victory. You confirm their hope, fill them with confidence in God, and help them to pray with a cheerful heart and perfect resignation: Thy will be done!

Health of the Sick, help me to realize that it is a great grace to be sick. May sickness lead me to a knowledge of my helplessness and teach me the virtue of humility. May sickness open my eyes to the vanity of all earthly things and direct my heart to those which are above. May sickness weaken the violence of carnal desires and remove from me the occasion of sin. May sickness teach me to pray with devotion; may it give me an opportunity to practice patience, obedience, humility, and confidence in God.

May I use sickness as one of the great means I have of atoning for my sins and of increasing my merits for heaven. Help me to thank God for sickness. Though I use the proper means for recovery, I wish to leave it entirely to God to do with me what He wills, since He knows what is best for me. Perfect resignation is the most acceptable sacrifice to God, as you have taught me in your own life.

(3) MARY, *you are the health of the spiritually sick.* In the days of their strength they live in forgetfulness of God, and when illness overtakes them they lie down with the poison of sin eating into their hearts. The gnawing worm of conscience, the fear of their approaching death, of the judgment to come, and of a never ending eternity, fills them with anguish and brings them to the verge of despair. May they, too, learn that you are the Health of the Sick. Obtain for them the grace of repentance and forgiveness and even bodily health.

Grant us, Your servants, we beg of You, O Lord God, that we may be blessed with health of soul and body, and by the glorious intercession of the Blessed Virgin Mary be freed from the sorrows of this present life and enjoy everlasting bliss. Through Christ Our Lord. Amen. (*Feast of Our Lady, Health of the Sick,* Saturday before the last Sunday of August) *Aspiration:*

> We fly to your patronage, O holy Mother of God; do not reject our petitions in our needs, but deliver us always from all dangers, O glorious and blessed Virgin.

5 years (333) *

35. Refuge of Sinners

Consideration:

Mary is called the Refuge of Sinners because She is *the Mother of the Good Shepherd* Who laid down His life for His sheep. He came to seek the lost sheep and to bring them to His sheepfold that there may be one flock and one shepherd. The conversion of sinners is this Shepherd's greatest joy, for He says, "There will be joy in heaven over one sinner who repents, more than over ninety-nine just who have no need of repentance" (Luke 15:7).

After God, no one knows *the malice of sin* more than Mary. Like her Son she understands that sin is the greatest evil in the world, an offense to the almighty God, a rejection of the Blood of her Son, the ruin of souls.

From the Cross *Jesus entrusted to the care of His Mother the souls He was redeeming.* She is eager to carry out His Last Will, especially by being a mother to sinners, who need her most. Her motherly love urges her to come to the rescue of sinners and to prevent their eternal damnation. She pleads with her Son in their behalf that they may be given the grace to repent and be saved. If there is left at least a spark of good will in the sinner, he will be saved through Mary's prayer.

What a source of hope this is for you, if you have often hurt God by sin in your lifetime! Mary is ever your Refuge when we have sinned and your most powerful Advocate before the Just Judge, to whom she can plead with a mother's unfailing prayers.

Prayer

(1) MARY, being the Mother of our Redeemer, *you receive sinners with loving kindness, and you do all you can to save them from damnation.* What sacrifices you made for us during your earthly life! For thirty-three years—from the time you laid the newborn Savior in the crib of Bethlehem to the day when you stood beneath the cross on Calvary and watched Him die—you suffered a con-

stant martyrdom, for the sword of sorrow continually pierced your soul. But you did not complain. You bore all these sufferings with patience because you knew that the salvation of men was to be brought about in this manner. You even willingly sacrificed Jesus that the sinful human race might be redeemed.

It is impossible for you not to have mercy on sinners. Now that you are in heaven, where you no longer have to make any sacrifices for their salvation, you cannot look on quietly and see how all that you and your Divine Son have endured remains without fruit, and how those souls perish on whose account your Son shed His Blood and you became the Mother of Sorrows. To the end of the world you will never cease to have mercy on sinners and to intercede for their salvation.

(2) MARY, if you confer upon us so many temporal blessings, *you will surely be all the more anxious about our spiritual welfare.* The sinner, were he even the outcast of the world, is never rejected by you, but you welcome him with motherly kindness and do not leave him till you have reconciled him to His Judge. As the devil goes about seeking whom he may devour, you go about seeking whom you may save.

As the Mother of Mercy, you are full of kindness and love, not only toward the just, but also toward sinners. Pray for the sinners of the world, especially for those farthest removed from God. Prepare them to receive divine graces. Stand between them and the just punishments of God. Plead for their sincere repentance that they may not be lost. Be their safe refuge and their hope for the sake of Jesus Who died for them.

(3) MARY, *how well you know that mortal sin is the greatest offense against God!* The infinite majesty of God is so great that all creatures in heaven and on earth are as nothing compared to Him. Teach me to understand that when I sin, I refuse obedience to God; I rebel against Him, even despise Him. I crucify Jesus anew by my sins, as the Apostle Paul reminds me, for by my sins I renew the cause for which my Divine Savior suffered the death of the cross. Help me to understand more and more the malice of sin that I may hate it above all things and avoid it as the greatest possible evil. Let me rather die than commit a willful mortal sin.

Refuge of Sinners, if I have the misfortune to fall into a grievous sin, let me have recourse to you at once. Obtain for me the grace of a sincere repentance and true contrition. With your help let me walk constantly in the way of penance so that as a penitent I may be saved.

O almighty and merciful God, Who in the Blessed Virgin Mary have given sinners a refuge and a help, grant us, who are protected by her, the forgiveness of all our sins and the blessings of Your mercy. Through Christ Our Lord. Amen. (*Feast of Our Lady, Refuge of Sinners*, August 13)
Aspiration:

> Our Lady of la Salette, Reconciler of sinners, pray without ceasing for us who have recourse to you.

300 days (435)

36. Comforter of the Afflicted

Consideration:

Mary's power to comfort the afflicted arises mainly from this, that *she above all others has known sorrow.* As the inseparable companion of Jesus, during the thirty-three years of His mortal life, She shared in His sufferings. And when the disciples forsook their Divine Master one by one, Mary followed Him faithfully even to Calvary, there to drink with Him to the dregs His bitter chalice. Having been afflicted more severely than any human being, her heart can sympathize with our pains.

Her own example reminds us that we must first bear the cross before we can wear the crown of glory. Though she was the Mother of God, she suffered much. She had to be the Mother of Sorrows before she became the Queen of Heaven. It is surely God's Will that she should therefore sympathize with the sufferings of humanity and, being the Mother of Mankind, that she should also be its comforter and consolation.

Mary knows the causes of sorrow and can remove them. She is eager to open for you the sources of true consolation when the cross weighs heavily on your shoulders. *She will not always remove the cross, but rather console and strengthen you to bear it patiently and even cheerfully.* Thus affliction can become joy when transformed by love. Mary fills your heart with this love that changes suffering to a noble sacrifice. When you turn to her for help, she will grant you the consolation found in conforming ourselves to the Divine Will as she has always done.

Prayer

(1) MARY, the Apostle Paul tells us that the source of all consolation is God: "Blessed be the God and Father of our Lord Jesus Christ, the Father of mercies and the God of all comfort, who comforts us in all our afflictions" (2 Cor. 1:3-4). But *after God, it is you who console us in our afflictions.* What unspeakable compassion fills your loving heart for us poor exiles from our heavenly home!

You have the heart of a mother who forgets herself to think only of her children. You know by experience what it is to be afflicted, for your whole life was a series of sufferings and trials. You now have the greatest sympathy with the sorrowful and hasten to comfort them.

Your loving Son invited the afflicted: "Come to me, all you who labor and are burdened, and I will give you rest" (Matt. 11:28). Since you are a true image of your Divine Son in all things, you also possess the most tender compassion and mercy for the afflicted, and you know no greater happiness than that of comforting them in their sorrows. Being also our Mother, given to us by Jesus from the cross, you are our best comforter.

(2) MARY, *you also comfort the afflicted by your example.* You are a model for us in all our sufferings and trials. Though you were the Mother of God and our Mother, you have suffered. I have no suffering which you did not experience. "Great as the sea" was your sorrow, and with it all you were resigned, calm, and wonderfully conformed to the Divine Will. Should God be less severe with me, an unprofitable servant, than with you, His own Mother? If I wish to be crowned with you in heaven someday, then God should not give me heaven on earth. Since you were patient and made every sacrifice with a most cheerful heart, even when it caused you the greatest pain, why should I be impatient and discouraged? I am consoled at the very thought of the tender interest, the sympathy, and the love for us which fills your motherly heart.

Comforter of the Afflicted, teach me to seek comfort in you when I stand in need of consolation. Your whole life was a martyrdom, and yet even the weight of a small cross presses too heavily on me. My suffering is short, but yours was long. You are the Queen of Heaven not only on account of your Divine Motherhood, but also because of the merits which you acquired as the Queen of Martyrs and the Mother of Sorrows. Let me ever remember that no path but the hard, rough way of Calvary leads to the blissful home of heaven. Help me to say always with all my heart, "Thy will be done on earth as it is in heaven."

(3) MARY, *you also comfort the afflicted by your help.* At the marriage in Cana you observed the disappointment of the newly married couple. You not only sympathized with them, but you removed the trouble by taking the matter to your Son, who changed

water into wine at your request. You comfort us in the same way. You remove evils and help us out of every difficulty by your intercession with Jesus. You have become all to all, and your affectionate heart is open to all, that all may find whatever they need: the sick his health; the afflicted, comfort; and the sinner, pardon.

Comforter of the Afflicted, teach me to imitate you by sympathizing with others out of love for God. I wish to console my neighbor in his affliction and even encourage him to find his peace and joy in God.

Lord Jesus Christ, Father of mercies and God of all consolation, grant in Your loving kindness that we who joyfully venerate on earth Mary, Your most pure Mother as our comforter, may deserve to enjoy with her the unending happiness of heaven. Who live and reign forever. Amen. (*Feast of Our Lady of Consolation*, Saturday after August 28)

Aspiration:

Mary most sorrowful, Mother of Christians, pray for us.

300 days (376)

37. Help of Christians

Consideration:

Mary has always been the Protectress of the Church. The Church Militant is always at war with the enemies who try to destroy her by perversion of truth, corruption of morals, and persecution. Through Mary's intercession calamities have been averted, fierce persecutions checked, the enemies of the Church defeated. Many of her feasts are an evidence of the gratitude of Christians.

Mary is the Help of Christians *in their spiritual needs.* She comes to our aid in temptation, confirms us in good, and obtains for us the grace of making progress in virtue, for she desires nothing more than that we may share in the fruits of the redemption won for us by her Son. Her mission is to help us lead a good life and save our souls.

Mary is the Help of Christians even *in temporal needs.* Her motherly love for us is now even greater and more compassionate than it was on earth, because she knows our misery better in heaven. She can help because her prayer is all-powerful with God, and she will help because she is our Mother and loves us more than any other mother can.

Prayer

(1) MARY, we invoke you as the Help of Christians because *you afford help to Christians even in all temporal needs.* If, without being asked, you do so much, what will you do if we invoke your aid? Though you are now enthroned in heaven, you still take an interest in our misery and relieve our wants. You are still the Mother of God in heaven as you were on earth; Jesus, Who is omnipotence itself, remains your Son for all eternity. Your love for us is now even more intense and more compassionate, because you know our misery better in heaven than you did in this mortal life. You obtain sweet rest for all who are laden with trouble and pain; you give comfort to the afflicted and healing to the sick.

Help of Christians, give me an unbounded confidence in you.

You *can* help me, for your prayer is all-powerful with God, and you *will* help me, for you are my Mother and you love me as your child. Let me pray to you with a pure and penitent heart, for I cannot expect help from you if I continue to offend your dear Son and even crucify Him again by my sins.

I wish to beg your help with perseverance, even though for some time I may receive no help. I know you will grant my petition at the right time. Teach me to pray with resignation to the will of God, Who knows what is best for me. Obtain for me at least the grace of bearing my cross with patience.

(2) MARY, *you bring us help especially in our spiritual needs.* You are a most merciful Mother who rejects no sinner, no matter how far he may have strayed. You lovingly interest yourself in his behalf and try to reconcile him to your Son. You assist us in temptations. You are continually crushing the serpent's head by breaking Satan's plans to capture souls by sin. God Himself has said: "I will put enmities between thee and the woman—she shall crush thy head" (Gen. 3:15). Instead of capturing others, Satan is himself made a captive by you; like a chained slave he must obey your commands.

You confirm us in good and obtain for us the grace of making progress in the path of virtue, for you desire nothing more ardently than that we all become partakers of the fruits of redemption, won for us by your Son. In our efforts to reach holiness, you support us and obtain for the grace of perseverance. I can ask nothing of you that will give you greater pleasure or that you will grant more willingly than the grace to do good.

Above all, you assist us in the hour of death, which is the most important moment in our life because upon that moment eternity depends. As the exalted Queen of Heaven you take the souls of your faithful servants under your protecting mantle, accompany them to the judgment seat of your Son, and there you become their intercessor.

Help of Christians, I know you do all in your power to save my soul. May I also do my part and allow you to save me. If I fall into sin, obtain for me the grace of repentance. If I am tempted, give me help to fight with determination against the temptation that I may overcome it. Be with me especially in the hour of my death, when the devil will put forth every effort to win my soul.

(3) MARY, *you are the Protectress of the universal Catholic Church.* Through your intercession calamities have been averted from Christendom, fierce persecutions have ceased to rage, and enemies have been humbled to the dust. Many feasts are expressions of gratitude toward you for the frequent and wonderful deliverance of Christian nations from the invasions of enemies, from schisms and wars, and from other sufferings.

Help of Christians, show yourself the Protectress of the Catholic Church and destroy the wicked designs of her enemies, especially in these times of persecution.

Almighty and merciful God, Who in the person of the Blessed Virgin Mary provided never ending assistance for the defense of the Christian people, grant, we beg of You, that, strengthened by such help, we may do battle during life and be able to obtain victory over the treacherous foe in death. Through Christ Our Lord. Amen. (*Feast of Mary, Help of Christians, May 24*)

Aspiration:
   Mother of Perpetual Help, pray for us.

                                                    300 days (426)

38. Queen of Angels

Consideration:

Mary is the Queen of angels, because *she is the Mother of Christ Who created the angels.* St. Paul says, "For in him were created all things in the heavens and on the earth, things visible and things invisible, whether thrones, or dominations, or principalities, or powers. All things have been created through and unto him" (Col. 1:16).

Mary is the Queen of Angels because *she is elevated far above them in dignity and glory.* To none of the angels did the Son of God say, "You are my Mother." To none of the angels did He render obedience. None of the angels entered so deeply into the mysteries of our salvation as the Mother of God. Angels are mighty heavenly spirits, but Mary is their Queen. Michael and the good angels conquered Lucifer and his rebel followers and continue to fight them on earth, but only Mary has crushed the head of the infernal serpent. Gabriel, the Power of God, stood in awe and reverence before Mary, whom he greeted as full of grace and the Mother of the Son of God.

In Heaven *all the angels pay homage to their Queen.* The seraphim and cherubim, thrones, dominations, principalities, powers, virtues, archangels and angels gather around her to greet her in person and praise her as the Mother of their Maker and their God.

Prayer

(1) MARY, *your dignity is higher than that of the angels.* Angels are God's servants, but you are the daughter of the heavenly Father, Who chose you to become the Mother of His Son. You are the Spouse of the Holy Spirit. Even an archangel bowed before you and greeted you reverently, "Hail, full of grace."

No dignity can be compared to that of being the Mother of God. No angel could ever say to the Son of God, "You are my Son." Because of this dignity the Church places you above all the angels and

calls you their Queen. The angels stand before the throne of God
with fear and trembling, covering their faces, while you approach
and pray for the human race to Him Who was born of you and calls
you by the sweet name of Mother.

(2) MARY, *you were more favored by God than all the angels*. If
God gives His graces to everyone according to his particular vocation, what measure of grace corresponds to the dignity of Mother
of God? You received such a fullness of grace that you approach
nearest to the Author of grace.

You were considered worthy of cooperating in the work of our
redemption, for upon your consent depended the Incarnation of the
Son of God. The angels were but messengers of the work of Redemption, but you were the Mother of the Redeemer. The angels
assemble around you in the greatest reverence and exclaim as the
Jews of old did to Judith: "Thou art the glory of Jerusalem; thou
art the joy of Israel; thou art the honor of our people" (Judith
15:10) .

(3) MARY, *you can and really do accomplish more for our salvation than the heavenly spirits*. You have greater power because you
are the Mother of God, while the angels are only His servants. You
are our Mother, while the angels are our friends and brothers of
ours in the family of God; hence you love us more tenderly.

Queen of Angels, help me to imitate the angels by being as eager
as they are to do God's Will and to serve mankind. Let me ever consider them as my best friends and protectors, who want to help me
save my soul. I want to be grateful especially to my guardian angel,
who never wearies in his faithful care.

Lord Jesus Christ, You have given us Your Mother Mary that she might
be our Mother of Perpetual Help, whose beloved image we venerate;
grant, we beg of You, that by earnestly imploring her motherly help, we
may deserve to enjoy at all times the blessings of Your Redemption. Who
live and reign forever. Amen. (*Feast of Our Lady of Perpetual Help,*
June 27)

Aspiration:

O Mary, bless this house where your name is always praised. Praise
forever be to Mary Immaculate, the Virgin Mother, blessed among
women, the Mother of Our Lord Jesus Christ, the Queen of Heaven.

300 days (298)

39. Queen of Patriarchs

Consideration:

Mary stands above the patriarchs in queenly majesty. Patriarchs were the ancestors of the human race, and in particular of the chosen people, like Adam, Noe, Abraham, and Jacob.

Mary cooperated in restoring to mankind what had been lost through Adam's fall. In her Immaculate Conception she was saved, not from a flood of water but from the flood of sin, and through her, as the ark of salvation, the human race was saved from eternal death because she has given us a Savior. As through Abraham and Jacob the chosen people grew into a great nation, and a kingdom through the royal house of David of the tribe of Juda, in her Divine Son not only one nation, but the whole of mankind became the chosen people of God, and members of His spiritual and eternal kingdom.

Mary is the greatest daughter of the patriarchs, for the faith and hope of the patriarchs, and all the promises given them, have been wonderfully fulfilled in and through Mary, whom they now acknowledge as their Queen.

Prayer

(1) MARY, *you far surpass the Patriarchs of the Old Law in dignity.* They were only the forefathers of one nation and one country; the land of Chanaan was promised to them as an inheritance. But you, as the Mother of the Redeemer, are the Mother of all the nations of the world. The Patriarchs were only the ancestors of Him through Whom all the nations of the earth were to be blessed, but you are the Mother of the promised Redeemer, through Whom the whole human race received grace and salvation.

God frequently appeared to the Patriarchs and assured them of His protection and love, but He assumed human nature from you, He lived with you for thirty years, and He obeyed you like a good

339

child. You alone had the privilege of calling the Son of God your son. You carried Him in your arms and loved Him as a mother loves her child. You shared with Him the pleasures and sorrows of thirty-three years. You saw Him die and rise again. By Him you were assumed into heaven, where you now reign with Him for all eternity.

Upon earth the holy Patriarchs beheld afar off and greeted with lively faith and firm hope that wonderful woman whom the Lord had announced from the beginning as the Mother of the Savior of the world. In heaven they now offer you with joy the tribute of their veneration and tender love, as to one who, through Jesus, brought them into the "everlasting dwellings."

Queen of the Patriarchs, you possessed in an intimate manner Him Who was their desire. Make me appreciate the happiness that I myself enjoy in possessing Him, together with all the graces of which He is the source, especially in the Most Holy Sacrament of the Altar.

(2) MARY, *you possessed all the virtues of the Patriarchs in a more wonderful degree.* The Patriarchs were men according to God's own Heart, who faithfully walked in the path of holiness and made it the first and most important rule of their life to do the Will of God in all things. Three virtues in particular shone like stars in their lives: in Abraham it was faith; in Isaac, obedience; in Jacob, patience. There is no virtue with which you are not adorned in an extraordinary degree.

Queen of Patriarchs, help me to follow in the footsteps of the Patriarchs that I may lead a virtuous life. Let me imitate in particular their faith, obedience, and patience.

(3) MARY, the Patriarchs enjoyed the favor of God on account of their piety. On various occasions God was pleased to listen to their prayers. But *God finds greater delight in you than in the Patriarchs.* You are holier and more intimately united with God because you are His Mother. You are the channel through which all graces come to us. You are all-powerful through your inter-cession. What you desire cannot remain undone; if you only will it, all is done.

Queen of Patriarchs, teach me to desire nothing so much as to preserve the grace of God in my soul, which makes me pleasing to God. If I do so, I am happier than if I possessed the favor of all the world, for God's grace infuses true peace into my heart and will make me happy for time and eternity. Because God bestows His favor on truly holy souls who consecrate themselves to Him without reserve, teach me to follow your example by mortifying all unruly love of the world and of self in order that I may love God with my whole heart and above all things. Obtain these graces for me through your all-powerful intercession.

O God, You were pleased to honor the Order of Carmel by the singular title of Your most Blessed Mother, Mary ever Virgin; grant, we beg of You, that she whose memory we solemnly venerate may favor us with her protection so that we may be found worthy to share in eternal happiness. Who live and reign forever. Amen. (*Feast of Our Lady of Mount Carmel,* July 16)

 Aspiration:
  O Queen, who are the beauty of Carmel, pray for us.

300 days (405)

OCTOBER—Third Saturday

40. Queen of Prophets

Consideration:

Mary is Queen of prophets because *all their prophecies concerning Christ are in a certain sense also prophecies concerning her,* His Mother. Isaias spoke of the Virgin that would conceive and bear a Son, of the Child that was to be born to us, the Son that would be given to us. Jeremias saw in vision the woman that would encompass a man; Ezechiel was shown the gate reserved for the Prince, the God of Israel.

Mary's excellence and greatness surpassed that of the prophets. Prophets made the prophecies but never saw their fulfillment. Mary, the object of their visions, not only saw the fulfillment but played a most important part in it.

Mary's activity surpasses that of the prophets. While the prophets were sent to rescue the Israelites from temporal and eternal ruin, Mary sacrificed her own life by giving her Son for the redemption of the world. Prophets fought against idolatry and immorality. Now as their Queen, Mary is active in heaven rescuing sinners in every age and place from the danger of eternal death.

Prayer

(1) MARY, the Prophets traced out the picture of the Messias many centuries beforehand. In describing the stages of the mortal life of Our Savior and the wonderful fruits of His mission, *they obtained a glimpse of you, the loving Mother of this God-Man,* the admirable daughter of Eve, whose glorious co-operation in the salvation of the world they knew that the Lord had announced at the beginning of the world. Your sweet and majestic person made their hearts beat for joy, while they wrote the prophetic history of your Divine Son. How deeply must those three—David, Ezechiel, and Isaias—have been moved, for to them was made known by special revelation your wonderful dignity as Virgin Mother of God!

342

Now, that in the abode of eternal glory they behold clearly your brilliant destiny, your dazzling crown as the "universal Queen of all creatures," with what joy do they pay homage to you, their Queen! With what veneration do they honor the excellence of the divine light with which you yourself have been favored by God!

Queen of Prophets, the Prophets of the Old Law had the most fervent desire for the promised Redeemer, your Son, and cried out with Isaias: "Drop down dew, you heavens, from above, and let the clouds rain the just one: let the earth be opened, and bud forth a Savior" (Isaias 45:8). Give me an ardent longing for Christ, especially through frequent Holy Communion and visits to the Blessed Sacrament.

(2) MARY, the Prophets were highly honored both by Jews and by Gentiles on account of their holy lives, their great zeal for the Law of God, and their miracles and prophecies. They had to endure many sufferings, and a number of them ended their lives by martyrdom. But *above them all in honor and suffering are you,* whom Isaias called the "prophetess" and "Virgin" and Mother of the Divine Redeemer, and David called "the King's daughter clothed in splendor."

You were a prophetess yourself. Through the Holy Spirit you predicted the occurrence of events which the distant future still held in its depths. The words which you spoke in the house of your cousin Elizabeth were a real prophecy and have been fulfilled at all times, even to the present: "From henceforth all generations shall call me blessed."

(3) MARY, animated by a lively zeal the Prophets put forth all their energy to rescue the Israelites from temporal and eternal ruin. They fought against the vice of idolatry and immorality. But *you have sacrificed your own Son to rescue sinners.* If you could have saved Him without injury to our Redemption, you would willingly have sacrificed your own life. And now, enthroned in heaven, so great is your love for us that you are ever active in rescuing sinners from danger and in saving their souls.

Queen of Prophets, help me to imitate the Prophets and your own example. They never sought the world with its pleasures, but God alone. They were willing to suffer for Him in their zeal to save souls. Teach me to be zealous for the honor of God and for the salvation of my soul and that of my neighbor. Help me to realize that the most divine of all divine things is to labor with God for the salvation of souls.

O God, in Whose Passion, as Simeon had foretold, the most sweet soul of Mary, Your glorious Virgin-Mother, was pierced through by a sword of sorrow, mercifully grant that we who reverently meditate upon her transfixion and her sufferings may obtain the blessed fruits of Your Passion through the glorious merits and prayers of all the saints faithfully standing at the cross interceding for us. Who live and reign forever. Amen. (*Feast of the Seven Sorrows of Mary,* Friday after Passion Sunday)
    Aspiration:
        Jesus, Mary, and Joseph most kind, bless us now and in death's agony.

                                                        300 days (273)

41. Queen of Apostles

Consideration:

Mary's Divine Motherhood was more sublime than the apostolic office of the apostles. The apostles were faithful followers of Christ, chosen by Him to assist in the establishment of His Church, but Mary's work was bound up with the eternal decrees of man's salvation.

Mary's Son is the Victim of our salvation. The apostles preached about Him and His doctrine to the world. But *it was chiefly under Mary's patronage and by her aid that the doctrine and laws of the Gospel have spread so rapidly* in spite of immense obstacles and difficulties, among all nations, setting up everywhere a new order of justice and peace. In her heavenly kingdom she is unceasingly working to maintain firm and fruitful the Catholic Faith. Guided by her inspirations and relying on her assistance, men eminent in holiness and apostolic zeal have risen to protect the rights of the Church and to lead souls to the holiness of Christian life.

At Pentecost Mary was with the apostles when the Holy Spirit descended upon them and filled the earth with His glory. She was the Bride of that Divine Spirit, the Mother of the infant Church, and the inspiration of the apostles. Through her the grace and the sanctifying gifts of the Holy Spirit are scattered abroad over the Church and Its members.

Prayer

(1) MARY, though the dignity of the apostles is great because Jesus made them His representatives on earth and conferred upon them the office of teaching, of the priesthood, and of pastorship in His Church, *your dignity as Mother of God is greater.* In this alone, that you are the Mother of God, you excel all greatness that after God can be imagined. Though the apostles were zealous servants of Jesus, they had various human weaknesses before the descent of the Holy Spirit. But you are adorned with every virtue, and there is no creature in heaven or on earth equal to you in sanctity.

(2) MARY, *you received, together with the apostles, the wonderful gifts with which they were endowed by the Holy Spirit.* The apostles began to labor zealously for the salvation of souls. They preached Jesus, Who is the Light of the world, the Way, the Truth and the Life, but you brought Him forth; you are His Mother. Without you we would not have a Gospel for the apostles to preach; we would not have Christ Who sent the apostles; we would never have seen an apostle nor heard the words of salvation. How fittingly are you called their Queen! The wonderful success which accompanied their preaching was in a large measure the effect of your constant prayer.

To this day you are ever zealous to enkindle the light of faith in the hearts of those who sit in darkness and in the shadow of death and to rescue their souls from damnation. With the Church I exclaim: "Rejoice, Virgin Mary, you alone have destroyed all heresies throughout the world."

(3) MARY, *the apostles and all apostolic men have honored you as their Queen.* The apostles regarded you as their Mother from the moment when Jesus gave you to John for a Mother. You were always in their midst as long as you remained in Jerusalem, giving them information about the wonderful conception of the Son of God, about His birth and about the years of His youth, for you "kept in mind all these words, pondering them in your heart."

The apostles were deeply devoted to you during your life. They hastened from far distant lands to receive your blessing before you died. Their veneration for you increased still more when they beheld the great miracles at your grave, which, with them, placed your glorious Assumption beyond a doubt.

The successors of the apostles, the Popes and bishops, and the most renowned priests and missionaries of the Catholic Church, have at all times paid the deepest veneration to you, greeted you as their Queen, and placed their apostolic labors under your protection.

Queen of Apostles, help me to respect the Holy Father, the bishops and priests, as God's representatives on earth. I shall always consider that every injury done to a priest is as if done to your Son Himself, Who expressly says, "He who rejects you, rejects me" (Luke 10:16). Help me to listen eagerly to the word of God and observe the teaching of my spiritual superiors. If I wish to be a good child of yours, I must show love and obedience to the priests, for they are not only special friends and representatives of your Son, but also my greatest benefactors, instructing me in the doctrine of salvation, purifying my soul and sanctifying me in the Sacraments, and offering up the Holy Sacrifice of the Mass for me. Bless the Holy Father, the bishops, priests, and missionaries of the Catholic Church. Help them to live worthy of their high calling. Bless their labors with success. Help them ever to be living images of your loving Son—other Christs!

O God, You have sent the Holy Spirit to Your apostles, who were united in prayer with Mary, the Mother of Jesus; grant us that, protected by the same Mother of ours and Queen of Apostles, we may be made worthy to serve Your Divine Majesty faithfully and proclaim Your glory by word and example. Through the same Christ Our Lord. Amen. (*Feast of Our Lady, Queen of the Apostles,* Saturday after the Ascension)

Aspiration:

Queen of the Apostles, pray for us.

300 days (437)

42. Queen of Martyrs

Consideration:

Suffering sufficient to cause death is martyrdom, even though death does not follow from it. St. Thomas says "that *to have the glory of martyrdom, it is sufficient to exercise obedience in its highest degree,* that is to say, to be obedient unto death." Mary was a martyr, not by the sword of the executioner, but by the bitter sorrow of heart.

All other martyrs gave evidence of their God in the anguish of a physical agony and death, but *the Mother of God died many times over in spirit,* in that extreme anguish which pierced her soul and crucified her Heart. Other martyrs sacrificed their own lives, the Blessed Virgin was martyred by sacrificing the life of her Son, a life which she loved far more than her own, and which exceeded all other torments ever endured by any mortal on earth.

Mary surpassed all martyrs in her love of God. This love made her feel the sufferings of her Son more keenly than if they had been inflicted upon her in all reality. Her martyrdom was life-long, because all her life she loved her Son and remembered His sufferings. The cross is the measure of God's love for us and the sum total of our love for God. Only when we have understood Mary's martyrdom will we understand the greatness of Christ's love for His Mother and the intensity of her love for her Son and for the souls for whom He died. She, too, was a victim of love for the salvation of others. Her Son suffered in the flesh; she in the heart.

Prayer

(1) MARY, *you are the Queen of Martyrs because of the greatness of your sorrows.* We think it almost impossible that man could endure the torments of the martyrs. But far more intense was your pain, for you did not, like the martyrs, suffer only bodily, but also spiritually. The sword of sorrow did not pierce your body, but your soul, as Simeon had prophesied: "Thy own soul a sword shall pierce" (Luke 2:35).

You suffered not only as a mother, but as the Mother of God. If a mother witnesses the sufferings of her child, these sufferings become her own. The scourging, the crowning with thorns, the nailing, all the tortures which tormented the Body of your Son, penetrated your heart to complete your martyrdom. You even witnessed the violent death of your loving Son.

You did not, however, feel the sufferings of your Son in the manner in which other mothers feel the sufferings of their children. He Whom you saw suffer and die was also the Son of God. Your sorrow at the Passion of Jesus was as great as was your love for Him, and you loved Jesus more than your own life, and would have sacrificed your life a thousand times if, without offending God, you could have rescued your Son from the sufferings of the Passion.

God poured into the hearts of the martyrs such consolations as enabled them to bear their pains more easily; but you suffered without consolation. Feeling, as you did, all the pains of your Son, you also experienced in your heart His want of consolation, and like Him you could exclaim: "My God, my God, why hast Thou forsaken me." It was this desolation that made your suffering so bitter and plunged you into a sea of sorrow.

(2) MARY, *you are the Queen of Martyrs on account of the long duration of your sufferings.* The tortures of the holy martyrs were very great, but passing; your martyrdom lasted from the moment that you took your Divine Son into your arms until you beheld Him expire on the cross. Your life was one constant scene of sorrow, because you so clearly understood the inner meaning of the predictions of the Prophets about the Passion of Jesus, and you were enlightened by a special revelation in the knowledge of the details of the Passion and death of your beloved Son. You were an eyewitness of all His sufferings. Even after the Resurrection of Jesus you still remembered His bitter Passion and death, and the remembrance of it always pierced your soul anew with the sword of sorrow. Your grief ceased only with your last breath.

(3) MARY, you are the Queen of Martyrs because *you took the holy martyrs under your special protection.* You prayed for them and obtained for them strength and courage to declare their faith in Christ fearlessly, to endure pain bravely, and thus to obtain the crown of martyrdom.

Queen of Martyrs, help me to suffer patiently the unbloody

martyrdom of self-denial. As long as I live, I am inclined to evil. Aid me in keeping a watchful eye on these inclinations and in fighting against them with earnestness that I may also obtain a crown like that of the martyrs. Give me strength and consolation in my own martyrdom so that I may bear my cross willingly for the love of Jesus and you.

Lord Jesus Christ, we offer You our prayers and sacrifices so that, while recalling Your sufferings we also may dwell on the bitter piercing through of the most sweet heart of Your Blessed Mother Mary, and through the most powerful and loving intercession of this Queen of Martyrs and of all Your saints gathered at the foot of the cross, we may deserve to be one day numbered with the blessed by the merits of Your death. Who live and reign forever. Amen. (*Feast of the Seven Sorrows of Mary*, September 15)
Aspiration:

> Holy Mother, pierce me through,
> In my heart each wound renew,
> Of my Savior crucified.

500 days (375)

43. Queen of Confessors

Consideration:

Confessor saints distinguished themselves by the holiness of their lives, but did not die a martyr's death. They practiced all the virtues in a high degree, especially, love of God and neighbor, prayer, detachment from creatures, and fidelity to duty. Mary is the Queen of Confessors because she *imitated Jesus most perfectly.* She fulfilled most faithfully the duties of religion, of her state in life, and of the love of her neighbor.

Not only love of God, but also love of neighbor is the foundation of our religious duties, for Jesus said that we shall be known as His disciples if we have love for one another. The saints were ever intent upon doing good to their fellow men in body and soul. But *Mary's love for her neighbor was greater.* She had given mankind a Savior, and with Him all the graces necessary for salvation. She shared in the very charity of Christ because she was associated with Him in the great work of the Redemption. She now continues to show this charity by constantly pleading to God for her children and obtains for them the graces they most need for their salvation and the blessings they want for their temporal happiness.

You can imitate the Queen of Confessors by being conscientious in all your religious duties according to God's Will. You will find time for prayer and the frequent reception of the sacraments. The salvation of your soul will be the most important concern of your life. Mary will be not only a model of holiness for you, but also the intercessor who will secure for you all the graces you need for the sanctification of your soul.

Prayer

(1) MARY, you are the Queen of Confessors, that is, the saints who in the various positions and states of life persevered in the confession of the faith and in the practice of virtue, and who proved themselves to be true and faithful followers of Jesus, not by the death of martyrdom, but by a holy life. You are their Queen be-

cause *you fulfilled most perfectly the duties of religion, of your state in life, and of the love of your neighbor, and made the most excellent profession of Jesus Christ.* The Gospel speaks of how fervently you fulfilled your religious duties at the presentation of your Child in the temple and at your celebration of the Passover in the temple of Jerusalem. After Jesus, you practiced the virtue of prayer more perfectly than all the saints. The Evangelist records how you "kept in mind all these words, pondering them in your heart". How beautifully you praised God in your Magnificat when at the visit to Elizabeth you exclaimed: "My soul magnifies the Lord, and my spirit rejoices in God my Savior"!

Queen of Confessors, help me to fulfill conscientiously all my religious duties according to God's will. Let me find contentment in prayer. I wish to regard it as the first and most necessary requisite for salvation, for without it I cannot live a virtuous life and die a holy death. But help me especially to be fervent in the reception of the Sacraments—to go to confession and to receive Holy Communion as often as possible.

(2) MARY, *with far greater fervor than the confessors you fulfilled the duties of your state of life.* In your single life you watched carefully over your virginal purity. All the virtues were outstanding in you: purity, humility, meekness, detachment, poverty, obedience, piety, fervent love of God, burning zeal for His glory, perfect submission to His adorable will, charity for your neighbor, and patience in every trial.

No mother among the saints ever fulfilled her duties with such devotedness as you did. You were devoted to your husband Joseph. At his word you hastened into Egypt and back again. You were devoted to Jesus and took care of His wants from early morning till late at night. How painfully you sought Him for three long days! Even after He had begun His public life, you were a faithful Mother to Him; and though you could not accompany Him everywhere, your heart was always with Him. You suffered contempt and torture with Him in your soul during His holy Passion.

In your widowhood the Mass, Holy Communion and the Real Presence of your Son were the heart and soul of your very existence. You merit the title of Our Lady of the Blessed Sacrament not only because you have given us the Eucharistic Christ, but also because you were the most devoted lover and adorer of Jesus in the Holy

Eucharist. You often visited the holy places sanctified by the sufferings of your Son and there prayed to God to have mercy on men. Your eyes were continually directed to things above; your only desire was to be one with Jesus, your Son.

Queen of Confessors, help me to be faithful in fulfilling the duties of my state of life as God wills. Let me be content with my state and patiently bear its hardships, for I am not in this world to enjoy a life of ease, but to merit heaven.

(3) MARY, the confessors, mindful of His words, professed faith in Jesus also by a sincere and active love for their neighbor: "By this will all men know that you are my disciples, if you have love for one another" (John 13:35). Inflamed with the most sincere love towards their fellow men, they were ever intent upon doing them good in body and soul. But *your love for your neighbor was even greater than that of the confessors.* Your greatest service to mankind was the gift of the Savior, from Whom we have received salvation and every grace we need to attain it. Your intimate part in the plan of Redemption associated you with your Son, and hence you share His charity for the souls of men. You showed this charity not only in your lifetime; you show it now in heaven by continually pleading to God for the children entrusted to you by Jesus on the cross.

Queen of Confessors, help me to imitate your spirit of charity toward my neighbor, for your loving Son receives every act of charity to others as if done to Himself. Only if I love my neighbor can I be regarded as His true disciple and your loving child.

Through Your mercy, O Lord, and the intercession of the Blessed Virgin Mary, may Your Church increase in the number of the faithful and ever shine forth in the manifold light of virtue. Through Christ Our Lord. Amen. (*Feast of Our Lady, Queen of the Apostles,* Saturday after the Ascension)

Aspiration:

To you, O Virgin Mother, who were never touched by any spot of original or actual sin, I commend and entrust the purity of my heart.

300 days (354)

44. Queen of Virgins

Consideration:

Our Lady was always a Virgin, but in her case perpetual virginity was marvelously combined with the Divine Motherhood. In the conception and birth of Jesus, Mary kept her virginity intact. She brought forth, while remaining a virgin. With the honor of virginity, she has the joy of mother-hood. St. Bernard, praising this privilege, says: "Mary chose for herself the better part. Clearly the better, because conjugal fecundity is good, but virginal chastity is better, but the best is virginal fecundity, or fecund virginity. The privilege of Mary will not be given to another, because it will not be taken away from her."

Mary is the Queen of virgins because *the consecration of her life to God is the most perfect,* her example most attractive and powerful. Consecrated virginal life implies a decisive victory over sensual nature, frees from human attachments and gives all time and energy to the service of God.

So great is the *grace* that was given to Mary, that not only did it preserve her own virginity, but *confers that wonderful gift of purity to those who are devoted to her.* Though not all are called to a virginal life, all are bound to be chaste, and in the devotion to the Queen of virgins they will find inspiration and strength for the observance of chastity demanded by their particular state of life. Scripture says, "O how beautiful is the chaste generation with glory . . . it triumphs crowned forever, winning the reward of undefiled conflicts" (Wisdom 4:1).

Prayer

(1) MARY, you are the Queen of Virgins because *you were the first among all the daughters of Eve to make the Lord the solemn promise of perpetual chastity.* Other holy Jewish virgins dedicated themselves to the service of the temple for a few years; after that they returned into the world and married, because a large number of children was considered a blessing of heaven, and virginity not

an honorable state, and barrenness a curse. The Holy Spirit, Who dwelt in you, urged you by the gentle influence of His grace to devote yourself without reserve to God and to unite yourself to Him forever in the purest love by a vow of perpetual chastity. You are truly the honor of virgins and the Mother of virginity.

(2) MARY, you are the Queen of Virgins because *by the splendor of your purity you far surpass all the virgins that have ever lived or shall live in ages to come.* No greater purity in a creature can be imagined than yours. You are compared by Holy Scripture to myrrh, which preserves things perfect and spotless. Your angelic purity was such as to prevent the least breath of impurity from poisoning the hearts of those who looked upon you, for which reason the words of the Holy Spirit are applied to you: "As the lily among thorns, so is my love among the daughters" (Canticle 2:2). The virgins of all ages come in triumph to offer you the lily of their purity and the palm of their victory.

Queen of Virgins, sweet Mother of that Divine Lamb Who is the leader and guide of virginity, how joyfully do we glorify you for having, by your example, given us a cause to develop so many wonderful virtues upon the earth! Increase more and more the number of your cherished daughters who adorn the Church like blooming flowers and fill it with a fragrance so rare that it can only come from heaven.

(3) MARY, you are the Queen of Virgins because *you infuse love for chastity into the hearts of Christians.* You assist them in their struggles and temptations, and by your prayers you obtain for them from God the grace of preserving this holy virtue spotless throughout their whole life. Knowing the great value of virginal purity, you esteem and love it above all things. You look upon virginal souls with particular favor and love, and you spread over them the mantle of your protection that they may suffer no harm.

Queen of Virgins, teach me that there is no virtue more noble and lovable than virginal purity, for it raises me above the weaknesses of nature, unites me most intimately to God and purifies my entire being. Help me to live a pure life that I may imitate the life of the angels. Guard me from violating in any way this holy virtue. If an impure temptation arises in my heart, give me strength to reject it immediately and direct my thoughts to God by considering the truths of religion and especially death, judgment, heaven, and hell.

Never allow an improper word to escape my lips. Keep me from the company of persons who may be an occasion of sin. Through the frequent reception of the Sacraments, through prayer and vigilance, let me overcome temptation and live a virtuous life in imitation of you that I may be blessed with the pure of heart who shall see God.

O God, since You stoop to the humble and dislike the proud, help Your servants to imitate with a pure heart the humility of the Blessed Virgin Mary, who was pleasing to You in her virginity, and because of her humility conceived Our Lord Jesus Christ, Your Son, Who lives and reigns with You forever. Amen. (*Feast of the Humility of Mary,* July 17)

Aspiration:

O Lord Jesus Christ, grant to us, Your servants, the grace to be protected at all times and in all places by the patronage of Blessed Mary, Your Virgin Mother.

300 days (91)

45. Queen of All Saints

Consideration:

Mary is the Queen of All Saints because *God Himself has willed that Mary should be the most perfect image of Jesus.* He has made her the masterpiece of His creation. No one ever belonged to Jesus in so nearly perfect a manner as His Mother. He lives in her more intimately than He does in all the angels and saints. She was always associated with Jesus in His mysteries.

Through Mary we reach Jesus, the Source and Model of all sanctity. God has laid no other foundation for our salvation, perfection and glory, for Jesus said, "I am the Way, and the Truth, and the Life." We mount to God by two steps: the first, which is nearest to us and most suited to our need, is Mary, our Mother; the second is Jesus, our Mediator and Elder Brother. Christ came to us by Mary, and it is through Mary that we must go to Him.

Mary is Queen of All Saints because *of all creatures she possesses the highest power in heaven as the Mother of God.* Her prayers are most powerful because they are a mother's prayers, and Jesus cannot refuse them. God has given her more power than He gave to all the saints, that she may obtain for us the grace to imitate her holiness in this world and enjoy the vision of God in heaven. How great then must be the confidence you should have in your heavenly Mother!

Prayer

(1) MARY, you are the Queen of all saints because *you made the most diligent use of the rich treasure of grace which God granted to you.* Your understanding was always occupied in learning to know and praise God; your heart loved Him above all things. You zealously accepted every inspiration to good. You never received a grace with which you did not faithfully co-operate, a thing which

cannot be said even of the greatest saints. Thus sanctifying grace
was increased in your soul in a most wonderful degree.

Because you were full of grace, you also excelled in every virtue
in a far greater measure than every other saint. In each of the saints
there shone some particular virtue, some trait of the life of their
Divine Master, but all the traits of Jesus were expressed in you as
faithfully as they could be expressed in any creature. Because of
the fullness of grace and the splendor of your virtues you are raised
above all the saints; you are their Queen.

Queen of All Saints, teach me to think frequently of the happiness
which the saints enjoy in heaven that I may never grow weary of
working for its infinite joys, for, as St. Paul reminds me, "Eye has
not seen nor ear heard, nor has it entered into the heart of man,
what things God has prepared for those who love him" (1 Cor. 2:9).

(2) MARY, *you are raised above all the saints in glory.* Chosen
from among all the children of men, you sit on a throne of surpassing splendor, in the words of the Scripture: "She shall be admired in the holy assembly, and in the multitude of the elect she
shall have praise; and among the blessed she shall be blessed"
(Ecclus. 24:3).

How beautiful does the Old Testament speak of your beauty
and majesty! The Jewish people admired most the cedar tree for
its strength, the cypress for its great height, the palm for its slender
growth, and the olive tree for its fruitfulness. To these trees you are
compared. "I was exalted like a cedar in Lebanon, and as a cypress
tree on Mount Sion. I was exalted like a palm tree in Cades . . .
and as a fair olive tree in the plains" (Ecclus. 24:17–18).

Since among the shrubs the vine is the most noble, the Scripture
puts these words on your lips: "As the vine I have brought forth a
pleasant fruit" (Ecclus. 24:23). Among the flowers the red rose is
the most beautiful: "I grew as a rose plant in Jericho" (Ecclus.
24:18). Among the spices cinnamon and aromatic balsam are the
most precious: "I gave a sweet smell like cinnamon and aromatic
balm" (Ecclus. 24:20). The beauty of your virtue surpasses that of
all the saints so that in the Canticle it is said of you: "Who is she
that comes forth as the morning rising, fair as the moon, bright as
the sun, awe-inspiring as an army set in array" (6:9).

Queen of All Saints, as you surpass all saints in the grace of a
virtuous life and merits, so you stand higher than all the elect in

the grace of glory and reward. After God there is no greater bliss for the blessed in heaven than to behold you, their glorious Queen.

(3) MARY, of all creatures *you possess the highest power in heaven as the Mother of God.* You pray, but not in the way the saints do; in a way you command. Though omnipotent, Jesus cannot resist the motherly authority He Himself gave you. To you all power is given in heaven and on earth. Nothing is impossible with you, for how can He resist your appeal Who has assumed flesh of your flesh? You use this wonderful power for the benefit of your children, especially those who tenderly love you and venerate you as their Mother.

Queen of All Saints, keep me ever mindful that God has created me to live a life of holiness in this world and to become a saint in heaven. He will give me enough grace to do this if only I have an earnest desire for holiness. I know that holiness does not consist in heroic deeds, but in doing the will of God perfectly, loving God with all my heart and my neighbor for God's sake, keeping my soul from sin, and being united with God through prayer and the sacraments. Since you have more power than all the saints, obtain for me this grace above all others, that I may imitate your holiness in this world and enjoy the vision of God and your presence for all eternity in heaven.

O God, You have given us the Blessed Virgin Mary that we might venerate her as the Queen of All Saints and the Mother of Fair Love; mercifully grant that under her protection we may love You above all things here on earth and enjoy the happy companionship of all Your saints in heaven. Through Christ Our Lord. Amen. (*Mary, Queen of All Saints,* May 31)

Aspiration:

O Virgin Mary, Mother of Jesus, make us saints.

300 days (303)

46. Queen Conceived Without Original Sin

Consideration:

It was fitting that Mary should be conceived without sin. The angels were created in the splendor of immaculate purity. Adam and Eve came forth from the hand of the Creator in the state of grace. It would be an insult to the Holy Spirit if the Mother of the Creator of all and Savior of men were denied the glory of such sinlessness.

But *faith* tells us that "in the first instant of her conception, by the singular grace and privilege of the Omnipotent God, in virtues of the merits of Jesus Christ, Savior of the human race, Mary was preserved from all stain of original sin." This dogma was defined by Pope Pius IX on the eighth of December, 1854.

This truth is founded on *the word of God* and upon the constant *tradition of the Church*. God Himself had announced from the beginning of the world that Mary was destined "to crush the head" of the infernal serpent; she could not have begun her life subject to his power. The archangel Gabriel called her "full of grace" because she was never deprived of sanctifying grace.

Prayer

(1) MARY, I believe the teaching of the Church concerning you that from the first moment of your conception you possessed sanctifying grace, even the fullness of grace, with the infused virtues and gifts of the Holy Ghost. Yet you remained subject to death and other pains and miseries of life that your Son Himself willed to undergo.

I believe that you were, "in the first instant of your conception, by the singular grace and privilege of the Omnipotent God, in virtue of the merits of Jesus Christ, Savior of the human race, preserved from all stain of original sin."

This article of faith is founded upon Scripture and upon the constant tradition of the Church. If God Himself had announced from the beginning of the world that you were destined "to crush the head" of the infernal serpent, you could not have begun your life by being wounded yourself by his poisonous bite and subject to his power. The archangel Gabriel called you "full of grace" because you never were deprived of sanctifying grace, and consequently you possessed this grace in the first moment of your conception.

The Fathers and writers of the Church compared you to the ark of Noe which alone escaped the universal deluge; to the thornbush which Moses saw burning, but was not consumed; to the enclosed garden; to the rod of Aaron which, when laid in the ark, budded and blossomed without having taken root; to the fleece of Gideon which remained dry while the ground all around it became moist with dew. They look upon you as the queen who came from the Most High, perfect, beautiful, and without original sin; as the paradise of innocence which God Himself planted and protected against all the attacks of the poisonous serpent.

(2) MARY, *reason, too, approves of your Immaculate Conception,* for this privilege corresponds with your sublime vocation. You were the throne of God, the wonderful palace in which the Son of God chose to dwell for nine months. Your womb was the chosen place honored by the mysterious working of the Holy Spirit. If everything that comes in contact with God must be pure and immaculate, what purity was necessary for you, the vessel in which the Son of God formed His Flesh and Blood? Your Immaculate Conception is a brilliant witness to the sanctity of Jesus, your Son.

If Jesus, the Son of God, could choose for His Mother her who pleased Him most, He would surely choose one acceptable to the Blessed Trinity and worthy of the great honor for which she was destined. You were, therefore, not only free from all actual sin, but you also remained exempt from original sin, otherwise, you would not have been a Mother suitable for Jesus Christ, the Son of God.

As Eve received natural life from Adam, you received spiritual life, the life of grace, through your Son. If Eve was originally immaculate, your conception as the second Eve could not be less immaculate. You who are superior to Eve in merits could not be inferior to her in dignity. Therefore, since Eve was immaculate in her formation, you must have been immaculate in your conception.

(3) MARY, it is an ancient belief and now an article of faith of the Catholic Church that *after your death you were admitted body*

and soul into heaven. This privilege corresponds with your exalted dignity and great merits. But the principal reason of your bodily Assumption into heaven was due to your Immaculate Conception. Because of original sin man was doomed to death and corruption; but, being exempt from the stain of original sin, you were not subject to corruption and were assumed into heaven body and soul immediately after your death.

God Himself has testified to your Immaculate Conception by miracles. Who can number the wonders which have been wrought at Lourdes, where you appeared eighteen times and declared to Bernadette and to the world, "I am the Immaculate Conception", just four years after this doctrine was defined as a dogma of faith, to declare to the whole world your approval of it and that you were not only immaculately conceived, but that you are the Immaculate Conception! How many miracles have been wrought also through the Miraculous Medal which bears your image!

Mary, conceived without sin, teach me to be grateful to God for the grace of Baptism by which I was cleansed from original sin and spiritually regenerated and sanctified. Help me to guard against every sin, above all against every mortal sin, lest I lose the grace of God, infinitely greater than all the riches of the world. Since I could not imitate you by entering the world free from sin, let me at least leave it free from sin.

O God, Who by the Immaculate Conception of the Virgin Mary has prepared a worthy dwelling place for Your Son, we humbly beg of You, that as through the death of Your Son, which You foreknew, You have kept her free from all sin, so by her intercession enable us also to come to You with pure hearts. Through the same Christ Our Lord. Amen. (*Feast of the Immaculate Conception,* December 8)

Aspiration:

O Mary, conceived without sin, pray for us who have recourse to you.

300 days (357)*

47. Queen Assumed into Heaven

Consideration:

It is a dogma of Catholic Faith that the immaculate Mother of God and ever Virgin *Mary was taken up into heaven body and soul*. This was solemnly defined by Pope Pius XII on November 1, 1950. The Mother of Jesus, as the new Eve, was always associated with her Divine Son in the struggle against the infernal enemy, and now shares in Christ's complete victory over sin and death.

It was fitting that Mary should be assumed into heaven with body and soul. By her Assumption God honored her body that was always the temple in which He dwelt by grace. Her holy and virginal body which gave flesh to the God of all sanctity and the Victor over death, should never experience the corruption of the grave. Death and corruption are a result of original sin, but Mary was preserved from original sin and its effects.

Mary is the Queen of heaven and earth. Since she shared in all the mysteries of our Redemption, Jesus crowned her with glory and power, and placed her at His right hand that she might dispose of the treasures of grace as the Mother of God and Queen of heaven and earth. Her glorious beauty should fill our hearts with a longing for the joys of heaven and with great confidence that she can obtain for us the graces we need to share in her glory.

Prayer

(1) MARY, you obey the law of death, but your death is rather a peaceful slumber, a gentle separation of the soul from the body. Your soul reaches such a degree of love that it seems unable to rest any longer except in the blissful embrace of the Blessed Trinity. It leaves your immaculate body and sweetly speeds to enjoy the blessed vision of God. But soon your fair soul is again united to your body which lies peacefully in the tomb, and suddenly you stand immortal and glorified, clothed in queenly glory.

363

As angels sing their hymns of praise, *you are raised on high to the kingdom of glory by God's own power.* Who can tell the sweetness of that loving embrace whereby Jesus welcomes and admits you, His own Virgin Mother, to unending union with Him in the glory of heaven! Your peaceful tomb has been opened by the apostles and found to be empty. Beautiful flowers whose sweet fragrance scents the air fill the place where your body has lain, and heavenly music envelopes your empty tomb. The apostles now realize that you have been taken up into heaven, soul and body.

(2) MARY, *it was fitting that you should be assumed into heaven with soul and body.* By your Assumption God honored your body that was always the temple in which He dwelt by grace. It was a gate through which the Son of God, the Divine Word, passed to earth and became Man. It was fitting that your holy and virginal body which gave flesh and blood to the God of all sanctity, the Victor over death, should never experience the corruption of the grave. Death and corruption are a result of original sin; but by your Immaculate Conception you were preserved from original sin and its effects. You offered yourself to suffering and your beloved Son to death for the Redemption of mankind; it was fitting that you should be united with Him in glory.

Queen Assumed into Heaven, I rejoice that after years of heroic martyrdom on earth you have at last been taken to the throne prepared for you in heaven. Lift my heart with you in the glory of your Assumption above the dreadful touch of sin and impurity. Teach me how small earth becomes when viewed from heaven. Make me realize that death is the triumphant gate through which I shall pass to your Son, and that someday my body shall rejoin my soul in the unending bliss of heaven. From this earth, over which I tread as a pilgrim, I look to you for help. When my hour of death has come, lead me safely to the presence of Jesus to enjoy the vision of my God for all eternity together with you.

(3) MARY, *I venerate you as the Queen of heaven and earth.* Your own Son led you to a throne of glory in heaven next to His own. As you tasted the bitterness of pain and sorrow with Him on earth, you now enjoy the sweetness of eternal bliss with Him in heaven. I thank Jesus for having put a most beautiful crown upon your head, while all the angels and saints acclaim you as their Queen.

Because here below you shared in all the mysteries of our Redemption, Jesus has crowned you not only with glory, but with power. He placed you at His right hand that you may dispose of the treasures of grace by a singular title—that of Mother of God. In the midst of all the saints you stand as their Queen and ours— dearer to the Heart of God than any creature in God's kingdom. You pray for your children and distribute to us every grace won by the loving Savior on the cross.

Queen Assumed into Heaven, may your glorious beauty fill my heart with a distaste for earthly things and an ardent longing for the joys of heaven. May your merciful eyes glance down upon my struggles and my weakness in this vale of tears. Crown me with the pure robe of innocence and grace here, and with immortality and glory in heaven.

Having been made partakers of Your heavenly banquet, we implore Your mercy, O Lord Our God, that we who celebrate the Assumption of the Mother of God, may by her intercession be delivered from all the evils that threaten us. Through the same Christ Our Lord. Amen. (*Feast of the Assumption,* August 15)

Aspiration:

Remember, O Virgin Mother of God, when you stand before the face of the Lord, to speak favorable things in our behalf and to turn away His anger from us.

300 days (308)*

48. Queen of the Most Holy Rosary

Consideration:

The rosary means literally "a garden of roses." In this garden are blooming the *white* roses of the joyful mysteries of our religion, in which the Word of God was made flesh, and Mary, the inviolate Virgin and Mother, performs her maternal duties for Him with a holy joy. In the *red* roses of the sorrowful mysteries we behold the agony and death of the suffering Christ, the price at which the salvation of our race was accomplished. The *golden* roses of the glorious mysteries direct our minds and hearts to heaven, for we see Christ's triumph over death. His Ascension into Heaven, the sending of the Holy Spirit, Mary's Assumption, and the everlasting glory of all the saints in heaven united with the glory of the Mother and her Son.

In her sixth and last apparition at Fátima, on October 13, 1917, the Blessed Virgin in answer to Lucia's question—"Who are you and what do you want?"—said: *"I am the Lady of the Rosary,* and I have come down to warn the faithful to amend their lives and ask pardon for their sins. Men must not continue to offend the Lord, already so deeply offended. *They must say the Rosary."*

Through the prayer of the Rosary *untold blessings have been showered down upon mankind throughout the ages.* Today as in past times of peril that have threatened civilization, Mary has again come to save mankind from the evils that overwhelm us, especially materialism and Communism. But the Rosary is especially *most salutary in bringing back home life to its full splendor,* by raising the family to a higher family circle where God is Father and Mary is Mother and we are all children of God. According to Mary's promises, the Rosary is a guarantee of her special protection and great graces, a happy death and eternal salvation.

Prayer

(1) MARY, *your Holy Rosary is very important in my spiritual life.* As a devotion of the Church it imprints a particularly Catholic

character upon my soul by constantly recalling to me the remembrance of Jesus and you. It expresses the three great phases in the work of our redemption—joy, sorrow, and glory. By saying the Rosary I desire to show my gratitude and love to Jesus and you, to praise God for the benefits of the Incarnation, to make reparation for the sins of the world, and to obtain grace and assistance for my soul and for all mankind.

According to your promises to your favorite children, the Rosary is a guarantee of your special protection and great graces, a happy death and eternal salvation. By the daily recitation of the Rosary may my own devotion to you grow more ardent, more earnest. Let no work prevent me from saying my beads. May my soul find rest, strength, and refreshment in the joys, the sorrows, and the glories of my Divine Lord, and you, His loving Mother. The fifteen mysteries form your crown. Queen of the Most Holy Rosary, may my Rosary lead me, crowned with an everlasting crown of glory, to your feet.

(2) MARY, through the prayer of the Rosary *untold blessings have been showered down upon mankind throughout the ages.* Through the Rosary today as in past times of peril that have threatened civilization, you have again come to save mankind from the evils that overwhelm us.

But make your Rosary most salutary in bringing back home life to its full splendor, by raising the family to a higher family circle where God is Father and you are Mother and we are all children of God. May the Rosary strengthen the unity of family life, so easily weakened by the modern way of living, and keep it from worldliness, and be a source of great blessing, the greatest of which is peace founded on love.

(3) MARY, *in your apparitions you expressed a desire that we pray the Rosary.* At Lourdes you appeared eighteen times and invited Bernadette to recite the Rosary with you. In each of the six apparitions at Fátima, you insisted on the recitation of the Rosary. You made your appearance with the Rosary in your hands and said, "*I am the Lady of the Rosary,* and I have come to warn the faithful to amend their lives and ask pardon for their sins. They must not continue to offend Our Lord Who already is so deeply offended. *They must say the Rosary.*"

You made known your Great Promise when you showed your Immaculate Heart to Lucy, the little shepherd girl of Fátima, and said, "I promise to assist at the hour of death with the graces necessary for salvation all those who on the first Saturday of five consecutive months go to confession and receive Holy Communion, *say the Rosary, and spend a quarter of an hour in meditation on the fifteen mysteries of the Rosary with the object of making reparation to me."*

Queen of the Most Holy Rosary, you have been pleased to come to Lourdes and to Fátima to reveal to us the treasures of graces hidden in the recitation of the Rosary. Inspire our hearts with a sincere love of this devotion, in order that by meditating on the Mysteries of our Redemption that are recalled in it, we may gather its fruits and obtain blessings for soul and body, peace for the world, freedom for the Church, the conversion of sinners, and the salvation of our souls.

O God, Whose only-begotten Son by His life, death, and Resurrection obtained for us the rewards of eternal salvation, grant, we beg of You, that meditating upon these mysteries in the Most Holy Rosary of the Blessed Virgin Mary, we may both imitate what they contain, and obtain what they promise. Through Christ Our Lord. Amen. *(Feast of the Most Holy Rosary,* October 7)
Aspiration:
Queen of the Most Holy Rosary, pray for us.

300 days (394)

49. Queen of Peace

Consideration:

This title was inserted into the litany by Pope Benedict XV during the First World War. It is a cry of mankind for peace—peace of heart and peace among nations.

Mary is the Queen of Peace because *she brought Jesus, the King of Peace, into the world.* By His death He atoned for our sins and restored us to the peace of the friendship of God. It is the peace of which He spoke, "Peace I leave with you, my peace I give to you; not as the world gives do I give to you" (John 14:27).

Jesus has brought peace to men of good will; but good will is found only in those who want to do the Will of God. The observance of the Ten Commandments brings peace to the heart and to the world. Peace lies in the avoidance of sin. Peace is found also in unwavering trust in Providence, since to those who love God all things work together unto good.

Mary appeared as the Queen of Peace at Fátima. She assured us that if we would do penance and amend our lives—say the Rosary, honor and consecrate ourselves to her Immaculate Heart, and receive Holy Communion in reparation to her Heart on five First Saturdays—that she would protect us from the just punishments of God and that she would bring peace to the world. She said, "If what I tell you is done, many souls will be saved and there will be peace." The Queen of Peace is the only hope for true peace in the world today. Devotion to Our Lady is a sure way to deep personal peace, because Mary is "the Way" to Jesus, the King and giver of Peace.

Prayer

(1) MARY, you are the Queen of Peace because *you brought Jesus, the King of Peace, into the world.* At his birth angels sang in the heavens, "Glory to God in the highest, and peace on earth among men of good will" (Luke 2:14). You gave us the Savior of the world

and the Prince of Peace, as the prophet had foretold: "A Child is born to us . . . and His Name shall be called the Prince of Peace" (Isaias 9:6). By His death Jesus atoned for our sins and restored us to the peace of the friendship of God. He is truly a Peacemaker. Above all, at prayer and Holy Communion He leaves with us the peace of which He spoke at the Last Supper, "Peace I leave with you, my peace I give to you; not as the world gives do I give to you" (John 14:27).

(2) MARY, *only after I have become like you, a lowly child, shall I have true peace in my soul and enter the kingdom of peace,* for Jesus said, "Unless you turn and become like little children, you will not enter into the kingdom of heaven" (Matt. 18:3). I cannot enjoy the peace of your Son unless I conquer my pride and remain humble. I rely too much upon myself. I freely boast of the little good that is in me as if it were mine by personal merit, whereas whatever good is in me really comes from God. My pride leads me into many sins and daily faults—sensitiveness, jealousy, rash judgment, uncharitableness, and anger. And yet your Son says, "Blessed are the peacemakers, for they shall be called children of God" (Matt. 5:9). Humble Handmaid of the Lord, be my model and teacher of humility, that I may find true peace.

Queen of Peace, through you peace came into the world. Though you may peace come into my soul by bringing Jesus to me, especially by Holy Mass, Holy Communion, and prayer. May the power of His grace conquer my pride, and may His Presence enable me to enjoy His peace and to spread it among others.

(3) MARY, *you appeared as the Queen of Peace at Fátima.* There you assured us that if we would do penance and amend our lives, say the Rosary, honor and consecrate ourselves to your Immaculate Heart, and receive Holy Communion in reparation to you on five First Saturdays, that you would protect us from the just punishments of God and that you would bring peace to the world. How earnest are your words! "If what I tell you is done, many souls will be saved and there will be peace. . . . If my requests are granted, Russia will be converted and there will be peace. . . . In the end my Immaculate Heart will triumph and an era of peace will be conceded to humanity."

Queen of Peace, you are the only hope for true peace in the world today. May there be a sufficient number of people to fulfill your requests so that disaster may be averted, the mental and spiritual ills of mankind cured, and a lasting peace secured. Pray for us and give to the world the peace for which all people are longing, peace in the truth, justice, and charity of Christ. Give peace to the warring nations and to the souls of men, so that in the peace of order the kingdom of God may be victorious.

Extend your protection to the infidels and to all those still in the shadow of death; give them peace and grant that on them, too, may shine the sun of truth so that they may unite with us in proclaiming before the one and only Savior of the world, "Glory to God in the highest and peace among men of good will."

Behold with kindly eyes and crown with success the fatherly care with which the Sovereign Pontiff, the Vicar on earth of your Divine Son, continually seeks to call together and unite the nations in peace. Grant that in childlike submission to our common Father, we may carry out wholeheartedly his salutary directions. Enlighten the rulers of our country as to those same directions. Promote and maintain peace and concord in our families, peace in our hearts, and Christian charity throughout all the world.

Queen of Peace, obtain peace and complete freedom for the Holy Church of God. Stay the spreading flood of modern paganism; enkindle in the faithful the love of purity, the practice of the Christian life, and an apostolic zeal, so that the servants of God may increase in merit and number.

We consecrate ourselves to your Immaculate Heart that your love and patronage may hasten the triumph of the kingdom of God, and that all nations, at peace with one another and with God, may proclaim you blessed, and with you may raise their voice to resound in the chant of the everlasting Magnificat of praise, love, and gratitude to the Heart of Jesus, where alone they can find truth and peace.

May the kind intercession of Your Immaculate Mother and Ever Virgin Mary aid us, O Lord, that, having been continually blessed with her favors, we may be freed from all dangers and enjoy peace through her kind prayers. Who live and reign forever. Amen. (*Feast of Mary, Mediatrix of All Graces,* May 31)

Aspiration:

Immaculate Queen of Peace, pray for us.

300 days (430)

Part III

THE HAIL MARY, THE HAIL HOLY QUEEN, AND THE MAGNIFICAT

The Hail Mary—*Ave Maria*

(*The Archangel Gabriel*)

"Hail [Mary], full of grace, the Lord is with thee. Blessed art thou among women" (Luke 1:28).

(*St. Elizabeth*)

"And blessed is the fruit of thy womb [Jesus]" (Luke 1:42).

(*The Church*)

"Holy Mary, Mother of God, pray for us sinners now and at the hour of our death. Amen."

Background:

After Our Lord's own prayer—the Our Father—no other prayer has a nobler origin and is more beautiful than the Hail Mary. Although God did not teach it to us by His own lips, He has done so by the lips of others.

The Hail Mary consists of three parts. The first, "Hail [Mary], full of grace, the Lord is with thee, blessed art thou among women" (St. Luke 1:28), are the words used by the angel Gabriel in saluting the Blessed Virgin. The second, "and blessed is the fruit of thy womb" [Jesus] (St. Luke 1:42), is borrowed from the divinely inspired greeting of St. Elizabeth. Finally, the petition, "Holy Mary, Mother of God, pray for us sinners now and at the hour of our death. Amen," has been added by the Church. "Most rightly," says the official Catechism of the Council of Trent, "has the Holy Church of God added to this thanksgiving, petition also and the invocation of the most holy Mother of God, thereby implying that we should piously and suppliantly have recourse to her in order that by her intercession she may reconcile God with us sinners and obtain for us the blessings we need both for this present life and for the life which has no end."

"Holy Mary, Mother of God," is an act of faith in the Divine Motherhood of Mary. In the fifth century, Nestorius, a heretic, asserted that in Jesus Christ there were two distinct persons, as well as two natures, and that Mary was the mother of the human person only and that, therefore, she should not be called the Mother of God. On June 22, 431, the General

Council of Ephesus, assisted by the Holy Spirit, condemned these errors and vindicated the dignity of Mary by a solemn definition proclaiming her "Mother of God." The whole Church rejoiced in singing the praises of Mary, the Mother of God. Each time you say the Hail Mary you profess your faith in this most important privilege of Mary, upon which all her other privileges rest.

The Hail Mary is the most perfect compliment which you can make to your heavenly Mother, because it is the compliment which God sent her by an archangel. This compliment won her heart and made her consent to be God's Mother. By the same compliment you, too, will infallibly win her heart.

Prayer

"Hail"

MARY, MOTHER OF GOD, from all eternity you were in the mind of God as the Mother of the future Redeemer of the world. At your conception God preserved you from every stain of original sin— you are the Immaculate Conception. He filled your soul with a fullness of graces, which made you holy and most pleasing to Him.

MARY, MY MOTHER, when the time of Redemption had come, the Holy Trinity entrusted the archangel Gabriel with the most important message ever given to a creature. He found you in prayer and greeted you with the joyful salutation, "Hail"! as if he wanted to tell you, "Rejoice, be happy, Mary! I am a messenger from heaven. I bring you happy tidings."

"Mary"

MARY, MOTHER OF GOD, next to the name of Jesus, no other name is so often on the lips of the faithful Christian as your name. Mary means "Sovereign Lady." How well it becomes you, for you are the sovereign Queen of heaven and earth, of angels and men! Your holy name strikes terror into the evil spirits, for from the beginning you crushed the serpent's head.

Your name means "Star of the Sea." When the waves of temptation surge round me and when I find myself amid the rocks of trials, I wish to follow the advice of St. Bernard: I shall look up to the star and call on you, O Mary! In all dangers, in needs, in doubts, I shall turn my thoughts to you. Let your name be ever on my lips and in my heart. If I follow you, I cannot stray; if I invoke you, I shall not lose hope; if you support me, I cannot fall; if you protect me, I have nothing to fear. With you as my Guiding Star, I shall safely reach the port of salvation.

MARY, MY MOTHER, help me ever to speak your sweet and holy name with love, confidence, and reverence, as it is spoken in heaven. You are my hope!

"Full of Grace"

MARY, MOTHER OF GOD, no stain of original or actual sin ever defiled your pure soul. This was your singular privilege among all the daughters of Eve. Never for one moment were you under the power of the enemy.

If God sanctified John the Baptist in his mother's womb because he was to announce to the world the Redeemer; if God sanctified the Prophet Jeremias because he was to announce God's revelations to the world, what sanctity and purity, what privileges and what fullness of grace must not the Almighty have bestowed upon you, who were to give to the Incarnate Word His very Flesh and Blood! If St. Stephen was "full of grace" and the apostles were "filled with the Holy Spirit" because they were to preach the Word of God, what fullness of grace must not God have showered upon you, in whose chaste womb the Eternal Word dwelt, and from whose Immaculate Heart He took flesh and blood.

MARY, MY MOTHER, in your womb was the grace of divinity, in your heart the grace of charity, in your hands the grace of mercy. You were truly full of grace, for through you men have received Redemption, the sick, health; the sorrowful, comfort; sinners, pardon; the just, grace; the angels, joy; the Blessed Trinity, glory and honor; and the Son of Man, His human flesh. Surely you, more than any other creature, have received all grace in its fullness.

"The Lord is with thee"

MARY, MOTHER OF GOD, the Lord was with you in a manner different from all other creatures on earth or in heaven. The Lord was with you at the very first moment of your existence, preserving your soul pure and immaculate from every stain of original sin. The Lord was with you also during your whole life, not only preserving you from the smallest venial sin, but enriching your soul at every moment with the choicest heavenly graces. Especially at the

Incarnation, and during the nine months of your pregnancy, the
Lord was with you in a way that no other creature ever possessed
Him.

The Lord was with you in a manner more intimate, more perfect,
and more divine than He ever was or will be with any other creature.
He was with you not by His essence, His presence, and His power:
He is with all His creatures in this manner. He was with you not
only with His actual grace, touching your heart and enlightening
your understanding. He was with you not only by His sanctifying
grace, making you pleasing in His sight: He is present in this
manner with all the just. He was with you not only by a special
protection guiding you in His ways and leading you securely to
salvation: He does this for each one of the elect. He was with you,
and with you alone in a most wonderful manner, for in you, and
of your substance, was formed His adorable Body; in you he reposed
for nine months, with His whole Divinity and humanity.

MARY MY MOTHER, your Immaculate Heart gave flesh and blood to
the Lord, and your chaste womb became His dwelling place. I praise
you for this sublime privilege, and I beg you to preserve my soul from
sin that God may always dwell in it by His grace.

"Blessed art thou among women"

MARY, MOTHER OF GOD, when you entered the house of Zachary,
and Elizabeth heard your greeting, the infant leaped in her womb
and, being filled with the Holy Spirit, she cried out with a loud
voice, "Blessed art thou among women."

You are more blessed than all other women. The curse that was
brought down upon us by Eve has been taken away by the blessings
we received through you. You are indeed blessed, because of the
fullness of grace we admire in you; blessed, because of the Majesty
of the Person Who became your Son; blessed, because of the glory
you deserved for being the Mother of God. When Jesus cast out the
devil and preached His heavenly doctrine to the Jews, a certain
woman from the crowd, lifting up her voice, said to Him, "Blessed
is the womb that bore thee, and the breasts that nursed thee." These
words of two women have found a response in the hearts of all true
Christians who with Holy Mother Church pray to you: "Blessed
is the womb of the Virgin Mary, which bore the Son of the Eternal
Father, and blessed the breasts that nursed Christ our Lord."

The Catholic Church, ever true to her Divine Founder, has ever called you "Blessed." She shall ever announce to her children your blessedness. You yourself foretold it when, inspired by the Holy Spirit, you exclaimed during your visit to Elizabeth, "My soul magnifies the Lord, and my spirit rejoices in God my Savior; because he has regarded the lowliness of his handmaid; for, behold, henceforth all generations shall call me blessed" (Luke 1:46).

MARY, MY MOTHER, I, too, join the millions of your faithful children and call you "Blessed," and I invoke your powerful intercession. Protect me during life, and obtain for me heaven beyond the grave, where I may continue singing your blessedness in God's kingdom.

"Blessed is the fruit of thy womb"

MARY, MOTHER OF GOD, you yourself were "blessed," but infinitely more "blessed" was the fruit of your womb, for the fruit of your womb was Jesus. Jesus is God, and God is infinitely blessed and worthy of the praises of men and angels for all eternity. The fruit of your womb was the source and cause of your blessedness. God preserved you immaculate in your conception and showered down upon you the richest treasures of heaven to prepare you to bear this precious "Fruit" which was to give life and salvation to the world. If the tree is known by its fruit, how holy, how blessed must that tree be, whose "Fruit" restored the dead to life, washed away sin, and is the pledge of life everlasting!

Jesus is the Fruit of your womb, and Jesus is the Way, the Truth, and the Life. Jesus is the Redeemer of the world, "the living Bread that came down from heaven," and "he who eats this bread shall live forever."

MARY, MY MOTHER, I thank you in the name of all mankind for this blessed Fruit of your womb. I thank you for Jesus Who is our hope and our salvation.

"Jesus"

MARY, MOTHER OF GOD, to the words of Elizabeth the Church has added, "Jesus," to declare that the fruit of your womb was the Redeemer of the world. The tongues of men or angels can pronounce no name more holy or more sweet than the name of Jesus. The archangel Gabriel brought this name from heaven when he told you, "Thou shalt call his name Jesus." You gave this holy name to your little Son at His circumcision.

The name you have given to your Son means Savior. Jesus is truly the Savior and Redeemer of the world, for He saved His people from their sins by His Precious Blood on the hill of Calvary. How great is the power and sacredness of that name! St. Paul says, "God also has exalted him and has bestowed upon him the name that is above every name, so that at the name of Jesus every knee should bend of those in heaven, on earth and under the earth, and every tongue should confess that the Lord Jesus Christ is in the glory of God the Father" (Phil. 2:9). Through the name of your Son Jesus we are saved. "Neither is there salvation in any other. For there is no other name under heaven given to men by which we must be saved" (Acts 4:12). And Jesus said, "If you ask the Father anything in my name, he will give it to you" (John 16:23).

MARY, MY MOTHER, teach me ever to love and praise the holy name of Jesus. May that name be ever on my lips and in my heart during life, and may it be my last word at death!

"Holy Mary"

MARY, MOTHER OF GOD, you are truly holy. The Gospel calls you full of grace and says that the Lord is with you, and four times calls you blessed. God seems to speak to you in the words of Scripture: "Thou art all fair, O my love, and there is no spot in thee" (Cant. 4:7). We call the saints and angels in heaven holy, but as your dignity is so much greater than that of all God's creatures, so the Almighty enriched your soul with holiness greater than that of all the saints and angels in heaven. At the very first moment of your existence, the grace of perfect sinlessness and intimate union with God was bestowed upon you. By being faithful to grace, you doubled and increased this great holiness at each act to your dying breath. You are holy beyond our power to understand.

MARY, MY MOTHER, through your holiness which prepared you to be God's Mother, pray for me that I may imitate your sanctity as far as I possibly can with the help of God's grace. May I always remain in God's grace and friendship and love throughout life, and someday merit to be united with Him forever in heaven where I shall better understand the holiness with which the Lord has blessed you.

"Mother of God"

MARY, MOTHER OF GOD, according to the Scriptures Our Lord Jesus Christ is God; then you, who are the Virgin Mother who brought Him forth, must be the Mother of God. This is the teaching of the apostles and of the Catholic Church. I believe that in your womb was formed a pure body, animated with a human soul, to which the Divine Word was united, and so Jesus became man in one and the same Divine Person. The sacred body of Jesus—His very flesh and blood—was formed from your Immaculate Heart. This title of Mother of God surpasses all your titles. It raises you in dignity beyond the angels, above any other creature that God has created or ever will create.

MARY, MY MOTHER, I rejoice with you because of the sublime dignity which is yours. May your name be ever on my lips and the memory of you be ever in my heart. With Holy Mother Church I wish to praise you as the Mother of God.

"Pray for us sinners, now and at the hour of our death."

MARY, MOTHER OF GOD, your Immaculate Heart gave Jesus flesh and blood. You watched over His infant years. You stood by the cross at Calvary, your Heart breaking at His sufferings. From the cross you heard Him say, "Woman, behold thy son." You received His dead body into your arms and with your own hands laid Him in the grave. Jesus could never refuse to grant the petitions of so faithful and devoted a Mother, especially when your requests promote the greater glory of God. On earth Jesus worked His first miracle at your request. But now you ask Him not to change water into wine, as you did at Cana, but to have mercy on souls redeemed by His Precious Blood. You ask Jesus to give strength to the weak, health to the sick, confidence to those who have lost hope, and heaven to the dying.

The saints assure me that a faithful client of yours will never be lost, because you can help him and want to help him. We are poor sinners, but do not let us lose hope. May we raise our eyes to you and be comforted, trusting in your motherly kindness and mercy. You will lead us from sin safely to Jesus and salvation. I beg you to pray for me. My sins of thought, word, deed, and omission are countless in the sight of God. With all earnestness I beg: Holy Mary, Mother of God, pray for us sinners—pray for me, a sinner!

MARY, MY MOTHER, I need the aid of your prayers at all times. I have three powerful enemies: the world, the flesh, and the devil. I want your aid especially at the hour of my death, the hour of my greatest need, because on it hangs an eternity of bliss or woe. When my misspent years, my deadly sins, my abuse of God's grace and mercy stare me in the face to make me lose hope, pray for me. Stand at my bedside; may the light of your presence banish the evil spirits. May the gentle touch of your holy hand and the sweet sound of your voice comfort me. In loving resignation to God's holy Will, and in humble but confident hope of a favorable judgment and a blissful eternity, may I go to meet my Judge. Beg Jesus to have mercy on me, for you are the Mother of my Judge. Many times during my life, in reciting the Holy Rosary, I have invoked you to pray for me at the hour of my death. I trust you have heard every prayer, and that you will not forsake your child when I shall need you most. For the love of Jesus, help me at my last moments, shield me from the enemy, and obtain for me a happy death, a favorable judgment, and the glory of heaven. Amen.

The Hail Holy Queen—*Salve Regina*

"Hail, holy Queen, Mother of mercy, our life, our sweetness
and our hope.
To thee do we cry, poor banished children of Eve.
To thee do we send up our sighs, mourning and weeping
in this valley of tears.
Turn then, most gracious advocate, thine eyes of mercy
toward us.
And after this our exile, show unto us the blessed fruit of
thy womb, Jesus.
O clement, O loving, O sweet Virgin Mary."

5 years (332)*

Background:

There are four so-called final antiphons of Our Lady which conclude the
Divine Office at Compline: the *Alma Redemptoris Mater, Ave Regina
Coelorum, Regina Coeli,* and *Salve Regina.* These antiphons developed
from the practice of joining to the Office of the particular day the Little
Office of the Blessed Virgin or some popular devotion in honor of Mary.
They are greetings of respect to the Mother of God, to which earnest petitions are joined. Through them the Canonical Hours of the Divine Office
are entrusted to Mary, our Mediatrix. They are remarkable for power of
expression, for the sublimity of their rhythm and the beauty of their melody.

The *Salve Regina* is the final antiphon used from the end of Eastertide
to Advent. It gives to the Queen of Heaven various titles of honor which
inspire us to place our confidence in her and to beseech her aid in the
trial and struggles of this life so that we may obtain the joy of the future
life. Mary is particularly called the "Mother of Mercy," because her Son
is the embodiment of Divine Mercy.

The *Salve Regina* was probably composed by Herman the Lame, a monk
of the monastery of Reichenau, a little island in the Lake of Constance,
enclosed by Germany, Austria, and Switzerland. He was the son of a
Suabian count. From birth he was lame and could not move without the
help of others. Herman, highly gifted and very pious, from early childhood showed a remarkable devotion to Our Lady. At the age of seven

383

his parents brought him to the Benedictine monastery of St. Gallen for his schooling. Later he entered the monastery of Reichenau, where he was ordained priest. He prayed the *Salve Regina* for the first time in the seclusion of that monastery. In this prayer he found consolation and strength in his bodily affliction. Considered one of the most prayerful and learned men of his time, he was a philosopher, poet, orator, musician, and theologian. Herman the Lame became an honor to the Church through his spirit of prayer and devotion to Mary, to whom he turned in his sufferings. He died in 1054.

The closing words of the Hail Holy Queen: "O clement, O loving, O sweet Virgin Mary," were added a century later by St. Bernard of Clairvaux. On Christmas Eve, 1146, Emperor Conrad III, with the highest dignitaries of the Holy Roman Empire, gathered at the cathedral of Speyer to make plans for another crusade. They were waiting for the great Bernard, abbot of Clairvaux, the soul and driving force of the whole undertaking. Amid the ringing of bells from all the churches of the city and the singing of hymns, the bishop, the clergy, and the enthusiastic people welcomed Bernard at the city gates and accompanied him to their cathedral. The emperor himself met him at the doors of the cathedral and accompanied him up the center aisle, while the choir sang the *Salve Regina*. Bernard was so deeply moved by this appeal to the Mother of God that immediately after the last words of the hymn he added, as if by some heavenly inspiration: "O clement, O loving, O sweet Virgin Mary!" From that time on these words were added to the Hail Holy Queen as a fitting ending. This perfect gem of prayer came down to us through the centuries as a moving appeal to the Mother of God for her help and protection.

Prayer

"Hail, Holy Queen"

MARY, MOTHER OF GOD, you are the Queen of heaven and earth since the day of your Assumption, when your Divine Son took you to Himself in heaven. Next to God, the Lord and Ruler of all, there is no one more powerful than you; your power is almost without limit.

You are already a Queen by your human descent. Your genealogy, which the Church reads in the Mass on your birthday, includes the most illustrious names of the chosen people. David is your ancestor. But far greater than your human relationship to the royal house of David is your relationship to the King of Kings. You are the daughter of the Heavenly Father, the Mother of the Divine Son, and the Immaculate Bride of the Holy Spirit. No wonder that all the angels and saints bow before you in deepest respect. Who can enumerate all the writers, musicians, artists, and sculptors who considered it their greatest honor to perpetuate your memory in word and song, on canvas and in stone.

MARY, MY MOTHER, you stand far above any creature in dignity; hence your Son made you Queen of Heaven and earth. I gladly submit to your rule, and I wish to serve you faithfully and lovingly. I have complete confidence in your queenly power and in your motherly care.

"Mother of Mercy"

MARY, MOTHER OF GOD, you gave birth to the Savior, the God of Mercy. God has entrusted to you the office of showing mercy. Your most fervent desire is to be merciful. There is no sternness in you, but only love, kindness, and mercy.

At times I, a poor sinner, may fear to approach the Heavenly Father. But He has given me His Son Jesus as Mediator. He is my Brother, Who became like me in all things except sin in order to have pity on me. Yet there may be times when in my sinfulness I fear even my Divine Brother and the majesty of God. Though He is man, He is at the same time my God and Judge.

Mary, you are my intercessor with Jesus. No matter how exalted your privileges, you are one of our race, created like me. Though you are the Mother of God, you are still my Mother, and I do not fear to draw close to you. Your Son listens to you, and the Father listens to His Son. These are the steps by which I, a sinner, reach God. I place all my confidence in you. You are my hope because you are the Mother of Mercy.

MARY, MY MOTHER, you are the hope of us all. Then obtain pardon for sinners, relief for the poor, cure for the sick, strength for the weak, consolation for the afflicted, and help to all in need and in danger.

"Our Life"

MARY, MOTHER OF GOD, I owe my life to you, not the life of the body, but that which is much more precious—the life of grace. You gave us the Savior Who brought life for our souls; hence you are rightly called the Mother of the living. Without you we would have remained in sin.

MARY, MY MOTHER, without you there would have been no salvation, for in the Redemption of mankind you were not a mere tool that had no will. God did not force you to become the Mother of the Redeemer. You became the Mother of God willingly. You were free to refuse. Your consent was necessary for the salvation of men. Therefore, we rightly call you "Our Life."

"Our Sweetness"

MARY, MOTHER OF GOD, in you I find all that is lovely and beautiful, all that is sublime and holy, all that is good and kind. You are the ideal of all virtue and sanctity. You are the spotless lily, the mirror of justice.

MARY, MY MOTHER, why should it not be sweet to think of you, to love you, to imitate you in everything, to belong to you in life and in death? As I look up to you, the Virgin most beautiful and Mother of God, my heart is filled with deep respect and love and devotion.

"Our Hope"

MARY, MOTHER OF GOD, Jesus your Son is truly our Hope because He is our Redeemer. In Him we hope to be saved for all eternity because we were redeemed by His most Precious Blood. But you, too, are our hope, since you gave us this Redeemer and you want to help us to be saved. Your Divine Son has given you to us as our Mother and has declared us your children.

MARY, MY MOTHER, it is with the confidence of a child that I approach you as my Mother. No mother will ever give up her child. You have always helped me in the past, as you have helped millions of your clients who have come to you in their needs. I shall always trust in you and rely on you as my hope.

"To thee do we cry, poor banished children of Eve; to thee do we send up our sighs, mourning and weeping in this valley of tears."

MARY, MOTHER OF GOD, through the sin of our first parents we lost paradise and were banished to this vale of tears. Through your sinlessness we have hope. We cannot escape suffering, for we are strangers on earth. Without suffering we would easily forget our real home in heaven. Trials remind us that we are only banished children.

MARY, MY MOTHER, my life is a way of the cross. I am a cross bearer along with all the other fellow travelers of mine in this vale of tears. Teach me never to complain in my sufferings. Never let me bear pain like a slave, but rather lift my heart to God, from Whom alone come help and salvation. But my way to God takes me first to you; then through you to Jesus, and through Jesus to the Father in heaven. You are my best intercessor and helper at the throne of God. Being the Mother of Mercy, you will not leave me helpless in my need. To you I send my sighs, mourning and weeping in this vale of tears. Hear me and have pity on me!

> *"Turn then, most gracious Advocate,*
> *Thine eyes of mercy toward us."*

MARY, MOTHER OF GOD, you possess mercy in the highest degree. Like your Divine Son, you sacrificed yourself—your whole life— out of love for mankind and for its Redemption. Your love was holy, like that of your Son, Who sacrificed Himself so that we might be happy.

You are merciful because of your relation to our Redeemer. Jesus came to redeem, to seek what was lost. He rejected no one but invited all to come to Him and be refreshed and strengthened. He is still the Good Shepherd Who goes after the lost sheep and the Father who receives the prodigal son with open arms and forgiving Heart. He is indeed the Goodness and Kindness of God. Being the Mother of Jesus, you, too, are kind.

You learned to know every kind of sorrow and suffering. But you also suffered together with Jesus. Though you did not die the outward death of a martyr, inwardly you suffered and died with your Son. Truly you are the Queen of Martyrs. You saw your Son going about doing good to the sick, the blind, the lame, the deaf, the mutes, the lepers, and many others afflicted with various diseases. Since contact with the sufferings of others makes one understanding and sympathetic, what sympathy must have filled your heart!

MARY, MY MOTHER, since Jesus gave you to us to be our Mother, He must have filled your heart with a love and compassion like His own. Your greatest desire is to help us in our miseries of body and soul, for you are the Mother of Mercy. Turn your eyes of mercy

toward me. I bring you my troubles of body and soul. You understand my need and can sympathize with me. Help me, for your heart
burns with love and mercy, like the Heart of your Son, Who is the
God of Mercy.

"And after this our exile, show unto us the fruit of thy womb, Jesus."

MARY, MOTHER OF GOD, how fortunate we are to have you with us
as our refuge at the hour of death! You are the most loving of
mothers. In you I find the purest love of a virgin and the sublime
strength and fidelity of a mother. In you there is no bitterness or
harshness, but only love, kindness, sympathy, and mercy.

MARY, MY MOTHER, in the hour of death, when I shall need you
most, help me, as you assisted St. Joseph at the hour of his death.
Bring Jesus to my side and plead for His mercy. Protect me from
the evil enemy and take me safely to yourself. Through your kind
prayers may I at last see the Fruit of your womb, Jesus, for all
eternity.

"O clement, O loving, O sweet Virgin Mary!"

MARY, MOTHER OF GOD, I love you because after God you are
most lovable. Because of your virginity you are the purest, the
noblest, the most beautiful creature. Endowed with all the beauty
that could be given to a human being, you are the fairest of all
mankind. You are the chosen vessel of divine grace. Your soul is
all-beautiful because the God of infinite and eternal beauty dwells
within you. You are the masterpiece of God's creation.

I love you because you are good. Next to God no one has ever
been so good to us. Without you we would be still sitting in the
darkness of sin. Through you we have become reconciled with God
and have been made His children and heirs of heaven. By becoming the Mother of God, by giving us your Son, you have become
the channel through which all the graces and merits of Jesus come
to us. God has made you the Consoler of the afflicted, the Health of
the sick, the Refuge of sinners, the Help of Christians. As God came
to us through you, so it is God's will that we should come to Him
through you. No mother could be more loving and merciful.

MARY, MY MOTHER, I love you with all my heart. But let me
prove my love by imitating you. The temptations of the world, the
flesh, and the devil afflict my soul, but you are my faithful helper.

Guard me from sin. Under your protection I can overcome temptation and the evil inclinations of my heart. Teach me to follow your example, that through you I may find Jesus, and through Jesus I may reach our Father in heaven, O clement, O loving, O sweet Virgin Mary! Amen.

The Magnificat

OUR LADY'S HYMN OF THANKSGIVING

(Luke 1:46–55)

I. (*Mary's gratitude for God's singular gifts and graces.*)

"My soul magnifies the Lord,
    and my spirit rejoices in God my Savior;
Because he has regarded the lowliness of his handmaid;
    for, behold, henceforth all generations shall call me blessed;
Because he who is mighty has done great things for me,
    and holy is his name;

II. (*The many benefits which God had bestowed at all times on the people of Israel.*)

And for generation upon generation is his mercy,
    to those who fear him.
He has shown might with his arm,
    he has scattered the proud in the conceit of their heart.
He has put down the mighty from their thrones,
    and has exalted the lowly.
He has filled the hungry with good things,
    and the rich he has sent away empty.

III. (*The promise made of old to the Fathers—the mystery of the Incarnation.*)

He has given help to Israel, his servant,
    mindful of his mercy—
Even as he spoke to our fathers—
    to Abraham and to his posterity forever."

3 years (320)*

Background:

The Magnificat is the only prayer, the only work, which the Blessed
Virgin composed, or rather, which Jesus composed in her, for He spoke
by her mouth when she visited Elizabeth. From Mary's soul burst that

eternally beautiful song, which humbly turns all praise and honor from herself and gives it to God. It is the greatest hymn of praise which God ever received from a pure creature.

Mary uttered her hymn of praise in Aramaic. It comes to us translated through Greek, the language of St. Luke. This, in turn, comes to us translated into Latin, and from Latin into English. Still so overwhelming is the thought, so exalted the theme that even in translation four times removed from the original, the words of the Magnificat thrill us by their power.

Mary's Magnificat comes from the abundance of *a heart aflame with zeal,* but it is also the work of *a mind alive with learning* and the love for Divine Wisdom. It reveals a mind steeped in the sacred writings of her people—the history, the prophecies, the poetry of Israel, and all in terms of the relation of these to God and of God to them. The phrases of her hymn echo the great lines of the Old Testament which record the highest moments of Hebrew history.

God looks for *the virtues of gratitude and humility* in His servants, and when found in them they draw down His favor and His gifts. Both these virtues are found in the Magnificat. God, Who is ready to confer on us every good thing, will have all His gifts return to Him by gratitude and will not allow us to deprive Him of glory when we attribute to ourselves through pride what belongs to Him alone. Pride and ingratitude repel grace from our souls; gratitude and humility unlock the treasure of heaven and draw down upon us God's choicest gifts.

Forgetful of herself, of her dignity and greatness, Mary thinks only of returning thanks to God. Lowly in her own esteem, she gives all praise to Him to Whom she attributes all her greatness and privileges. God had exalted her above all creatures. She thinks only of glorifying Him, "her Benefactor." Her spirit rejoices in God alone, Whom she calls "her Savior." God had raised her to the highest dignity in His power by choosing her to be the Mother of His Son made Man. She, in her humility, looks upon herself as His lowly "handmaid." "All generations," she prophesies, "shall call me blessed." She attributes blessedness to God, Whom she calls essential Holiness: "Holy is His name." "Great things," she acknowledges, "have been done in her." The glory of this she attributes to the Almighty. God's mercy, His power, His justice, His charity—all are praised in that sublime canticle.

The Magnificat shows the wonderful appreciation the Blessed Virgin had of the infinite goodness and mercy of God in the great work of the Incarnation of His Son. She joins her exceeding great joy with love and praise. She is grateful for having been freely chosen by the Divine Goodness to be the happy instrument of God in bringing about that wonderful work. And in her most profound humility, she ascribes nothing at all to herself, but gives all the glory to God.

The Magnificat is taken to be Mary's song of humility. But it is also *a song to the supreme humility of God.* He Who is mighty has done great things for His most lowly handmaid. He has lowered Himself to the dust. Our Lady, in giving us this song of her Heart, brought forth from that storehouse of her soul things old and new. Not one of the old songs of Israel fails to find its echo in this new song of the Mother of the Messias.

This is a wondrous song, this canticle of God's Mother, full of simplicity and depth. Marvelous notes they are, and though mingled with chords from ancient times, yet new and strange and mysterious, on account of their relation to Christ's kingdom. It is a song very dear to all children of Mary, who first sang it under the guidance of the Holy Spirit. To thank God for the graces He has given to Our Lady, her devoted children will often say the Magnificat. We should join our voices to hers in her eternal Magnificat, for her triumph is also, in a measure, our triumph. Would that we might always say it with the same devotion, piety, and loving enthusiasm with which the great soul of the Mother of God poured it forth for the first time.

THE MAGNIFICAT—The Song of Praise of the Redemption

(LUKE 1:46–55)

The Magnificat is in its character and substance the most appropriate song of praise of the Redemption, as the Blessed Virgin Mary herself says, "My spirit has rejoiced in God my Savior."

1. Mary extols the glory of the Redemption *with regard to God.*

The Redemption is *a work of God's power:* "Because he who is mighty has done great things for me, and holy is his name." "He has shown might with his arm, he has scattered the proud in the conceit of their heart" (49, 51).

The Redemption is *the work of God's mercy:* "And for generation upon generation is his mercy, to those who fear him." "He has given help to Israel, his servant, mindful of his mercy" (50, 54).

The Redemption is the *work of God's fidelity:* "Even as he spoke to our fathers—to Abraham and to his posterity forever" (55).

2. Mary extols the glory of the Redemption *with regard to herself.*

From the lowliness of her nature, rank, and sex, she is raised by her share in the work of the Redemption to a great dignity, inward holiness, and external glory: "Because he has regarded the lowliness of his handmaid; for, behold, henceforth all generations shall call me blessed; because he who is mighty has done great things for me, and holy is his name" (48).

3. She then reveals the glory of the Redemption *with regard to the heathen world and the kingdom of Satan.*

Unhappily, a part of the Israelite nation also belonged to the kingdom of

Satan. This kingdom of arrogance, earthly might, and independence is confounded, cast down, and stripped of its power: "He has shown might with his arm, he has scattered the proud in the conceit of their heart. He has put down the mighty from their thrones, and has exalted the lowly" (51, 52).

4. Mary extols the work of Redemption *in that wondrous kingdom of God, the Church.* The cornerstone of the Church is laid in the Incarnation.

a. The foundation of the Church, promised and fulfilled: "He has given help to Israel, his servant, mindful of his mercy, even as he spoke to our fathers, to Abraham and to his posterity forever" (54, 55).

b. The Church's laws and means of power, poverty, and humility: "He has put down the mighty from their thrones, and has exalted the lowly" (52).

c. The spiritual and temporal benefits given by the Church, Sacraments and blessings: "He has filled the hungry with good things, and the rich he has sent away empty" (53).

Prayer

The Magnificat

My soul magnifies the Lord,

MARY, MOTHER OF GOD, you saw nothing great but the Lord. Your soul acknowledged Him as the Creator of the angels and men and the universe—the Supreme Being Who is above all creatures. He is eternal because He always was and always will be and always remains the same. He is all-knowing because He knows all things, past, present, and future, even our most secret thoughts, words, and actions. He is all-present because He is everywhere. He is almighty because He can do all things. You praised one God in three Divine Persons—the Father, the Son, and the Holy Spirit. You praised the Blessed Trinity for the Incarnation—the greatest expression of God's infinite love for man. All love tends to become like that which it loves; so God became man because He loved man. You praised the Lord for the privilege of being His Mother.

MARY, MY MOTHER, I join you in thanking God for all the great things He has done for you and, through you, for all mankind. I thank the Divine Word, the Second Person of the Holy Trinity, for taking flesh of you and for becoming man to save my soul. I thank Jesus for having chosen you to be His Mother.

and my spirit rejoices in God my Savior;

MARY, MOTHER OF GOD, your whole life found its reason and joy in your Divine Son. Your union with Jesus brought peace and joy to your heart because of the wonderful fruits of grace His presence produced in your soul. There was opened to you a world of life, light, and love, a gracious outpouring of the treasures of the Sacred Heart of Jesus, the Fount of all grace, holiness, and joyfulness. You were carrying the very source of joy in your own body so that you experienced the joy Jesus promised to give the apostles after His resurrection and especially in heaven: "You therefore have sorrow now; but I will see you again, and your heart shall rejoice, and your joy no one shall take from you" (John 16:22). He encouraged them to ask for the spiritual joy that you already felt: "Ask and you shall receive, that your joy may be full" (John 16:24).

MARY, MY MOTHER, teach me to find my joy in Jesus, my Savior. Never let me lose Him by sin. Ask Him to open the treasures of His Sacred Heart to me so that my soul may be filled with grace and peace and spiritual joy. May my joy become full in seeing Him by faith in the Eucharist and face to face in heaven.

Because he has regarded the lowliness of his handmaid, for, behold, henceforth all generations shall call me blessed;

MARY, MOTHER OF GOD, in taking the title of servant, you merited the title of the Mother of God—and this title brought upon you the everlasting praise of all the faithful. You never exalted yourself because of heavenly gifts: as you became more and more acquainted with heavenly mysteries you fixed your mind more firmly in humility, answering the angel, "Behold the handmaid of the Lord." You did not mean to praise the virtue of your own humility, but to declare that God had looked upon your nothingness and that, out of His pure goodness, He had been pleased thus to exalt you. You united in your heart a humble opinion of yourself with great purity, innocence, and fullness of grace!

Among all Heaven's saints you are the most humble; yet you excel them all in the splendor of your grace and in the fire of your love. You were the instrument of God's mercy and power, because He regarded your humility and saw in you nothing to render you unworthy to co-operate with Him in the great work of man's Redemption. Though you considered yourself as nothing in your own eyes, God considered you worthy enough for the Divinity.

What you said was the simple truth. Your soul did glorify God. Your spirit, which had already been united with the Incarnate Word, was actually so closely united with Him that you carried the Son of the Most High in your womb.

As for the future, into which you looked with prophetic gaze when you said that all generations would call you blessed, you saw the glorious praise which would be given you down the ages and through the nations.

Yet frank as your statements were concerning yourself, you referred everything to God. You were lifted up; but God has lifted you up. He has regarded you, but only because in you He saw a little handmaid. The ages will call you blessed only because the mighty God did the wonderful thing that changed an unknown virgin into the Mother of God. You did not deny your gifts, but you insisted that they were gifts—gifts from God. The highest humility has become the clearest truth.

MARY, MY MOTHER, teach me to be truly humble, to have a humble opinion of myself, yet to be grateful for all of God's gifts. I wish to refer to God all that is good in me and to acknowledge as my own all that is sinful and unworthy. Let my only glory be the privilege of being able to glorify God in all that I do or think or say. Someday I hope, through your intercession, to obtain the grace of being called "blessed" by Jesus in His kingdom, and to be among those to whom He will say, "Come, blessed of my Father, take possession of the kingdom prepared for you from the foundation of the world" (Matt. 25:34).

Because he who is mighty has done great things for me, and holy is his name;

MARY, MOTHER OF GOD, in utter humility you acknowledged that all was God's: the plan of Redemption was His; the choice of a Mother was His; the action was His. It was your humility to know and proclaim that all in you was the work of God and was for the work of God; so you accepted all and offered all. The only exaltation that meant anything at all to you was exaltation by God Himself.

Indeed, God has done great things for you. In view of your dignity as Mother of God, you were chosen from all eternity. You alone were conceived immaculate among all the children of men, born full of grace and blessed among women. Your Immaculate Heart was completely free of anything evil. All the virtues that could ripen in a human soul through the abundance of divine grace were found in you. Next to Jesus, you are the most perfect likeness and image of God, the clearest mirror of His beauty and goodness, the most cherished of all God's children, in possession of the highest fullness of all the divine and moral virtues as well as of the seven Gifts of the Holy Spirit. Oh, the depth and fullness of the working of God in your soul in which He wished to achieve all that His almighty power and highest love could achieve in a mere creature to make you in some way worthy of the Divine Motherhood!

MARY, MY MOTHER, teach me from your conduct in your supreme exaltation to give glory to God, to Whom alone it belongs. Help me to preserve humility in the midst of the blessings God may have showered on me and to return unceasing thanks to Him for His many favors, and thus be worthy of a reward forever.

I bow in admiration before you, the sanctuary of God; and I thank Him with you for the great things He has done for you. As He has glorified Himself in you more than in all others, so may I too glorify Him most by revering you whom He Himself has honored so much. Join your thanks to mine in praising God for the great things He has done for my own soul. May my best gratitude be loving, faithful, and generous service to God till my dying breath!

And for generation upon generation is his mercy, to those who fear him.

MARY, MOTHER OF GOD, you are the channel by which the most precious mercies of Christ are poured into the hearts of the faithful. Since you co-operated in the Incarnation, you also co-operated in the Redemption and in all the graces resulting from it, and hence in our sanctification and salvation. Associated with Jesus in the work of our sanctification, you merited these graces, not in the same manner as Christ, but secondarily, that is, under Christ and because of Him, for He conferred upon you the power of meriting for us.

This was only fitting, for you gave Jesus His very flesh, that human nature which made it possible for Him to acquire merit; you co-operated with Him by your acts and suffering in the work of Redemption, for your will was ever in accord with God's will and with the will of your Divine Son. You suffered in your soul what Jesus suffered in His Body, and in union with Him you offered yourself as a victim for our sins.

It was truly most fitting that you should have a share in the distribution of the fruits of Redemption. You are the Mediatrix of all graces. It is God's Will that we should receive all graces through you. You are "Suppliant Omnipotence," because through your prayers before an omnipotent God you can do all things, for He, as it were, entrusted His omnipotence to your keeping.

MARY, MY MOTHER, you are my hope. Through you I hope to obtain all the graces Jesus has destined for me through His merciful Redemption. Pray for me, Suppliant Omnipotence, that I may use God's graces well for the sanctification and salvation of my soul and that I may praise His infinite mercy to me in union with you for all eternity.

He has shown might with his arm, he has scattered the proud in the conceit of their heart.

MARY, MOTHER OF GOD, from the abundance of your Heart you praised the greatness of God's power, holiness, and mercy. You declared that God is all-powerful, all-holy, and ever merciful. Like a prophetess you spoke of the nature, power, and works of God.

How beautifully you proclaimed that the full strength of Christ is shown forth in the mystery of the Cross, which is the sign of salvation to the humble and an obstacle unto destruction to the proud!

God has scattered forever all the demons who, exalting themselves in the conceit of their heart, had risen up against Him.

MARY, MY MOTHER, may the power of the grace of God strengthen me against the enemies of my soul: the world, the flesh, and the devil. Through the Sacraments and prayer, may the strength of divine grace, like the sap flowing from the vine into the branches, penetrate my soul, enlightening my mind by fixing it more firmly in faith and imparting supernatural energy to my will. Through your prayers I hope to share in the power of Christ. May He show might with His arms also in my behalf, by giving me courage to undertake difficult tasks, contempt to despise the things of earth, patience to bear suffering, strength to resist temptations, and earnestness to strive for virtue.

He has put down the mighty from their thrones, and has exalted the lowly.

MARY, MOTHER OF GOD, you teach me that pride is always a barrier to the blessing of God, for only to the humble does He grant His graces. Your humility was the basis of your holiness. You had a sense of utter dependence on God; hence He filled you with an abundance of His graces.

At the Annunciation, you humbly submitted to the Will of God and uttered the most gracious act of humility that ever fell from human lips: "Behold the handmaid of the Lord; be it done to me according to thy word." You called yourself the servant of Him Who for thirty years would be subject to you. The very moment of your exaltation, the highest to which God could raise a creature, found you deeply conscious of your own nothingness. Fully acknowledging your unworthiness to be the Mother of Christ, you accepted the wonderful privilege only in obedience to the Divine Will. The Lord exalted you because you were lowly.

MARY, MY MOTHER, never let my pride keep the grace of God from bearing fruit in my soul. May your humility ever be an inspiration to me to subject myself to the Divine Will with some of the child-like confidence with which you have always subjected yourself. The only glory I desire on earth is the privilege of dedicating my body and soul to serving God in my state of life, so that I may be still more privileged to continue praising His mercy and love for me for all eternity in heaven.

He has filled the hungry with good things, and the rich he has sent away empty.

MARY, MOTHER OF GOD, through you Jesus, the Bestower of all good gifts, was born into the world—and only those who hunger and thirst after Him shall receive their fill.

He once said, "Blessed are they who hunger and thirst for justice, for they shall be satisfied" (Matt. 5:6). No one ever hungered for sanctity more than you, and no one was ever more filled with divine grace.

You must have looked into the future Eucharistic life of the Church as you pronounced your prophetic words. You are the Mother of the Savior Who said, "I am the Bread of Life. . . . If anyone eat of this bread he shall live forever; and the bread that

I will give is my flesh for the life of the world" (John 6:52). It was from you that Jesus took the flesh and blood with which He feeds us in the Sacred Host. The grace of the Eucharist also comes to us through you, since you are the Mediatrix, the channel, through which God's graces reach us. No one ever hungered for this Bread of Life as you did, and you were the first to live the Eucharistic life. You are indeed Our Lady of the Blessed Sacrament.

MARY, MY MOTHER, it is the will of God that I become holy. Make it my will also, and the object of my most ardent and enduring longing. Through your help I want to maintain this desire as long as I live. May your Son be able to notice in me, as He did in you, a genuine hunger and thirst for true justice, for perfect contempt of the world, for absolute purity of conscience, for generous self-denial and holiness.

Give me a great hunger for the Bread of Life so that I may partake of it as often as possible. Help me to know Jesus better, to love Him more, and to center my life around the Eucharist. Through your prayers may I enjoy the richest graces of this Sacrament for the sanctification of my soul.

He has given help to Israel, his servant, mindful of his mercy—Even as he spoke to our father—to Abraham and to his posterity forever.

MARY, MOTHER OF GOD, you speak here for all the faithful, for as Abraham was the Father of believers, you are the Mother of all those who have accepted Christ, and you ever obtain Christ's greatest mercies for those who remain faithful to you.

Your hymn of thanksgiving proclaims to us the virtue which every follower of Christ should have and which was supremely present in you: joyful zeal for God's Majesty and for the salvation of souls. Your mission in life was to do all in your power that God's mercy might reach us from generation to generation; that God's bounty might fill us, and not let us be sent away empty; that God's justice might rule as in fulfillment of His promise which He gave to our fathers, to Abraham and his posterity forever. How marvelously you have fulfilled your mission and continue to fulfill it in giving us a Savior in Whom your soul rejoices. He has given us Redemption, and grace and eternal life. May we always join you in praising the mercy of God shown to us through you.

MARY, MY MOTHER, help me ever to be grateful for the mercies of God shown toward my own soul. May my gratitude prove itself in generous zeal to make God known and loved in the souls of men. Grant that out of this apostolic zeal may come one great sustaining spirit of joy—joy in working for God and souls, joy in the Lord, so that I may join in your glorious *Magnificat* in the spirit of joyful gratitude in which you spoke it.

Part IV

ENTIRE CONSECRATION TO MARY

O Virgin Mother, daughter of thy Son,
Created beings all in lowliness
Surpassing, as in height above them all:
Term by the eternal Council pre-ordained
Ennobler of thy nature, so advanced
In thee, that its great Maker did not scorn
Himself in His own work enclosed to dwell.

—DANTE

Entire Consecration to Mary

Jesus Christ is the one Source of our holiness. He Himself said, "I am the Way and the Truth and the Life." God has laid no other foundation for our salvation, perfection, and glory. Christ must be the last end of every devotion. Therefore, your aim should be to reach Christ, for you are holy only in so far as you become similar to Him, in so far as you belong to Him in perfect consecration. Now, God Himself has willed that Mary should be the most perfect image of Jesus. He has made her the master-piece of His creation. Moreover, no one ever belonged to Jesus in so nearly perfect a manner as His Mother. Mary is always associated with Jesus. Without Him she would cease to be what she is. He lives in her more intimately than He does in all the angels and saints. It follows that *no other devotion can make you resemble Jesus and consecrate you to Him so perfectly as the devotion to His Blessed Mother.*

The purpose of true devotion to Mary is to lay a more solid foundation for devotion to Jesus Christ and to put forward an easy and secure means for finding Him, for loving and serving Him faithfully. Holy Church has taught us through her saints that "the way of coming to Christ is to draw near to Mary." We mount to God by two steps: the first, which is nearest to us and most suited to our need is Mary, our Mother; the second is Jesus Christ, our Mediator and Elder Brother. Christ came to us by Mary, and it is through Mary that we must go to Him.

You are but a child in the spiritual life, clothed in the weakness of your human nature, troubled by temptations of the flesh, the world, and the devil. You find it so hard to preserve in yourself the graces and treasures which you have received from God. Consequently, as in the order of nature you have need of a mother's care and tenderness, so, too, in the order of grace. Be firmly convinced of the fact that Mary's fondest desire is to unite you to Jesus; and that Jesus' fondest desire is to have you come to Him through His holy Mother, for *perfect consecration to Jesus Christ is none other than an entire consecration to His holy Mother.*

True devotion to Mary consists in giving yourself entirely to Jesus through Mary. You consecrate yourself to Mary, that you may belong to Jesus in a more nearly perfect manner. You give her your body and soul, all material as well as spiritual goods—that is, your merits, graces, and good works, past, present, and future. This you do without any exception,

403

without hoping for any other reward than the honor of belonging to Jesus Christ through and in Mary. You entrust to her your merits, graces, and good works that she may keep and increase them for you, because these you cannot share with anyone. But in so far as the fruits of your prayers, penances, and atonements can be applied to others, you give them to Mary that she may apply them to whomsoever she wishes, according to God's will and for His greatest glory. This is at one and the same time a consecration to Jesus and to Mary, a perfect consecration to Jesus through Mary, inasmuch as *you give and consecrate to Him everything through Mary's hands, even the right of disposing of your spiritual goods.* Therefore, all that you have belongs to Mary. She has the full right of disposing of everything that can be given away. You entrust to her care whatever you cannot give to others.

True love is a gift of self and all we have. How well then is true love proved by the practice of this special devotion to Mary! You give everything you have to Mary in order that you may in as nearly perfect a manner as possible give all to Jesus for His greatest glory through the hands of His own Mother. Such unlimited generosity cannot but make you truly devoted to Jesus and Mary, to the extent that you will become the object of Their tenderest affection, the recipient of Their choicest favors.

If among men generosity is repaid by generosity, how much more is this the case when there is question of generosity to Jesus and Mary! If you are generous to Them, They will be generous to you in this life and above all in the next. How can it be otherwise? Mary, your Mother, gives herself to you in the same spirit that you give yourself to her. She gives her whole self to you, just as you give all that you are to her. She purifies all your good works and adorns them with her own merits and virtues. She presents these good works to Jesus and persuades Him to accept them, even though they be poor in themselves. Jesus looks kindly upon them because they are presented to Him by His beloved Mother. Mary employs the value of all your good works for the greatest glory of God, for she does nothing except for this most noble end.

This devotion is an expression of highest charity toward your neighbor, since you give souls on earth and those in purgatory what is most precious to you—namely, all the spiritual assistance that you can possibly give to anyone. However, it is not true to say that you cannot help those whom you love and for whom you pray if you have given all to Jesus through Mary's hands. On the contrary, Mary, who knows how to assist your loved ones better than you do, will reward the generosity you have shown her by your consecration. Besides applying your merits in the wisest possible manner to those who are most in need of help, some of whom are perhaps dear to you, she will most assuredly be particularly kind to those for whom you pray. You need not fear that you will fail in your obligations to those for whom you promised your prayers. You confidently entrust your promises and spiritual bouquets to Mary's care. She, the kindest of mothers, will attend to all as she herself knows best.

It is well to remember that this entire consecration to Mary can be made to last for definite periods of time, for example, from one feast day to another. It can, moreover, be revoked by a simple act of the will. You do not bind yourself under sin, but simply pledge your love to Mary by the complete gift of yourself to her. It is advisable to renew this consecration, preferably on every first Saturday of the month or on one of Mary's feast days, either by using a long form of consecration or by means of some shorter expression of entire consecration.

The practice of this devotion simplifies your acts of piety. It imparts to your spiritual life a liberty, childlike abandonment, and loving confidence such as our Lord referred to when He said: "Amen, I say to you, unless you be converted and become as little children, you shall not enter into the kingdom of heaven."

Prayer of Entire Consecration to Mary
(Detailed Form)

I. NATURE

Jesus, my Savior, *I give myself entirely to You through Mary.* That the gift of myself may be most pleasing to You and more nearly complete, I consecrate myself entirely to Your dear Mother Mary, and I wish to live and act in perfect dependence on her for the remainder of my life. May she, in turn, make me wholly Your own!

II. EXTENT

Mary, my dearest Mother, I give myself over to you and through you to Jesus.

1. I give you *my body with all its senses,* pledging myself not to use them except in accordance with your good pleasure and that of Jesus. Moreover, I accept beforehand whatever God may have in store for me as regards sickness and health, life and death.

2. I give you all the *possessions* I have in the world. I wish to use them only in dependence on you, for your honor and the glory of God.

3. I give you *my soul with all its faculties,* dedicating them under your guidance to the service of God and the good of souls. At the same time I renounce whatever may stand in the way of my sanctification or endanger my salvation.

4. I give you all *my interior and spiritual treasures.* I surrender to you:

a) The meritorious value of my acts. The merits by which I procure for myself an increase of grace and glory, and which I cannot give away, I present to you, not in order to apply them to others, but that you may hold them in trust for me and give them increase.

b) The satisfactory value of my acts. The satisfactory value of my acts, which supplies for the punishment due to my sins, as well as the indulgences I may gain, you may dispose of and freely apply to whomsoever you will since I can give all this to others.

c) The impetratory value of my acts. Even the impetratory value of my acts and prayers, by which I can intercede for others, I give to you.

Mary, I beg you to favor according to your good pleasure those to whom I am bound by ties of affection or relationship and to whom I am under special obligation. Loving Mother, I entrust to you all those who are near and dear to me. I am all yours and you are mine! All mine is yours! Draw on what I have given you, but more still on the treasury of your own merits and those of your dear Son, in order to help those I have entrusted to your motherly care.

III. EXCELLENCE

Accept, dearest Mother, my consecration as an act of childlike abandonment and self-surrender to your motherly care.

1. I wish that my consecration may be *an act of religion toward God,* the Word-Made-Flesh, *and toward you,* Mary, Mother of God. By it I wish to acknowledge God's absolute dominion and my own nothingness, and proclaim at the same time, with heart and soul, those rights over me which God has given to you.

2. I wish that my consecration may be *an act of humility,* for by it I want to acknowledge my nothingness and helplessness. I divest myself of everything that I have received from God, and restore all to the Giver through your hands, Mary, for through your Divine Son and you I have obtained every good gift from God.

3. I wish that my consecration may be *an act of confiding love for you,* because love consists in the gift of self, and to give myself entirely and unreservedly presupposes firm confidence and living faith.

IV. FRUIT

1. My dearest Mother Mary, by my consecration I wish *to glorify God and you* in the highest possible manner, for I give myself to God forever with all that I am and all that I have, without measure or selfishness. I do so after the manner of Divine Wisdom—that is, returning to God in the very way He chose to come to me, and hence in the way that is most pleasing to Him.

2. By my consecration I wish *to secure my own sanctification.* I know, dearest Mother, that you are most willing to help sanctify one who, having disposed of his person and goods in your behalf, is, so to say, your own property. I trust that you will most assuredly secure for me choice graces to safeguard my little spiritual treasure; that you will make it grow and have it bring forth fruit until the hour of my death. I am sure that you will help me by means of your own rich merits and satisfaction and through your powerful intercession with God.

3. By my consecration I wish *to ensure the sanctification of my neighbor.* I know that, having left the apportioning of my merits to your good pleasure, everything will be done with greater wisdom, for you are by far more prudent, thoughtful, and devoted than I can ever be.

Mother, I put all my trust in you. I rely entirely upon you because I love you sincerely. Amen.

(According to St. Louis de Montfort)

Mary, in the presence of all the heavenly court I choose you this day for my Mother and Mistress. I deliver and consecrate to you, as your slave, my body and soul, my goods, both interior and exterior, and even the value of all my good actions, past, present, and future; leaving to you the entire and full right of disposing of me and of all that belongs to me, without exception, according to your good pleasure, for the greater glory of God, in time and in eternity.

O admirable Mother, present me to your dear Son as His eternal slave, so that as He has redeemed me by you, by you He may receive me!

O faithful Virgin, make me in all things so perfect a disciple, imitator, and slave of the Incarnate Wisdom, Jesus Christ, your Son, that I may attain, by your intercession and by your example, to the fullness of His age on earth and of His glory in heaven. Amen.

(According to St. Vincent Pallotti)

IMMACULATE MOTHER OF GOD, Queen of heaven, Mother of mercy, Advocate and Refuge of sinners! Enlightened and inspired by the graces obtained for me so richly from the divine treasury through your motherly affection, I resolve this day and always to place my heart in your hands to be consecrated to Jesus.

Most Blessed Virgin, I now give you my heart in the presence of the nine choirs of angels and all the saints. In my name, consecrate it to Jesus. Because of the childlike confidence which I have in you, I am certain that you will do all you can to make my heart belong entirely to Jesus now and always, so that I may imitate perfectly the example of the saints, and in particular that of Saint Joseph, your most pure spouse. Amen.

3 years (370) *

Consecration to the Immaculate Heart of Mary

O Mary, Virgin most powerful and Mother of mercy, Queen of Heaven and Refuge of sinners, we consecrate ourselves to your Immaculate Heart. We consecrate to you our very being and our whole life: all that we have, all that we love, all that we are. To you we give our bodies, our hearts, and our souls; to you we give our homes, our families, and our country. We desire that all that is in us and around us may belong to you and may share in the benefits of your motherly blessing.

And that this act of consecration may be truly fruitful and lasting, we renew this day at your feet the promises of our baptism and our first Holy Communion. We pledge ourselves to profess courageously and at all times the truths of our holy Faith and to live as befits Catholics who are submissive to all the directions of the Pope and the bishops in communion with him. We pledge ourselves to keep the commandments of God and His Church, in particular to keep holy the Lord's Day. We pledge ourselves to make the consoling practices of the Christian religion, and above all, Holy Communion, an important part of our lives, in so far as we shall be able to do so.

Finally, we promise you, O glorious Mother of God and loving Mother of men, to devote ourselves wholeheartedly to the spreading of devotion to your Immaculate Heart, in order to hasten and assure through the queenly rule of your Immaculate Heart, the coming of the Kingdom of the Sacred Heart of your adorable Son, in our own hearts and in those of all men, in our country and in all the world, as in heaven so on earth. Amen.

3 years (390)